In *Sociological Jurisprudence*, Roger Cotterrell convincingly argues that we need a broadly interdisciplinary, empirically grounded understanding of the social not only to understand how law actually operates in everyday life but to guide jurists in pursuing law's practical projects in the world. His insights are particularly useful for conceptualizing the very nature of a legal system given that legal and quasi-legal authorities inevitably operate in negotiation with each other and often do so without stable hierarchies to guide them. Providing both a summation of Cotterrell's prolific career and a forward-looking roadmap for scholars and jurists, *Sociological Jurisprudence* is a must-read for all who are interested in understanding and advancing law in the 21st century.

Paul Schiff Berman, *Walter S. Cox Professor of Law,*
The George Washington University

Cotterrell offers a sustained statement of the vital role of the sociologically-informed jurist in exploring the general idea of law, and applies his account, suitably developed for the twenty-first century, to emerging transnational legal phenomena and the clarification of legal values. This book is essential reading for anyone interested in general questions about law, both within and across states.

Michael Giudice, *Associate Professor and Graduate Program Director,*
Department of Philosophy, York University, Toronto

For much of the last century, jurisprudence has been pre-occupied by the question of its relationship to law as a social phenomenon. In this impressive volume, one the key figures in the debate builds a compelling case for the need for a sociological jurisprudence capable of articulating the idea of law amid diverse contexts and changing conditions for law's authority, systematicity and unity.

Nicola Lacey, *School Professor of Law, Gender and Social Policy,*
London School of Economics and Political Science

SOCIOLOGICAL JURISPRUDENCE

This book presents a unified set of arguments about the nature of jurisprudence and its relation to the jurist's role. It explores contemporary challenges that create a need for social scientific perspectives in jurisprudence, and it shows how sociological resources can and should be used in considering juristic issues. Its overall aim is to redefine the concept of sociological jurisprudence and outline a new agenda for this.

Supporting this agenda, the book elaborates a distinctive juristic perspective that recognises law's diversity of cultural meanings, its extending transnational reach, its responsibilities to reflect popular aspirations for justice and security, and its integrative tasks as a general resource of regulation for society as a whole and for the individuals who interact under law's protection.

Drawing on and extending the author's previous work, the book will be essential reading for students, researchers and academics working in jurisprudence, law and society, sociolegal studies, sociology of law, legal philosophy and comparative legal studies.

Roger Cotterrell is Anniversary Professor of Legal Theory at Queen Mary University of London. Educated as a lawyer and a sociologist, he has written widely on sociology of law, jurisprudence and comparative law and is a Fellow of the British Academy and of the (UK) Academy of Social Sciences.

First published 2018
by Routledge
2 Park Square, Milton Park, Abingdon, Oxon, OX14 4RN

and by Routledge
711 Third Avenue, New York, NY 10017

Routledge is an imprint of the Taylor & Francis Group, an informa business

© 2018 Roger Cotterrell

British Library Cataloguing-in-Publication Data
A catalogue record for this book is available from the British Library

Library of Congress Cataloging-in-Publication Data
Names: Cotterrell, Roger (Roger B. M.), author.
Title: Sociological jurisprudence : juristic thought and social inquiry /
    Roger Cotterrell.
Description: Abingdon, Oxon [UK] ; New York : Routledge, 2017. |
    Includes bibliographical references and index.
Identifiers: LCCN 2017030178 | ISBN 9781138052833 (hardback) |
    ISBN 9781138052840 (pbk.) | ISBN 9781351683234 (epub) |
    ISBN 9781351683227 (mobipocket)
Subjects: LCSH: Sociological jurisprudence. | Law—Philosophy.
Classification: LCC K370 .C684 2017 | DDC 340/.115—dc23
LC record available at https://lccn.loc.gov/2017030178

ISBN: 978-1-138-05283-3 (hbk)
ISBN: 978-1-138-05284-0 (pbk)
ISBN: 978-1-315-16752-7 (ebk)

Typeset in Bembo
by Apex CoVantage, LLC

For Albie and Kaja

CONTENTS

PREFACE

The term 'sociological jurisprudence', once familiar in the literature of legal thought, is now often neglected or misunderstood. What can it mean today? Using it here, I seek to link the ideas developed in this book with a century-old tradition of Anglophone jurisprudence. But the legal world today is very different from the one in which the American jurist Roscoe Pound famously announced his programme of 'sociological jurisprudence' at the dawn of the twentieth century – as a new approach to juristic theory and practice that, he claimed, would actively engage with the social sciences. Law in the twenty-first century is dramatically changed in its doctrines, institutions, and socioeconomic and political contexts. So too are juristic practice, legal philosophy, and the social sciences.

So, the orientation of sociological jurisprudence today must be very different from the one that Pound and his followers assumed. Nevertheless, this term is a good one to indicate the outlook that unites the studies in this book. Drawing them together here and integrating them, I hope to show that 'sociological jurisprudence' is a useful label for an approach to legal inquiry that is essential at the present time. The two words joined in it indicate the linked foci of the book: on the one hand, to explore the nature of *jurisprudence* as juristic knowledge and practice; on the other, to clarify the place that the *sociological* must occupy in the juristic enterprise.

With these foci, this book has two main aims. The first is to examine the nature and tasks of jurisprudence as a theoretical resource of jurists. Jurisprudence, I argue, is not identical with legal philosophy nor, indeed, with a social science of law. It is a theoretical tool oriented solely towards helping jurists to fulfil their practical professional tasks. These are not the tasks of every lawyer or other professional who works with law. Jurists can be seen as legal scholars with a particular concern for the general well-being of the idea of law as a value-oriented structure of regulation. So, I suggest, they should have a theoretical interest in such a general idea of law, yet always with a primary focus on practical regulatory issues in the particular legal system or systems that they serve.

A clear sense of the nature and purpose of jurisprudence depends on a clear conception of juristic work. This is not to suggest that one can really generalise about the work that jurists do in all legal systems – even all contemporary Western systems – because juristic roles in practice will be varied and the meaning of 'jurist' differs in different legal cultures. But progress can be made in thinking about jurisprudence if some explicit working conception of what a jurist is – an ideal type – is elaborated. Such an approach makes it possible to explore, for example, how far values should be the concern of jurists and in what ways, as they try to make the idea of law practically meaningful. The nature of jurisprudence and the juristic role is the focus of Part I of this book.

A second aim is to show that sociology – understood here not as a distinct, professionalised academic discipline but in a broad sense as any systematic, sustained, empirically oriented study of the social – can aid juristic tasks and, indeed, must do so. Sociological perspectives should be an important part of contemporary jurisprudence. How can such a claim be justified? It can be based in part on the incontrovertible fact that the context in which law exists is changing in very important ways and law itself seems to be assuming new forms or is, at least, being used in strikingly new ways. These changes in the context and forms of law open a space for new intellectual resources in juristic thought. They undermine old certainties, especially about the structures of legal authority and the nature of legal systems.

For example, how far can law still be thought of in terms of distinct *systems* when new or newly important forms of powerful, authoritative regulation are created outside – or at least are not limited within – the jurisdictions of nation-states, jurisdictions that in modern times have fixed the familiar, relatively settled boundaries of legal systems? How far is it becoming realistic to think of law in terms of diverse, intersecting, interacting networks of regulation rather than self-contained systems?

These developments disturb settled hierarchies of legal authority. How far is legal authority becoming a matter of negotiation between (or mutual support by) parallel or competing regulatory authorities existing in no settled hierarchy? How are jurists to deal with the phenomenon of legal pluralism, which requires some kind of normative order to be created within a plurality of legal regimes existing in the same social space? How can normative order be juristically established when relations between legal regimes are unclear or when the 'legal' character of some of these regimes is disputed and there is no unchallengeable juristic authority to end such disputes?

Many juristic issues present themselves once law spills out beyond the borders of state jurisdiction or where jurisdictions overlap or are of indefinite or contested scope. Can jurists assume an agreed understanding of what law is in such conditions? Can there be a single, governing concept of law to put to use in negotiating legal pluralism? Can such a concept be satisfactorily developed by specifying philosophically an a priori *essence* of law, so that particular kinds of regulation can be judged legal or nonlegal simply by reference to this? Alternatively, should the approach be first to study empirically the great variety of regulatory regimes that actually exist and make effective claims to authority – that is, claims generally accepted within the regulated population? Generalising from such empirical evidence, should the jurist then assume a provisional working model of 'law' to facilitate initial juristic assessment of these regimes and a basis for negotiating with them?

The 'a priori' approach is in danger of failing to recognise processes of change occurring in the regulatory landscape and the need to engage juristically – indeed, experimentally – with them. The 'working model' approach is more realistic. It can support constant juristic sensitivity to wide-ranging sociolegal change and a sociological view of the contemporary regulatory landscape. Conceptual inquiries certainly remain very important on this view – but mainly to facilitate empirical understanding and wise legal evaluations and juristic strategies.

The chapters in Part II of this book all indicate that jurisprudence needs new resources. It must take full account of the social and political contexts in which problems about system, authority and plurality arise if it is to adapt to address effectively the developing transnational and international dimensions of law – as well as to recognise ways in which legal thinking inside nations is becoming diversified. Law's authority has long been parasitic on the political authority of the state, legitimated by democratic processes. But this may no longer be sufficient. It is necessary to consider more carefully how authority can arise and the various forms it can take. Sociological inquiry reveals authority being created in patterns of social interaction not necessarily regulated or supervised by the state and often unknown to or ignored or misunderstood by state officials and jurists.

Much juristic work is concerned with *values* that law serves and it might be thought that social science has little to offer the jurist here. Sociology is concerned with 'is' not 'ought', with understanding facts, not applying values. But I argue that a sociological perspective can clarify much about the role of values in law and society. This is the main focus of the chapters in Part III. Sociological inquiry cannot resolve value questions, but it can explain much about ways in which these questions arise, the forms they take, and why some become important to law and therefore prominent in juristic thought, in certain times and places.

Certain values are argued for in this book as particularly important to a juristic idea of law: values of justice and security as popularly understood in a variety of ways and solidarity as the value that law must serve if it is oriented towards integrating social life and limiting conflict. If efforts are made to promote these (or other) values in legal regulation, sociological resources may be important in helping to show how far and under what conditions these efforts can succeed. In this book, primarily Durkheimian sociological traditions are invoked to support such claims. Other sociological resources could certainly be used, but I try to show in Part III that Durkheimian ideas are especially instructive. They illustrate well some analytical resources of a sociologically oriented jurisprudence.

The following chapters can be treated to some extent as independent essays addressing different aspects of a set of interrelated problems. They indicate challenges facing jurisprudence and illustrate a sociological approach to this field. They are intended not to suggest that all problems of jurisprudence are sociological but rather to assert that a sociological perspective must be part of the jurist's outlook.

This is certainly not a claim that jurisprudence must accept dependence on any social science discipline (or, indeed, any other academic discipline). Its allegiance is simply to law as an idea of specific values to be embodied in regulatory practice. The task of the jurist is to expound and defend this idea. This entails recognising law's responsibility to reflect popular aspirations for justice and security and its integrative tasks as a general resource of regulation for important communal networks and for individuals interacting under its protection.

Despite advocating a sociological perspective, this book does not set out to explain comprehensively the social character of law in empirical terms. The juristic role is to promote law's well-being as an idea, not to observe it scientifically as a practice. But, in promoting law in this way, the jurist has to make the fullest possible use of systematic, empirical studies of law as a field of practice and experience, a social phenomenon in a social context. Sociologists need juristic knowledge if they are to understand law as ideas informing practice, but jurists need sociological insight if they are to fulfil their role in all its aspects.

Various chapters incorporate in extensively revised form material published elsewhere. I am grateful for permission to adapt content from the following journals and books: *Ratio Juris* (Wiley) vol 26 (2013) 510–22 (Chapter 3); *Jurisprudence* (Taylor & Francis) vol 5 (2014) 41–55 (Chapter 4); S. Taekema, B. van Klink and W. de Been eds, *Facts and Norms in Law* (Edward Elgar, 2016) 242–62 (Chapter 5); N. Roughan and A. Halpin eds, *In Pursuit of Pluralist Jurisprudence* (Cambridge University Press, 2017) 20–39 (Chapter 6); S. Donlan and L. H. Urscheler eds, *Concepts of Law* (Routledge, 2014) 193–208 (Chapter 7); *Law & Social Inquiry* (Wiley) vol 37 (2012) 500–24 (Chapter 8); R. Cotterrell and M. Del Mar eds, *Authority in Transnational Legal Theory* (Edward Elgar, 2016) 253–79 (Chapter 9); V. Mitsilegas, P. Alldridge and L. Cheliotis eds, *Globalisation, Criminal Law and Criminal Justice* (Hart, 2015) 7–23 (Chapter 10); *International Journal of Law in Context* (Cambridge University Press) vol 4 (2009) 373–84 (Chapter 11); *Social & Legal Studies* (Sage) vol 20 (2011) 3–20 (Chapter 12); K. Dahlstrand ed, *Festskrift till Karsten Åström* (Juristförlaget i Lund, 2016) 111–29 (Chapter 14).

Among the many people who have in various ways helped my recent work for this book I particularly want to thank the following: Reza Banakar, Maksymilian Del Mar, Michael Freeman, Werner Gephart, Rosemary Hunter, Valsamis Mitsilegas, David Nelken, Richard Nobles, Stanley L. Paulson, Nicky Priaulx, David Schiff, Phil Thomas, Kenneth Veitch, Matthew Weait, and Mauro Zamboni. Finally, my love and gratitude, as ever, to Ann Cotterrell, who continues to give the support and encouragement that underpin all my work.

1

INTRODUCTION

Recovering sociological jurisprudence

A view across a century

A century ago it was considered self-evident in the most progressive fora of Western legal scholarship that jurisprudence – juristic perspectives on the nature of law – would and should draw on the then newly emergent science of sociology, as well as on the developing social sciences in general. In a time of rapid legal and social change it could hardly be doubted, except by those who wished somehow to stop the clock of history, that legal scholarship needed resources from the new sciences of social life. By this means, legal thought could learn from social theory and reshape itself to confront the modern challenges for law arising in complex, diverse, industrialised Western societies.

At the beginning of the twenty-first century, however, social science has lost much of the lustre that, in its pioneer decades, attached to it as a new set of resources for understanding social life. Economics, not sociology, gradually established itself as the most prestigious among the various social sciences that could be called on to inform policy analysis. It seemed to offer objective technical knowledge to inform the management of modern capitalist societies, their increasingly elaborate financial systems, and eventually their interactions in a global system – this system appearing to have its own dynamics that have come to be called the processes of globalisation. But even economics – despite being attractively, from the policymaker's point of view, oriented to 'efficiency' – has now lost much of its prestige in many quarters as it has seemed to fail in predicting far-reaching economic crises and offering clear solutions to them or ways to prevent their recurrence.

Sociology was once seen as the master social science, embracing all others, because it studied social relations *in general* or 'society' *as a whole*, rather than specific aspects of society (e.g. the economy or polity) or specific types of social action (e.g. economic calculation). But it has tended to retreat from its early ambition to develop firmly empirically oriented, historically grounded social theory, that is, theory that could map the broad contours of social change, the basic frameworks of order and cohesion enabling societies to exist, and the shifting patterns and structures of social relations. Instead, sociology has become, to a large extent, a fragmented intellectual discipline, split into distinct specialisms (e.g. sociologies of race, gender, class, sexual orientation, work, education, organisations, politics, religion, deviance, family life, popular culture). And the field of social theory has often been relinquished to philosophical speculation.[1]

However, insofar as jurisprudence has been seen as theoretical knowledge aimed at giving jurists an overall perspective on law in general (at least, law as understood in the legal systems the jurists serve), ambitious empirically oriented social theory, giving a perspective on social existence at large (not any particular region of it), has always been seen as potentially the most useful sociological contribution to jurisprudence. The generality of social theory's perspective on social life could mirror and inform the generality of jurisprudence's perspective on the whole life of law as jurists encountered it. Jurisprudence, on this view, ought to be able to draw on empirically oriented social theory to put its perceptions of law into a larger socio-historical perspective, just as it ought to draw on various strands of philosophy to put them into a broader intellectual, political, and ethical context.

Amenable to these ideas, jurisprudence, a century ago, looked to sociology for perspective. Thus, the early outlook of Roscoe Pound's sociological jurisprudence was significantly influenced by a broad idea of 'social control' (Pound 1942), especially as expounded by the pioneer American sociologist Edward Ross (Ross 1901; Hunt 1978: 19–20). Ross analysed types of such control (e.g. public opinion, custom, education, personal beliefs, moral sentiments), which he saw as guaranteeing the cohesion of social life in modern societies. He identified law as especially important among them – 'the most specialised and highly finished engine' of social control (Ross 1901: 106).[2] Thus, for jurists seeking to locate their subject, law, in a larger intellectual universe, sociology could seem to offer the potential to tie legal scholarship firmly into much wider regions of social inquiry; and it could validate law as an important topic for social analysis. As the epitome of a new kind of social inquiry offering enlightenment about the nature of contemporary society, sociology could help to place jurisprudence alongside the other leading sciences of modern life. To the extent that jurisprudence was sensitive to the new currents of social science, it had the prospect of being supported by them.

Today, sociology can still perform something of this integrative function for jurisprudence but only if it is appreciated just how radically the context for this has changed. Current resources of sociology for law are entirely different from what they were when the idea of a sociological jurisprudence was introduced in the Anglophone world and

---

1 See e.g. Elliott and Turner eds 2001, in which many chapters are devoted to the work of theorists who would usually be characterised as philosophers.

2 On the complex ambivalence of Ross's concept of social control, none of which is reflected in Pound's appropriation of it, see e.g. Ross 1991: 235–40. Social control became an enduring if variously interpreted concept in sociology, also widely invoked in sociology of law. See especially Black 1976; 1998.

explored in continental Europe in the decade before World War I.[3] Also, the nature of jurisprudence – its scope, tasks and relation to other spheres of knowledge – is now understood very differently. The idea of jurisprudence as the jurist's theoretical understanding of the nature of law needs much clarification after a century of transformation of legal theory and of reassessment of the resources on which it can draw.

Sociology in the study of law

Sociological jurisprudence was, and remains, an enterprise of *jurists* appealing to social science for aid in their own projects of analysing legal doctrine and institutions and improving juristic practice. But social scientists interested in law have certainly not remained content just to be on call to serve such juristic purposes. Sociologists have taken law as a topic of research for their own disciplinary projects. The special scientific enterprise of sociology of law evolved during the twentieth century, initially as a mainly speculative, theoretical inquiry built on the ideas of such thinkers as Karl Marx, Émile Durkheim, Max Weber, and Ferdinand Tönnies and, later, Georges Gurvitch, Talcott Parsons, Theodor Geiger, and Niklas Luhmann. However, from around the midpoint of the twentieth century, in the United States, Europe, and elsewhere, detailed empirical studies of the working of legal systems began to proliferate – especially studies of courts in operation, the varieties of lawyers' practice, the work of administrative and enforcement agencies, the processes of law creation, and citizens' experience of law. This research – often now termed 'law and society' scholarship or sociolegal studies – soon drew on the resources of all or any of the social sciences and has flourished especially in Anglophone countries. Law has become a major focus for empirical social scientific research. But this burgeoning research enterprise has rarely made links with jurisprudence.

As sociology of law has increasingly drawn on the social sciences at large, it has seemed unimportant for most purposes to distinguish it from explicitly multidisciplinary 'law and society' or sociolegal studies. So 'sociology' as a resource for research on law is now often seen in practice as a 'transdisciplinary' form of sociology. In other words, it is a compendium of theory, methods, and traditions of inquiry that, while certainly owing most to sociology's heritage as an academic discipline, is not tied to the protocols, priorities, and professional outlook of that discipline or any other. Instead 'sociology' in this context can be taken to refer to any inquiry that seeks to study some facet of the social world (for example its legal aspects) systematically and empirically, with a serious concern to identify *social variation* (Cotterrell and Selznick 2004: 296) – that is, the characteristics that distinguish social environments from one another – and the effects and causes of that variation. This is the way in which sociology is understood in the context of this book.

While most sociological study of law, in this sense, has studied observable social action (e.g. the practices of lawyers, police, administrators, legislators, litigants, or

---

3 See Pound 1907. The most influential of the theories of the 'free law' school in Germany, Austria, and France in the period before World War I pointed strongly to the need for sociological resources to be used in juristic practice and judicial decision-making: see generally Wigmore et al eds 1917.

citizens seeking informally to resolve disputes or get redress), there is no reason why *legal ideas* cannot be studied sociologically. Indeed, they should be so studied, if sociological inquiry is to be able to portray law realistically as practice and experience. It is possible, for example, to examine why and how legal ideas emerge in particular times and places, why certain issues become legally significant while others do not, why legal doctrine develops in certain directions rather than others, why legal ideas sometimes seem to reflect social change and sometimes seem to resist it. Sociology can, in such ways, illuminate the progress of legal thought in particular sociohistorical contexts and offer insight into legal problems.

There can – and should – be a sociology of legal ideas, and it can even be said that sociology of law is not complete without it. Sociologists need to study law as doctrine (rules, principles, concepts, values) as well as law as a focus for official or citizens' action if they are to be able to take into account juristic understandings and engage with law as normative ideas informing practice and experience.

Crucially, however, a scientific sociology of legal ideas is not, in itself, sociological jurisprudence. While in practice there might be much overlap in approaches and results, these are in essence different projects. A sociology of legal ideas has to justify itself as a disinterested, explanatory, social scientific study – although one that may often produce knowledge of great juristic interest. It is true that legal scholars have contributed to the development of sociology of law, turning themselves into social scientists for the purposes of inquiry. And sometimes their intention in doing so has been to produce scientific knowledge of the social character of law that might be juristically useful.[4] But sociological jurisprudence as a scholarly enterprise cannot purport to be a disinterested social science. It is necessarily always in the practical service of the jurist. Today, as a century ago, it needs to be understood not as a science in itself but merely as a way of doing jurisprudence, a way of intellectually informing juristic practice, contributing to the fulfilment of practical juristic tasks.

In this perspective, sociology, like philosophy, history, or any other field of knowledge, is just a resource on which the jurist – magpie-like – can draw for inspiration and enlightenment in the practical tasks of making law work. Jurisprudence, seen in this way, is not an academic discipline but a kind of bricolage – an assembly of bits and pieces of insight about law that can ultimately be of potential value for juristic practice, putting it into a broadening perspective.

This view of jurisprudence is developed in Chapter 4. A full justification of it, however, depends on an understanding and defence of the very specific role of the jurist which it presupposes. Chapter 3 is devoted to exploring this role. And, as a preliminary to that, an even more basic inquiry has to be pursued: it needs to be asked what special expertise jurists can and should claim and how far their expertise

---

4 A classic case is the work of one of the founders of sociology of law, the Austrian jurist Eugen Ehrlich, whose pioneer sociology (Ehrlich 1936) was intended in part to produce social knowledge that could inform the operation of state law, especially as applied by state courts. But, as sociology, it set out to explain the regulatory structures of social life, finding them in diverse forms of social association with variable relations to state law.

is to be understood as the (complex and perhaps elusive) expertise that every lawyer professes. So, in Chapter 2, the nature of lawyers' expertise is considered, and this exploration sets the scene for the discussion in the following two chapters of the juristic role – presented as an ideal type, not as an attempt to generalise about jurists in all times and cultures. Then, in Chapter 5, discussion returns to the question of the place that sociological inquiries can and should occupy in juristic practice.

In the rest of the present chapter, and as a prelude to these further discussions, two remaining questions need to be answered. First, how does the general conception of the nature of jurisprudence introduced earlier and elaborated later in this book correspond with currently dominant views of theoretical inquiries in law? In other words, how does jurisprudence, at least in the contemporary Anglophone world, stand? Second, what can be learned about the possibilities for new linkages between jurisprudence and sociology today from past experience of efforts to develop a sociological jurisprudence? What is worth retrieving (or perhaps reinterpreting) from this historical experience, and what past mistakes need to be avoided (or perhaps reassessed in the light of changed conditions for both jurisprudence and social science today)?

Jurisprudence declining, theory flourishing?

'It is ironic that at the same time that jurisprudence in the sense of a formal subject for study seems to be vanishing from the sight-line of the law school, theory has become more and more important to the legal academic' (Leith and Morison 2005: 147). This view, recently expressed in a United Kingdom context, entails two claims, both controversial but both substantially correct.

The negative claim is that jurisprudence as a taught subject for prospective law-yers has lost its way. Its purpose has become unclear and therefore its position in legal education has become uncertain. Indeed, this uncertainty may always have existed. A general, rather vague idea of jurisprudence as the 'lawyer's extraversion' (Stone 1968: 16) – that is, a theoretical perspective affirming the unity of the juristic craft while linking it to larger bodies of knowledge and wider culture – might have significance; in certain circumstances it might help to enhance the status of law-yers' legal thought and practice in both professional and political terms (Cotterrell 2003: 11–13). But jurisprudence has perhaps become less amenable to these kinds of professional and political uses – whatever their significance in the past – as it has been transformed in the Anglo-American legal world in the second half of the twentieth century into a self-consciously professionalised legal philosophy. As such, it presents itself as a branch of philosophy seeking legitimacy from the academic discipline of philosophy, rather than from any assumed direct practical relevance to lawyers' professional experience and thought. In Chapter 4 this transformation of jurisprudence into a subfield of philosophy is analysed and it is argued that while the benefits of this development in terms of philosophical credibility and status may be undeniable, the consequences for jurisprudence *as a resource for jurists* have been much less beneficial.

If legal philosophy essentially seeks intellectual legitimacy from the discipline of philosophy rather than from the requirements of lawyers' legal studies, its position in the law school is likely to be insecure. As jurisprudence in the law school curriculum has significantly allied itself with academic philosophy (for which law is just one topic for philosophical study among others) its relevance for juristic legal studies has become uncertain. Insofar as legal philosophy chooses its topics of study for their philosophical interest rather than for their juristic importance in the world of legal practice, its intellectual orientation can easily appear to be at a tangent to the jurist's or lawyer's professional orientation – a situation that has been explicitly recognised (and even welcomed) by some leading legal philosophers.[5]

The argument developed in subsequent chapters of this book is certainly not that contemporary legal philosophy is unimportant to jurisprudence; it is merely that these intellectual enterprises should not be confused. Jurisprudence is too important to be allowed to wither because its purpose has ceased to be understood. The decline of jurisprudence might easily appear as an unacknowledged marker of the loss of a clear, unambiguous recognition of the distinctive responsibilities – intellectual, ethical, political – of juristic work itself. The place of jurisprudence in the formation of the lawyer ought to be, amongst other things, a reminder that training in the arts and crafts of legal practice is not only a matter of technical efficiency in the interpretation, manipulation, and organisation of rules (important though that technical competence is).

It should be a means of affirming that (i) for all lawyers law is ultimately to be understood as involving value choices (expressed especially in the form of legal rules) for which they must take responsibility, and (ii) that the integrated, value-oriented *idea of law* (complex, fluid, and variable as that idea is) is something to be nurtured and endlessly rethought by those legal professionals who are willing to undertake the role and responsibility of jurists.

Much of what follows in this book – especially in the chapters in Part I – is intended to elaborate this now often underemphasised idea of a specific juristic consciousness. It follows that jurists – for whom jurisprudence is a necessary theoretical resource – are certainly not restricted to academic specialists who profess jurisprudence as a distinct law school subject. Indeed, to the extent that taught jurisprudence has been turned into professionalised legal philosophy, jurists will not necessarily and certainly not always be found among self-identifying jurisprudence specialists. They will be found among all kinds of committed lawyers with theoretical sensibilities who seek to develop broad perspectives on their intellectual practice in law. Today there are many such lawyers. Hence, as the earlier quotation states, 'theory has become more and more important to the legal academic', but also to practising lawyers, judges, and other professionals working with law who share the juristic outlook.

Juristic theory is, however, only one kind of legal theory and – as noted earlier – is a bricolage kind of knowledge packaged to be a useful compendium of insights for

5 See Chapter 4, pp 54–5.

juristic purposes. Theory can be of other kinds. It can also be theory that structures, orients, and legitimises distinct academic disciplines or knowledge-fields organised for purposes of scientific or philosophical inquiry. So, legal theory will mean something different in the context of legal philosophy from what it means for jurisprudence. In one formulation, it might mean 'the clarification of legal values and postulates up to their ultimate philosophical foundations'.[6] Similarly legal theory in sociology of law serves different purposes again; here it is scientific theory – empirically oriented, explanatory theory of law as a social phenomenon – properly oriented to the needs of disinterested social scientific inquiry.

All of these kinds of academically developed theory can sometimes be useful for juristic purposes but their nature and the reasons for their development should not be confused. The fact that they so often have been confused has resulted in much fruitless argument about what is 'genuine' legal theory or what can properly be admitted to the pantheon of theoretical inquiries about law.

On the one hand, legal theory is many mansions, juristic, philosophical, and social scientific. On the other hand, these distinct theoretical endeavours do not exist in inevitable isolation from one another. There is no reason why legal theory developed in different disciplines and practices cannot be used in common debates around law, as long as the purposes for which theory has been created in different regions of intellectual life are recognised and respected.

Revisiting early sociological jurisprudence

A century ago jurisprudence – as juristic legal theory – had a very different intellectual profile as a knowledge-field from the one it has today. Before its modern professionalization as a branch of the academic discipline of philosophy, it was a relatively open intellectual terrain in which the speculations of jurists on the nature and functions of law could be gathered and compared with scant regard to any need to organise these speculations as a rigorously defined discipline, unified by common aims, accepted methods, and tightly policed canons of philosophical rigour. It was not necessary to have been trained as a philosopher to be able to contribute to jurisprudence. One needed only to be a jurist with something of interest to say about law as a focus of juristic practice and social experience. One could, indeed, 'philosophise' about law without being a philosopher, and for many jurists their speculations about law in general were merely a complement to their practical activities in expounding legal doctrine or promoting law reform.

So, it was easy to use the terms 'jurisprudence' and 'legal philosophy' interchangeably to indicate a potentially unlimited range of topics for and approaches to speculation about law and to include in the scope of jurisprudence any studies in political theory, social theory, moral philosophy, ethnology, political economy, history, or other intellectual fields that could be considered to be relevant to the practical

6 Gustav Radbruch, quoted in Friedmann 1967: 4.

workings of law (e.g. Berolzheimer 1912). Such an approach courted many dangers – of dilettantism and superficiality – and the philosophical professionalization (and narrowing) of Anglophone jurisprudence from the mid-twentieth century, influenced by English analytical philosophy, was widely welcomed by scholars acutely conscious of these dangers. This development was initially seen by some of its supporters as helping legal studies to achieve full academic respectability in the university environment through their demonstrable disciplinary integrity founded on unifying, sophisticated legal theory and systematic, explicit methods of legal analysis.

From another point of view, however, the philosophical professionalization of jurisprudence could often be considered an impoverishment. Along with much disorganised, derivative, and directionless literature of bricolage jurisprudence created in the period before this modern professionalization, some works of great and wide juristic vision, insight, and imagination were produced.[7] The openness of 'pre-professionalised' jurisprudence at least allowed juristic thought to engage freely with many intellectual fields: the consequence was the easy production of hybrids such as historical jurisprudence, ethnological jurisprudence, psychological jurisprudence, and sociological jurisprudence. In all cases their potential was greater than their achievement, yet their greatest scholarly products are properly seen as juristic classics.[8]

What should be learned from the development of a sociological jurisprudence during this period prior to modern philosophical professionalization? What insights did it establish that are of lasting value? And what prevented its fuller engagement with modern social studies of law? This last question will be looked at in some detail in Chapter 5 as a prelude to considering how sociology today can be used for juristic purposes. Here it is important to focus more on the other questions – especially because few attempts have been made in recent times to defend the early projects of sociological jurisprudence, as set out most famously and influentially in Roscoe Pound's work.

Pound's reputation has suffered primarily because his programme of sociological jurisprudence was overtaken by more radical intellectual enterprises (first, legal realism and, second, sociology of law) that revealed it as conservative and intellectually compromised although it had at first been seen, with some justification, as daring and innovative (Wigdor 1974; Hull 1997; Hunt 1978).[9] Legal realism, with its detached, unromanticised view of the judicial process and its willingness to emphasise the all-too-human limitations of judges, was rejected by Pound insofar

---

7 Even after the advent of contemporary positivist legal philosophy, this continued to some extent. See e.g. Friedmann 1967, a wide-ranging, consistently thoughtful survey text that can still be consulted with profit.

8 A small, indicative sample from this literature might include Gierke 1950, Jhering 1913, Petrazycki 1955, Duguit 1921, and Gurvitch 1932.

9 Pound's work was extremely influential in popularising the idea that law's normative reasoning and processes should not be regarded as intellectually self-contained but must be informed by empirical social understanding. For recent reevaluations of Pound and early sociological jurisprudence in this respect in various contexts see Knepper 2016, Brock 2011, Astorino 1996. See also Simon 2008 (calling for a renewed sociological jurisprudence); Fischman 2013 (importance of linking normative legal analysis and empirical social research).

as it challenged his ultimate faith in common law judges' ability to safeguard the virtues and values of law. Sociological jurisprudence initially called in aid sociological insights into social conditions to reveal inadequacies in the administration of justice by courts and in the social policies that both legislatures and courts seemed to promote, but ultimately Pound saw judicial wisdom and the judicial function as the irreplaceable heart of Anglo-American law. So, sociological jurisprudence, as Pound promoted it, aimed to serve and improve the judicial process but not to undermine a basic faith in its soundness.[10]

Pound saw less of a threat from developing sociology of law, which he associated most often and most approvingly with Eugen Ehrlich's pioneer empirical studies of social norms (in Ehrlich's terminology 'living law') – norms that, for Ehrlich, courts and legislatures must take into account if state law is to work effectively (Ehrlich 1936; 1917: 77–81). But the effect of the development of sociology of law was eventually to bypass jurisprudence – making a sociological jurisprudence seem irrelevant – because legal sociologists rightly saw that legislators, not courts or jurists, would be the most powerful agents of change in modern law, and sociology of law could have most relevance and power if it guided and critiqued legislative and administrative action on the basis of empirical research, rather than focusing on the interpretation of legal doctrine by judges as Pound's sociological jurisprudence tended to do.

The major limitation of Pound's sociological jurisprudence in the context of its time was its almost exclusive court focus, even though in his early work he called on legislatures to correct the failings of courts and help to adapt the law to emerging socioeconomic conditions. By contrast, modern sociology of law, sociolegal studies, and 'law and society' research have developed a much wider view of law, certainly not ignoring the work of courts but seeing law existing in many other environments than the courtroom. Indeed, one of the primary contributions of modern empirical sociolegal research has been to show that much experience of law and much of the operation of law takes place entirely outside the purview of courts. Yet the early history of sociological jurisprudence shows it as very strongly associated with problems of judicial decision-making.

Pound's work puts immense confidence in the ability of judges, properly guided and sometimes corrected, to develop law in accordance with social needs (with those needs perhaps clarified by using the resources of sociology). But this is not merely an Anglo-American common law outlook. Comparable developments in continental Europe early in the twentieth century show a similar orientation. The theorists of 'free law finding' (*freie Rechtsfindung* or *libre recherche scientifique*) in Germany, Austria, and France (Wigmore et al eds 1917) argued that where gaps existed in the law as expressed in legislation or code provisions, the judge should fill those gaps creatively and responsibly, balancing the interests at stake within the

---

10 Tidmarsh (2006: 522) notes that Pound 'always believed that an independent judiciary should be the principal organ for transmitting social scientific principles into action'.

framework of the legal provisions, and sociology would be among the important resources available to the judge in doing this.[11] Judges should not 'mechanically' apply legal provisions without carefully considering their social effects. The 'free law' arguments of continental European jurists were in this respect essentially identical with Pound's (1908) strictures against the myopic 'mechanical jurisprudence' of some American common law judges.

Moral distance as a juristic problem

Although, in its time, the fixation of sociological jurisprudence with the judicial function may have been a limitation (putting too much ultimate faith in judges and too little emphasis on the modern creation of law outside courts), it might not be seen in quite the same way today. The pervasive loss of faith in legislation as an instrument of change, the recognition of the limits of governmental regulatory power, and the ebb and flow of distrust in administrative processes and bureaucracies[12] have all tended to renew scholarly interest in debating how far courts (or less formally organised tribunals) might be intermediaries of some kind between the political regulatory processes of the state and the expressed or unexpressed interests and aspirations of diverse social and cultural groups.[13]

Courts surely have many inherent inadequacies in taking on any such intermediary role. But the idea of identifying some locus at which state regulation and everyday social experience are brought into direct, mutually respectful contact is not unimportant. What the sociological jurists sensed was a need for some kind of ongoing, regular *communication process* between the perceptions and ambitions of regulators and the experience and expectations of the regulated. The problem of moral distance (a many-sided problem of communication failures, inadequate information, regulatory hubris, and frequent popular alienation) between state policymakers and regulators, on the one hand, and the populations they purport to regulate, on the other (Cotterrell 1995: 302–6), seems to grow more serious as contemporary societies become more complex and diverse and as transnational pressures influence regulatory policies in many states seemingly irrespective of the wishes of their populations.

---

11 In a common law context outside the United States, the writings of the Australian jurist Julius Stone, following Pound's lead, 'suggested that the courts should identify the social interests or demands underlying legal disputes and . . . strike an appropriate balance between them . . . [so that judges would] avoid relying on categories of illusory reference . . . and . . . articulate . . . the real reasons for their decisions' (Aroney 2008: 132).

12 For a sample of views see Rottleuthner 1989, Teubner 1992, Yeager 1993, Delgado and Stefancic 1994, Banakar 2016: 55–8, noting (p 57) that the 'insight that law was not the effective vehicle for social engineering which many public policymakers and legislatures had envisaged or hoped for is shared commonly by various approaches within legal sociology'.

13 See e.g. Collins 1986 and Redlich 1988 (courts as agents of democracy), Galanter 1983 (courts' diffuse social influence), Mirchandani 2008 (social role of 'problem-solving' courts), Dumas 2018 (legislature and courts can represent the same public but in different ways).

Sociological jurisprudence, in implicitly recognising aspects of the problem of moral distance, assumed that well-functioning courts with able, socially aware judges – 'the intellectual and social flower of the nation', as Ehrlich (1917: 74–5) expansively put it – could be part of the answer. It never really tested this assumption and, in Pound's case, dismissed the American legal realists' efforts to do so (Pound 1931). So its answer to the problem of moral distance remained undeveloped and ultimately reliant on an unexamined faith.

Despite such limitations, what is of continuing importance about early sociological jurisprudence is that it saw problems of relating state regulatory ambitions to popular aspirations and experience as central to *juristic* responsibilities (perhaps the most important part of them). By contrast, sociology of law has often tended to see these only as *political* problems about the efficient formulation and implementation of state regulation, on which social science might advise. So, the fundamental lesson of sociological jurisprudence is that the need to make legal regulation socially responsive, properly informed about social conditions, and aware of popular sentiment and experience, is a necessary and fundamental concern for jurists, and not just for politicians, legislators, and administrators.

The need to obtain reliable empirical social knowledge and insight to address the problem of moral distance therefore points towards the significance of sociology in the administration of justice at all levels, as well as in the main processes of state law-making. It points to the importance of renewing and refurbishing some aspirations of sociological jurisprudence, but with a much more serious and sustained engagement with contemporary social science than happened in Pound's time.

It is, indeed, easy to pinpoint the stage in Pound's work at which the appeal to social science was permanently discarded (though he continued to label his jurisprudence as sociological). Pound saw the task of law as to balance conflicting interests – individual, social, and public – that were being pressed for recognition and protection. Law selects the interests it will recognise, the means of weighing them, and the degree of protection it will give to them. The crucial problem for law – and for sociological jurisprudence – is how to identify interests arising in social life and confronting the legal system.

An ambitious and genuinely sociological approach would have been to look behind the interests being presented directly by litigants in court so as to identify the social forces that such interest claims reflected. Some 'free law' theorists advocated just such a step. But Pound, no doubt conscious of the pioneer limitations of early twentieth-century sociology, stepped back from using sociological inquiries to address juristic problems directly. The sociological vagueness and opacity of the concept of 'interest' would be bypassed, in his work, by the strategy of looking merely at the kinds of interests pressed in court and in legislative lobbying.

Instead of a rich picture of social life, the 'scheme of interests', as Pound called it, would represent claims actually already brought to the attention of the judicial and legislative systems. Sociological jurisprudence, in this way, turned in on itself, away from sociological inquiry and back to the existing experience of lawyers and officials. Despite the limitations of social science at the time, it is not obvious that early sociological jurisprudence had to sheer off its sociological promise so completely in this way.

Legal values and sociological jurisprudence

Classic sociological jurisprudence developed some insights that need re-emphasising. Pound rightly stressed that law is much more than just rules. Today, jurists and legal philosophers are familiar with Ronald Dworkin's (1978) critique of the 'model of rules' as the essence of the concept of law and his claim that law must also be seen in terms of principles, standards, and values. But while this critique has usually been understood as part of a debate about the intellectual identity of law and the criteria of unity and autonomy of a legal system, for Pound the reason for insisting that law was not just a matter of rules was to present law realistically as part of the value structure making up the civilisation (we might now say the culture) of the society in which it exists (Pound 1923: 141–51; 1958: ch 8).

So, law is less a matter of rights than of the recognition and ordering of interests by society's regulatory institutions. And law is directionless if thought of in terms of rules unless the rules link to principles and standards guided by and reflecting societal values. The experience of developing legal ideas within a larger framework of cultural values (what Pound called the jural postulates of law) is as important to the logical structure of law as is the positivist ordering of rules in juristic categories.

While sociology of law can concern itself with legal values, it cannot directly guide their appropriate development. It can only try to clarify the context of value debates, the conditions under which such debates seem relevant, and the consequences of seeking to implement particular values through law.[14] But jurisprudence, serving the jurist's professional commitment to law as an affair of values, can and should use the resources of sociology, along with any other intellectual resources that can be helpful, to inform its project. This does not mean that sociology, in the transdisciplinary sense proposed in this chapter, should be put into a distinct compartment on the jurist's shelf of available resources, separated from other potential inputs into juristic thought. The sociological perspective cannot monopolise juristic thought but has to *inform* all aspects of juristic thinking. The jurist has to understand law as a social phenomenon using all available resources for studying that phenomenon empirically, seeing it as a particular regulatory aspect or field of social life.

This is why sociological jurisprudence is not *a particular kind* of jurisprudence or a particular theoretical region within jurisprudence. It is not, for example, a 'third theory' of law to be set alongside (and quarantined from) legal positivist theory and natural law theory.[15] These other approaches to theory need also to be sociologically informed and

---

14 See especially Chapters 5 and 12.
15 This kind of categorisation is widespread in the literature, often as an attempt to mark out a secure place for sociological approaches in jurisprudence but also often with the implication that they are separate from other approaches. Thus Tamanaha 2015 sees 'social legal theory' as a 'third pillar of jurisprudence', requiring recognition and development as a sociological jurisprudence; Stone 1968: 18–20 distinguishes sociological or functional jurisprudence (or law and society), analytical jurisprudence (or law and logic), and critical, censorial, or ethical jurisprudence (or law and justice), consigning the treatment of each to separate books. Separate classification of sociological approaches from other jurisprudential approaches, however, facilitates their marginalisation in jurisprudence.

subjected to sociological critique, just as sociological perspectives need to be informed and critiqued by them. The term 'sociological jurisprudence', ideally, should indicate no more than jurisprudence *in general* that is aware of its responsibility to link law's enduring value commitments to a systematic, empirically grounded understanding of the diverse contexts of legal experience.[16] That is, it should indicate jurisprudence consciously oriented to address the need for sociological awareness in all its inquiries.

Part II of this book attempts to survey some newly prominent conditions that make this awareness especially important today. In the book's final part, an effort is made to illustrate, through particular inquiries about contemporary law, how sociological insight can illuminate specific juristic problems or clarify various fields of juristic interest.

How then should contemporary sociological jurisprudence differ most fundamentally from its pioneer forms? Above all, it must engage with sociological research far more seriously than it did a century ago, when there was perhaps some excuse for underestimating sociology's potential, given its fledgling intellectual status, the relative paucity of its empirical research, and the hesitant steps of its early creators. Today, the scope and ambition of sociolegal inquiry is immense. There is no shortage of theoretical and empirical contributions to the social study of law.

It is not necessary, however, to become a practising social scientist in order to be a jurist and to use and contribute to jurisprudence. What is necessary is to adopt a consistent interdisciplinary sensitivity; to read widely and carefully in sociologically oriented studies of law; to be prepared to explore and to seek out helpful guides; above all, to discard any idea that jurisprudence can be a self-contained discipline, a closed-in body of knowledge not dependent for its vitality on the progress of social inquiry. The closely interlinked studies in the rest of this book are intended to suggest how that broad sensitivity can be nourished in jurisprudence and to offer a sample of current work that shows some of the urgent challenges that jurisprudence faces today as well as some of the resources available to help in meeting those challenges.

Ironically, this effect may in turn tend to marginalise jurisprudence from other fields of legal inquiry in which insights from social science have now become familiar components of study.

16 If jurisprudence fully and universally embraced this responsibility, the consequence would be that the term 'sociological jurisprudence' would become redundant. For the present, however, it signals an emphasis in (not a branch of) jurisprudence that, so this book argues, needs to be nurtured and generalised.

PART I
The juristic point of view

2
THE NATURE OF LEGAL EXPERTISE

Dichotomies

Before we ask more specific questions about juristic roles and the nature and challenges of contemporary jurisprudence, a preliminary inquiry is needed. What kind of special skills and knowledge can and do lawyers, in general, profess? Like other professionals, lawyers are recognised as having expertise. But what is it, and how is it assessed? This chapter argues that the nature of legal expertise is complex and problematic. Its character is best brought to light by exploring dichotomies – polarities in the nature and range of lawyers' work that suggest sharply contrasting, even mutually incompatible features of the professional practice of law.

One such dichotomy contrasts a conception of 'legal science' or legal *scholarship*, as a highly specialised intellectual accomplishment focused on legal doctrine, with powerful but more diffuse ideas of lawyer *craft-skills and wisdom*. While important, the latter may be just refinements of citizens' everyday techniques of reasoning in coping with problems and managing their worldly affairs. A second dichotomy contrasts the idea of law as a *public* resource and cultural possession with that of law as arcane technicality and know-how appropriated for purely *private* advantage.

The argument here will be that legal expertise involves much more than knowing legal rules and regulations and how to access them. But its further aspects remain difficult to summarise in general terms because they are validated by different kinds of clients or audiences. However, as subsequent chapters will argue more fully, it is possible to specify more precisely what might be called *juristic* expertise – the perspective on law adopted by one particular kind of legal expert. This focuses on law as an idea structured by values. Juristic expertise is a knowledge and practice committed to the well-being of this idea of law. It involves interpreting and promoting, by means of regulatory techniques and in the light of regulatory experience, basic values of justice, security, and solidarity reflected in typical demands made on law. Legal expertise properly emphasises a 'method of detail' in legal analysis. But there is a place too for a juristic expertise aimed at seeing the 'big picture' in a legal system which is the context of the jurist's work. For the moment, however, our focus is on legal expertise.

Public and private faces of expertise

Legal expertise is sometimes acknowledged in oblique ways. One way, sometimes too little noticed (but very instructive), is evidenced in the familiar phenomenon of jokes about lawyers. In America, lawyer jokes have apparently become so pervasive that the legal sociologist Marc Galanter could build a vast collection of them and go on to write a substantial book (including 300 such jokes) to explore what they tell about lawyers in society (Galanter 2005). Everyone knows the kind of joke: 'Question: How many lawyers does it take to change a light bulb? Answer: How many can you afford?' Or: 'Did you hear that terrorists took a hundred lawyers as hostages? They said that if their demands weren't met they'd start releasing the lawyers one by one.'

Lawyer jokes are even the subject of jokes. The late US Chief Justice Rehnquist said that he often used to begin speeches with jokes that caricatured lawyers but 'I gradually realised that the lawyers in the audience didn't think the jokes were funny and the non-lawyers didn't know they were jokes' (quoted in Stein 2006: 398). Lawyers as a professional group have been singled out for criticism throughout history, but some American scholars have asked why jokes have, in recent decades, become such a pervasive vehicle for this criticism in their country – one in which, far more than in most other countries, legal expertise is seen as central to the national culture, an essential resource in addressing problems in almost all aspects of life.

Lawyer jokes are said to 'represent a broad discontent with the legal profession', 'a broad public disillusionment' (Overton 1995: 1099, 1107). Yet, surveys have shown that lawyers are also respected for their skill, their ability to solve problems, and perhaps especially for their devotion to client interests (Galanter 1998: 808–10; Post 1987: 380). And in the United States, where jokes against lawyers are apparently most prevalent, the most extreme *reverence* for law itself as an idea also often seems to exist, though its extent waxes and wanes at various times. There is some significant popular sense that the nation is founded on law and that law is central to the national character. If, as Robert Post (1987: 379) writes, the 'most striking image of the lawyer in popular culture is the intense hostility with which it is invested', this seems to go along with a deep-rooted if not necessarily evenly distributed respect for law, or at least a firm and broad public recognition of its indispensability.

Post emphasises, in this context, a duality of popular thinking which is surely not restricted to the American context. It will be argued here that it is an important key to the ambiguities of legal expertise. On the one hand is a notion of law as *technical know-how which lawyers manipulate* or circumvent for clients in sometimes valuable, sometimes threatening and dangerous ways ('a strict if dubious legality') (Post 1987: 382). On the other is the image of law as a public resource, the means of justice and *the embodiment of values of a community*, law as a crucial integrative structure of society. 'Popular culture,' Post argues, 'is filled with the contradiction between these two kinds of law,' 'between reasons that are hair splitting, and reason that is absolute' (1987: 383, 384). But rather than two kinds of law, perhaps what is identified here are two aspects of lawyers' legal expertise that exist in permanent tension – a tension that may explain in part why lawyers seem to be far more often the victims of jokes than are other professionals (Galanter 1998: 816). One might dramatise the tension by saying that the lawyer's expertise is that of both the *priest* and the *magician* – on the one hand, purveyor of a benevolent knowledge that, for those who believe in it, both transcends and supports individual life; on the other, master of a secret art that can turn right and wrong upside down.

The religion-magic metaphor is less bizarre than it might seem. Émile Durkheim (1995) theorised religion as a crucial means by which societies have represented themselves to themselves. He thought that where no official religions exist, unofficial ones might need to take their place. Postmodernist theory sometimes claimed that, if in contemporary conditions there is nothing else left for people to believe in, law might remain the sole possible object of faith (Cotterrell 2003: 250–2). And human rights have often been called a modern religion, the sole remaining universal object of faith for secular society (e.g. Cole 2012; Féron 2014). A long tradition of literature compares lawyers with priests – the point often being to suggest some mystical influence of lawyers' work.[1] But the priest metaphor can also evoke the idea of an expert whose task is to link the universal and the particular, the big picture of life in society with the local detail of everyday problems, the transcendent with the mundane, in a way that serves both the common good and the particular individual who needs help.

Magicians in the Durkheimian view are radically different from priests: Durkheim's followers Marcel Mauss and Henri Hubert saw magic as derived from religion but a *corruption* of religion's openly recognised, public worth, a siphoning off of its power for private, secret ends (Mauss 1972) – like covertly tapping into the public electricity supply to run a private generator, stealing a public resource for private gain. The essence of magic is arcane knowledge, kept from public scrutiny, safeguarded by impenetrable mystique, creating an awe of the power it controls for good (white magic) or ill (black). Thomas More wrote in his *Utopia* of lawyers as 'people whose profession it is to disguise matters' (quoted in Post 1987: 379). And Karl Llewellyn, never afraid of blunt prose, declared that the idea that the heart of lawyers' work lies in their 'peculiar knowledge of the law . . . gives us [lawyers] a sort of standing as monopolists in a secret lore; and it may be we have discovered that the priests of any black art can make the uninitiated pay well for mystic service'.[2]

---

1 See e.g. the classic polemic of Arnold 1935, especially pp 59–71; and noting (p 224) 'the comforting belief of a legal paradise' that could be reached 'if we only had time and money' to attain it.

2 Llewellyn 1962: 318. Cf Yale law professor Fred Rodell in 1939, quoted in Strickland (1986: 203): 'In tribal times, there were the medicine-men. In the Middle Ages, there were the priests. Today there are the lawyers. For every age, a group . . . learned in their trade and jealous of their learning, who blend technical competence with plain and fancy hocus-pocus to make themselves masters of their fellow men.'

These polemics will not be further pursued here. But the idea they provoke of a potential conflict between two aspects of legal expertise is important. On one side is legal knowledge as a cultural, communal resource which the lawyer can tap into and interpret to the citizen, perhaps ideally almost like a conscientious priest whose practice of addressing mundane problems is based on a grand transcendent scheme of thought and conviction. On the other side is an obscure, technical 'artificial reason' of law which perhaps only the lawyer can know and which, as Edward Coke famously wrote, 'requires long study and experience, before that a man can attain to the cognisance of it'.[3]

Law as craft and as science

Because many different kinds of legal practice exist, and there are many different roles that involve professing knowledge of law in some sense, there are surely many different kinds of legal expertise. Llewellyn follows his rejection of the idea of legal expertise as 'a secret lore' by outlining what he sees as the practising lawyer's *real* claims of expertise. He writes that it is not enough to know the law, essential though that is, because

> the essence of our craftsmanship lies in skills, and in wisdoms; in practical, effective, persuasive, inventive skills for getting things done, *any kind of thing in any field*; in wisdom and judgment in selecting the things to get done; in skills for moving [people] . . . into desired action. . . . Our game is essentially the game of planning and organising management (not of running it), except that we concentrate on the areas of conflict, tension, friction, trouble, doubt – and in those areas we have the skills for working out results.
>
> *(Llewellyn 1962: 318, emphasis added)*

These kinds of skills can be expressed in a wide range of terms: the lawyer as fixer, business counsellor, family relations adviser, participant in drafting corporate plans and deals, custodian of other people's property, political actor, freedom fighter, administrator, management consultant, trouble shooter, general adviser on life problems, hired gun, and so on. Some such roles involve much reference to legal rules and procedures or at least awareness of them, but others involve little use of 'law' in any technical sense (cf Arnold 1935: 26) and no thought of litigation or courts; in some cases the lawyer's task may be only 'continuing negotiation', perhaps never producing legal finality but merely aiming to keep deals afloat (cf Flood 1991: 67). One might say that there is little law here or that what there is stays out of sight. The aim is to avoid it, to keep as far away as possible from the use of legal knowledge in ways that might produce contention, to structure arrangements so that law does not intrude. The expertise being employed is partly a matter of background understandings.

---

3 *Prohibitions del Roy* (1608) 12 Co Rep 63, 65.

However, when legal expertise is thought of in academic contexts or many judicial contexts, it is usually considered primarily to be centred on *communicable knowledge of legal doctrine* (rules, principles, and concepts of law, and specifically legal ways of reasoning with these). The question then becomes: what is the nature of this expertise in legal doctrine? Coke's famous seventeenth-century claim that the 'artificial reason' of the common law was not something the king could know just through his legally untrained reason is an unambiguous assertion that special knowledge of legal doctrine is what founds the expertise of legal professionals. This arcane learning is considered to reflect communal wisdom somehow but is 'worked pure'[4] through the intricate reasoning of generations of lawyers and judges. Many writers have tried to pinpoint the nature of this common law learning. It is not just an ability to access the provisions of statutes or the contents of law reports, because, although the ability to find legal provisions in their numerous sources is an essential basis of this expertise, others apart from lawyers can gain this access, if sometimes with difficulty.

It is *creative reasoning* in legal doctrine that seems crucial. What is special about legal expertise in this sense is the ability to work with legal ideas securely, linking them in accepted patterns of reasoning, drawing inferences from them that will be recognised as legally appropriate, and understanding how rules interrelate to create webs of legal meaning. It is a matter of being able to work out new or different interrelations and argue persuasively for them. On these bases, the legal expert can make reliable predictions as to how courts may decide, not only in cases where the rules and their interaction have been established in advance but also in cases where they have not. All the vast literature on legal reasoning and legal argumentation is aimed at explicating the special nature of legal expertise in this sense or relating it to forms of reasoning and kinds of knowledge that are not thought of as specifically 'legal' but may be considered to be of general philosophical interest. Two themes from such discussions of legal reasoning are crucial in this chapter. One is the effort to pinpoint what is truly *unique* in the lawyer's methods of reasoning in legal doctrine; the other is the strong claim that *nothing* at all is unique in them.

In the first category, Charles Fried (1981: 57) has insisted that there 'really is a distinct and special subject matter for our [legal] profession' and that, while philosophers and economists also analyse law, only lawyers and judges are masters of the artificial reason emphasised by Coke. When 'general philosophical structures and deductive reasoning give out, overwhelmed by the mass of particular details', lawyers work with precedent and analogy, applying 'a trained disciplined intuition where the manifold of particulars is too extensive to allow our minds to work on it deductively. This is not a denial of reason' but 'a civilised attempt to stretch reason as far as it will go. The law is to philosophy . . . as medicine is to biology and

---

4 See *Omychund v Barker* (1744) 1 Atk 21, 33: 'the common law, *that works itself pure* by rules drawn from the fountain of justice' (argument of Solicitor-General Murray, later Lord Mansfield; emphasis in original).

chemistry. The discipline of analogy fills the gaps left by more general theory.'[5] For Fried, these methods make law's rationality a kind of 'rationality apart' (1981: 58).

One could agree, at least, that this rationality resides in a 'method of detail' (Twining 1974) which cannot appeal to theory for an ultimate resolution when a specific case problem must be confronted. And this is not an impenetrable magic art but perhaps one important aspect of the lawyer-craft that Llewellyn had in mind, one that he sometimes wrote about in terms of 'situation sense' (e.g. Twining 2012: 216ff.): the shaping of law to make sense in the instant case while simultaneously embodying enough consistent principle to make legal doctrine an adequately integrated intellectual structure capable of being mapped and taught.

This seems especially an Anglophone common law orientation in which addressing reason to factual case particulars is emphasised more than developing the aesthetics of a conceptually pure legal science. But other analysts are not at all convinced that legal expertise is built on any 'rationality apart' (e.g. Fontaine 2012: 30). Larry Alexander (1998: 517) writes: 'thinking like a lawyer is just ordinary forms of thinking clearly and well'; it 'boils down to moral reasoning, empirical reasoning and deductive reasoning' and lawyers 'reason in these ways exactly as everyone else does' (and see Alexander and Sherwin 2008). Appeals to analogy, he claims, depend on this everyday thought and are not a special kind of reasoning that lawyers practise. But to treat legal reasoning as lacking any uniqueness is not at all to minimise its importance or difficulty; it is merely to strip it of mystique and counter 'obscurantist claims on its behalf'; if lawyers lose 'a bit of our special priesthood aura in the eyes of others', he concludes, this is no bad thing (Alexander 1998: 533).

It is, in fact, to present a realistic view of what lawyers have to offer: not special, arcane techniques but ordinary reasoning developed, it may be hoped, to very high levels of competence. On such a view, thinking 'like a lawyer' is in principle like the reasoning of anyone else. But perhaps, one can suggest, it is done by lawyers with a *special self-awareness*, so that techniques of this everyday reasoning are consciously picked out, nurtured, fine-tuned, and emphasised; these techniques include distinguishing and narrowing issues to avoid confusion and manage complexity, deciding on material facts among a host of irrelevances so as to identify what is really important in a problem to be solved, presenting arguments with maximum persuasiveness and sharp attention to opposing lines of thought, tailoring argument precisely to issues and to results sought, and generally aiming for coherence and consistency in thought and action.

Alexander is surely right to insist that to label such reasoning techniques as 'ordinary' is in no way to diminish their importance or difficulty when developed by lawyers to a high level. They can then be seen as the crucial intellectual tools

---

5 Ibid. Among many discussions of analogy in legal reasoning see especially Weinreb 2005, and Brewer 1996 who claims that 'there is inevitably an uncodifiable imaginative moment in exemplary, analogical reasoning' but 'this imaginative moment is not unfamiliar in other areas of reasoning in whose rational force our intellectual culture has placed great confidence – namely, both the empirical and the demonstrative sciences' (p 954).

that support the craft-skills and practical wisdom that Llewellyn sees as the mark of able lawyers and the real essence of their expertise. The 'legal point of view' (cf Samek 1974) is not different in kind from other viewpoints; it is ordinary reasoning developed in certain ways that are sufficiently valuable in practical affairs to be rightly seen as special expertise.

Legal and other philosophers often explore the general character of legal knowledge and reasoning to try to judge how far it is distinctive. But for most lawyers this will not be important unless legal expertise is *directly challenged* by expertise claimed by other professional groups in competition or unless law promoted as an academic discipline is confronted by and must engage with other academic disciplines. Where law is institutionally well insulated as a knowledge-field from other such fields, issues about its epistemology are not likely to be seen as crucial and may not even be widely recognised as worth serious exploration.

If, for example, the idea of a 'legal science' – a science of legal knowledge and reasoning – is very firmly entrenched under conditions that allow this science to be organised in substantial isolation from other intellectual work, no comparisons with other knowledge-fields or practices may need to be made; issues about the distinctiveness of legal reasoning by comparison with other kinds of reasoning may seem unimportant to most practitioners of such a pure legal science. Then it may be only observers of this science from 'outside' – for example those with access to different intellectual traditions – who will examine carefully how far its epistemology reflects or relies on ways of thought shared with other knowledge-fields (e.g. Samuel 2003; 2009a).

The opposite end of the spectrum of conceptions of legal expertise from Llewellyn's craft-wisdom approach is the idea that legal expertise is mastery of some such pure legal science. Rudolf von Jhering wrote satirically in a continental European civil law context a century ago of a 'heaven' of concepts (*Begriffshimmel*) (e.g. Hart 1983: ch 12) to which some jurists seemed to appeal – a 'heaven' because it was a system of legal thought existing only in conceptual constructs unrelated to any empirical inquiries about life on earth – in effect, an object of faith. Roman law has been described as 'a self-contained form of knowledge' (Samuel 2003: 25) which 'divides naturally into self-contained and self-referential blocks' (ibid, quoting Alan Watson). Law in this view can appear as 'forms of knowledge . . . with their own logic . . . independent of the facts of society' (Samuel 2003: 25). To the extent that this outlook on law influences modern civil law thought and the interpretation of Continental codes (ibid: 29), it is not hard to see it as inspiring the application to modern law of autopoiesis theory which portrays this law as a self-referential, self-reproducing communicative system normatively closed to all other knowledge-fields.[6]

Legal interpretation in the modern French tradition has been described as aiming 'to analyse and to explain in a coherent and logical manner a legal text or court

---

6 For a convenient summary see Luhmann 1988.

decision' and by that method alone to 'guide the reader towards future outcomes' (Samuel 2009b: 435). Such a legal science acquires 'disciplinary stability', Geoffrey Samuel suggests (ibid: 440), insofar as no appeal to 'nonlegal' knowledge-fields is required in it (or, indeed, juristically allowed);[7] so, legal expertise seems unique, sharply defined, and easily recognised and can be powerfully defended. Even when frontiers of the legal science are disputed and transgressed, they stay strong, Samuel claims, because of (i) a clearly defined object of study (e.g. the *corpus juris civilis* of Roman law tradition), (ii) firm institutional roots with a body of professional jurists, and (iii) the 'apparent coherence and rationality' of law's doctrinal structure centred on timeless fundamental concepts – of persons, actions and things (ibid: 440–2).

This is legal expertise seemingly grounded not in a craft of getting practical jobs done for clients, with one eye on legal doctrine and the other on the messy, disordered ways of the world. It is legal expertise that interprets the world as an ordered, comprehensive conceptual universe of legal ideas rationally structured and reassuringly managed. But the legal science at the heart of this assumed expertise is based on a 'circular' epistemology. Legal science constructs and presents legal doctrine as a unique, comprehensive unity, but it is only the (usually unexamined) *assumption* of this unity that gives legal science its distinct object of study and its warrant to exist as a unique science (Cotterrell 1995: 55).

Defences and dilemmas of expertise

For the idea of legal science as an autonomous enterprise to be plausible, certain empirical conditions must be satisfied. Ultimately they come down to institutional and political conditions. A seemingly 'closed-off' legal science, essentially unrelated to other knowledge-fields and existing as self-standing scholarly legal expertise, surely requires that the scholarly guardians of this expertise be themselves institutionally set apart from the purveyors of other kinds of (potentially competing) knowledge. Otherwise perhaps the possibilities for infiltration of legal scholarship with other knowledges, other approaches to epistemology, other views of the connection between ideas and the empirical world – and thus other claims of scholarly expertise – might proliferate (Balkin 1996). Where legal scholars have been firmly embedded in the state legal complex[8] and sometimes influential in it, as, for example, in the case of prominent juristic commentators in some Continental civil law systems (Duxbury 2001: ch 4; Jansen 2016: 204–8), their *institutional location* and organisation in the legal structure[9] may provide a fortress from which the claims of

---

7 Many efforts over the past century have been made to challenge this tendency to insularity and to demonstrate the interdependence of juristic and 'nonlegal' bodies of thought. For a recent illustration see Encinas de Muñagorri et al 2016.

8 A complex made up of 'the different occupations, usually legally trained, that belong to the legal and judicial institutions of a given society and whose tasks are to create, elaborate, transmit, and apply . . . [state] law' (Karpik and Halliday 2011: 220).

9 On which see e.g. Fontaine 2012: ch 2.

autonomous legal science can be strongly defended; indeed it may ensure that in general these claims need no defence.

In common law contexts, too, there are institutional conditions for autonomy. University law schools today are sometimes physically separate from other university departments, even located in their own buildings, and may also be separately funded and managed. In such conditions they may enjoy much practical independence from the rest of the university. However, at least in common law environments, academic legal scholars are not necessarily consistently integrated into the state legal system. The university environment in the United Kingdom and other parts of the common law world is one in which leading academic lawyers today, as compared with their predecessors in past generations, often see themselves as much less firmly situated in the state legal complex and much more as part of a multidisciplinary academic community (Cownie 2004; and see Edwards 1992). Also, legal studies may exist in close proximity to social sciences and other research clusters; and opportunities for cross-disciplinary collaboration, or at least influence, may flourish.

In such settings legal expertise is a more complex idea than seems often to be assumed in Continental legal science. It is an academic expertise seeking the same kind of legitimacy as that of other university researchers, using scholarly methods to explore designated fields of experience. And these fields are marked out not only by established disciplinary assumptions but also according to ultimately managerial criteria, that is, by the practical division of the university into administratively convenient departments. Academic legal expertise thus becomes, in part, mastery of a particular, conveniently designated research specialism alongside all the others that the university contains.

Again, institutional divisions do not necessarily protect the autonomy of law as science or discipline. Well-endowed law schools in the common law world sometimes have the resources and incentive to employ nonlawyers as academic staff, bringing multidisciplinary work physically inside academic law as an institution. And, insofar as the institutionalisation of law in the university raises different considerations from the professional organisation of legal practice or from lawyers' interests in affirming a distinct legal expertise, universities sometimes actively promote cross-disciplinary work. They support multidiscipline research centres, collaborations across different knowledge-fields, and styles of research (for example empirical sociolegal studies in law departments) that may bring welcome external grant income for the university as a whole but further blur conceptions of a distinct disciplinary practice of law.

Despite these developments, and uncertainties about the distinctiveness of legal thought and reasoning, it is generally accepted whatever the differences between legal cultures that law is a powerful knowledge-field, easily recognised as such and possessing generally high status in public perceptions. The crucial reason is surely not ultimately an intellectual one: it lies in the *political positioning* of law, in its obvious, indisputable significance for government. Law as a knowledge-field is powerful because legal knowledge is essential to the state. It amounts to official knowledge of crucial general techniques of government and of official control in regulating social and economic life.

However fragile may be law's ultimate disciplinary autonomy, however unsure its ultimate claims of special expertise as a form of reasoning or social inquiry, it consists of techniques, procedures, and types of institutional knowledge about the agencies and processes of government, administration and official dispute processing that are crucial to the modern state. Those having elaborate knowledge of these techniques and forms of knowledge are undeniably important experts. Their expert knowledge is essential not only for the work of state officials and functionaries in all fields of government but also for citizens living in the shadow of these state structures. So it is *the link between law and state power* (now being extended internationally and transnationally in new forms) that makes legal expertise unique and guarantees its security, whatever doubts about its nature arise from uncertainty about its claims to intellectual autonomy.

In this perspective, those who claim expertise in law can be seen, in part, as custodians of the regulatory techniques of government.[10] They intellectually organise and classify these techniques, refine and reform them, rationalise and justify them as systems or collations of knowledge. They advise those who need to rely on and use them and provide information to those who need to organise their affairs in the shadow of government regulation. They identify flaws and failings in these regulatory techniques, invent and propose modifications to them, and explore and explain the meaning and significance of legal regulation judged against the interests, aspirations, and expectations of those affected by it. Because many different kinds of officials and professionals are engaged with law in one or more of these many different ways, the purveyors of legal expertise are not limited to those recognised as professional lawyers; they also include, for example, administrators, legislators, legal journalists, political activists, and campaigners of various kinds. Of course, some criminal offenders and other law-breakers also become expert in the legal fields of which they have experience.

In some cases, expertise is directly linked to problem-solving and the use of legal knowledge to achieve specific social or economic purposes; in others it is more closely tailored to building this knowledge as an integrated structure or system of thought. Such integration allows the regulatory structures of government to be understood as a coherent whole – not necessarily governed by any all-embracing rationality but with a 'piecemeal' rationality tailored to making the various areas of regulation as predictable and intellectually coherent as possible, despite the fact that the techniques of government and the uses to which these are put are always changing.

The crucial point, however, is that the combination of institutional location and political positioning of activities focused on law is an especially important determinant of the relative autonomy of legal expertise. Emphasising this, it is possible to bypass many debates about the nature of legal reasoning and legal epistemology and about the balance between craft skills of the kind Llewellyn emphasised and formal

---

10 Fontaine (2012: 44) claims that the primary image of the jurist is as technician and (often) as agent of power.

scholarly learning of legal doctrine as the essence of legal expertise. The expert in law is most obviously someone who can get close enough to the regulatory power of the state – in some or all of its many forms – to understand its *mechanisms* and use or pass on this understanding in any ways that the legal expert's clients or audiences – including citizens, corporations, governments, administrative agencies, courts, police, students, and nonlawyer researchers – may value.

This formulation may be the only one that allows us to conceptualise modern secular legal expertise in entirely general terms. It does not cover the case of experts in religious law where different kinds of institutional structures and constellations of power may guarantee the significance and scope of legal expertise. And it does not apply to stateless societies where the meaning of law – and the identity of law's expert guardians (if any) – raises issues beyond the scope of this chapter. More fundamentally, this formulation says nothing as to how expertise might be assessed: what, for example, counts as being a 'good lawyer' rather than the appropriate butt of lawyer jokes.

If we return to Galanter's analysis of the context of these jokes, one thing stands out as especially relevant here. It is the – at first perhaps disconcerting – revelation that many such jokes are told by lawyers themselves (Galanter 1998: 831ff.). He suggests that telling them serves several purposes. It is a means by which members of a politically and institutionally powerful profession try to defuse criticism of their position by deflating its importance in self-deprecating talk. And it is a way for lawyers sensitive to criticisms of their profession to try to differentiate themselves as good practitioners from the bad ones who behave unethically and deserve public criticism.

So, telling lawyer jokes is a way of saying: 'I know the things that the public perceives as wrong, but I use my expertise (however that is defined) for good. I can tell the good lawyer from the bad.' But another perspective is also possible. Telling jokes may be a practice of 'laughing at life' while recognising that it is not going to change; that good and bad are hard to separate in reality and sometimes depend on context and perception; that perhaps the lawyer's deployment of expertise cannot do other than create resentment and criticism even as it earns respect and gratitude; so that lawyer-priest and lawyer-magician are not necessarily to be seen as different people.

Legal values and juristic expertise

So far, the argument of this chapter has been that while the exact nature of legal expertise is somewhat elusive, it is not difficult to identify *institutional conditions* that enable certain occupational groups to establish themselves as experts in law. These are not just features of modern academic organisation as discussed earlier; they are also more generally the historic conditions of existence in many countries of what Max Weber (1968: 784–808) termed legal 'honoratiores' or juristic notables. Nor is it difficult to recognise how the intimate relationship between legal knowledge and skills and the regulatory requirements of the state mesh to provide *political conditions* that confer special status on those with a high degree of understanding of technical mechanisms for conducting government by means of rules.

Beyond this, the claim being made here is that legal expertise can be described only in terms of apparent dichotomies. One dichotomy is between elaborate legal scholarship, on the one hand, and practical craft skills, on the other. The latter may have an indeterminate relation to knowledge of legal doctrine – perhaps extensive knowledge is claimed, perhaps relatively limited knowledge – but the centre of expertise lies in practical wisdom and wide awareness of human affairs, not in scholarly virtuosity. Another dichotomy is between the practice of law as a resource of the common good and its practice as mastery of regulatory techniques for private client advantage. In the former case the lawyer's service is not necessarily to be seen as high-minded and altruistic but merely as well attuned to the general priorities of orderly integration and management of a society. In the latter, the primary focus is on client interests in isolation from wider concerns, and legal doctrine is an instrument for private advantage or an obstacle to be avoided in pursuing it. These two dichotomies might be labelled *scholarship v. craft* orientation and *societal (public) v. client (private)* orientation.

Whatever the balance of these orientations in particular contexts, it is easy to accept that some element of both the scholarship and client orientations is needed. As regards the first, one clearly cannot claim to be a legal expert without certain kinds of *legal learning*. A sense of the anatomy of legal doctrine is needed. That entails knowledge of basic organising concepts in legal doctrine;[11] awareness of broad accepted classifications of legal fields; understanding of criteria of legal authority and ability to discover, recognise, and evaluate sources of law; knowledge of judicial and administrative procedures relevant to mobilising law; and competence in what can be called 'rules of legal discourse' (Bell 1986: 48–50) – rules that govern appropriate terminology, argument, and types of justification. Beyond this, comprehensive knowledge of legal doctrine is impossible, so the legal expert specialises in particular doctrinal areas, practices, and procedures. Leaving aside all questions about the unique qualities of the legal reasoning needed to make use of these components of doctrinal knowledge, the components make up a recognisable object of learning.

The question that should then arise is: what is this knowledge and reasoning for? Answering it involves clarifying the idea of *client focus*. Who does legal expertise serve, and how? Some scholars argue that the idea of the lawyer's commitment to a common good or public welfare has disappeared. Nostalgic, but surely largely mythical, images of the 'lawyer-statesman' as an effective past model of legal professionalism are invoked to suggest an old yardstick of public-spirited practice of law that is thought to be past recovery (Kronman 1993). Some writers claim that client orientation has got out of hand to such an extent that any link between legal expertise and the promotion of a common good has almost entirely disappeared (Tamanaha 2006).

But much legal practice at least in highly individualistic, liberal societies *cannot avoid* being directed firmly towards the interests of private clients. Otherwise, for most lawyers, an orientation to public service means an orientation to the state as

---

11 For example, concepts of contract, tort, and restitution in common law: see Fried 1981: 39.

the ultimate client. If the figure of the lawyer-statesman has been a past reality, as scholars such as Anthony Kronman argue, this reality has been that of the legal expert as loyal servant of the political power and purposes of the state. A focus on client orientation is a reminder that professional expertise is something that ultimately is defined, validated, and measured only by its clients – those it addresses.

So far nothing has been said here about ideals or ultimate values that lawyers might be required professionally to serve. Could the legal expert, as such, be expected to have any special competence in protecting or promoting basic *values or ideals* sometimes projected onto or thought to be implicit in law? This is a matter not of the use of legal expertise being guided by appropriate values (as professional ethics requires) but of the use of expertise *to realise* values through law. This links, in part, to the idealistic image of the lawyer-statesman but also to the image of the lawyer as priest of a secular religion of law. Could the promotion of ultimate values, for example of justice or security (the values most often associated with law), be seen as part of the responsibility of legal expertise?

Many legal experts see themselves as guided by values which they wish to see expressed in law. Some see law as a vehicle for furthering values and work to influence law to achieve this; others see law as acting against such values and understand part of their role as to criticise legal doctrine because of this. This orientation to ultimate values as a concern for law is characteristic not only of many practising lawyers, judges, and academic legal scholars but also of other kinds of people who may have legal expertise – journalists, legislators, administrators, political and social activists, and so on.

Client orientation (which includes orientation to any of the expert's audiences) is important again here. If values are important, it has to be asked how they are important to those whom legal experts address – those who, as suggested above, ultimately define the recognised scope of expertise. How do, for example, values of justice and security vary in significance and meaning for different client groups? How does the balance between such values vary in the aspirations and expectations of the legal expert's clients and audiences – in various public or official perceptions; in certain social groups as contrasted with others? How does it vary in the perspectives of various agencies of the state or in the regulated citizenry, among academic audiences of students and scholars of law, or among diverse popular audiences outside the academy? And how far can any legal expert speak to society at large as the ultimate client or audience?

As important as client orientation is scholarship orientation. In an era of specialisation, no legal expert can see the whole of law in all its detail – whether as fields of practice or bodies of doctrine. So it is necessary to speak of many kinds of expertise centred on different kinds of legal knowledge and skills. Who can see an overall picture, and what kind of picture could it be? Is there any kind of legal expert who can take an overall view of the scope of law as an idea? Anyone who could do so would almost necessarily need to ask and find some answers to the question: what is law for? It would not be enough to portray law as an intellectual structure – for example a union of primary and secondary rules or an abstract norm system – without addressing this question, because the legal expert has to keep a client orientation in view. For whom is it useful to portray law in this way? For whom is this knowledge of law valuable? And if it is valuable, why and in what ways?

Undoubtedly people project values on to law and see it as oriented to values in certain ways; they project on to it hopes and fears, aspirations and expectations. Because of law's 'method of detail' and its vast terrain of doctrine, most legal experts see only the value orientations that law presents in *particulars*, in the issues of a single case or cluster of cases, a specific law reform issue, or the organisation and orientation of a certain field of doctrine. And citizens project their aspirations for justice, security, or other values onto the limited legal experience they have or learn about.[12] Criticism of lawyers has been shown to be greater among Americans with higher socioeconomic status than among those with lower status (Galanter 1998: 810). Why? Perhaps because the rich make use of lawyers more than the poor, and they experience the ways in which lawyers' expertise can give client benefits but also create serious threats. The poor may experience lawyers rarely, and mainly as defenders or advisers when they face trouble; their adverse views of law may focus more on police and administrative officials. So, expectations and perceptions of legal expertise are differentiated socially.

Is there any expert role which involves seeing law as a whole, in terms of values that justify law's existence? Is there a category of legal expert who speaks critically but consistently for the very *idea of law*, an expert whose expertise is focused on the *well-being* of this idea? I do not mean legal philosophers as such. They may or may not be committed to this well-being and may see law only as a phenomenon of philosophical interest. And their focus may be on law as a universal form rather than as an idea given significance by the conditions of particular legal systems. A focus on law's well-being will be concerned as much with the way Llewellyn's lawyer-craft skills work and with the nature of general practical wisdom in the use of legal resources as with technical legal knowledge. It will be a focus on law as potentially a vital collective possession of society no less than as something that finds its significance in sorting out dilemmas of individuals in everyday life. And, because this overarching expertise aims to see law as a whole, it must not be lost in (although aware of) the endless detail of rules and regulations in a legal system. It has to see the big picture of such a legal system.

It would be wholly unrealistic to ask busy lawyers to take on all these responsibilities in their practice. Nevertheless, a focus on explicating and critiquing underlying values of a legal system – that is, examining them in the light of both popular and professional concerns for values of justice and security – should find a place somewhere in discussion of legal expertise. And sensitivity to the great diversity of popular aspirations for and understandings of *justice and security* would have to go along with an equal sensitivity to the need for social integration of society through law. In other words, the jurist in ever more complex and diverse modern societies

---

12 On this popular projection of values and its consequences for legal policymakers, see Chapter 14.

must also promote a *value of solidarity*. This requires law to be an instrument morally and equally integrating – as equally valuable subjects of law – *all* those living within the jurisdiction of a legal system.

Expertise in exploring conditions for the well-being of the idea of law in this wide but essential sense could be seen as the special legal expertise of the jurist – drawing on the resources of philosophy, on social science, and crucially on the experience of lawyers and citizens in relation to law.

The next chapter discusses in detail what this juristic expertise involves. It cannot be dissolved away into everyday reasoning, or explained as the effect of institutional and political conditions, or treated as an accumulation of technical know-how. Juristic expertise as the committed promotion of a value-oriented idea of law adapted to the specific, varying conditions of law's sociohistorical existence is the most distinctive, perhaps ultimately the most difficult, form of legal expertise. It is the kind that addresses most directly the various powerfully implied dissatisfactions that get brought to light in the funniest and the most disturbing of the lawyer jokes.

3

THE JURIST'S ROLE

Who guards the idea of law?

The meaning of the term 'jurist' is vague and varies with different national legal traditions. In common law systems it often suggests a role somewhat higher in intellectual status than does the term 'lawyer'. Jurists tend to be thought of as *scholars* of law,[1] which entails more than being legally well informed or skilled. Not every lawyer is necessarily a jurist. Many Anglophone practising lawyers would not call themselves jurists and might even be embarrassed or puzzled by the title. But theorists of law, whose work is often considered of much less everyday significance than that of legal practitioners, are sometimes called jurists.

What's in a name? The term 'jurist' can be given many different kinds of significance. This chapter harnesses it for a particular purpose and uses it to identify a particular role in relation to law – one that is hard to define with precision but nevertheless important. To see this role as the specifically 'juristic' one – the special responsibility of the jurist – is a starting point for clarifying it and giving it a prominence that it presently lacks. The role is that of maintaining *the idea of law* as a special kind of practice and enabling that idea to flourish. One might say that the jurist's role, on this understanding, is to safeguard and promote law's general *well-being*. This cannot be a simple matter because conceptions of this well-being will vary greatly. It is important to try to unpack it as far as possible, while recognising that different jurists will understand it in different ways. This entails also distinguishing this role from other roles touching on law with which it can be confused.

One such role – strange as it might seem to distinguish it immediately – is that of the legal philosopher. Writers on law do not necessarily treat jurisprudence, typically

---

1   Duxbury 2001, addressing both common law and civil law contexts, largely equates jurists with academic lawyers.

seen in the common law world as what jurists profess, as identical with legal philoso-phy. Julius Stone (1968: 8) wrote that: 'Most of the problems of jurisprudence . . . are in substance different from those of philosophy . . . any writer who pretends to bring . . . [jurisprudence's] full range within any particular philosophical tradition is deceiving at least himself.' The jurist, on this view, is not primarily a professional philosopher, even a philosopher of law; and not a sociologist of law either. The idea at the base of Stone's claim is that the jurist's responsibility is to *law* as such, as a broad, diverse field of practice and experience, and not to any intellectual discipline (e.g. philosophy, sociology) for which law may be one object of study among others.

The jurist's work is certainly allied with that of other legal professionals such as practising lawyers and judges. But, to use Stone's (1968: 16) term, it is a form of lawyers' 'extraversion', a turning out beyond everyday practice to a wider, more broadly informed view of the nature of law. So the jurist's ultimate responsibility might be considered to be to *law generally*, not to any particular aspect of its practice. Judges, for example, may be but are not necessarily jurists. The jurist's scholarship is not confined by the demands of deciding particular cases or applying law to specific disputes. It is not required to limit itself within (though, to be realistic, it must take account of) the bounds of precedent or codes, parliamentary sovereignty, or existing legal or constitutional structures. It certainly does not involve uncritically defending any of the law in force – currently existing legal provisions. And it is not bounded by the requirements of legally advising or representing specific clients (individuals, groups, organisations, governments, administrative agencies) as practising lawyers do.

The jurist's focus could be said to be on *law as a practical idea* in general, or as embodied in the legal system (or type of legal system) which the jurist serves. The focus is on the worth of law, its meaningfulness as a social institution. To this extent, a juristic perspective goes beyond the everyday practice of law in courts or lawyers' offices but is one of *committed*, not disinterested, analysis or observation of law; it is concerned with all aspects of law's well-being, for example its clarity, coherence, fairness, consistency, reputation, accessibility, enforcement, and effectiveness. That suggests a theoretical sensibility, but not necessarily adherence to any wide-ranging theoretical system. Rather, if the concern is with law in general, the jurist will need some general but flexible practical framework of thought, a way of envisaging or modelling law as a phenomenon, at least provisionally *in relation to the time and place* – that is, in the particular political and historical context in which he or she works.

Modern legislators and administrators may seek to use legislation to codify, sim-plify, systematise, consolidate, or clarify law or to reform procedure to make the administration of justice through law work better. But often they make or use law purely as a tool of government and governance, and policy is the exclusive focus of attention. Thus, legislative or administrative responsibility is not necessarily focused on the value of law as a social institution. Again, practising lawyers have a respon-sibility to the legal system in which they work, but their role is also to serve the interests of their private or governmental clients in relation to law. How the balance is struck – between allegiance, on the one hand, to the general well-being of law and, on the other, to client interests – can be studied empirically but may be hard to theorise outside the context of particular cases or types of practice. In Chapter 2 we saw how complex and variable this balance can be.

Equally, legal journalists may be committed to law reform and exposing legal scandals, but their job is also to get a good story and satisfy the expectations of those who employ or commission them to write. Again, not all *legal scholars* are jurists according to the conception followed here: academic lawyers, legal theorists, and social scientists may or may not have a commitment to law, to its worth and well-being. Their primary commitment may be to scholarship *rather than* to law, and a distinction can be drawn between those whose scholarship is intended to enrich or sustain law and those whose intellectual aim is to unmask or debunk it[2] or just to find out about it and convey knowledge of it.

Thus, the idea of law seen in terms of a concern for and commitment to its general well-being is hard to view as an exclusive focus for any specific category of professionals, unless this idea can be set at the centre of the jurist's work. If this is done, 'jurist' becomes not merely an honorific title. It can be the label to attach to a specific role which entails serving law, in all its complexity, contradictions and ambiguities, in a comprehensive and exclusive way. The jurist's role, on this view, sits between broad philosophical or social scientific visions of law, on the one hand, and the specificities of legal practice and reform, on the other – distinct from yet linked to both, in a shifting, variable relationship. The remainder of this chapter explores what such a juristic commitment to law entails.

Juristic outlook: Radbruch and Dworkin

It is surely unrealistic to think of juristic responsibility as if it were the same in, say, a police state, a theocracy, and a liberal democracy, an unstable polity or a stable one, or a society whose history has been one of violence and disorder as compared with one that has long benefited from relative internal peace. The jurist's responsibility exists *in specific historical contexts*, usually in relation to a particular legal system or type of legal system and with a concern for the kinds of legal practice that exist or are possible in that system or type. And it will be a multifaceted responsibility, reflecting law's multifaceted character. But how to clarify that responsibility when law itself can be seen from so many points of view, with so many tasks assigned to it, and such diverse expectations attached to it? And how to do so when those tasks and expectations vary with historical and political context?

The work of the German legal scholar Gustav Radbruch in the first half of the twentieth century, informed by the political turmoil of the Weimar period and the Nazi experience and still much neglected in the Anglophone world, offers useful pointers in trying to answer such questions. Radbruch does not explicitly demarcate

---

2   A classic case is that of the Soviet legal theorist Evgeny Pashukanis (1978), a learned and profound scholar of law, who, following Marx's teaching, saw his role as to pave the way for law's *demise*. In the Anglo-American world, some extreme forms of critical legal studies writing can similarly be seen as legal scholarship beyond the jurist's role as this book presents it.

the jurist's special role in the way this chapter aims to do, but his work nonetheless exemplifies that role. It also suggests how to solve a dilemma in conceptualising it: on the one hand, to specify what is *distinctive* about the role; on the other, to allow for great *variability* in the way it can be played. In what follows, some of Radbruch's key ideas about law and its well-being are used as a starting point for developing this chapter's themes.

He is significant here for three reasons. First, he consistently emphasises the role of jurists as one of moral responsibility for the well-being of law. Second, he presents the jurist's view of the idea of law as necessarily highly malleable or fluid in important respects, adapted to context and varying as that context changes. Third, he doubts the utility for the jurist of any seemingly timeless philosophical 'system' whose abstractions exist independently of empirical inquiries about social variation. The jurist, it might be said, is not a 'hedgehog' but a 'fox': not committed single-mindedly to one value orientation, such as the pragmatic pursuit of chosen social 'purposes' of law, or the elaboration of a philosophy of 'justice', or the preservation of established 'order' at all costs. Instead, the jurist's commitment is to a permanent but ever-shifting relationship among ideas of justice, order, and purpose implicated in law.

Erik Wolf, discussing the 'practical bent' of Radbruch's jurisprudence, sees him as sympathetic to sociology, as understood in the German context in the first half of the twentieth century (Wolf 1958: 11). For Radbruch, jurists cannot be uncommitted sociological observers of law; however, they should recognise that, for the most part, justice and other legal values do not have timeless content but must find their meaning in specific sociohistorical contexts. More precisely, the space for realistic debate around those values would be set by this context, by what Radbruch calls 'the nature of the objective situation' (*Natur der Sache*) (Radbruch 1950: 53–5, 172–4; Van Niekerk 1973: 241).

Important parallels can be noted between Radbruch's juristic outlook and that of Ronald Dworkin. First, both insisted that law is a *value-laden cultural phenomenon*. It expresses fundamental values, rooted in the political community. It is the jurist's responsibility to bring these to light and to work out their interrelation in the ongoing business of plotting law's practical development over time and keeping legal/judicial practice in step with what Dworkin (1986) terms law's 'integrity' and what Radbruch (1950: 73) calls the 'idea of law' – law as doctrine expressing a distinctive combination of values.

Second, Radbruch sought a jurisprudence to engage with specific *legal issues in time and place*. He tried to do this by treating as variable the relationships between what he saw as the fundamental values of law and asking how these relationships might alter with circumstances and how the content of the values themselves could change in different conditions. Dworkin also tried explicitly to make his jurisprudence of principle a practical tool of commentary on changing law. He applied it as a public intellectual, criticising, for example, decisions of the United States Supreme Court that he saw as 'unprincipled' and, as such, as undermining the integrity of American law.[3]

---

3   For example, among many publications, Dworkin 2011a; 2008.

Third, for both writers, the juristic role seems to assume an *ongoing evolution of law's values*. For Dworkin this evolution occurs in the continual reinterpretation of law: the effort (especially by judges) to see the legal system in terms of the 'soundest' theory they can develop, which will allow the 'best' reading of legal doctrine and the most 'attractive' integration of legal standards in their application to specific cases or issues. Law as an integrated system of principle is built 'from the inside', so to speak, in ongoing interpretation and application of its precepts. Potentially, as the common lawyers once insisted, law 'works itself pure'.[4] That is, 'integrity' characterises the relation between the value elements expressed in legal doctrine at any given time.

For Radbruch, too, what seems important is a shifting reconciliation of legal values in time and place. Nevertheless, ultimately this is very different from Dworkin's idea of a systematic integration of values. Often the relationship between legal values as Radbruch portrays them is one of irreconcilable *tension*, sometimes *conflict*; the issue is often how to *compromise* them against each other, the terms of the compromise changing over time. And it seems that sociology as well as philosophy can serve the jurist in understanding how this compromise may be achieved and under what conditions (Van Niekerk 1973: 241). For Radbruch there is a need in any legal system to balance values of order, justice, and suitability for societal purpose in law, and this balance may well vary in different contexts. This suggests a comparative dimension of the concept of law: between different legal systems and between historical phases of law's existence (Wilhelmine, Weimar, Nazi and postwar Germany, in Radbruch's case).

Juristic style: Radbruch and his critics

Law's 'well-being' is, therefore, a variable notion, not definable in any timeless fashion. There is the sharpest possible contrast between Radbruch's hesitant, uncertain, often provisional outlook (sometimes seen by critics as inconstancy) and Dworkin's confident ultimate intellectual commitment to a fully integrated, comprehensive, philosophical system of values (Dworkin 2011b). So, Dworkin states that the role of moral and political philosophers is 'to try to construct self-conscious articulate systems of value and principle out of widely shared but disparate moral inclinations, reactions, ambitions and traditions' (2011b: 109). Thus, when law is seen, as he eventually saw it, as 'a subdivision of political morality', it takes its place as one region in 'a large and complex philosophical theory' that 'proposes a way to live' (2011b: 1, 405), a total philosophical system focused on a rational elaboration and integration of ultimate values.

This is very far removed from Radbruch's outlook. Accepting contradictions and compromise reflecting actual legal life, rather than building a system of thought to explain 'a way to live', Radbruch's jurist is wracked by self-questioning: 'we are to believe in the profession of our life and yet . . . in some deepest layer of our being,

---

4 See *Omychund v Barker* (1744) 1 Atk 21, at 33; Dworkin 1986: 400.

again and again to doubt it' (Radbruch 1950: 139). Indeed, the relativistic (or existential) aspect of his outlook (ibid: 55–9; Friedmann 1960: 198–9) may be what is most important about his juristic thought, distinguishing its exploratory, interrogatory style and also accounting for a remarkable polarisation in evaluations of his work. This is important because it illustrates differences between juristic and (some) legal philosophical outlooks.

Some scholars, especially those of continental European origin writing in (or translated into) English, emphasise the respect in which Radbruch was held as a jurist (Friedmann 1960: 192, 209). One praises the 'wisdom which permeates the whole of his work . . . a thoroughness of erudition, a sincerity of tolerance . . . a total absence of the slightest intellectual arrogance' (Chroust 1944: 23). Wolf (1958: 8, 9) lauds 'his attitude of open-mindedness . . . his constant readiness to listen to others and to consider other viewpoints as valid', his wish to keep apart 'from that type of legal philosophy which had hardened into a "professional discipline"' . . . 'his disdain for polemical discussions' . . . his 'rejection of the demand for a closed legal philosophical system'.

These are statements about *a way of doing jurisprudence*, not about the substance of a theory. They indicate ways of thinking that, from a certain philosophical standpoint, might be devalued or even treated as indicators of intellectual weakness. Thus, Radbruch's willingness to rethink his prewar views after 1945 in the light of the Nazi experience has, for H. L. A. Hart, 'the special poignancy of a recantation' (the assumption being that he had disowned his earlier legal theory),[5] but his 'passionate demand' (rather than intellectual argument?) addressed to the German conscience was linked, so Hart claims, with 'an extraordinary naivety'; Radbruch, he goes on confidently to declare, had 'only half digested the spiritual message of liberalism' (Hart 1983: 72, 74, 75).

Yet it should be emphasised that Radbruch's juristic experience had, in important respects, been *far wider* and perhaps more profound than that of many of his critics. He had served honourably in government and been active as a liberal scholar and social democrat during the turbulent Weimar republic. After expulsion from his teaching position by the Nazis, he had lived through the Hitler era in Germany to welcome the post–World War II rebuilding of his country and to assist at its beginning. Perhaps a much more nuanced judgment on his thought is possible,[6] one that envisages the jurist 'in the thick of events', trying to hold to the idea of law while acutely aware of the contexts of its application, rather than the distanced philosopher elaborating concepts that might claim a validity independent of changing

5   An assumption that may be unjustified, as argued later in this chapter.
6   Cf. A. P. D'Entrèves writing to Lon Fuller: 'I share your feelings about Hart's "strokes of the oar". I confess that in both hearing and reading his strictures on Radbruch . . . I could not help feeling sorry for the incurable smugness of our English friends' (quoted in Lacey 2010: 22). On Radbruch's political views and activities especially in the Weimar period see the excellent discussion in Herrera 2003: 147–71. On his courage as a lonely juristic voice publicly condemning Nazism as it rose to power see Kaufmann 1988: 1633; Van Niekerk 1973: 238–9.

conditions. But if jurists are not philosophical system-builders or seekers after timeless abstract truth, it is necessary to ask what kind of practical framework of thought can serve their task.

The jurist needs a *flexible* way of thinking about law – one that recognises that law's form and substance can be very variable but does not lose sight of viable ultimate criteria of law's worth and measures of its well-being, relative to time and place. That is, jurists need criteria and measures that can embrace, in some way, everything valued in law by those who live under it and appeal to it. Radbruch provides, up to a point, a model for such a way of thinking. I take him as presupposing that because jurists' focus is on 'law' (an idea which *they* have the task of expounding in relation to their experience), no single 'external' system of thought (economic/ utilitarian, theological, sociological, moral, or political) can be allowed to dominate this focus. The jurist is left to work out an independent practical meaning for the idea of law and the realisation of that idea in particular contexts.

Juristic focus: law's variable geometry

The idea of law can be thought of juristically as a 'triangle' of three central values – a triangle that can be stretched into different shapes depending on context; we might say that law as a structure of values has a *variable geometry*. Thus, for Radbruch, the idea of law is a balance of the values of (i) *justice*, (ii) *order*, or security or certainty, and (iii) (fitness for) *purpose (Zweckmassigkeit)*, or expediency or utility. Justice is fundamental, the 'specific idea' of law (Radbruch 1950: 75, 90) as equal treatment of equals and different treatment of different cases. But this cannot be sufficient: the 'purpose' of law (purpose being a value given content in sociohistorical time and place) determines who and what are to be considered equal and different and how justice is to be measured and realised (ibid: 90–1). Order, the third value of law, is, in one sense, even more fundamental. Without order, ideas of justice and purpose become meaningless. Even where the judge cannot do justice through law, there is an obligation to serve the value of order, which demands certainty in legal doctrine and predictability in legal decisions. Doing justice and pursuing aims through law presuppose law's stability. To that extent, providing order is the first task of law (ibid: 108).

The variable geometry of law may well explain Radbruch's so-called recantation – his apparent change of outlook on the conditions of law's well-being after the experience of Nazism. It is probable that he thought, in Weimar times, that *order* was ultimately the non-negotiable value. Without it – in a Hobbesian state of disorder – there could be no society and no law. Weimar's irresponsible anti-constitutional politics, its prejudiced judiciaries failing to apply the letter of law consistently, and its gangs of street thugs dispensing everyday nonlegal 'justice' and pursuing their political 'purpose' might well have suggested that a realistic jurist *in such a context* must privilege order, even though (Radbruch insists) the central value of the idea of law is always justice. But his emphasis on the need for consistent, predictable application of legal doctrine predates the Weimar period (Paulson 2006: 34–6).

He is very explicit: 'It is more important that the strife of legal views be ended than that it be determined justly and expediently' (Radbruch 1950: 108). What law in this image (reflecting a dread of social collapse) stands against, as law's opposite (its total denial), is *chaos* and *anarchy*. Yet there is no 'absolute precedence' of 'legal certainty . . . fulfilled by any positive law, over the demands of justice and expediency, which it may . . . have left unfulfilled' (ibid: 118).

Later, a different opposite of law (perhaps wholly unforeseen as a modern European phenomenon) seems to be revealed to Radbruch by Nazism: law's opposite or total denial now becomes *barbarism* resulting from *total unconcern for fair treatment*, the complete abolition of justice as a value. The emphasis in Radbruch's outlook certainly shifts – the geometry of the triangle has changed: its centre of gravity has moved from the 'order' point towards the 'justice' point – but surely neither his method nor his theoretical frame of reference changes in any significant way. The value triangle still represents the idea of law, its values held in tension, but the balance between them alters with circumstances, and the wise jurist in extreme crisis times must, it seems, focus especially on what might destroy the whole triangle. The complete disappearance of one point of the triangle would mean that the idea of law could no longer be sustained.

Those who defend Radbruch against charges of inconstancy (especially the charge that he discarded a prewar legal positivist position in favour of a natural law position after 1945) tend to stress a continuity in his thought that is capable of embracing revision and reinterpretation in the light of experience.[7] The argument seems highly plausible. He argued after 1945 that where 'there is not even an attempt at justice' in positive law, so that 'equality, the core of justice, is deliberately betrayed', a statute may lack 'completely the very nature of law' (Radbruch 2006: 7). His argument about Nazi law can be treated as identifying an end-state, one in which the extremely variable *conditions of justice* (justice being a value always fundamental to law as an idea) have been shown, in particular historical circumstances, to have reached their limit of existence. So, what seems, from one viewpoint, philosophical inconstancy appears, from another, as the jurist's constant effort to preserve a flexible but ultimately non-negotiable idea of law in changing political conditions.

An approach such as this cannot specify what law's well-being is. It merely sets parameters and guidelines – a framework of thought in which jurists are to work. But the guidance is firm (order and justice are the values that jurists must *always* serve), even if it is strictly limited. Only at the extremes (the collapse of order or the disappearance of all semblance of justice)[8] does it seem to call on the jurist's conscience to protest the destruction of the idea of law. In 'normal' times, everything, it seems, is left to personal judgment on the optimal balance of order and justice in law.

---

7   Paulson 1994, 1995, 2006; Wolf 1958; Friedmann 1960; and Van Niekerk 1973. Cf Spaak's (2009) contrary view.

8   Or, we might speculate, the *total* dominance in law of policy-driven pragmatism, expediency or instrumentalism – but Radbruch does not seem to address this issue, except to note that '[b]y no means is law anything and everything that "benefits the people"' (Radbruch 2006: 6).

The idea of law in its cultural setting

Can one say anything in general terms about what might be 'good' or 'wise' juristic judgment in such matters? Radbruch contributes here in discussing the third point in the triangle of law's values – law's orientation to 'purpose' (*Zweckmassigkeit*). He sees order (as legal certainty) and justice (as equal treatment of like cases) as permanent, constant (if formal) legal values (Radbruch 1950: 108–9). So, they are within the jurist's province to analyse and apply. But law's 'purpose' is given *culturally*, by the prevailing ideas of the times: that is, law is guided in different sociohistorical contexts by different conceptions of 'the good': these give rise to different views of the individual's relation to state and society or to different allegiances or orientations – for example to individual freedom, to the good of state and nation, or to the building of human culture more widely (ibid: 90–5).

Thus, purpose refers to *objectives set for the idea of law by sociohistorical conditions*; purpose sets criteria for justice as a value served by law. It affects the social meaning of this value (determining, for example, which kinds of cases are to be considered legally alike and which different). So, it would appear that the jurist's concerns cannot be limited to purely technical reconciliations of order and justice (as in the rule of law which combines legal certainty and equality before law). The jurist has to look beyond law's technical efficiency to its existence as an idea embodying cultural expectations. Order and justice are, at one level, fundamental (technical) values that must always animate law's practices and procedures. At another level, they are expressions of law's significance relative to time and place. A continuum seems to link the technical and social aspects of order and justice. What Radbruch does not make clear, however, is how far jurists can be expected to contribute to the realisation of these social values, in other words, how far they may venture into the terrain of social theory or moral and political philosophy.

Radbruch's thought can, it seems, take us no further, but it is not necessary to stop with him. In dealing with order and justice as technical legal matters, the jurist is on firm ground. As often portrayed in positivist legal thought, these are purely matters of efficiency in the working of a system of rules, and the rule of law as the reconciliation of these technical values can appear not necessarily as a social (or moral) good but as merely the condition of a working rule system (Raz 2009b: 210–29). At another level, however, the realisation of order and justice as *social* values in *some* combination is always demanded from law (Cotterrell 1995: 154–5, 316–17).

Individuals no doubt interpret these values differently in different sociohistorical contexts. One might ask, for example, how much order is possible and what will order be taken to mean – in a peaceful or stable state, in a chaotic or corrupt state, in a tyrannous state, or in conditions of war. What will justice as equality or fairness relate to – in a society structured by classes, castes or ranks, a slave society, or a liberal democracy? How far will people privilege order over justice (as they understand these values) or the reverse; how much of one or the other will they be satisfied with? The relative importance of these values may vary greatly with time and place.

What this points to is the need to think juristically in nondogmatic, relativistic ways (cf Radbruch 1950: 55–9) – emphasising flexible frameworks of thought about law's well-being. Radbruch's 'idea of law' is such a framework – instructive in implying a variable geometry of legal values. Others, in more recent times, are John Finnis's (2011: 276–81) idea of a 'focal meaning' of law and Nigel Simmonds's (2007: 52) idea of 'archetypes' of the legal 'to which actual instances of law merely approximate to various degrees'. Above all, one might refer to Lon Fuller. For Fuller, it is only at the direst extreme that law's existence becomes an all-or-nothing matter (when law does or does not conform to *minimum* demands of a 'morality of duty'). Far more practically important (because applicable to all legal systems) is his claim that social order can be *more or less* 'legal', that legality is *a matter of degree* and the task of the jurist is to *build* legality as a moral value structure (Fuller 1969: 122–3).

Just as Radbruch was sometimes criticised for vagueness or indeterminacy, Fuller is criticised for not being able to specify *exactly* what legal excellence means, or how conflicting attributes of legality are to be reconciled, or when law begins or ceases to exist. These are demands for a *system of thought* to explain law comprehensively as a phenomenon. But the addressees of these demands here are writers (such as Fuller or Radbruch) who, it must be stressed, are not really interested in such systems.

They think of their legal theory as aiding a *juristic craft*, as offering not timeless or conclusive answers but only a framework for practical time-bound ones.[9] Thus, *juristic craft and philosophical system seem almost antithetical ideas.* Karl Llewellyn, far from being a system-builder, insisted that rigid conceptualisation is 'bad jurisprudence' and eventually put the idea of juristic craft at the heart of his legal theory (Llewellyn 1962: 83; Twining 2012: 199–200, 561–8, 572; Llewellyn and Hoebel 1941: 297– 309). Juristic wisdom is merely this craft practised at the highest possible level.

Here then is surely the most constructive way to think of 'purpose' in law from a juristic perspective: not in terms of a conclusive *theory* of law's purpose, as though law had a single, timeless purpose to be discovered, or as if a systematic elaboration of such a purpose were possible. A juristic view of purpose in law is surely no more than constant empirical concern in the jurist's work for its specific sociohistorical context, insofar as that context informs the content and conditions of citizens' aspirations and expectations for order and justice. Attention to purpose involves not a philosophical effort rigorously to expound social values but a *sociological* attempt to identify patterns of experience in the jurist's sociohistorical environment, so that the idea of law can be advanced in *that* context, in relation to *those* aspirations and expectations. It demands sensitivity to the ways that values of order and justice are understood and experienced in a given society at a particular time.[10]

Why take account juristically of these popular aspirations and expectations? The answer is that jurists, if they are to promote law's worth and well-being, will work to show its social significance. So they will be led to shape and present law as far as possible as a unifying force (Cotterrell 2003: 8–11) socially and politically in their

---

9 For Fuller's 'affirmations of the middle-range' in theory and his unequivocal juristic rejection of 'complete' philosophical systems see Winston ed 2001: 61–3, 305–13. See also Soosay 2011.

10 For an illustration of how such an approach might operate in a sociohistorical context very different from Radbruch's, see Cotterrell 2016.

society – a social institution that potentially benefits all. The idea of law must, on this view, confront social diversity and conflict without attempting to reason it away or merely replicate it. Law itself must be made to appear *juristically* as a unity[11] in which social diversity is accepted, ordered, stabilised, and balanced. Law as an idea 'here and now' must relate not just to myriad individual interests; it must appear as a convincing framework for social life, serving *the whole* of society. If it cannot be so portrayed, cynicism about it spreads, a threat to the well-being which the jurist seeks for it (Tamanaha 2006).

So, the jurist has to hold the justice-order-purpose triangle of law together in a way that not only promotes law's unity and coherence as a structure of values but also promotes social unity or an overall solidarity in the society the jurist serves. Thus, the key juristic task is to interpret and influence law so that it mediates the diversity of popular senses of justice and of popular aspirations for security but does so while maximising regulatory conditions for such a society-wide solidarity.

Juristic responsibility

My argument is that jurists must speak for the idea of law as a flexible but distinctive and unifying value structure – as something like the variable geometric structure that Radbruch's juristic thought evokes. If *no one* speaks forcefully and influentially for law in this sense but people generally seek only to make use of it for their political or personal ends, history shows a range of risks, ultimately including that of constitutional collapse, as in the Weimar republic. In the United States, related dangers have been noted. Dworkin (2006a: 1) wrote of the country as being in 'a period of special political danger' in which US citizens 'are no longer partners in self-government; our politics are rather a form of war'. Even at the highest judicial levels, a view of law that seems to deny any possibility of a consensus around it has sometimes been expressed.[12] The idea of law as something distinct from government or from the pursuit of specific interests – something of general juristic importance – needs its advocates, it seems.

Dworkin's solution was to seek deep unifying principles which reasonable people might be persuaded to acknowledge despite differences in ideologies and world views and to reason politico-legal ideas from them.[13] But why should it be

---

11 That is, a single coherent, practical regulatory framework appropriate to the time and place. Ongoing juristic efforts to portray law's regulatory unity are identical with efforts to portray its authority as conclusively settled. This search for regulatory unity is to be distinguished clearly from any philosophical deduction of a 'unity of value' (Dworkin 2011b: 1) in which different ultimate values are finally harmonised.

12 See Toobin 2007: 237, quoting former US Supreme Court Chief Justice William Rehnquist in private conversation with an unnamed colleague in 2004: 'Don't worry about the analysis and the principles in the case. Just make sure the result is a good one this time around – because those principles you announce will be ignored in the next case.' See, more generally, West 2005.

13 Dworkin (2006a: 9) seems to admit that this is not necessarily a juristic response to the issues, noting that in this context, 'my main interest is in political principle, not law.'

assumed that there are deep principles on which people could be persuaded to agree? What if there are only different outlooks and ideologies? What if 'irrationality' (in the sense Max Weber meant in characterising some habitual and emotional action) or *different* rationalities confront philosophical reason (Weber 1968: 25; Brubaker 1984: 50–1)?

The jurist's task is not to try to rationalise conflict away but to identify where it lies and how law can respond to it; the question is how to preserve law as a universal good in the face of moral and political disagreement or simply in the face of popular disinterest in questions about ultimate values. In short, the juristic issue is how the idea of law can survive in the sociohistoric conditions it faces. So the jurist's concerns are sociological as much as philosophical, but neither philosophy nor sociology can *remove* these concerns; they remain the jurist's responsibility.

To give the term 'jurist' a special meaning as this chapter has done is a means of assigning this responsibility. The idea of the juristic role as discussed here refers to an ideal type in Max Weber's sense: that is, it provides a kind of model which may approximate, to some degree, the role that many (but certainly not all) who are called jurists actually play. What is presented here is a thought experiment. It asks: what would follow if there was such an accepted specialised role of guardianship of the idea of law and its well-being? What issues would then present themselves? How then would juristic work be judged?

This approach suggests that the jurist's role as guardian of the idea of law is more than guardianship of law's intellectual techniques. It embraces law's responsibilities for reflecting aspirations for order and justice in a cohesive society. Thus, the juristic role presented here is not only a Weberian pure type, a conceptual model to interpret aspects of reality. It is also an ideal in the more usual normative sense. The claim is that this role is important; an ideal that ought to be pursued. That does not mean that the juristic role must be monopolised in practice by any particular professional group. Philosophers, judges, academic lawyers, client-focused practitioners of law, and others sometimes more or less readily slip in and out of the juristic role. Jurists are certainly not debarred from filling other roles in relation to law, and others don the cap of the jurist in parts of their work. Even if the role is seen as distinct, the professional allegiances of those who fill it need not be.

But it is necessary to identify a distinctive professional commitment to guardianship of the idea of law, especially when the moral aspects of many public roles are widely seen as requiring clear definition. The juristic role exists alongside many other kinds of intellectual and practical engagement with law. Often it has been obscured by those other kinds. Yet, if the idea of law is valued in itself, the jurist's role in the sense discussed here could be the most fundamental engagement of all. In the next chapter I consider the nature of the theoretical knowledge that specially serves this role.

4

WHY JURISPRUDENCE IS NOT LEGAL PHILOSOPHY

Defending jurisprudence

This chapter argues that jurisprudence, as a body of theoretical knowledge about law, is a necessary resource to support the role of the jurist. But the nature of jurisprudence needs much clarification and, in fact, has been widely misunderstood. A deep uncertainty about its nature has made jurisprudence hard to defend intellectually. Perhaps because of this, it has increasingly, over the past few decades, been treated as having been incorporated or redefined into something with a different name – legal philosophy. Indeed, jurisprudence and legal philosophy are often considered synonymous. But I shall argue here that they are not.

Legal philosophy, as that term is now understood in Anglo-American scholarship, designates a field of theory that presents itself as having a clear identity and strong intellectual underpinnings located in philosophy. Its methods, choice of problems, forms of argument, and criteria of relevance are seen as validated by philosophy as an academic discipline. Legal philosophy, understood in these terms, is the branch of philosophy that takes law as its object. As such, it is often seen as having higher intellectual status than that which jurisprudence possessed before its incorporation or redefinition.

In fact, many self-identified Anglophone legal philosophers now view jurisprudence, insofar as it is *not* legal philosophy in this contemporary sense, as unworthy of serious scholarly attention. And it is true that jurisprudence has often seemed to be a disconnected package of insights about law drawn with little discrimination from 'nonlegal' academic disciplines in the humanities and social sciences and from lawyers' theoretical speculations on their own legal professional knowledge and practice. So, in the past it seemed important for legal philosophers to attack jurisprudence's 'syncretism of methods' (Kelsen 1967: 1), the unsystematic package of approaches that characterised it in its primitive (pre-philosophical) state.

Today, these attacks are usually considered unnecessary. Legal philosophers see the battle for intellectual rigour as won as far as they are concerned. Contemporary

Anglophone legal philosophy tends its furrow, unconcerned with the nature of jurisprudence insofar as this could be anything different from what legal philosophers do;[1] jurisprudence might be acceptable merely as the name for a pedagogic package of ideas to broaden the minds of undergraduate law students, but this would not validate it as a serious field of academic research.

In this chapter I shall defend jurisprudence as something more than a pedagogic package, and also as an enterprise distinct from legal philosophy. It will be argued that, however undisciplined (in academic terms) and philosophically inept its literature may often have been, jurisprudence is properly seen as an important body of thought about law that aims at exploring, aiding, and developing the *prudentia* of jurists. A dictionary search reveals that *prudentia* can mean acquaintance, knowledge, sagacity, prudence, discretion, and foresight, which will serve as a provisional set of meanings here:[2] one to attach to an ideal juristic understanding of law.

On this basis, jurisprudence is not an academic field, certainly not a modern academic discipline. It is, at best, a patchwork of insights related to the idea (and ideal) of law as a practice of regulation to serve social needs and social values, as these are recognised in particular times and places. So jurisprudence, on this view, is an exploratory enterprise aimed at serving an ongoing, ever-changing juristic practice. It is not aimed at finding ultimate truth about law's nature or timeless, 'essential', or 'necessary' characteristics of the legal.

What may be timeless is the *task* for which jurisprudence should provide enlightenment: a task of making organised social regulation a valuable practice, rooted and effective in the specific contexts and historical conditions in which it exists but also aimed at serving demands for justice and security through regulation as these perennial values are understood in their time and place and as they might be further clarified and reconciled as legal ideals. Jurisprudence, on this view, is aimed at informing those who are enduringly (usually professionally) concerned with the well-being of the idea of law as a theoretically guided practice in this sense, equipping them with the means of promoting that well-being (itself a matter for interpretation).

In the previous chapter such legally committed individuals were identified as taking on a specific role in relation to law – the role of the jurist, here understood in ideal typical terms – and the aim in this chapter is to defend jurisprudence as a contemporary enterprise whose raison d'être is to gather and organise knowledge to assist them.

Bricolage jurisprudence and its enemies

How could such an idea of jurisprudence be unpacked? *Lloyd's Introduction to Jurisprudence* (Freeman 2014), edited through many editions by Michael Freeman, has been the textbook used by generations of jurisprudence students in the UK and

---

1 Thus the *Oxford Handbook of Jurisprudence & Philosophy of Law* (Coleman and Shapiro eds 2002) treats its subject as legal philosophy and makes no reference to jurisprudence as a field.

2 The diversity of meanings suggested by these words is important here. They usefully imply that jurisprudence cannot be systematically codified as an ethical or other programme but rather promotes or serves a cluster of (not necessarily easily integrated) juristic virtues.

many other countries. The book primarily serves 'pedagogic' jurisprudence – it relies on educational justifications which, as noted earlier, this chapter aims to go beyond[3] – but in doing so *Lloyd* defends a vision of jurisprudence that rejects the claim that this should be equated with legal philosophy.

The approach adopted can, following the suggestion in Chapter 1, be called theoretical 'bricolage'[4] – a bit of this, a bit of that, with each different theory or set of ideas given a hearing; never defined *ab initio* as outside the agenda of debate; not required to show its prevalidated ticket of entry into the 'province of jurisprudence' as 'an exclusive field of inquiry' (Halpin 2011: 184). The approach is merely open-minded curiosity as to what could be inspiring, what might show law in a new light.

Dennis Lloyd (1965: xvi) stated in presenting his textbook that he wrote 'as a lawyer and not as a philosopher'. Clearly he did not regard this as a fatal flaw, but it raised the issue of how the jurisprudential project should be related to the legal philosophical one. He contented himself with rejecting, as early as 1959, what he saw as excessive claims for linguistic philosophy as a route to legal enlightenment (Lloyd 1965: xvi–xvii). His approach continued a jurisprudential tradition that was not oriented towards defending itself in modern academic disciplinary terms. As he made clear, his reference points were law (as an immensely important social, political, and moral idea) and lawyers, and not the specific disciplinary orientations of any of the humanities or social sciences.

The implication was that jurisprudence did not need the credentials of these disciplines to support its validity. But this would certainly not be the only acceptable (or even necessarily the most important) way to approach law theoretically, because clearly law is not just to be studied for juristic purposes. Defending a kind of bricolage jurisprudence *á la Lloyd* is entirely compatible with championing legal philosophy (in collaboration with moral and political philosophy) and legal sociology as powerful enterprises aimed at the theoretical study of law and legal phenomena for mainly nonjuristic purposes (but which might produce much juristically valuable knowledge along the way).

'Open-minded curiosity' is not, however, enough to justify jurisprudence. Open-mindedness and curiosity can lead in many directions represented by the plethora of approaches to legal scholarship existing today in Anglophone countries, which have often seemed to leave jurisprudence as a backwater. In part it is because of a failure to demarcate and defend jurisprudence with sufficient clarity as a project that a need was felt to replace it with an academically rigorous legal philosophy – validated by philosophy as a profession. Despite this, many scholars have insisted on the nonequivalence of jurisprudence and legal philosophy, but usually in ways that put jurisprudence in a position of relative weakness.

Jurisprudence, wrote Julius Stone (1968: 16), is 'the lawyer's extraversion' – but how far this turning outwards should go, what it is a turning outwards from, and

---

3 I have discussed the specific value of pedagogic jurisprudence in Cotterrell 2000.
4 On bricolage in jurisprudence see Hull 1997: 8–13.

what is to be gained by this he did not adequately explain. He was clear that most jurisprudential problems were different from those of philosophy (ibid: 8) but not about what linked those problems into a coherent enterprise. William Twining (2002: 3), also refusing to equate jurisprudence with legal philosophy, defines it as 'the general or theoretical part of law as a discipline'. But this begs the question of the nature and boundaries of law as a discipline, and what is still needed is a unifying aim for the jurisprudential project.[5] Twining (1979: 575) once listed at least five distinct functions that jurisprudence may perform for the discipline of law. These can be summarised as integrating it, facilitating its relations with other disciplines, philosophising about law's nature and functions, 'middle order' theorising about law as a practice, and exploring the intellectual history of legal scholarship.[6] On Twining's view, legal philosophy is part of jurisprudence. But what the whole adds up to is a set of tasks without any very clear relationship between them; jurisprudence is thus described but not systematically justified.

A popular contemporary jurisprudence text takes a different approach: 'Jurisprudential questions, while "theoretical", are the sorts of questions about "the nature of law" to which any lawyer or judge might be expected to provide a reasonably intelligent answer' (Penner et al 2002: 4). This has the virtue of linking jurisprudence not to any particular disciplinary protocols or academic field but to law as a diverse, ever-changing range of practices. It comes closest to the argument this chapter seeks to make, but more needs to be said about the kind of contribution jurisprudence can make to these practices. And must *every* lawyer be expected to have answers to jurisprudence's questions?

By contrast, legal philosophers are often very clear. 'Jurisprudence,' writes Brian Leiter, is 'the study of philosophical problems about law,' and 'distinctively *philosophical* problems . . . define the discipline of jurisprudence.'[7] These problems are given by a certain understanding of the nature of philosophy. Beyond this, on such a view, there may be no worthwhile legal theory, and jurisprudents – for example critical legal theorists, feminist legal theorists, the antipositivist Lon Fuller, postmodernists, critical race theorists, and economic analysts of law – 'as opposed to legal philosophers', have purveyed 'so many half-baked ideas' (Leiter 2007: 100–1). But this 'philosophical view' of jurisprudence (Twining 1979: 574) has its costs.

The following sections of this chapter sketch characteristics of the dominant outlook (rather than the substance) of contemporary Anglo-American legal philosophy, focusing initially on its positivist core and then considering it more broadly. I argue that these characteristics disable it from standing in for jurisprudence as the *prudentia* of jurists and have made it largely unconcerned to try to do so. One consequence has been to make the juristic value of much legal philosophy controversial and even denied altogether in some quarters. In the legal world, it seems that the question

---

5 There is a similar problem in treating jurisprudence as 'the epistemological basis of legal knowledge' (Tur 1978: 158) when the *scope* of legal knowledge remains to be clarified.

6 For a broader but perhaps more diffuse listing see Twining 2009: 9–10.

7 Leiter 2007: 84, 137, emphasis in original.

of what legal philosophy has to offer is now rarely answered. From such sceptical views of current legal philosophy (based here mainly on a collation of critiques from within the ranks of legal philosophers themselves), the chapter goes on to elaborate jurisprudence's special function and why this research field needs no specific justification from any of the particular academic disciplines that contribute to it.

Contemporary legal positivism

Generalisation is risky but sometimes required to attempt to gain some overall perspective on an intellectual field, a sense of its shape and orientations, and an insight into the directions of its development. So it is necessary to try to identify here some dominant characteristics of legal philosophy despite the variety of work it encompasses. Within it, what is often seen as its central part, around which much of the rest is organised or engages, can be called contemporary legal positivism (hereafter CLP).

This enterprise of description and analysis of the conceptual structures of law is unified most obviously by its adherents' recognition of H. L. A. Hart's *The Concept of Law* (1994) as its originating text. CLP has been said to stand 'as victorious as any research programme in post-World War II philosophy' (Leiter 2007: 2). Its founding proposition, as formulated by John Gardner (2001: 199), is that in any legal system 'whether a given norm is legally valid, and hence whether it forms part of the law of that system, depends on its sources, not on its merits'. This proposition is held to differentiate CLP from what it understands as opposing projects in legal philosophy associated with natural law theory. Thus, natural law thought is, for CLP, a theoretical 'other' against which it asserts its identity. The consequence of accepting CLP's founding proposition is that conceptual inquiries about law can be conducted in a way that largely excludes any substantive moral or political concerns.

Indeed, it is tempting to see CLP as defined mainly by what it excludes from consideration. Gardner (ibid: 223–4) is explicit about this, noting that CLP's founding proposition addresses only the issue of law's *validity*; other philosophical questions about law exist beyond this but are not specific to CLP and hence not part of its unifying project of exploring the implications of its central proposition. This entails a commitment to the idea that what counts as law in any society is determined by the existence of certain social facts (Leiter 2007: 122).

Interpretation of CLP's founding proposition produces its two opposed factions, 'exclusive' (or hard) and 'inclusive' (or soft) positivism, the former claiming that what determines legal validity *cannot* include purely moral criteria, the latter asserting that, while some (or many) legal systems might in reality exhibit moral criteria of validity, a legal system not relying on any such moral criteria *could* be envisaged (so, law is still analytically separable from morality). A huge literature now explores the ramifications of these and related claims. The focus of attention is thus on developing a rigorous concept of law based on a correct interpretation of CLP's founding proposition.

Concern here is not with CLP's debates around these matters but only with what from a juristic point of view appears as their *narrowness*. While, as Gardner insists, they occupy only a part of legal philosophy, the intensity, intricacy, and assumed crucial importance of arguments around them divert attention from other philosophical issues about law. Many theorists[8] have noted (and regretted) the narrowing of the concerns of positivist legal theory over time: from Bentham, to John Austin, to Hart, and on to Hart's current CLP successors. Early legal positivism, treating law as 'posited' from identifiable political sources rather than produced through revelation, nature, or speculative reasoning on the human condition, might be seen as providing a liberating basis for many theoretical inquiries about law's role in relation to morality and politics. But gradually 'the needs of a detached, descriptive jurisprudence were . . . relentlessly separated from the world of political theory, in which so many contestable conceptions of human nature strove endlessly with one another. This separation was not simply a dogma, open to debate, but a determination of the field of inquiry itself' (Coyle 2013: 401–2). Tightening philosophical protocols, internalised throughout CLP, have encouraged and justified this narrowing, transmuting jurisprudence into a confined arena of debate, policed not by criteria of social or legal significance but by canons of technical sophistication in argument.

Legal philosophers outside the CLP camp, and some within it, have noted this situation. Ronald Dworkin (2006b: 213) wrote that CLP risks 'intellectual insularity', that it understands legal philosophy as 'distinct not only from the actual practice of law, but also from the academic study of substantive and procedural fields of law', from 'normative political philosophy' and from 'sociology of law or legal anthropology. . . . It is, in short, a discipline that can be pursued on its own with neither background experience nor training in or even familiarity with any literature or research beyond its narrow world and few disciples. The analogy to scholastic theology is . . . tempting.'

More restrained complaints are widespread. On one view, the legal positivist tradition has produced 'exclusivity and disengagement' through its particular conceptual and definitional focus, but 'the frailty of the endeavour which rests a restrictive understanding of law on a single insight is obvious to everyone' except those pursuing it (Halpin 2011: 200–1). The narrowing of English positivist legal philosophy has left it only 'a shrinking audience within the academy'; it fails 'to communicate its ideas to those outside its own caste' (Richard Cosgrove, quoted in Duxbury 1997: 1996). Anglophone legal philosophy has become a 'small, hermetic – and rather incestuous – universe' (Leiter 2007: 2).

For some critics, the real indictment is that CLP has *lost touch with the practice of law* and its social and political contexts. To counter this, it is necessary to discard the idea 'that the deepest questions confronting the doctrinal lawyer must await the "solution" of prior philosophical problems. A different viewpoint

---

8 See e.g. Halpin 2011: 200, Schauer 2011, Priel 2015, Dyzenhaus 2000, and Twining 1979: 558.

must prevail: one must begin from the lawyer's perspective, the administration of justice at the concrete level' (Coyle 2013: 418). The natural lawyer John Finnis, whose work has often been seen in the past by CLP scholars as compatible with (because distinguishable from) their projects, has now passionately condemned Hart's CLP legacy for its complacency, blindness, or narrowness of outlook, leading to its refusal to address what Finnis sees as vital and urgent political and moral issues surrounding law in contemporary society (Finnis 2009: 180–5).

An answer to these criticisms might be that, even if they point to limitations of CLP's projects, they do not invalidate these projects *on their own terms*. At worst they might indicate their insignificance as seen from some viewpoints (e.g. Dyzenhaus 2000: 715). Other criticisms, however, bite at CLP projects themselves. Brian Leiter (2007: 1–2) argues that CLP's view that philosophy requires a 'method of conceptual analysis via appeal to folk intuitions (as manifest, for example in ordinary language)' has been undermined by the 'naturalistic' revolution in Anglophone philosophy from the 1960s. While CLP has recently featured debates on method, these have been 'idiosyncratic and narrow'; they have been divorced from wider debates in philosophy fundamentally challenging the epistemic viability of conceptual analysis and of reliance on intuitions. But, in Leiter's view, CLP has usually unquestioningly assumed this viability of both matters as fundamental to its practice (ibid: 164–75).

The kind of conceptual analysis that has been central to CLP has also been challenged by Finnis on the ground, essentially, that conceptual analysis presupposes a choice (not a discovery) of concepts (such as a concept of law) and any such choice depends on the *purposes* for which concepts are sought. Hence CLP's projects of conceptual inquiry about law require an elaboration of these purposes and therefore require the opening of CLP to matters (including moral or political matters) outside its self-imposed analytical remit.[9] Efforts to go a little way towards this 'opening' while holding to CLP's fundamental tenets lead to much complexity.[10] Otherwise, CLP sometimes attracts criticism for making assumptions about the nature of law's social and political contexts (e.g. Coyle 2013; Twining 1979: 564) – assumptions that it does not see as controversial because of its lack of concern to study these contexts empirically and comparatively. The issue becomes how far CLP, even accepting the validity of its narrow project, is based on sufficiently firm foundations in pursuing it.

The utility of CLP for any idea of jurisprudence as a broad, open inquiry is also put in doubt by criticisms of its typical modes of argument. Andrew Halpin (2011: 180–5) has discussed three ways of arranging argument that are relevant here. One is 'axiomatic disengagement', in which the acceptance of a certain theoretical approach to a defined subject-matter eventually makes meaningful communication with other theoretical approaches impossible. Another is the promotion of a particular 'insight' (such as CLP's founding proposition) so extensively that it is held

---

9 Finnis 2011: ch 1, Finnis 2009: 163–6. Cf Endicott 2001, Gardner 2007.
10 See e.g. Raz 1994: 326–40 on the place of moral reasoning in, about, and through law; Dickson 2001 on 'indirectly evaluative' theory.

actually to *define* the relevant field of inquiry; nonacceptance of the relevant insight or failure to see its full significance produces exclusion from the field of argument. The third approach, 'splitting the subject-matter', assigns opposing views to different categories of inquiry (so that they need not engage with each other). Halpin's example of this last approach is Hart's claim that his work and that of Dworkin represent entirely separate projects. What is important for our purposes here is that these three approaches (which Halpin sees as having helped to shape CLP) are all ways of *excluding argumentative engagement*, rather than encouraging the challenge of different perspectives.

An outward-looking, curious, exploratory jurisprudence is not served by the approaches Halpin identifies, which limit 'external' engagement and exploration beyond predefined fields. As regards the debates that *do* take place with critics or even sometimes 'internally' within CLP, what can be observed is their frequent intensity and aggressiveness. As one commentator notes, 'positivists and their critics have extracted innumerable technical satisfactions from their exploration of the weaknesses of each other's positions' (Coyle 2013: 404). How far does this amount to *point-scoring*, to what Edward Shils (1985: 168) describes as the sharpshooter approach of 'those who regard intellectual activity not as the extension of understanding but a game in which the prizes go for rigour and elegance of formulation and proof, and for proving the other fellow wrong'?[11] This style, associated with certain kinds of lawyers' debates, seems to carry over to the type of philosophy that finds a home in some law schools.

As Shils claims, intellectual sharpshooting is not always the best way to understanding: 'Discoveries are not made in this way, least of all self-discoveries and the discoveries of the self in one's fellow-man' (ibid). But the language of much debate around CLP evokes the sharpshooter image.[12] Indeed, the image was explicitly invoked by one weary protagonist in a long debate around CLP's view of legality, seeing its culmination as the final showdown of a 'High Noon' encounter (Simmonds 2011). But the irony only emphasises the destructive setting of debate.

Why legal philosophy is not jurisprudence

If contemporary Anglophone legal philosophy is viewed *beyond* its positivist core, the problems for its jurisprudential utility appear differently. Certainly, it contains a vast diversity of projects. Definitional limitations on its scope can be fixed only by reference to philosophy as its parent discipline and to some kind of concern with law as

---

11 See also Collini 2006: 113, discussing H. L. A. Hart's philosophical environment: 'Seeing things in the form of "propositions", and then conducting a stiff philosophy tutorial on their clarity and coherence, could indeed dispose of a lot of fuzzy thinking, though it was perhaps less well adapted to doing justice to matters of deep human interest that could not without loss be formulated in a series of neat "propositions"'.

12 Describing opposing ideas as 'demolished', 'dismissed', 'happily defunct', 'ridiculous', 'absurd', 'asinine', 'preposterous', 'spectacularly wrong-headed', 'silly', and 'a joke', to take a few examples: see Kramer 2011: 116; Leiter 2004: 176; Leiter 2007: 4, 20, 59, 100–1, 174; and Gardner 2001: 225.

its focus. In earlier times, when philosophy was less professionally compartmentalised in the academy, it was easy to treat legal philosophy and jurisprudence as synonyms; what made problems 'philosophical' could remain a matter of little concern. In principle, as noted in Chapter 1, nothing stopped jurists from declaring any of their general musings on law to be legal philosophy. Today, with legal philosophy's identity fixed by its relationship to philosophy as an academic field, matters are different.

This introduces a new criterion for assessing the worth of legal theoretical inquiries on the basis of whether or not they are 'philosophically interesting' (cf Twining 1979: 569–70). And ideas that could be of juristic interest – because relevant for a general understanding of legal practice or experience – sometimes appear as 'a philosophical mess' (Leiter 2007: 60). Indeed, legal philosophical issues can, it seems, be pursued *irrespective of any reference to law's actual settings*. For example, on one view, 'the' concept of law can be elaborated philosophically in terms of law's 'essential' qualities whether or not these qualities exist in any particular social conditions; if the evidence of conditions reveals that the regulatory forms do not conform to the philosophical concept of law, it is not the concept that needs adjusting; the conclusion should rather be that in those conditions there is no law (Raz 2009a: 25, 91–2). What is philosophically essential is not governed by what contingently exists.

There are several problems here for any jurisprudential project concerned with 'the idea (and ideal) of law as a practice of regulation to serve social needs and social values, as these are recognised in particular times and places'. To philosophise about law irrespective of experience in particular times and places may show limited concern for juristic relevance. Legal philosophy mainly seeks universal truths rather than knowledge rooted in the particularities of social context,[13] and it is sometimes assumed that obtaining the latter would require 'life-consuming empirical studies' and 'a mountain of data' (Dworkin 2006b: 166–7). So, when legal philosophers refer to 'sociological' considerations, they usually mean claims that can be made about the relevance of social conditions without actually studying these conditions. A famous instance is Hart's claim in *The Concept of Law* to be engaged in a project of 'descriptive sociology' (1994: vi). This means, for him, mainly speculation on how people actually use language – but without any empirical inquiry about this, any examination of its sociological significance, or any recognition of possible social variation in language use.

However, what usually insulates legal philosophy from systematical empirical inquiries is ultimately not the purported difficulty of the latter but a conviction that empirical research is uninteresting as compared with efforts to discover context-free

---

13 See e.g. Raz 2009b: 104, describing what he sees as 'the difference between legal philosophy and sociology of law. The latter is concerned with the contingent and with the particular, the former with the necessary and the universal.' As used by legal philosophers, however, this way of characterising the distinction implies misleadingly that sociology of law (unlike legal philosophy) is not concerned with or does not provide general legal theory. In fact, the key issue is: what is the object to be theorised? Is it law as experienced in particular kinds of society or civilization or law as some kind of pure form detached from social context?

truth or to conceptualise what is essential in law, these efforts being guided by intuitions as to what is philosophically significant or what are reliable foundations for inquiry.

Our concern here is not to debate whether a philosophical search for truth, the universal, or the essential in law (or in anything else) is appropriate as a philosophical project. The issue is whether it is appropriate as a *juristic project* and whether any effort at finding knowledge of the legal world that has timeless validity can be conducted without the kinds of empirical inquiries that philosophers regard as uninteresting or practically impossible. Can one speculate in any useful way about timeless or essential characteristics of law without studying the variety of forms that social regulation can take, as well as the variety of social and historical contexts that influence the ways in which theoretical issues are formulated and how far these are seen as important and meaningful as juristic concerns?

If jurisprudence is understood as juristic knowledge focused on promoting the well-being of the idea of law as a socially valuable practice of regulation, this knowledge must represent regulatory practices in their time and place, reflecting the variability of sociolegal conditions. Certainly, jurisprudence, understood in this way, has no need to ignore broad speculations in moral and political philosophy; it can surely find much inspiration in efforts to portray values and ideals of law as capable of transcending particular cultural contexts. But these wide horizons of theory need juristically to be judged against and explicitly related to local circumstances. Any pretention to timelessness and universality needs to be discounted against empirical sociolegal study of the circumstances in which juristic tasks have to be performed.

In such a juristic outlook, theoretical resources appear as a continuum, involving different levels of generality, different scale and scope. But they are unified by an overarching project of serving the theoretical needs of juristic practice in its time and place, broadening this practice while keeping it rooted in changing experience and encouraging critical imagination in it by an open search for comparative and philosophically ambitious insights about legal doctrine and the contexts in which it is created, interpreted, and applied.

Leaving aside contemporary legal positivism, the main juristic problem with those parts of the contemporary legal philosophical enterprise that are integrated with moral and political philosophy is not narrowness but perhaps its opposite – the expansive ambition of the effort to find truth about some aspect of human experience. It might be said that many philosophical projects involve no more than working out the results of rigorous reasoning from certain accepted premises. Nevertheless the product is often *systems* of thought – for example theories of social justice, of liberalism as a value system, of democracy, or of the moral good – which claim or assume universal validity in relation to the matters they address. Such philosophical systems are surely of interest for jurisprudence, but they are not normally directed to juristic purposes. This is certainly so if, as discussed in Chapter 3, juristic tasks require a pragmatic, provisional managing of conflicts of values and understandings and the pursuit of legal ideals in the light of experience, with awareness of law's operational limits.

Relations between legal philosophy and empirical sociolegal inquiry are certainly matters for debate. Leiter (2007: 4, 176), assuming a context of positivist legal philosophy, insists that philosophy must be 'continuous with empirical science', proceeding 'in tandem' with it 'as a reflective attempt at synoptic clarity about the state of empirical knowledge'; in other words, philosophy's task is to organise intellectually what empirical study reports as existing. The naturalistic critique entails that positivist descriptive legal philosophy depends for its validity on being grounded in empirical inquiries about law. That must surely mean grounded especially in the related enterprises of comparative law and sociology of law: the former insofar as it reveals the empirical variability of law's doctrinal and institutional forms, the latter insofar as it studies legal practices, institutions, and experience systematically and empirically as social phenomena. In some ways, Finnis's challenge to conceptual inquiry, noted earlier, is even more fundamental because it denies the possibility of separating CLP's projects from legal philosophy in a larger sense, integrated with moral and political philosophy. And behind everything is the problem of the role of *intuitions* in determining what counts as important as a starting point for inquiry. Perhaps a key to progress is to insist that intuitions be made explicit and justified. Such a protocol would be almost guaranteed to widen the scope of intellectual discussion.

It is possible to interpret all these contemporary critiques as nudging legal philosophy in the direction of a receptiveness to an indefinite range of types of knowledge about law as an idea, a set of practices and institutions, and a field of social experience: *broadening* it (into wider moral and political concerns) and *deepening* it (to assess sociolegal conditions). A legal philosophy changing in these ways would come closer to the orientation that I am associating with jurisprudence. For the moment, however, these kinds of critique remain only at the edges of the contemporary Anglophone legal philosophical enterprise. So, this enterprise does not provide the range of knowledge and insight to serve fully the theoretical *prudentia* of jurists. Legal philosophy's protocols divide, limit, and insulate it from an outward-looking curiosity about the whole range of theoretical issues that might be raised in relation to law and about the relevance of empirical and comparative inquiries about law seen as a matter of juristic practice and social experience, varying with time and place.

Current legal philosophy's focus is not on juristic experience in all its practical complexity, ethical ambiguity, and contextual specificity but on abstract problems defined by philosophical interest. Its dominant positivist approaches avoid or marginalise important moral and political dilemmas that surround the practice and experience of law. Its typical focus on the universal or the necessary blinds it to social variation revealed by empirical studies of law in society and the resources of sociolegal theory. Its tendency to see its concerns as relatively independent of those of lawyers in practice and academic lawyers in general[14] isolates it from many everyday juristic

14 Gardner 2001: 203, Leiter 2004: 178. Cf Coyle 2013: 415, Twining 1979: 562.

concerns.[15] But jurisprudence, I shall suggest, has to find its unity and purpose by recognising how these matters together make up the jurist's theoretical universe.

Jurisprudence and jurists

The structured character of legal philosophy today presents a striking contrast to bricolage jurisprudence. Lacking firm methodological commitments, this jurisprudence has collected insights from anywhere they can be found – including, for example, English analytical jurisprudence, Scandinavian legal realism, many kinds of American and continental European theory, moral and political philosophy, economic analysis, Marxism, feminism, the comparative speculations of historical jurisprudence, and the legal anthropology of stateless societies. Linguistic limitations often confine jurisprudence's practical reach, but no disciplinary protocols do so. And it can draw on everything that legal philosophy has to offer, but it is a 'philosophical mess' (cf Leiter 2007: 60). What can unify it?

It is not enough to defend it in the way that pedagogic jurisprudence is often defended: as important for the 'liberal education' of lawyers. One might ask why lawyers need a liberal education, what that is, and why jurisprudence (rather than other subjects of study) is needed to provide it. Also, for reasons suggested earlier, it is not enough to advocate the lawyer's 'extraversion' (a close relation of the liberal legal education argument). Nor is it enough to state all the varied things jurisprudence might encompass in a checklist. Something must hold all this together, but what that is cannot be the theoretical or methodological protocols of an academic discipline. Jurisprudence is not an application to law of the protocols of disciplines such as philosophy, sociology, economics, or anthropology. Its orientation is not a *focusing down* from one or more of these disciplines to the special topic of 'law'. It has to be a *projection up* from law as regulatory practice and experience into any realms of theory that can support that practice or make sense of that experience.

It is easy to suggest how this shifts the focus of theoretical questions from a 'legal philosophical' orientation to a juristic one. For example, instead of asking abstractly 'Is there a general obligation to obey the law?' one might ask how law can best be made fit to attract a sense of obligation from those who serve it professionally and those who appeal to it or are addressed by it as citizens. Instead of asking 'What is the nature of law as a system of rules?' one can ask how rules operate (and should operate) in lawyers' practice and citizens' experience of law. Instead of asking 'Does the concept of legality entail moral commitments?' one might ask what moral

---

15 This situation might be altered if the study of legal interpretation and reasoning became more central in current legal philosophy: see Halpin 2011: 197–8. That it is not (despite important contributions by legal philosophers) may reflect the difficulty of addressing such matters convincingly without assessing the relevance of various moral, political, or other evaluative criteria that are avoided in the dominant positivist approaches to conceptual analysis. Similarly, in its dominant forms, contemporary legal philosophy has resisted studying the processes of legislation and administrative lawmaking: see Dyzenhaus 2000: 719–21.

significance legality should be expected to have and how that might be achieved in specific sociolegal conditions. Instead of asking generally 'Is unjust law still law?' one might consider how far law can be just and what 'just' can mean (and for whom?): what should be understood in practice and in a particular time and place by the idea of law's 'flourishing', and how can such flourishing be promoted? Instead of asking how legal philosophy affects the world (e.g. whether legal positivism has promoted liberty or tyranny) one should ask jurisprudential questions: what in juristic practice has promoted quiescence in the face of tendencies to authoritarianism in particular societies and what could help to counter such tendencies?

From this perspective it is easy to see why some of the legal theory most often disparaged in legal philosophy can appear as among the most enlightening jurisprudentially. Examples are the work of Lon Fuller and Karl Llewellyn. Very different theorists, they were nevertheless indisputably jurists rather than philosophers, and their focus was on law as a practice and, indeed, a craft of regulating. As one writer suggests, jurisprudence for them was 'the love and pursuit of a sort of lawyer's wisdom' (Soosay 2011: 32). For Llewellyn, the problems of jurisprudence arise from the need for society, through its legal specialists, to fulfil what he called the 'law-jobs' – practical tasks of dispute-processing, fixing lines of authority, social coordination, 'smoothing friction' with 'vision and sense', and integrating all the dimensions of legal work (Llewellyn and Hoebel 1941: 290–3; Llewellyn 1962: 322). For Fuller, these problems are about subjecting conduct to the governance of rules, involving the promotion of core social values in the practice and experience of law (Winston ed 2001).

The idea of law as a craft may be incompatible with the idea of it as represented by any philosophically coherent system of thought. At one level, the juristic issues are about ensuring the efficiency of the tools of law for the social tasks to which it is to be directed and understanding the technical character and limits of those tools. At another, the issues are about aspirations to elaborate and promote ultimate social values through law and to understand and assess the practice and experience of law in terms of those values; so, jurisprudence is concerned with asking about the juristic meaning of such values. In one aspect, therefore, it points towards a need to clarify the nature of legal ideas as lawyers (and nonlawyers) understand these; in another it points towards exploring what the philosopher F. S. C. Northrop (1959) called the complexity of legal and ethical experience (a matter for which both philosophy and the social sciences are needed).[16]

The essential point is that, however wide these jurisprudential inquiries become, they start from and must relate back to conditions of legal practice and experience in their particular time and place. This is why jurisprudence is unlikely to become a pursuit of universal knowledge. For that to happen, juristic experience would itself have to become uniform – perhaps in some future era of genuinely global law. Juristic practice would have to become a universal enterprise, crossing all national and cultural borders. How far it already has some limited characteristics

---

16 See Chapter 5, where Northrop's ideas are discussed.

of this universality depends on how its nature is understood. I argued in the previous chapter that the jurist's role might be seen as entailing a wider vision than that which many lawyers require for their everyday work and a different focus than that typically needed by legislators, law reformers, and most judges. So, perhaps it might be possible to envisage a flexible, context-sensitive juristic idea of law that can cross frontiers – one that holds to certain legal values (justice, security, solidarity) in combination but avoids dogmatism about the possible forms which law can take. Yet any such juristic perspective has to be rooted in narrower professional (e.g. lawyers', legislators', judges') and popular (citizens') perspectives on law.

The broader the jurist's vision, the more universal the knowledge required to support it, and so the more comprehensive the reach of jurisprudence should be. Its theoretical bricolage, its package of insights selected for their potential juristic relevance, can be unified only by the particular vision of the juristic role that the package supports. But the ideal of wide-ranging intellectual curiosity about legal experience, which may be jurisprudence's most attractive feature, should surely be encouraged. By that means it might help to promote a more universalistic – or at least more broadly comparative – understanding of the juristic role without denying its grounding in specific sociolegal contexts. But how are those specific sociolegal contexts to be understood theoretically in jurisprudence? The next chapter looks at sociological resources that can help to promote such understanding.

5

SOCIOLOGY IN JURISTIC PRACTICE

Two intellectual worlds

Can sociological inquiries play an important role in addressing juristic issues? It might be far from obvious that they can. Juristic inquiries and sociological inquiries seem to inhabit different worlds of knowledge. The juristic study of law centres on normative argument, interpretation, and analysis; sociological study typically does not.

Contrasting priorities seem obvious. A juristic focus will be on legal phenomena understood primarily in ways that Hart (1994) associated with a normative 'internal' view of rules. Typical juristic concerns are with the organisation (systematisation, generalisation) and interpretation of legal rules, principles, and concepts; the clarification of legal values; and the orderly management of doctrinal change. Juristic responsibilities can include evaluating, improving or expounding legal rules, or applying them to judge social relations. Social scientists, however, typically do not have any such primary focus. They are concerned with observing and understanding social phenomena and with describing and explaining the nature of social life – either in relatively general terms (as social theory) or in specific aspects or fields. They can identify rules and norms as recognisable commitments of individuals whose action they observe or as structural elements in social institutions (such as those of law). But they are not committed, as social scientists, to adopt a particular interpretive attitude to these.

Jurists professionally inhabit a world of legal doctrine – rules, norms, principles, concepts, and values – as insiders; sociologists' focus may certainly include normative phenomena, but their world of professional inquiry is the social at large, of which law is a part. Their concern is to make sense of the social – even if that involves, as one (perhaps important) aspect, studying law's role in structuring social relations.

This demarcation may seem superficially clear, but even stating it in these terms implies issues that might threaten to undermine it. For example, can a totally clear line be drawn between norm and fact, between description and evaluation, or between participants in legal practices and observers of them? I shall suggest that although genuine distinctions are certainly to be drawn and maintained between juristic and sociological perspectives on law, these are much less sharp and absolute than is often assumed or claimed.

Indeed, in important ways, juristic and sociological inputs into the practice, explanation, and interpretation of law can be closely linked and can interact closely. Sociological inquiries cannot *solve* normative problems of law (although they have been invoked to do so in juristic contexts and have sometimes been used to try to avoid these problems). However, and crucially, they can reveal and explain much about the contexts in which juristic problems are addressed. They can sometimes also show why these problems take the form they do, why certain kinds of juristic arguments tend to prevail over others, and what the parameters of meaningful juristic debate are likely to be in specific contexts.

I shall argue that, by such means, sociological perspectives can and should help to explain the *meaning, scope, and significance of juristic controversies*, at least in some contexts. For these reasons, at least, jurists need these perspectives if they are to be well informed and best equipped to fulfil their tasks of understanding, interpreting and applying legal doctrine. But there are also some other kinds of juristic-sociological interdependence that are or have been claimed, sometimes with misleading consequences, and in developing this chapter's arguments it will be necessary to examine the most important of these other claims.

The use of social science in the courtroom

The most familiar situations in which social science has been accepted into the world of juristic practice are those in which courts consider social scientific evidence and purport to rely on it as a partial or total justification for their decision. In United States courts and those of several other countries this practice has become widespread (Hughes and MacDonnell 2013; Rathus 2012; Naveen 2006; Yovel and Mertz 2004). The 1908 case of *Muller* v *Oregon*[1] is often cited as the first instance of very extensive citation to (and acceptance by) the US Supreme Court of statistical, social scientific, or psychological studies as evidence. Such evidence had featured in earlier cases, but in *Muller* almost the *entirety* of counsel Louis Brandeis's brief to the Court was made up of such material. Just two of its 113 pages addressed legal authorities bearing on the issue in the case: whether a statute of the state of Oregon limiting the working day for women employees to ten hours was a valid exercise of state authority under the US Constitution.

Reading the Brandeis brief now,[2] it is impossible not to be amazed by the overwhelming, almost chaotic hotchpotch of materials – a massive evidential blunderbuss of (often later discredited) opinion and fact statements: extracts from books

---

1   208 US 412 (1908).
2   The entire text is available at https://louisville.edu/law/library/special-collections/the-louis-d.-brandeis-collection/the-brandeis-brief-in-its-entirety. The term 'Brandeis brief' was widely used after *Muller* to refer to any such use of social science or social statistics by counsel in court as a major basis of argument.

on factory conditions, women's physiology, hygiene and infant mortality, quotations from dozens of US and foreign official reports and commissions, labour statistics and economic analyses, organised under such headings as 'Bad Effect of Long Hours on Health', or safety, or morals; 'Good Effect on Individual Health', home life, or general welfare; 'Effect on Output', on regularity of employment or scope of women's employment; and 'Opinions' of physicians, employers, and employees on the reasonableness of a ten-hour working day.

What should be made of this kind of argumentation before courts, which has become more sophisticated but not necessarily changed its fundamental character since *Muller*? Does it represent an infiltration by social science of the juristic world? At first glance, the answer is surely negative. What is presented is purportedly just evidence. Like all evidence, it provides raw material around which juristic argument can be organised or to which it can be applied. The complex relation of legal analysis to fact finding seems the same in this kind of case as in any other. But can the material presented be entirely understood only as evidence? Can it sometimes present an authority that challenges the court?

In *Muller* the issue was whether Oregon's statute infringed what had been held to be Fourteenth Amendment guarantees of freedom of contract or whether it fell within an exception allowing reasonable state controls to protect health, safety, or the general welfare. The juristic issue was thus made to centre on the *reasonableness* of state action. Insofar as what is reasonable depends on the state of knowledge at the time, the matter could be settled by appeal to a survey of that knowledge in the form presented in the Brandeis brief. Richard Lempert (1988: 187–8) has noted that 'the Court could not go wrong in relying on social science' because it was ultimately immaterial whether the evidence was sound or not; what was important was that it represented the *best available* knowledge and so showed conclusively what it was reasonable for a well-informed legislature in 1908 to see as dangers to health, safety, or welfare.

'Reasonableness' is an empty concept whose content is to be supplied from contextual (in this case social scientific) knowledge. It remains a juristic concept,[3] a part of legal doctrine, but social knowledge is imported to give it meaning. In such circumstances law creates a space for social science – not merely as factual evidence but actually *as part of juristic normative understanding*.

Certainly one could say, as a Luhmannian systems theorist might argue (e.g. Luhmann 2004), that juristic discourse always retains the power to decide for itself in terms of its own priorities what is reasonable; it can 'trump' all nonjuristic experts or providers of evidence. Nevertheless, in practice, once 'reasonable' has been established juristically as a guiding concept in analysis, it is hard to exclude available evidence of what is widely thought to be reasonable.[4] This evidence does not just

---

3 And not just in Anglo-American legal thought: see Taekema 2003: 186–7. For a wide-ranging survey of invocations of 'reasonableness' in continental European legal systems see Zorzetto 2015.

4 It is not easy to reinterpret 'reasonable' to mean only what lawyers professionally might consider to be such without reference to wider non-professional opinion. An appeal to what Edward Coke, in

support juristic evaluations of what 'reasonable' means; in practice it *colours* those evaluations or even may *control* them. Even if a juristic decision about what is reasonable is made on other grounds, so that the evidence of a Brandeis brief merely helps to rationalise it, this in no way lessens the juristic importance of the latter insofar as it provides grounds which the court can declare to support its decision.

Such a merging of juristic and social scientific perspectives might, however, seem a special case. Social science evidence was famously relied on by the US Supreme Court in *Brown v Board of Education of Topeka*[5] to show the pernicious effects on black children of racial segregation in 'separate but equal' education in US public schools. Findings in social-psychological literature about these effects were treated by the court as sufficient to justify its decision that this segregation denied black children 'equal protection of the laws' as required by the 14th Amendment. *Brown* contains *almost no juristic argument*. It dismisses an appeal to the original intent of the 14th Amendment on the grounds that this is unknowable. It finds no directly relevant prior legal authority except *Plessy v Ferguson*,[6] which upheld as constitutional 'separate but equal' communal facilities, and it overturns *Plessy* purely on the basis of social scientific evidence, which, interestingly, it refers to as the 'modern authority' that amply supports its finding of the law. The evidence is treated as showing that racially separated educational facilities produce unequal consequences for black and white children.

This is a very different use of social science from that in *Muller* and, it can be suggested, from a juristic point of view, an unwise one, however well motivated. Here, juristic argument is largely *replaced* by social science; jurisprudence vacates a space for decision, which it leaves to be occupied by social science. The social scientific literature, through its findings, presents the court directly with an answer as to whether 'separate' education of different races can be 'equal'. Social science decides the law.

As has often been remarked, the strategy is dangerous as far as judicial legitimacy is concerned (e.g. Yovel and Mertz 2004: 414–6; Lempert 1988: 189; Chesler et al 1988: 22–4). If the social science turns out to be unreliable, discredited, conflicted, or controversial, so does the juristic process that has relied on it. In *Brown* it might have been better to argue juristically that legal equality is always undermined by legally sanctioned racial segregation: that racially differentiated legal entitlements *by their nature* deny equality before the law.

From a sociological perspective, Lempert (1988: 188–9) has distinguished three functions that social science evidence can perform for courts – an *enlightenment* function (helping to show courts as widely receptive to knowledge of the social world), a *legitimising* function (providing, as in *Brown*, a plausible, publicly understandable basis for the decision reached), and a *strategic* function (supporting an

---

Prohibitions del Roy (1608) 12 Co Rep 63, 65, famously called the 'artificial reason' of the law (lawyers' learning) is quite different from what is in effect an appeal to broad culturally situated common sense.

5   347 US 483 (1954).

6   163 US 537 (1896).

argument or a strategy that judges wish, for reasons unconnected with the social scientific evidence, to follow anyway). If, however, juristic responsibility is thought to include a concern for the integrity and consistency of law as a structure of norms, concepts, and values, deliberate reliance on social science must be risky because there is no reason why social scientists should share these juristic concerns.

Only Lempert's 'enlightenment' function (for example as operating in the determination of 'reasonableness' in *Muller*) seems fully consistent with (and supportive of) juristic responsibilities in this sense, while the legitimising function (to a considerable extent) and the strategic function (to a lesser extent) may represent juristic temptations that are best avoided.

Thick ethical concepts and the fact-value divide

It is necessary to return to 'reasonableness', but now from a different standpoint. As some philosophers and sociologists have emphasised, there are many concepts that seem to combine factual and normative elements in a way that makes these inseparable (Williams 1985; Thacher 2006: 1665–7; Selznick 1961). 'Reasonableness' is clearly a normative idea. However, it presupposes a wide range of *factual experience* that makes it possible, in a given time and place, in a certain culture, on the basis of available knowledge of circumstances, to give content to the idea of 'reasonable' behaviour, as in the familiar concept of the 'reasonable person' of English common law thought (Saltman 1991; Zorzetto 2015: 117–9).

'Friendship', 'courage', 'treachery', 'gratitude', and 'brutality' are other such ideas said to have 'both descriptive and evaluative dimensions that cannot be disentangled' (Thacher 2006: 1665; see Williams 1985: 129–30, 140–5). 'The way these notions are applied,' writes the philosopher Bernard Williams (1985: 129), 'is determined by what the world is like (for instance, how someone has behaved), and yet, at the same time, their application usually involves a certain valuation of the situation, of persons or actions.' Language, including legal language, does not always distinguish fact and value, description of the social world and normative or ethical assessment of it. What Williams calls 'thick' ethical concepts[7] bridge these distinctions.

The sociologist Philip Selznick has used somewhat related ideas in analysing the idea of legality and treating it as the central focus of sociology of law. Like Lon

---

7   As contrasted with 'thin' ethical concepts such as 'good' or 'virtuous' that are 'general and abstract' and do not require concrete factual contexts to give them meaning (Williams 1985: 152). On the relevant philosophical debates see e.g. Carson 2011, concluding (p 14) that the 'thick ethical concepts structuring our evaluative experiences of generosity, cruelty, and the like stubbornly resist evaluative and descriptive dissection'.

Could 'equality', as in the 14th Amendment, itself be a thick ethical concept in this understanding? I suggest not. The idea of equality of treatment makes sense *as an idea* irrespective of context. For this reason I think, like many commentators, that *Brown* could, as a matter of juristic analysis, have been decided without recourse to social science evidence, or with this evidence performing only an 'enlightenment' function. In such a controversial case, however, the temptation to bolster the decision's legitimacy through an appeal to the authority of social science must have been considerable.

Fuller, whom he often cites, Selznick treats legality both as a matter of *normative ideals*, especially the progressive reduction of arbitrariness in the application of rules (something to be striven for as a juristic project), and as a set of *factual conditions* involving predictability and consistency in official action – things that legal sociologists can study empirically. Institutions, including legal institutions, are patterns of behaviour that social science can observe, but they may get their distinct identity from the fact that they are organised around ideals (Taekema 2003: 148–9).

For Selznick, legal sociologists do not necessarily have to approve the ideals he sees as enshrined in the concept of legality, but they must recognise them and understand that the features of law that they study empirically in terms of the behaviour of lawyers, judges, administrators, etc. gain their fundamental meaning and coherence only from some relation to the inbuilt values of legality. From this point of view, a sharp line between the concerns of the jurist and the legal sociologist should not be drawn, and sociology of law, for Selznick, should be aimed at understanding the conditions and character of legality.

Ultimately, I think that, although Selznick is right to emphasise a certain interrelation of fact and value, some of his key arguments are very problematic.

- First, can it be said that law always serves specific ideals that can be characterised as 'legality'? Surely the sociological study of law be organised around other basic concepts than that of legality (such as power, conflict, dispute, coordination, control).
- Second, as legal positivist critics of Fuller have long insisted, legality *need not* be thought of as involving anything more than certain technical prerequisites for the effective operation of any legal order with or without ideals (e.g. Hart 1983: 349–51; Raz 2009b: 224–6).
- Finally, if legality is indeed a matter of ideals, are these ideals the same in all times and places? Does law everywhere always have the same ultimate destiny towards legality as understood in certain developed Western legal systems? Or, if law as an institution is structured around a unifying, if often unstated, set of ideals, why not suppose that such ideals are not absolute and universal but relative to time and place? In the latter case the idea that law is oriented to legality would seem to become either a truism (legality is whatever, in any given context, law is expected to aim at) or too tied to context to characterise 'law' in any abstract general sense (legality is just what 'we' take it to mean).

Selznick dismisses cultural relativism, insisting that relativists, who celebrate the diversity of ultimate value commitments among humans, assume in practice a universal cross-cultural ideal of respect for humanity in all its diversity, a commitment to absolute respect for others as human and to general principles for showing this respect (Selznick 1961: 25). But, in answer, one might say that they affirm *their* particular value of respect for all others as human, but this does not demonstrate any such value as universal or accepted throughout the world.

Selznick's apparent absolutism with regard to values such as legality seems at odds with sociology's commitment to the empirical study of variation – to an assumption that social science does not philosophise about timeless absolutes (of legality or anything else) but examines how norms, values, and institutions vary depending on the social and historical context in which they are found. Sociology's focus on empirical variation should clearly distinguish it from philosophy's tendency to seek absolute truths about the world, including about the nature of law.

Selznick's ideas are very different from those of most legal sociologists, who have preferred to leave inquiries about legal values to jurists. Not recognising legality, as Selznick does, as values inbuilt, if rarely fully realised, in law as a sociologically observable practice, they are usually ready to affirm the fact/value distinction, the separation of a world of social facts from a juristic realm of normative interpretation. Selznick's writings on sociology of law mainly address sociologists, especially to persuade them take note of juristic and philosophical issues about legal values.[8] They do not seem obviously addressed to jurists, and they do not engage much with juristic issues about the nature of legal interpretation and juristic understandings of legal values.

Selznick's concern with the idea of legality is not with interpreting it. This is because he sees it as in some way natural, a part of the empirical character of law and hence a phenomenon that sociology can treat as a matter of social fact as well as of legal values.[9] Because it is natural in this sense, it is not necessary to ask *who* fixes its meaning. But if this question were to be asked, the main answer would probably be that jurists and judges have the responsibility for fixing its meaning: in doing so they 'control' the idea of legality through their interpretations of law. Selznick's effort to portray legality naturalistically as values inbuilt in law as a social phenomenon is an effort to bring it within the purview of social science, but its analysis and definition surely remain the monopoly of jurists.

I think that the same may be true of all 'thick ethical concepts' that are a part of legal doctrine. Juristic interpretation needs to fill these concepts with factual content and may do so by appealing to social science or many other sources. But generally it *ultimately controls* their normative meaning in law.

This is not necessarily a straightforward matter, however, as a case such as *Muller v Oregon* shows. As noted earlier, it may often not be practically possible (even if this were desired) to fix the meanings of an idea such as 'reasonableness' juristically in isolation from wider cultural understandings, including knowledge presented through social science. The ethical 'thickness' of some legal concepts may make it

---

8   His own major sociological study of legality (Selznick 1969) is especially concerned with its relevance in aspects of the internal processes of large-scale organisations such as corporations, aspects that have often been treated as largely outside the scope of juristic concern.

9   He does not deny that the practice of legality varies in time and space as law itself does, so the sociologist will need to study this variation. But Selznick's (1999) view seems to be that legality remains a single constant idea (if somewhat vague in his exposition): it is law's ultimate moral destiny wherever legal phenomena are found.

impossible for juristic analysis to separate out a realm of normative analysis (which it could treat as purely its own) from a realm of factual inquiry that gives space for many kinds of knowledge beyond juristic control to contribute to legal interpretation. Such a contribution might be impossible to reject even if juristic interpreters might wish to do so.

In this important sense juristic understandings are potentially 'socially porous': they remain in principle not just cognitively but also *normatively* open to influence from social scientific insights (cf Luhmann 2004: 106–8).

Sociological jurisprudence and sociology of law

Selznick's work might suggest an ambition to explore the possibility of *integrating* or perhaps even *fusing* the projects of legal sociologists with central juristic concerns.[10] And much other sociologically oriented scholarship can be seen as having been aimed at scientifically supporting juristic tasks, improving the intellectual conditions in which these tasks could be undertaken, or even taking on the tasks themselves. In the space available it is possible to refer to only a sample of these contributions.

An important case is that of Pound's sociological jurisprudence, already discussed in Chapter 1. Pound thought jurisprudence should be guided by sociology. Society could be seen as an arena of conflicting interests, and the juristic task would be to balance these interests so as to minimise social 'friction' and 'waste' (Pound 1942: 63–80). But Pound's initial serious interest in sociology was short-lived,[11] and his jurisprudence, always retaining the 'sociological' label, developed its essential prescriptions for juristic practice from philosophical speculation. The term 'sociological jurisprudence' has been associated ever since with legal philosophies seeking some kind of legitimacy from social science but offering little or no real engagement with it. As noted earlier, Pound was at first drawn to the work of sociologists such as Ross. But his primary guiding insights came from such imaginative, socially aware jurists as Rudolf von Jhering and Josef Kohler.

After Pound, the idea of sociological jurisprudence usually suggested only a *potential* of drawing on sociology for juristic purposes or an unsystematic sampling of social science literature with no ambition for genuine partnership between jurists and legal sociologists (Cotterrell 2008a). Thus it has satisfied neither camp: giving neither sociological foundations for juristic work nor incentives for legal sociologists to engage with juristic issues. Among leading legal sociologists, only Selznick

---

10 He instituted at the University of California at Berkeley a successful programme in 'Jurisprudence and Social Policy', aiming to integrate juristic, sociological, and humanistic perspectives in its teaching: see Selznick 1980.

11 One reason may have been that, while sociology initially sometimes privileged law among the mechanisms of social control (see Chapter 1), it later put far more emphasis on informal controls, and so could no longer be seen by Pound as useful support for his programme of sociological jurisprudence. Cf Hunt 1978: 19–20.

spoke warmly about Pound's programme, while regretting its unfulfilled promise (Cotterrell and Selznick 2004: 297, 298–9).

While Pound thought that sociological insight could help jurists, he devoted little attention to asking what *kind* of insight this might be and what *methods* could be used to gather it. These issues are addressed directly with some rigour in the unjustly neglected sociological jurisprudence of the philosopher F. S. C. Northrop (1959). Northrop sees social science as having resources to reveal social rules that actually govern social life (whether or not these are recognised by jurists and courts). Early in the twentieth century, the primary founder of sociology of law, Eugen Ehrlich (1936), called these rules 'living law', and Northrop saw Ehrlich as having been guided by a belief that juristic interpretation and development of law must take *systematic* account of this living law. The problem was how to identify it and use it juristically, given its complexity and diversity (Northrop 1959: 15, 29).

Northrop's book (1959) on sociological jurisprudence focuses directly on this problem. He starts by asking why existing social norms should, in any case, be seen as an appropriate guide for juristic practice. What if widespread social practices and expectations seem, from a juristic viewpoint, misguided? Northrop's solution is to look beneath the detail of social norms (which might or might not be worth following juristically) to the deeper cultural realities they reflect (which jurisprudence cannot ignore). The juristically relevant living law is to be found in *deep cultural patterns* (1959: 35) to be understood partly through sociological research but also through philosophy 'which is nothing but a name for the basic concepts which a person or people uses to conceptualise the facts of experience' (1959: 15).

Northrop's naturalistic 'philosophical anthropology' is presented as a method by which humanistic and social science methods combine to build essential understandings of the cultures in which law must operate, understandings that must inform juristic practices if these practices are to connect with social life. He sees this as especially important in the development of international law (and, we might add today, transnational law) which must straddle radically diverse cultures but often operates in ignorance of them.

One might doubt that Northrop's approach is juristically practicable. His project of identifying relevant living law was perhaps too vast and open, too uncertain as to its benefits, and too costly in time and effort. Yet what remains extremely important here is the idea that *culture* (or whatever we might wish to call the social patterns Northrop seeks to grasp) puts very important limits on juristic movement. Juristic practices that are not informed by systematic knowledge of these diffuse cultural elements may be like rudderless ships buffeted by waves of social expectations and demands that they cannot convincingly interpret.

The problem of rooting juristic practice in common social experience does not disappear because the project of a sociological jurisprudence identifying deep cultural patterns might seem daunting. Indeed, in recent times, the relations of law and culture have been firmly placed on the jurist's agenda (e.g. Nelken 2007). But the particular ambitious project Northrop indicated – of conceptualising and interpreting culture in a juristically adequate and comprehensive way – still remains to be achieved.

The minimal impact of Northrop's book is surely connected with the fact that it was published in 1959, at a moment of major intellectual transition. Just two years later, Hart's *Concept of Law* (Hart 1994) appeared and gradually spurred the powerful new philosophical professionalism in juristic thought examined in the previous chapter. Legal philosophy, especially in the Anglophone world, thereafter gradually marginalised, in terms of intellectual status, what it saw as philosophically uninformed or amateurish earlier juristic thought. Especially subject to attack were projects aimed at crossing disciplinary boundaries, such as sociological jurisprudence. Legal realism, which in the first half of the twentieth century had held open in juristic outlooks the real possibility of collaboration with the social sciences, now tended to be disparaged as philosophically uninteresting.

At the same time, the social sciences were being increasingly professionalised as distinct academic fields. Sociology of law emerged in many Western countries from the early 1960s as a self-consciously professionalised and organised enterprise of empirical research. For many, though not all, legal sociologists, the idea of advancing by liaising with jurists was marginalised in favour of strong identification with the established academic discipline of sociology.

These developments explain why substantial mutual disinterest between jurists and sociologists of law existed by the last quarter of the twentieth century. However, this is not the whole story. Certainly, the juristic world, with high status and considerable political and organisational strength, might, after these adventures, have little interest in liaising with sociologists. But sociology, with its relatively low professional status (as compared with legal studies), might still be seen by some of its practitioners as possibly able to benefit from association with the world of law. This is surely one reason for the immense success of the 'law and society' and socio-legal movements over the past half century, also promoted by a growing conviction among policymakers and grant-awarding bodies that law is too important as a social phenomenon and tool of government to be left entirely to the care of jurists.

Perhaps encouraged by this conviction, Donald Black's (1989) 'sociological justice' represented a dramatic attempt by sociology of law to confront the juristic world – indeed to invade it aggressively. Black aimed to reshape (even make redundant) many juristic arguments and concepts through what he calls the 'sociology of the case'. Legal sociology, he argues, shows 'equality before the law' as impossible in practice. This is because it reveals empirically how cases emerge, are litigated, argued, adjudicated, and resolved. In doing so, it shows that what is understood juristically as consistency and equality in invoking and being addressed by law is often unobtainable because numerous social factors that are not and perhaps cannot be taken into account in juristic analysis shape every aspect of case handling by lawyers and courts.[12]

---

12 A similar insight (assumed rather that empirically demonstrated) underpins the fierce attacks on jurists' traditional 'method of justice' that are central to Vilhelm Lundstedt's realist jurisprudence (Cotterrell 2016).

Black writes: 'The rules provide the language of law, but the social structure of the case provides the grammar by which this language is expressed' (1989: 19). Without an adequate understanding of grammar the language may be unintelligible. So, legal sociology 'offers a new understanding of legal life by studying what jurisprudence ignores: the social structure of the cases' (1989: 94). Radical conclusions follow: jurisprudence's pursuit of legality is socially meaningless if it does not understand the social conditions to which juristic concepts are actually applied and in which they acquire practical meaning. Indeed, juristic administration of justice will create social injustice unless the sociology of the case is fully recognised in the operation of law.

Ultimately Black's sociology of the case may not add much at the level of theory to what the most radical legal realists suggested many decades before. What is of special interest is that these ideas are now presented by a legal sociologist, not a jurist, and are supported by systematic empirical research. Whereas legal realism represented an 'internal' warning to the juristic community from some of its own members about the inadequacy of its established methods, Black's sociology of law is an 'external' attack on the juristic world. Yet his work has had little effect on this world. The reason is not that his arguments lack cogency. It is that they are not aimed at engaging directly with juristic discourse; they do not propose how it might be altered to reflect the numerous social prejudices, discriminations, barriers, and inequalities that affect legal processes. Black does not engage in any big juristic conversation about the best meaning of law such as Dworkin's (1986) approach might envisage. He criticises the viability of the juristic project from the outside, as a sociological observer.

This outcome in no way indicates that sociology of law cannot engage with jurisprudence; it shows only the weaknesses of a *positivist* approach to legal sociology, which sees law, from a sociological standpoint, only as behaviour (governmental social control) and not as ideas (Black 1976). Because Black adopts this strictly behavioural view of law, he cannot debate with jurists about the social nature, conditions of existence and meaning of legal ideas.

The essentially 'anti-juristic' sociology of the case might be seen as an approach foreshadowed by that of *Brown* v *Board of Education* (following this chapter's interpretation of *Brown*). Not only is it hard to imagine how such an approach could become general practice, but also its adverse effects on law's legitimacy as an integrated normative system would be considerable. Yet it is no less disturbing that the many practical insights of the legal realist jurists are in danger of being forgotten in today's juristic theory because of pressures to orient this theory towards a correspondingly 'anti-sociological' philosophy of law.

Why jurists need sociology of law

The examples considered earlier of meetings between juristic and sociological perspectives suggest a spectrum. At one extreme (Pound), juristic thought dabbles with sociology but ultimately is barely affected by it; at the other (Black), sociology of law considers juristic concerns but ultimately proclaims the total superiority of its own approaches over juristic analysis. In the middle of the spectrum are approaches that suggest that social scientific knowledge (as systematic knowledge of law's cultural contexts) is, indeed, necessary for juristic tasks to be fulfilled: social science, on this view, can *support* juristic practice but must contribute *on its own terms*, not just as a resource 'on tap' for jurists.

These 'mid-spectrum' approaches are surely the most promising. They assume genuine interaction on a basis of equality between jurists and sociologists. Focusing on juristic responsibilities in general and not only on judicial ones, they are best seen as generalising or extending Lempert's 'enlightenment' function of social science beyond the courtroom context to all juristic discourse – but taking full account of the pervasiveness of thick ethical concepts in this discourse.

So, social science as enlightenment will be much more than factual evidence – raw material – for jurists to work with. In a genuine partnership with juristic thought it may have the potential to influence that thought in profound and productive ways once it is recognised that a sharp line between fact and value (between social observation and normative analysis) cannot be drawn to isolate sociological from juristic inquiries. The interpenetration of norm and fact, or valuation and description, in law's thick ethical concepts (such as the concept of reasonableness) sufficiently suggests a blurring of that line.

None of this is to deny that legal sociologists and jurists have distinct and contrasting professional responsibilities, research methods, guiding concepts, and primary intellectual concerns. It is only to suggest that (i) many intellectual arguments typically used to suggest that social science cannot contribute to solving juristic problems or to juristic development of law are ill founded, and (ii) that the at least partly negative results of some earlier attempts to link the worlds of the jurist and the legal sociologist should not deter the pursuit of new links.

What, then, might legal sociology be expected to contribute to juristic inquiries? Sociology has long debated whether its studies of moral phenomena can themselves be morally neutral (Abend 2008). As has been seen in the contrasting approaches of Selznick and Black, similar issues about dealing with the normative have arisen in sociology of law. Normative questions are certainly not foreign to sociological inquiries about law. Perhaps ultimately, neither a full sociological engagement in normative juristic analysis of law nor a total distancing of legal sociology from this kind of analysis is desirable.

Émile Durkheim, who saw sociology as a science aimed at objective empirical inquiry, nevertheless thought that 'science can help in finding the direction in which our conduct ought to go, assisting us to determine the ideal that gropingly we seek' and that, having observed reality, 'we shall distil the ideal from it' (Durkheim 1984: xxvi). Taken in isolation, these words might suggest something like Selznick's naturalistic view of values embedded in social institutions. But Durkheim's sociological practice was actually closer to Lempert's 'enlightenment' function of social science in which this science informs, guides, and assists moral and legal decision-making without pretending to be able to prescribe value solutions.

The best approach to the use of social science *in the courtroom* is surely this one which leaves the jurist's interpretive responsibility intact but informs it with wider, perhaps deeper understanding of the contexts of decision-making. In some circumstances this widening and deepening may be of such a character that social scientific understandings clearly point the way to appropriate decisions or modes of reasoning. As with the 'common sense' invoked in some judgments about 'reasonableness', it may be hard to resist these understandings and may seem obviously inappropriate to do so. In such conditions, social knowledge does not replace juristic judgments but becomes *part of them* – fact and value being integrated both in conceptualising the conditions in which adjudication is to take place and in the presentation of issues to be resolved through it.

The argument can be taken beyond adjudication to juristic practice more generally. Suppose, for example, that the juristic interpretation and development of legal doctrine treats as one of its guiding values the pursuit of social solidarity – what Durkheim described as the moral cohesion and functional integration of social life: then Durkheimian sociology offers many ideas as to how solidarity might be achieved and enhanced, what its limits might be in any given type of society, what consequences might follow from its pursuit, and what kinds of law and legal institutions might most effectively promote it.

In other words, this kind of sociology of law would not attempt to set the aims that juristic practice should seek, but its findings might suggest the social consequences of pursuing particular aims (such as enhancing solidarity); it might point out the most socially feasible ways of pursuing them, and the strengths and weaknesses of law and of particular legal strategies in doing so.[13] It might do more: it might clarify what as a practical matter solidarity can be taken to mean, by suggesting the kinds of solidarity that may have some prospect of realisation in particular kinds of society and that are likely to seem meaningful as part of social experience in them.

Jurists might debate whether to adopt such a sociological perspective. But it is available as a resource, reflecting, to some extent, experiences of social life among the populations law regulates. In Northrop's terms, such a perspective will relate in some way to a deep culture of understandings about the world in which law exists. The same is true of all major forms of social theory, some of which offer very different kinds of social insight from Durkheim's.[14]

In some ways Northrop's insights about the significance of deep cultural understandings are already being clearly reflected in contemporary juristic thought. In a sense, culture has now invaded juristic consciousness, and to this extent juristic understandings have become more directly sociological. If Ehrlich's 'living law' remains a sociological and not a juristic idea, the broadening and deepening of this idea into a category of 'cultural understandings' allows it to become important in some areas of contemporary legal thought.

13 Paul Fauconnet's classic (1928) study of the evolution of ideas of criminal responsibility is, in part, a very early effort to pursue aspects of such a project.
14 For extended discussions of ways in which Durkheimian sociology can contribute today to the clarification of legal and moral ideas and issues in a variety of practical contexts see Chapters 12 and 13.

For example, juristic practice in some contexts now explicitly embraces the assertion of 'cultural rights', the protection of 'cultural heritage', and the pleading of 'cultural defences'. Surely these usages imply Northrop's insight that law can (perhaps must) draw on deep ideas about 'culture'. But whereas Northrop seemed to refer to the broadest cultural underpinnings of law, state law in most Western societies is now faced with the diverse (perhaps conflicting) specific cultural understandings of different population groups within its jurisdiction. The invasion of law by culture nevertheless presents a situation in which juristic thought must surely gain sociological insight if it is to remain relevant to a changing social environment.

Sociology can give normative analysis something to work on simply through its 'enlightenment' function. But to some extent it can potentially also take advantage of what was earlier called the social porosity of juristic understandings. Thus, one can say that the sociological interpretation of legal ideas involves deliberately extending in carefully specified directions the ways in which many lawyers and other legal participants already typically think about law. Thus, to some extent, juristic analysis is *systematic* (it usually has a concern to develop integrated doctrine), *empirical* (it must make sense of the specific context to which legal doctrine is to be applied), and *social* (its concern is to regulate social life).

Sociological perspectives can build on each of these familiar characteristics of juristic thought, extending each of them in various ways (Cotterrell 2006: 54–63). By this means sociological inquiry may sometimes show why doctrinal development takes one direction rather than another or even why it reaches impasses – with causes rooted in social conditions (Cotterrell 1992). In other words, it may help to clarify (systematically, empirically, socially) the nature of juristic normative environments.

Ideas about the need to contextualise juristic arguments are familiar in legal scholarship. For example, critical legal scholarship emphasised how political factors and forces lead to legal ideas being 'tilted' one way or another or 'reified' – that is, fixed in juristic understandings and doctrines as though the possibility of contesting them could no longer even be imagined by most people (Gabel 1980). Recently the American constitutional lawyer Jack Balkin has written about what he calls *constitutional historicism*. This is the idea 'that the conventions determining what is a good or bad argument about the Constitution, what is a plausible legal claim, and what is off-the-wall [not to be taken seriously as a legal argument] change over time in response to changing social, political, and historical conditions' (Balkin 2011: 177).

Jurists need to know how these conventions change and the direction in which they change. They need to understand them in a cultural context. Juristic understanding of that context may be systematic, empirically grounded, and socially insightful to varying degrees. And the more it shows those features in a consistent way, the more sociological in character it can be considered to be.

Interestingly, neither Balkin's account of constitutional historicism nor, for the most part, the critical legal studies literature invokes sociology in explaining the conditions under which juristic practice takes place and how those conditions change, or can be changed. Most of the scholarly talk about these things has been in terms of politics. Alongside that, to some extent, economic analysis of law has provided explanations of a different kind. But sociological perspectives theoretically systematic, empirically oriented, and centred on a consistent concept of the social offer potentially the widest, most all-embracing explanations, the broadest available perspectives. In some sense, they should incorporate and further contextualise political and economic explanations, linking them and reinterpreting these in a wider social picture but without dissolving them away.

Social science can not only provide evidence for use in juristic contexts but also help to show the parameters of interpretive possibility available to jurists in analysing law. What are the boundaries of juristic practice in a particular time and place? What determines the acceptable range of possible legal argument; as Balkin puts it: what is juristically 'off-the-wall' or on it (Balkin 2011: 179–82)? Sociological study of law has the potential to explore these matters by showing law as an aspect or field of social life and by clarifying its relation to the cultural understandings of its time and place. In such ways it can show how 'culture' limits and creates possibilities for developing legal ideas. By revealing the parameters of interpretive possibility available in juristic practice, sociological inquiry can serve the jurist's most central task: to explore the meaning and social value of the idea of law in its time and place.

PART II

Transnational challenges to juristic thought

6

WHY LAWYERS NEED A THEORY OF LEGAL PLURALISM

Impacts of transnationalism

Transnational regulation, reaching across state boundaries, has proliferated in recent decades. And legal relations not confined within the jurisdictional boundaries of states have been taking increasingly intricate forms and becoming more pervasive in many fields – especially those of trade and finance. These developments pose new challenges for jurists, as for others – legal philosophers and legal sociologists – who have different kinds of theoretical commitments in legal studies.

Many lawyers now engage in transnational legal practice. The everyday life of law goes on within state legal systems but also between (or even irrespective of) such systems. For many theoretically oriented lawyers, transnationalism in law reshapes familiar juristic concerns and raises new issues, for example, (i) about the relationship between state and law, (ii) about the kinds of regulation that should or should not be juristically recognised as law, (iii) about the ultimate authority of law and its bases of legitimacy, (iv) about the nature of the populations law addresses and from whom it demands allegiance, (v) about the limitations of legal concepts developed in the state law context when these are applied transnationally, and (vi) about methods of navigating juristically across and within a plurality of regulatory regimes.

In this and the following chapters in Part II, the impact of transnationalism on these and other issues is examined. This chapter considers specifically the challenges of *legal pluralism* – the normative management of interacting, coexisting, superimposed, or conflicting legal regimes or systems – in contemporary Western contexts. Its argument is that because of important changes in the regulatory landscape lawyers now need a theoretical perspective on legal pluralism, and jurists should aim to provide one.

I shall argue that legal pluralism, as a normative project of negotiating the relations of irreducibly distinct regulatory regimes, has the potential to undermine the orthodoxies of modern juristic thought in two fundamental ways:

- by destabilising any idea that law has some 'true', essential, or timeless nature that philosophy could reveal or lawyers could assume;[1] and
- by reviving the idea that legal authority is not revealed by applying positivist pedigree tests of validity but is to be built pragmatically through communication and compromise between different normative orders and practices.

Juristic thought presently lacks the resources to deal with these emerging challenges. Confronting them demands an alliance between lawyers' analytical techniques and sociolegal empirical studies of regulatory practices. I hope to show that a particular theoretical view of legal pluralism, one that is centred on a *minimal* and *flexible* provisional model of law and an enlarged understanding of authority, is needed to inform this alliance.

A pluralist landscape

Legal pluralism is a term of varied meanings. Juristically it represents a variety of possible normative responses to the *fact* of legal 'plurality' (Roughan 2013: 44). Nowadays it is obvious that many varied kinds of legal regimes regularly interact or confront each other in the same 'social space'. Indeed, legal plurality usually exists in some form even in what lawyers would recognise as highly integrated legal systems. For example, relations between different traditional doctrinal fields (e.g. contract, torts, criminal law) are not always clear; doctrinal conflicts arise as legal reasoning develops normative ideas in a certain legal field but without any clear integration in other such fields beyond (Van Hoecke 2014: 53; Davies 2005: 96). And different forms of rationality (e.g. formal, substantive, instrumental, expressive) can exist in a single legal system (cf Dalberg-Larsen 2000: 105).[2]

Within the municipal legal systems of independent political societies (states), a deliberately maintained plurality of legal regimes or systems is commonplace. Often this is mainly geographically structured, as with federal, regional, provincial-national, state-tribal, or local-central divisions of jurisdiction. In many state legal systems there exist, or historically have existed, jurisdictional divisions based on personal statuses: religious and secular, colonist and colonised, citizen and alien,

---

1 Cf Zumbansen 2013: 118 ('The rich accounts of legal pluralism . . . can be read as strong signals that law itself has an identity crisis, a crisis regarding its own nature and function').

2 Legal sociologists and others have also examined institutionally produced state legal plurality – that is, the situation in which different parts of the state apparatus create regulation independently and interpret state law differentially. See Dalberg-Larsen 2000: 103–14, Davies 2005: 96, Roughan 2013: ch 12. This plurality may remain unless mechanisms are available, and steps taken, to identify it and select a final 'official' legal position.

noble and commoner, and many variables within these distinctions. These types of plurality are normally well understood. Yet they rarely produce wholly unproblematic divisions of labour between jurisdictions; often important jurisdictional disputes and enduring problems of interpretation exist. But such intrastate legal controversies are not juristically strange; they are part of the usual familiar fare presenting itself for normative processing by lawyers, judges and legislators.

Beyond these intrastate contexts, some other less traditional forms of legal plurality seem much less like juristic 'business as usual'. Relations between EU law and Member States' law or between EU law and WTO law are not always merely routine interpretive matters but can often provoke debate about the fundamental nature of the legal regimes involved. In such contexts perhaps a growing sense of juristic disquiet can be detected. The potential conflict between international law and the law of nation-states long ago inspired monist-dualist theoretical debates on the location of ultimate legal authority to control such conflict. But this could remain a largely impractical concern as long as, *in actual regulatory experience*, state law wholly dominated international law. Juristically, any authority of international law could be presented (and so controlled) as merely an extension of state legal authority through treaties and the consensual establishment of international legal bodies.

However, the question of how to handle the relations of state and international legal systems operating in the same social spaces has become more acute, insofar as international law (i) has sought greater 'independent' authority less easily subsumed into state authority, for example via assertions of *ius cogens* (e.g. Cassese 2012), (ii) has become more prominent in the regulatory landscape by developing in many new or newly significant doctrinal fields (such as human rights, trade and finance, environment, and intellectual property), and (iii) now sometimes (as with international criminal law) directly addresses the citizens of particular states. Further, as international law has increasingly appeared fragmented into a diversity of legal regimes whose relations are sometimes unclear, the old (usually practically insignificant) theoretical monism-dualism debates give way to (practical) monism-pluralism debates. So the idea that legal plurality has emerged as a theoretical issue for jurists (and not just a familiar commonplace) is now well established.

Beyond all this, many further dimensions of regulatory plurality are widely recognised by legal sociologists and an increasing number of sociologically oriented lawyers. Much regulation created in (often transnational) networks of social interaction – such as merchant communities,[3] corporate groups, industries, financial systems, Internet developers, 'private' NGO movements,[4] religious or ethnic communities,[5] or sports organisations (Duval 2013) – has been shown empirically to be at least as practically powerful as much juristically recognised law and as authoritative for those subject to it. Much of it is characterised by unions of primary and

---

3 For a wide-ranging recent discussion see Zumbansen 2013.
4 See e.g. Culver and Giudice 2010: 75–7, discussing the Greenland Conservation Agreement as an example of transnational legality created by NGOs.
5 For an excellent recent empirical study in a British context see Tas 2014.

secondary rules, such as H. L. A. Hart associated with a legal system. Some lawyers, indeed, speak of 'transnational private law'[6] to include at least some regulation created wholly or partly in these kinds of groups or networks.

But the commonest juristic stance has been to exclude much of this regulation from recognition as law. As long as lawyers can remain united in their basic assumptions about the attributes of law, such an approach remains viable. In borderline areas, fudging tactics can be used: concepts such as 'soft law' can signal the possibility of some, usually unspecified, juristic relevance in normative materials not conforming to shared assumptions about law (Terpan 2015). And, whatever concepts of law legal philosophers produce and however much evidence legal sociologists accumulate of the landscape of 'living law' (actually operative regulation), it can seem dangerous juristically to do anything other than hold the line against the unfamiliar – that is, against new types of regulation that, once recognised, would raise numerous juristic issues about their authority, legitimacy, and scope.

How lawyers approach legal plurality

It would be misleading to underestimate the power of orthodox juristic techniques for dealing with legal plurality or the determination with which they are being used today to defend against newly destabilising forms of plurality that threaten to escape juristic control. These techniques can be broadly summarised as four:

- *ultimate monism* – the assumption or construction of a single overall normatively integrated regulatory structure or system to provide a unifying umbrella over plurality,
- *hierarchical ordering* – the settling of permanent hierarchies of authority in or between regulatory regimes or systems,
- *ad hoc resolution* – pragmatic solving of particular doctrinal conflicts without any attempt at a more general and enduring settling of relations between regulatory regimes or systems, and
- *statist analogies* – use of juristically familiar characteristics of state law to interpret non-state forms of regulation by analogy or extension and so assess their juristic significance.

Legal scholars continue to rely on these techniques in addressing the whole range of contemporary regulatory plurality – the realm of what is now often called global legal pluralism.[7] Because they are part of the Western lawyer's normal stock in trade, they are for the most part well known and well understood. Appeals to monism are used (for example in considering relations of EU law to international law or to Member States' law) to conceptualise, integrate, or articulate one system or regime

6 Discussed in Chapter 8.
7 See Chapter 7.

from the juristic perspective of another. Appeals to hierarchy organise a vast range of codes, standards, practice rules, disciplinary norms, and organisational rules in relation to the authority structures of juristic law. By this means they can be juristically assessed. Pursuit of ad hoc resolution is found, for example, in efforts to develop and rethink conflict of laws principles and practices to deal with clashes between regulatory regimes or systems as they arise (e.g. Joerges 2011; Muir Watt 2016). State-law models of legality are widely applied (Culver and Giudice 2010: 143–4), and even proponents of constitutional pluralism or global administrative law, who are determined to recognise legal phenomena far removed from the limitations of state law jurisdiction, tend to appeal to constitutional or public law principles and concepts derived from the juristic experience of Western state law.[8]

Insofar as these techniques continue to be effective they obviate any need for a theory of legal pluralism – that is, a theory aimed specifically at conceptualising and normatively organising legal plurality. However, they have their limits. Thus, *ad hoc resolution* (however practically useful in the short term) is ultimately no solution to the juristic problem of making sense of the idea of law as an organised social practice and guiding its development. Its pragmatic resolutions merely postpone addressing the task of ordering plurality.

Much significant new regulation arises from what lawyers typically think of as 'private' sources, within associations and organisations of civil society, or through arbitration and dispute processing in commercial networks. Of the four techniques, *hierarchical ordering* has been the standard juristic approach to defining relations between private and public regulation. But this has been successful only to the extent that private regulation has needed recognition or guarantee from state law or other juristically familiar public regulation. The more recent scenario has been one in which this recognition is not necessarily sought. Yet the proliferation, prominence, and effectiveness of regulation produced from nonstate sources in organisations, associations, and networks are such that lawyers increasingly feel the need to take juristic account of them.

Monistic approaches seem no less unsatisfactory because monism presumes a perspective from which all legal reality can somehow be structured and integrated in an overall unity (e.g. Weyland 2002). But there is no Archimedean point from which a single juristic world can be envisaged and constructed (cf Walker 2002: 338). Monism presupposes an authority that can establish it; fulfilment of the juristic monistic dream in a globalised legal world must surely await the emergence of a global state.

As regards the use of *statist analogies*, I have suggested that this also includes the use of assumptions built out of Western experience with state law even when committed attempts are being made juristically to recognise nonstate forms of regulation. But the problem here is the rootedness of this approach to legal plurality in Western juristic experience. It may be almost impossible for Western lawyers effectively to

---

8 See e.g. Walker 2002: 342–3 (invoking 'constitutional discourse', 'citizenship', and 'sovereignty') and Kingsbury 2009 (emphasising attributes of 'publicness'). See further pp 125–6.

survey developing global legal pluralism without imposing on it the inheritances of their own legal cultures. But global legal pluralism is not an exclusively Western phenomenon and will surely become steadily less Western-focused as it continues to develop. The question is whether juristic methods can 'bootstrap' themselves up largely from the experience of Western legal cultures to address a genuinely global plurality (Menski 2014: 105).

The reasons why juristic techniques are no longer effectively neutralising legal pluralism as a problem are easily summarised. Much regulation that is widely seen as having juristic significance – for example, international law, transnational private law, standard-setting soft law, religious (e.g. Islamic) law, and other types of regulation often given the name 'law' – can no longer be assessed for this significance in terms of whether it can be incorporated into state law, seen as an extension of state law, or authorised or controlled by state law.[9] It appears to derive, wholly or partly, from nonstate sources of authority. When it is interpreted by analogy with state law or in terms of characteristics associated with state law this often seems to distort its nature and obscure the sources of its effectiveness and legitimacy.

The experience of Western jurists has been that of municipal state legal systems, which ultimately (because of their political integration) lend themselves to explanation in terms of ultimate monism or a hierarchical ordering of authority within them. While both monism and hierarchy may be problematic juristic constructions, the idea of the modern, autonomous, centralised Westphalian state easily inspires them. However, as this idea of the state is undermined in various ways, the juristic techniques that reflect it – the quests for monism or hierarchy – lose their solid experiential foundations.

Under the pressures of globalisation many states now seem less autonomous in their law-making authority. Their practical law-creating and law-applying sovereignty is weakened because of pressure imposed on them by more powerful states or groups of states (e.g. Simpson 2004),[10] and clearly some of this pressure is applied through law (for example extraterritorial legal effects, extradition arrangements, subjection to obligations as convention signatories). So, the sovereignty of some states extends, while that of others contracts; the interplay of legal effects among international authorities (for example the WTO), regional authorities (for example the EU, NAFTA), and state authorities is so complex that monistic or hierarchical conceptions of legal authority and legal system seem to need much qualification or supplementation. Intrastate (communal or religious) authorities can also contribute to this perception, insofar as they support ambivalent responses of cultural groups to state law – sometimes mobilising it, sometimes de-centring it (Barzilai 2008: 405–6), simultaneously recognising and not recognising its normative supremacy.

Legal pluralism can best be seen as an *ecological* problem, a matter of laws fighting for space in the regulatory landscape. More 'powerful' law pushes out less 'powerful'

---

9 But see Michaels 2005: 1227–37, discussing state control of nonstate law in the context of conflict of laws.

10 In Europe, European Union commitments are one source of such pressure: see Clifton 2014.

law. Different laws compete as to which should be recognised or suppressed (Cover 1983: 40–4). The label 'law' is approved or refused for regulation – in other words, the legal *validity* of regulation is decided. Claims to authority are successful or unsuccessful, in the sense of whether or not they are accepted, so that authority attracts legitimacy.[11] A juristic view of legal pluralism can be realistic[12] only if it recognises and can therefore evaluate the processes and conditions in which what is *legally* significant is decided, and in which *authority* is claimed and recognised. So, the remainder of this chapter introduces these related matters: issues of regulatory authority considered from a specifically juristic perspective, and issues about what is to count as 'law' in addressing legal pluralism. Subsequent chapters will further develop these initial ideas.

How should authority be understood in legal pluralism?

Legal authority may present itself as a topic of interest for a variety of distinct theoretical reasons, and the perspectives of those viewing the topic from various philosophical, sociological, or juristic standpoints may differ significantly.

From a *philosophical* standpoint, the primary aim seems often to be to conceptualise it in general or universal terms so as to specify an essence that is always present whenever the concept is correctly invoked. Thus, one could distinguish generally between types of authority (for example practical or epistemic) or bases of authority (for example substantive or procedural) and analyse the relations between them, thereby isolating distinctive characteristics of legal authority. Such an approach could be entirely unconcerned with examining empirically how authority is understood either by those who claim it or those who accept it. A philosophically interesting concept of authority has to be plausible in relation to *some* presumed general experience, but it should also be useful for assessing the correctness of assertions of authority made in practice.

By contrast, a *sociological* approach is likely to see authority as a matter of practice and experience, especially the practices and experiences of those making, accepting, or rejecting authority claims.[13] It would include study of the conditions under which such claims are made and the criteria that determine what types of claims are realistically possible in particular circumstances. So, a concern with actions in specific social conditions would be central. Thus, Max Weber's (1968: vol 2) account of authority as legitimate domination centres on identifying different types of authority claims and the particular sociopolitical or cultural conditions that these presuppose. Because of this focus, only provisional conceptualisations (ideal types)

---

11 In this context I treat authority as something *claimed* and legitimacy as something *conferred* on authority claims by their acceptance by individuals (or by groups): see Chapter 9. For further discussion see Cotterrell and Del Mar 2016a.

12 That is, attuned to the social and political contexts in which the jurist works.

13 This approach and the conclusions to which it leads are considered in Chapter 9.

or working models of authority are required as a basis for empirical study of the ways in which authority is claimed.

A *juristic* approach – serving the well-being of law as an idea and ideal – is likely to be different again. A juristic view would be analytical (concerned to conceptualise authority) and also normatively focused and capable of judging when and whether authority is properly claimed; it would not be satisfied with sociologically recording actions and experiences – observing authority claims and reactions to them. But, equally, it would need to see authority as an idea that has meaning in the specific contexts of its use. So, jurists faced with the challenges of legal pluralism should have only limited interest in projects of formulating essential, absolute, universal, or 'true' characteristics of authority and in 'legislating' abstractly correct uses of the term without precise reference to context. A wise strategy would seem to be to keep an open mind about the variety of possible forms that legal authority might take, to adopt an exploratory approach seeking and interpreting information as to how authority claims are actually being made and received.

This approach involves sociological inquiry but certainly does not entail that the jurist become a legal sociologist. Instead it suggests that juristic approaches should rely heavily on empirical studies of law and regulation and that jurists should shape their evolving normative responses to authority in legal pluralism by reference to them. Insofar as this involves an ongoing accumulation of information and interpretation, juristic invocations of legal authority in conditions of regulatory plurality must, for the foreseeable future, often be provisional and tentative. They necessitate a rejection of philosophical orientations towards conceptual universalism or essentialism because these could only close off the possibility of jurisprudence becoming, through its ongoing practice, a continual learning process.

From this perspective, legal authority appears as something that takes many forms, varies greatly in jurisdictional reach, is subject to limiting pressures and requirements for accommodation, and derives from many disparate sources. In juristically familiar settings of municipal (state-focused) law, orthodox understandings of legal authority (usually involving elaborate hierarchies and divisions of jurisdiction) require little disruption. Beyond this, however, authority is a matter for negotiation, learning, and gradual adjustment of juristic perceptions in interaction between regulatory regimes.

Nicole Roughan (2013) has argued that in contemporary legal pluralism distinct putative legal authorities necessarily interrelate and limit each other's claims to authority. Thus, the authority they claim has to be shared in some way, becoming 'relative'. In such conditions the overall legitimacy of this authority has to be found in normative principles (a 'relativity condition') to govern their interrelation. In effect, the relativity condition operates to justify the authority of any one regime or system by reference to other such regimes or systems with which it is normatively intertwined. In this specific sense, legitimate authority is 'relative authority'.

Roughan seeks definitive conceptualisations that are not tied to specific types or contexts of authority claims. She seeks, first, a universal 'test' to justify authority (2013: 134) and, second, an equally universal and essential 'relativity condition' to determine how authority can be shared and reciprocally legitimated (2013: 143).

Juristically one could see this as an excellent specification of ideal normative conditions which jurists might envisage and aim to promote. Yet, while it surely advances philosophical conceptualisation, it could be criticised as failing to recognise fully the chaotic reality of global legal pluralism and the fact that jurists must work in an environment where regulatory plurality must be negotiated.

In this environment no general *acceptance* exists for any single 'test' by which to justify authority. And jurists can hardly hope to see a universal 'relativity condition' invoked to settle the legitimacy of normative arrangements between competing authority claimants. The jurist has to balance pursuing conceptualisation with observing the varied, actually existing, shifting, often conflicting and contradictory practices and experiences of authority.[14]

Weber's sociology emphasises that not all authority resides in rule systems, though he saw authority derived from rationally formulated rules and procedures as the dominant type in modern Western societies. Claims of authority can also be founded in charisma (the authority claims of individuals or regimes to possess special qualities justifying allegiance) or in tradition (an appeal to the familiarity of the established). It is not difficult to argue that much regulatory authority today is charismatically based (for example in the claims to personal *expertise* of technical standard setters, adjudicators of disputes in particular fields, or learned interpreters of doctrine). As such, it often arises from what lawyers typically see as 'private' sources (for example in transnational networks centred on commerce, religion, environmental protection, sport, or the promotion of technological development).

While this is sometimes set aside as epistemic (cf Roughan 2013: 20) or theoretical (Raz 1994: 211–12) rather than practical authority, it could be unwise to conceptualise it out of the picture in considering legal authority. This is not only because such charismatically claimed authority is extremely widespread and powerful, given the range and scope of transnational standard-setting authorities, but also because it often competes directly with juristically familiar law, marginalising it in practice or compensating for its absence as effective regulation. To ignore it in the juristic landscape is to leave a large void in the jurist's picture of the regulatory terrain.

So, how can authority in legal pluralism be understood juristically? A philosophical approach such as Roughan's, however sensitive to the facts of plurality, seeks universal governing principles, and these may persuasively organise but will not necessarily *represent* actual regulatory experience. By contrast, a sociological approach might see legitimacy merely as a *fact*: the subjective acceptance of authority claims by those to whom they are addressed or who observe such claims being made. It would aim to study empirically the constituencies (networks, groups) over which authority is claimed and the way regulation works within them. In state legal systems, hierarchies of authority-conferring rules define what Weber characterised as legal-rational authority. Normally jurists can leave to political theorists the task

---

14 Recently, Roughan (2016) has emphasised a necessary interdependence of philosophical and sociological approaches, presumably to address this juristic need.

of examining democratic or other means of legitimating this. But in contemporary legal pluralism this is more problematic. Jurists trying to negotiate the 'relative' authority of competing intranational, transnational, or international regulatory regimes may need the help of sociological analyses to understand the communal networks[15] which these regimes address or in which they arise.

None of this, in itself, solves the problem of juristically evaluating competing authority claims. But jurists have to keep in view an idea (and ideal) of law as a socially valuable practice and seek to promote, develop, and interpret that idea under the conditions that exist in the particular contexts in which they operate. The jurist's idea of law naturally reflects ongoing juristic experience and does not lend itself to definition in absolute terms, though it may well be coloured by philosophical ideas existing in the jurist's own culture. In Chapter 3, I suggested that Radbruch's idea of law, embodying flexible but resilient values of justice and security (or order) and adaptable to guiding social purposes and cultural assumptions of the time, gives some focus for juristic responsibilities in rapidly changing conditions. In contemporary legal pluralism this normative orientation has to be combined with an awareness of what empirical sociolegal inquiry can reveal about proliferating forms of authority and their significance in the contexts in which they exist.

Concepts of law in legal pluralism

A relatively loose, flexible, Radbruch-inspired, juristic idea of law – worked out in practice but shaped by values understood in their cultural contexts – contrasts with dominant approaches to conceptualising law in contemporary Anglophone legal philosophy. These continue to seek some universally valid understanding of the nature of law, some ultimate 'truth' even while recognising that conceptualisations can vary depending on their purpose (Raz 2001: 10), or some fundamental essence of the 'legal' (cf Patterson 2012). Certainly, some writers focus only on necessary features of 'our' – presumably their expected readers' – concept of law or assume a particular evidentiary basis for their conceptualisation. But these limitations are usually left vague and, if mentioned at all, seem to be of little concern, hardly inhibiting very general claims about the nature of law.[16] From a practical juristic viewpoint, efforts to conceptualise law without ongoing reference to the evolving features of regulatory plurality noted earlier in this chapter can seem puzzling: one might wonder what such context-free conceptualisations are for, but usually no explanation is given. 'What is law?' is seen as a self-evidently important universal question.

By contrast, sociologically oriented approaches to contemporary regulatory pluralism often simply discard the what-is-law question as unhelpful.[17] Close to this position

---

15 On the concept of communal networks as a focus for regulation see Chapter 8.
16 For full discussion see Culver and Giudice 2010: 80–94.
17 See e.g. Berman 2009: 237 ('the whole debate about law versus nonlaw is largely irrelevant in a pluralist context because the key questions involve the normative commitments of a community and the interaction among normative orders that give rise to such commitments, not their formal status');

is Brian Tamanaha's (2001: 166) view that the issue of correct conceptualisation of law in a world of vast regulatory diversity can be solved by accepting as law, for the purposes of inquiry, whatever people in a particular environment identify and treat in practice as such. This approach, which turns the what-is-law question into a descriptive inquiry (Berman 2009: 238), might seem a natural response to 'the enormity of the subject-matter' that normative plurality presents (Halpin 2014: 181). From a sociological viewpoint it might indeed be productive to prevent any drawing of sharp conceptual boundaries that could inhibit open-minded research about regulatory plurality. Andrew Halpin (2014: 181) properly notes, however, that the 'almost universal rejection' of Tamanaha's theoretical approach results from its lacking 'any analytical or explanatory bite'. It gives no analytical purchase on the idea of law (Cotterrell 2008b: 8; Culver and Giudice 2010: 146–7); yet law as an idea cannot, for juristic purposes, be discarded. Amongst many other problems with Tamanaha's conventionalism, it is not clear *which* people's views as to what is law are to count when disagreements on this matter exist in any particular place and time. Surely any empirical inquiry claiming a legal focus must make clear what specific idea of law guides the inquiry.

It seems that a juristic approach to conceptualising law in legal pluralism has to occupy a position somewhere between a sociological focus on merely describing regulatory diversity and a philosophical effort to analyse and propound legal universality. If Tamanaha's 'give it up' approach to conceptualisation is discarded, one might nevertheless seek some minimal idea of law, 'as thin and formal a sense of law as possible' (Melissaris 2014: 113) that could have the prospect of being universally valid as a lowest common denominator of global legal pluralism. But such a conceptualisation, retaining the legal philosophical ambition of universality, would have to be so 'thin' as to embrace every known and presently unknown putative legal form.

The question becomes what analytical power can such a thin idea of law have? Is the search for the essential and the universal retained at the cost of a conceptualisation offering no guide to the jurist in the practical task of navigating regulatory plurality? And, even in such a cautious approach, certain kinds of experience of legal plurality might be too quickly ruled out. Thus, Emmanuel Melissaris, understanding 'law in terms of shared normative experiences of the participants in a community' (2009: 123), still assumes it to be an affair of rules and rule following (2014: 109, 115, 118). Yet even juristically recognised law is not always a matter of rules; standard-setting authorities that are powerfully significant in contemporary regulation and difficult for jurists to ignore are, as noted earlier, not necessarily structured around Weberian formal legal rationality. A thicker non-universalism might be much preferable to a thin universalism that is either controversial or lacks much analytical power.

A very different but no less thoughtful approach is shown in Keith Culver's and Michael Giudice's (2010) 'inter-institutional theory', inspired in some degree by

---

Parker 2008: 355 (noting that '[o]ne of the strengths of regulation and governance scholarship is that it is not preoccupied with what counts as "law" in its empirical studies of how regulatory regimes interact').

Neil MacCormick's institutionalist legal philosophy. They aim to offer 'a descriptive-explanatory picture of legality as variegated combinations of legal institutions, institutions of law, and function-oriented content-independent peremptory norms and associated normative powers' (Culver and Giudice 2010: xxviii). Institutions of law are purpose-focused clusters of related norms (ibid: 120); legal institutions focus and deploy these but need not require 'officials' in any Hartian sense or depend on hierarchical organisation or monistic structures.

So, what is envisaged as legality is a variable and often thick interweaving of norms and institutions seen in terms of their interrelations. The aim is to avoid any assumption that hierarchies, systems, and officials are essential aspects of legal phenomena, while recognising that these are often dominating features of the most juristically familiar types of legal regimes. The analytical focus in legal pluralism should be not on relations between different legal systems claiming to be comprehensive, supreme and open (claims that do not reflect the reality of law today) but on 'the diverse ways in which distinct institutions coordinate their normative practices and share normative powers' (Culver and Giudice 2010: 58). In some respects this approach parallels Roughan's concern with relations between authorities. The focus is on finding legality in processes of interaction and negotiation between institutional centres of diverse kinds.

How far could such a focus serve juristic needs? Culver's and Giudice's idea of legal institution suggests agencies of many different kinds in which norms are created, interpreted, organised, and applied. However, in their wish to free the idea of law from any necessary tie to officials, they refer to 'institutional actors' (certainly not just 'state-based actors') whose interactions can amount to 'the setting of law' (2010: 157). The idea of officials is deliberately marginalised here because it suggests public roles within systems which officials serve. There seems much merit in trying to escape from the official, the systemic, and the hierarchical as necessary features of legality. However, from a juristic point of view, the problem with Culver's and Giudice's approach may be that – in sharp contrast to Melissaris's thin universalism – it is *too rich* and thickly descriptive and, with such complex openness, gives few guides for juristically negotiating regulatory plurality as a practical matter.

A model of law as institutionalised doctrine

This juristic negotiation surely has to solve two basic problems that demand assistance from theory. The first is that of identifying the kind of regulatory normative materials (or *doctrine*) that lawyers should take into account within the pluralist landscape. In this, the role of the jurist is to make some mapping of the range of this doctrine and to recognise the extent of its authority over those it regulates. This has to be done bearing in mind that the sources of authority traditionally nurtured and stabilised in the context of state law can no longer be assumed to apply to all forms of law in global legal pluralism. To recognise the authority of doctrine means here to judge how far legitimacy is actually being conferred on doctrine's claims to authority in the specific communal networks it purports to regulate.

The other closely related problem is that of identifying for juristic purposes the *agencies* that create, interpret, develop, and enforce regulation in the many different forms it can take in global legal pluralism. The juristic need to identify these agencies arises simply because they are the authorities (the producers, controllers, and managers of normative doctrine) among which legality may need to be negotiated. Beyond the familiar hierarchies of authority in state law and its extensions, this negotiation of legality will surely have to take place in the kind of interactive 'inter-institutional' processes on which Culver and Giudice focus. Seen in a different perspective, these agencies are the diverse 'authorities' with which a shared or limited legal authority might need to be worked out in something like the manner that Roughan's conception of relative authority suggests.

To treat these problems as juristically central in addressing global legal pluralism, a basic theoretical focus would be on (i) normative doctrine, and (ii) the agencies that institutionalise it. So, for juristic purposes a suitable minimal model of law is that of law as 'institutionalised doctrine' (Cotterrell 1995: 37–40).

Doctrine in this model is not to be seen as necessarily limited to rules but could include principles, concepts, and values. Nor must it be peremptory, as Culver and Giudice require. In global legal pluralism, doctrine can readily shade between the prescriptive and the advisory (in legal terms, 'hard' and 'soft') and can be interpreted and applied accordingly. So, doctrine as a category can embrace codes, guidelines, standards, and protocols, and there might be no reason why lawyers should avoid involvement in managing regulation that entails integrating these kinds of doctrinal elements with more juristically familiar structures of rules. As regards institutionalisation, this refers only to the idea that specific agencies of some kind exist with the task of creating, interpreting, or enforcing normative doctrine. In developed state legal systems, agencies such as courts, legislatures, administrative boards, and police exist to carry out each of these tasks or to combine them. In other kinds of legal regimes, not all of the tasks may be fulfilled by specific agencies, or they may be fulfilled only partially. Hence, the institutionalisation of doctrine as law can be a matter of degree.

Such a thin, sketchy model is certainly not to be held out as a universal concept of law or a specification of law's essence or true nature. For juristic purposes it merely suggests where to focus the communication processes (identification, interaction, negotiation, compromise) by which legality can be developed in global legal pluralism. For legal sociologists it is a starting point from which to indicate provisionally a legal focus in empirical studies of regulation. For legal philosophers it is surely far too limited to contribute to their ongoing search for definitive conceptualisations and clarifications. For the future of jurisprudence – the juristic enterprise of theoretically managing the idea of law and serving its well-being as a socially valuable practice – the model of law as institutionalised doctrine would need to be combined with reflection by jurists on the *values* they associate with law and which they interpret in terms of their cultural experience. It would also need to be combined with sociolegal study of the *conditions* in which institutionalised doctrine develops and the *forms* it takes, as well as about the ways in which claims of *authority* are made and legitimated in the populations that today are subject to juristically significant regulation.[18]

Conclusion

Where does all this lead? It might be said that lawyers are less in need of a systematic theory than a *method* of approaching legal pluralism (cf Zumbansen 2013: 131–3, 137–8) using the resources indicated in this chapter. It has been said that, beyond asking the what-is-law question in legal pluralism, 'we should ask who makes law, in which structures, through which agents, and for what purposes' (Barzilai 2008: 416). All of these are juristic as well as sociolegal questions. So jurisprudence should be closely allied with (though never reduced to) social science. Mark van Hoecke (2014: 54) suggests that 'concepts of law should go beyond positivistic sets of rules and include the law's context', but one could go further and say that, in legal pluralism, context is what actually creates juristically useful understandings of law, adding flesh to a skeletal model of institutionalised doctrine, enabling juristic identification of normative doctrine and institutionalising agencies.

Therefore, empirical sociological research on the vast range of communal networks in which regulation is created or to which it is addressed is indispensable for pluralist jurisprudence. And, crucially, this context of regulatory networks is ever *broadening* and increasingly *non-Western*. The universalist-essentialist tendencies in contemporary Anglophone legal philosophical thought actually pull against the flexibility which jurisprudence needs – a continual willingness to learn and pragmatically to revise its ideas on the basis of diverse, evolving regulatory experience. A jurisprudence tailored to global legal pluralism has less need for comprehensive systems of theory than for thoughtful and imaginative extensions of the lawyer's craft skills – skills of building or navigating the rationality of legal doctrine in 'piecemeal' fashion, with an awareness of the values of the cultures in which law is practised. And, as earlier chapters have stressed, the juristic role implies a commitment to aspirations for justice and security – multifaceted values that in Western legal cultures inform diverse hopes for and expectations of the rule of law.

---

18 For further discussion of the model of law as institutionalised doctrine see Chapter 7.

7

A CONCEPT OF LAW FOR GLOBAL LEGAL PLURALISM

Is a general concept of law needed to embrace the range of regulatory regimes developing in a world in which transnational and intranational regulation are increasingly significant – a world now often characterised as one of global legal pluralism?[1] Does global legal pluralism require a concept of law? What purposes might such a concept serve?

Taking a closer look at the complexity of global legal pluralism, this chapter elaborates much more fully ideas sketched in the previous one about a juristic concept of law. It asks, first, why it might be useful to conceptualise law in *general* terms at all. It goes on to consider problems that the sheer diversity of transnational regulatory forms poses for such a project. The social rule approach of H. L. A. Hart's concept of law is taken here as a starting point, and some of its crucial limitations in the context of global legal pluralism are examined – in particular, limitations that can be brought to light by reinterpreting politically and sociologically Hart's familiar analogy between legal rules and the rules of sports and games. Finally, in the light of these considerations, I shall suggest key elements (political, communal, institutional) that must be present in any concept of law that can recognise appropriately the full range of contemporary national and transnational regulation.

Controversies about conceptualising law

Hart (1983: ch 1) famously insisted that trying to define law in general terms is fruitless. Yet, even if much legal philosophy, following his lead, now discards the quest for definition in favour of an effort to understand how law is talked about in

---

1 See e.g. Snyder 1999, Perez 2003, Snyder 2004, Berman 2012, and Giudice 2014. The term is used in various ways. I adopt it here because it suggests the diversity and polycentricity of transnational regulation. It does not imply any single globalising process in relation to law, any emerging unified global legal regime, any homogeneity of transnational regulation, or any theoretical presuppositions about the form or scope of this regulation.

specific contexts, it still seeks to describe or explain the characteristics that typically, or even universally, identify practices, forms, or ideas as legal. Scholars engaged in this task suggest many reasons why such marks of law's distinctiveness need clarification: for example to explain (i) the possible or necessary bases of authority of law (Leiter 2007: 129–31), (ii) the criteria that give legal systems their identity (Raz 2009b: ch 5) or distinguish law from other forms of normative regulation (Marmor 2001; Howarth 2000), (iii) the forms of understanding essential to law as an intellectual and social practice (Hart 1994: 81), (iv) the nature of law's distinctive kind of normativity (Kelsen 1967), or (v) the basic moral or political implications of law's existence (Murphy 2001). These kinds of issues, which it is often assumed can be raised wherever and whenever law is thought to exist, inspire attempts to explain its typical or essential features.

The effort to explore such questions clearly need not entail a search for a universal or global juristic concept applicable to what jurists might recognise as 'law' in any time or place. John Austin (1885a: lect 11) restricted his project of general jurisprudence to 'the ampler and maturer [legal] systems of refined societies' – a practical, culturally conditioned limitation of scope, hardly different from that assumed since his time in much comparative law scholarship[2] and legal philosophy.[3] The appropriateness of a concept of law will surely depend on its intended scope of application, and this matter can be settled not in the abstract but only by reference to the aims and cultural contexts of particular inquiries.

If, for example, the aim is to generalise or compare 'across two or more legal traditions or cultures (or even jurisdictions)' (Twining 2003: 202, 246), rather than to develop an idea of law applicable in all times and places, a concept of law to inform the inquiry will surely still be needed. But many elements in it may be self-evident and shared among the traditions, cultures, or jurisdictions compared. They will not require explicit statement. To articulate such a concept may, however, seem important when apparently fundamental characteristics of law in one environment are absent in another (which nevertheless seems worthy of juristic or sociolegal comparison) or else take such radically different forms that their nature or significance as legal phenomena becomes controversial. In fact, in any theoretical generalisation or comparison of phenomena selected for their legal relevance, a concept of law will be implicit or explicit in the inquiry.

Studies of, for example, the nature of dispute processing, norm enforcement, or various kinds of regulation which, it has been suggested (Twining 2003: 242), could be undertaken in a renewed general jurisprudence must rely, insofar as they are studies in *legal* theory, on their reference to a concept of law appropriate to the inquiry in hand. The problem will be to specify the nature of 'the legal' flexibly enough to

2 For example, among leading early modern comparatists, Raymond Saleilles saw useful legal comparison as restricted 'to the civilised world'; Edouard Lambert saw its scope as practically restricted to modern European civil law systems: see Jamin 2002: 715–6.
3 Discussion of the issue seems rare in Anglo-American legal philosophy, but Joseph Raz (2009b: 50) acknowledges the primacy of 'contemporary municipal legal systems' in informing his concept of law.

allow for revision in the light of research experience. A concept of law will have to be adequate to organise a project as an inquiry related to law but not so fully elaborated as to close off inquiry in advance about diverse phenomena that it might be illuminating to treat as legal in some sense.

For some scholars, such as Ronald Dworkin, the search for a concept of law to help describe or explain the nature of law has seemed fundamentally misguided, at least as a legal philosophical project in the tradition of analytical jurisprudence. Dworkin saw the juristic task as to understand and engage reflexively in interpretive practices by which law's validity or truth in specific contexts is determined. A jurisprudential project aimed at theorising generally about or systematically comparing legal phenomena might seem remote from this task. When such a project seeks descriptive knowledge of law through comparison, generalisation, and conceptual clarification, it will consider what gives practices or rules their identity as legal phenomena. It will ask 'what makes a particular structure of governance a legal system rather than some other form of social control' (Dworkin 2006c: 97). But Dworkin labelled this question 'sociological' and saw it as having 'neither much practical nor much philosophical interest' (ibid: 97–8; and see Dworkin 2006b: 228).

Whatever the merits of this last claim, it at least raises the issue of why general conceptual inquiries about the nature of law are significant. From a Dworkinian standpoint, they do not help to resolve practical questions about whether rules are valid as part of a specific legal order or whether statements of the law in such a context are true; they do not aid juristic practice in this sense. Another way of putting the matter is that they do not resolve, or even help to resolve, questions about the ultimate location of the authority that validates law for the purposes of juristic or official practice (see also Dyzenhaus 2006: 114).

Dworkin (2006b: ch 7) argued that the impossibility of using a Hartian concept of law to explain the sources of legal validity reveals the difficulty for any such explanatory concept of law. The open-textured, potentially incomplete and plural character (Raz 2009b: 93–7) of the rule of recognition – the ultimate criterion of law's validity – in Hart's concept of law may suggest that efforts to identify the basis of legal authority by means of a general, descriptive, explanatory concept of law have been unproductive. And disagreements between 'inclusive' and 'exclusive' legal positivists about the rule of recognition's theoretically possible content may point in the same direction.

Those stressing such difficulties often claim that practical problems of legal authority or validity are resolved not by applying pedigree tests of 'the legal' (derived from a concept of law) but, rather, in a collectively understood process of argument about provisionally identified legal materials. Nevertheless, it should be emphasised that any such process of argument presupposes certain conditions. It presupposes especially a *discursive arena* in which it can take place. For Dworkin, for example, it presupposes a particular community, which in some way sees itself as the author of its law.

For distinct, territorially bounded legal systems, such as those of nation-states, it may seem easy to assume the scope and character of a discursive arena in which legal argument and interpretation take place. But the matter is much more complex when many kinds of intersecting transnational regulatory regimes are under consideration. Then it may be important, and perhaps difficult, to define the discursive arenas in which interpretation of regulation and debates about the validity and authority of law occur. Who is included in the various communities of interpreters? What collective understandings about methods of attributing validity and authority to regulation link them? Assumptions of normal legal practice may be hard to make. Questions about the scope, identity, and differentiation of regulatory regimes become practically important. If they are not answered, the claim that law is a matter of interpretation becomes an unenlightening truism. Everything depends on the assumptions on the basis of which that interpretation takes place.

Some purposes of a concept of law

Conceptual inquiries about law's identity – in Dworkin's (2006c: 97) terms, how far it is 'a particular structure of governance' distinguishable from any 'other form of social control' – surely have juristic significance, whether or not they are philosophically interesting. And certainly, as Dworkin notes, they are sociologically interesting. Indeed, the fact that he characterises them as sociological, while many Hartian positivists see them as central to legal philosophy, suggests that clear demarcation lines separating juristic, legal philosophical, and sociological inquiries cannot now be drawn without controversy. This is hardly a new claim. Eugen Ehrlich, setting out his programme for sociology of law early in the twentieth century, saw the comparative conceptual inquiries of Austin's general jurisprudence as indicating 'a part, at least, of the material which the practical science of law will be able to pass on to the sociological science of law' (Ehrlich 1936: 485), though he sought a distinctively sociological way of understanding law's identity.

Juristically, the development of a concept of law as a marker of law's identity can serve at least two distinct purposes. First, it can be used to make explicit the underlying *framework of legal understandings* in relation to which comparisons of law-related ideas and practices across or between different regulatory regimes or jurisdictions can be undertaken. Second, it can be used to conceptualise *boundaries of 'the legal'* (e.g. legal doctrine, institutions, arguments, methods, problems) in relation to nonlegal or extralegal considerations. Such a conceptualisation does not necessarily suggest either (i) that the boundaries of the legal are fixed (so that they cannot change or are similarly located whatever legal order is considered), or (ii) that they should be fixed in a particular way (as a timeless, context-free ideal).

Reasoning out the boundaries of law in a certain way with certain criteria in mind can be, instead, a challenge to consider how to relate those boundaries to particular contexts (Howarth 2000). This challenge can be accepted not only by theorists seeking to understand the nature of law but also by lawyers asking how far, for example, moral or economic efficiency arguments might be legitimately made in particular contexts of legal reasoning or how far various kinds of public or private regulation, 'soft law', or 'persuasive' authority (Glenn 1987; cf Lamond 2010) might be relevant as legal material. A concept of law might, in other words, offer a framework for arguing out boundary problems of law systematically and comparatively.

For both juristic and sociological purposes (whatever their exact relation), a practically useful general concept of law is likely to have similar qualities. It will not be a definition of the subject-matter that marks an endpoint of inquiry. It will be, rather, *a starting point: a framework for study, a provisional setting of parameters*, a means of identifying and clarifying key questions about law that can be raised in a variety of contexts.

Viewed in this way, a concept of law is relevant to inquiries about law's authority or validity. Such a concept drawn up on the basis of observation and experience of law in a range of settings may not answer questions about the validity of specific rules or other precepts as law or about the truth of statements of the law in a particular jurisdiction. But it may provisionally suggest the parameters in which legal authority and validity can be debated or their sources located. Indeed, it may suggest conditions required for legal authority and validity to be meaningful ideas at all. Its main contribution may be to inspire challenges to assumptions made in particular legal contexts about any of these matters.

While these are practical juristic considerations, they are relevant also to sociological studies of the authority structures of law. Indeed, juristic and sociological inquiries are often interrelated. Legal practitioners need, as part of their professional skill, to be able to make sociological sense of their observations of the environments in which law is practised and to incorporate those observations as part of their practical knowledge of law. Correspondingly, many sociological inquiries about law as an aspect or field of social experience will need to synthesise the understandings of professional and other participants in legal processes.

Dworkin (2006b: ch 6) attacks positivist efforts to specify a concept of law for descriptive or explanatory purposes in a general jurisprudence on the grounds that there is no 'neutral', 'uncommitted', or value-free standpoint from which such a concept can be proposed. This is an appropriate reminder that any concept of law will reflect specific values or experiences. But such a concept can still aid communication with people who have different regulatory experiences and value commitments insofar as expressing the concept helps to reveal the standpoint it embodies.

In fact, the viewpoint reflected in a concept of law is not necessarily confined by the legal environment in which it has emerged. Limits may certainly be set by the project for which it has been created (how much generalisation of legal experience is envisaged? how extensive are the legal comparisons to be made?), but it is not pointless to seek a concept of law to suggest an indefinite, broadening range of regulatory contexts. The insurmountable limits of any such concept are not those of experience but those of imagination. A concept of law might be a means to broaden perspectives beyond those gained through any particular practical legal experience. It might also express an aspiration towards such a broadening.

'Law' in global legal pluralism

Contemporary transnational regulation presents striking normative diversity. Referring mainly to economic transnational regulation, Francis Snyder notes 'a startling variety of new legal forms and regimes', 'a variety of institutions, norms, and dispute resolution processes located and produced, at different structured sites, around the world' (Snyder 2004: 624; 1999: 342). There is now a (surely far from level) 'global legal playing field', including 'a novel regime for governing global economic networks', but the many sites of global legal pluralism 'do not make up a legal system' (Snyder 1999: 343, 372, 374). There is no uniform jurisdictional reference point, no single discursive arena in which legal reasoning takes place. Instead, regimes of different kinds intersect, conflict, compete, and overlap.

It is not necessarily clear what, following a positivist approach, should be looked for as appropriate 'pedigree tests' of normative validity in these diverse areas of regulation. Wolf Heydebrand (2001: 120) writes of a need to redefine notions of 'law' and 'legal' in considering 'quasi-legal, regulatory mechanisms at the global level'. Much significant transnational regulation is 'soft law',[4] and the legal quality of the contemporary *lex mercatoria* is subject to 'seemingly eternal dispute' (Zumbansen 2002: 401). Similarly, the 'legal substructure of international finance and banking is remarkably underdeveloped, characterised for the most part by a set of recommended "best practices" exhibiting little formality or clarity', while regulation emphasises 'open-ended, flexible guidelines' (Scheuerman 1999: 255).[5] In fact, '[m]any of the substantive norms of international business law are directly determined by the huge "industry leaders" who dominate the market. . . . More and more, [multinational] corporations exercise "sovereign" powers of law-making' (ibid: 257). Codes of practice, operating in some respects like multilaterally negotiated treaties, are 'applied as standard-form contracts laid down by the leading firms in a particular market' (Snyder 1999: 363).

In general, in transnational arenas, regulatory regimes of great diversity – public and private, state and international, 'soft' and 'hard', legislated and negotiated, centralised and diffuse – coexist, often in very unclear relations with each other. While some are rooted in territorial jurisdiction, the scope of others is functionally defined. Some operate through 'horizontal' coordination (especially by standardisation of contractual terms in the process of transnational business dealings), while others operate more 'vertically' through hierarchies of authority located in specific rule-making or adjudicatory institutions.

The inclination to deny that some, or perhaps much of this regulation is law derives from deep-rooted assumptions about law's nature: for example that it can be created or controlled only by state institutions and agencies; that it is essentially public and not private regulation; that it aims (even if sometimes unsuccessfully) to achieve clarity and relative constancy in the form of fixed rules, not flexible standards; that it is a supreme form of regulation, dominating other regulatory regimes; that it is comprehensive in its social field; and that it consists of imperative demands or specified permissions, not negotiated understandings. Each of these assumptions about law is challenged by developments in transnational regulation, insofar as this

---

4 See e.g. Snyder 2004: 630–1, Senden 2005, Trubek and Trubek 2005, and Schäfer 2006.
5 Scheuerman 1999: 255; and for reasons for this state of affairs see e.g. Rixen 2013 and Titolo 2012.

regulation is now often labelled 'law', seen as legally important, or increasingly integrated with national or international law.[6]

Is it possible and useful to impose, as a template on this diversity, a transnational concept of law? Would this help to broaden perspectives on the significance of new or newly prominent regulatory regimes that do not fit traditional ideas of nation-state law? It is not fruitful just to accept theoretically as law whatever regulatory practices are given the label 'law' by those who participate in them. As noted earlier, that would be to abandon the analytical purposes for which a concept of law should be designed; it would be to provide no guiding framework on which comparative or theoretical inquiries could be built. At the same time, there is no reason (from either juristic or sociological points of view) to give up the effort to conceptualise law in the face of growing transnational regulatory complexity and as part of an effort to understand that complexity.

Juristically, the most obvious problem that transnational regulation poses is that of structuring meaningful argument about the validity of regulation and its sources of authority – a problem of knowing how to reason normatively and systematically in transnational arenas. How is it possible to create a discourse to integrate transnational normative structures and impose juridical order on them? By contrast, from a *sociological* point of view, the need is to conceptualise law in ways that are helpful (i) in tracking the variable, fluctuating power of nation-state regulation, and (ii) in surveying the field of transnational regulation in relation to the social, economic, and political forces shaping it.

Hart and the rules of games and sports

In contemporary Anglophone legal theory, an approach informed by Hart's legal philosophy might seem initially promising as a basis for addressing analytical problems of transnational regulation. Hart's concept of law has been found useful not only by jurists but also by some legal sociologists and anthropologists. Neil MacCormick (1993) explored its usefulness in characterising the transnational law of the European Union and escaping limits imposed by traditional ideas of sovereignty.[7] Yet, for MacCormick, '[d]espite the pluralistic or polycentric potentialities [Hart] . . . points to in developing his theory, pluralism remains more a potential than an actual virtue of his own work' (1993: 9).

Like most other legal philosophers, Hart largely assumes that nation-state boundaries correlate with legal-system boundaries and limit the discursive arena of legal reasoning on questions of legal validity. The pluralist potential of his theory lies only in the fact that he does not *explicitly* tie his concept of law to the state's territorial jurisdiction. Unlike, for example, Hans Kelsen, Hart offers no analysis of the relation of law and state (Raz 2009b: 98), the closest he comes to this being the important

6 See Chapter 8.
7 And see MacCormick 1999: ch 8. A conceptualisation of legalisation in international relations that finds some inspiration in Hart's concept of law is suggested in Abbott et al 2000.

role his theory gives to 'officials'. But these are theoretically identified not as state officials but only as officials in relation to the legal system they serve.

In considering the kind of concept of law that could be useful in global legal pluralism, it is worth noting the limits as well as the advances of Hart's concept of law. It replaces Austin's theory of sovereign and subject, linked by legal commands, with the idea of an impersonal structure of rules making up a legal system. The main advance here for legal theory is to make it possible to separate the concept of law from particular structures of state-centred political power. It becomes possible to imagine, for example, international law and customary law as, in some sense, law, even if less developed than the law of nation-states. But the price paid for this – the remarkable *vacuum at the centre of Hart's concept of law* – is the difficulty of clearly distinguishing legal rules from many other obligation-imposing social rules. It is necessary briefly to illustrate this problem before showing how it arises and how it must be avoided in studying global legal pluralism. My illustration is in terms of the relationship of legal rules and rules of games or sports.

Having identified law as the union of primary and secondary rules, Hart specifies the minimum conditions for a legal system to exist as being (i) that citizens in general regularly obey the primary rules, and (ii) that 'officials' adopt an internal (critical, reflective) view of secondary rules, applying them as meaningful guides for their own conduct and that of others (Hart 1994: 116). Rejecting the idea of defining law, he claims only that this conceptualisation identifies central cases of typical invocations of the idea of law. Yet he has been widely assumed to be concerned with identifying law in contrast to other social phenomena. Frederick Schauer (2006: 871) claims, for example, that 'Hart helped us see why law is different not only from the state-sanctioned application of force, but also from norms, values, habits, practices, and a host of other determinants of behaviour that . . . remain crucially different from law.' The sophistication of Hart's approach has often been seen to lie partly in his refusal to identify law in political terms as Austin did. Instead of tying law to sovereign power, he emphasises its normativity (as rules) and its reality as social (especially linguistic) practices.

As is well known, this emphasis leads him (and other legal philosophers) to make frequent analogies between legal rules and the rules of games. But, remarkably, at no point does he clearly identify what distinguishes law as a species of social rules from the rules of games.[8] He discusses games only to explain common features of rules, including legal rules. This seems odd. Legal sociologists (unlike most jurists) are sometimes prepared to recognise 'private legal systems' (Evan 1990: 123–37) and many varieties of social rules as law, but they would usually not hesitate to

---

8 Dworkin (2006c: 100) notes that Hart's concept of law as the union of primary and secondary rules does not distinguish legal systems from such institutions as organised sports. More generally, secondary rules have long been recognised (e.g. Colvin 1978: 201) as a feature of institutionalisation in many organisations and are in no way unique to 'the legal world'. For an attempt to argue that a Hartian concept of law could dispense with secondary rules see Daniels 2010. For an elaborate discussion of the nature and organization of rules of games see Raz 1975: 113–23.

distinguish law from the rules of games or sports. It is strange if Hart gives no theoretical resources to make this distinction. Yet this matter has received little comment.

Legal rules for Hart are obligation-imposing, but rules of games can also have this character for the players. In any case, not all legal rules, he notes, have all the attributes that he sees as creating obligations (Hart 1994: 174, 175, 229). Further, organised games or sports certainly do not necessarily lack secondary rules, the emergence of which marks, for Hart, transition 'from the pre-legal to the legal world' (ibid: 94). Often there are elaborate, rule-governed processes supervised by 'officials' for creating, recognising, debating, changing, and adjudicating the primary obligation-imposing rules of games and sports (e.g. in cricket, bridge, or chess). Rules of games, no less than of law, are viewed from internal and external viewpoints. Indeed, the rules of some sports and games (e.g. cricket, bridge, croquet) are typically called laws.

Could it be said that games and sports are essentially, in some sense, trivial whereas law is concerned with matters of fundamental social importance? Joseph Raz (2009b: 116–20) has emphasised law's dominant social importance, its regulatory comprehensiveness, its claim to supremacy over other norm systems and its role in supporting them. But he admits these are traits of 'the legal' that can vary in degree (ibid: 116), and, in fact, each of these suggested marks of law's distinctiveness can be challenged with regard to law's social conditions of existence in particular contexts (Tamanaha 2001: 139–40). Many acknowledged laws address only highly specialised, technical matters of minor regulation.[9] On the other hand, often much turns on the outcome of games or sporting contests, in terms of reputations, prizes, opportunities, sponsorship, and careers. Much attention is often paid to management of the rules of sports and the adjudication of disputes. Much money may be at stake in organised sports. Indeed, the outcome of some sporting contests may be a matter of national economic, cultural, or political importance and of intense popular interest in a way that decisions on issues of law rarely are.[10]

The point to be made here is not that the rules of games and of law cannot be satisfactorily distinguished theoretically. It is that an approach to conceptualising law that seeks to avoid consideration of empirical questions about law's specific social contexts so as to address it more abstractly – for example by exploring the structuring of rules or norms – may not provide resources for understanding legal experience in general or for the variety of forms of law that currently exist. A concept of law that, for example, cannot clearly show that, for all their similarities, legal systems and the normative organisation of sports events are *fundamentally* different social phenomena lacks the power to guide appropriate studies of

---

9 Hart notes (1994:170) that game-rules concern 'activities for which there are only intermittent opportunities, deliberately created'. But this applies no less to many activities regulated by law. Elsewhere (1994: 174, 175, 229), he admits the insignificance of many laws.

10 For a critique of the idea that sports regulation does not involve matters of general governmental significance see Anderson 2006.

law, both by those who practise it juristically and those who study its character sociologically.

A concept of law in its contexts

The 'games problem' in the concept of law points to what is often missing from contemporary legal philosophy – an adequate recognition of the inseparability of any practically useful idea of law from its political and social contexts of application.

Dworkin implied interestingly in his early work (1978: 24–5) that law can be distinguished from the rules of games because rules *dominate* games as enterprises in a way that is not true of law; by contrast, rules do not dominate law because other standards (e.g. legal principles) are fundamental. Again, for Dworkin, games (or at least some of them) are *autonomous* institutions (ibid: 101), existing for their own sake, whereas law is not; it is thoroughly implicated in its wider social and moral context.

I think this is not quite correct, though it hints at something of great importance. It is not true that games are regulated only by rules; they are often also considered to be governed by other standards. The 'spirit of the game' may be very important (e.g. Fraser 2005: chs 6 and 7) and related to a sense of purpose, fairness, and playing properly rather than undermining the game or 'bringing it into disrepute'.[11] Again, games are not necessarily autonomous institutions: they may be pursued for many wider purposes, including the development of skills, fitness, or social contacts and may be viewed, like law, from many perspectives (Weber 1977: 116–24). But it is right to stress that law cannot be fully understood in terms of rules entirely divorced from the *specific moral contexts of their development and use.*

The problem in following Dworkin's approach to emphasising this law–morality connection is that, for him, it is to be pursued entirely within the confines of experience of a particular legal community. But contemporary regulatory complexity requires the recognition of an intense *interaction* between many different regulatory communities, often with fluctuating, partly shared memberships. It is this interaction (not necessarily governed by any shared authority or common understandings) that now produces the complexity of global legal pluralism. Global legal pluralism can be understood only by recognising that the participant experience of interpreters in any regulatory regime must coexist with (and will shape and be shaped by) their observation of other regulatory regimes that overlap, relate to, and possibly conflict with it. Participants in global legal pluralism will experience a

---

11 A classic case is the notorious 1933 'body-line' controversy in cricket. For a brief account see Blythe 1983: ch 7. See also generally Alldridge 2015. It has been suggested that 'law, unlike a game, purports to bind us morally' (Gardner 2001: 227). But this purported distinction begs the question of what morality can be. The idea of 'the spirit of the game' indicates a morality of its practice which it is not difficult to see as analogous to the morality that holds other kinds of networks of social relations together.

variety of regimes, jurisdictions, and systems and will do so simultaneously as both observers and interpreters.

While Hart's expulsion of political power, in the form of Austinian sovereignty, from his concept of law explains its inability (or refusal) to relate law and state or even to see law as more than a game of rules, Dworkin's distinguishing of law from game-rules in terms of law's wider moral significance points to law's essential ties to structures of community, that is, its deep immersion in the social. The lesson to be learned is that a convincing concept of law must emphasise directly and explicitly law's *political* dimensions or its *communal* dimensions, or both. And it must do so sociologically, recognising (especially in the contexts of global legal pluralism) the variety of law's practices and the empirical variability of its political and communal conditions of existence. It is to these matters that it is necessary, finally, to turn.

A concept of law should be judged by its fitness for the specific purpose for which it has been created. Whether treated as a model, framework, ideal type, or embodiment of a 'focal meaning' (Finnis 2011: 276–81), it should be seen less as making 'a claim to truth' (cf Marmor 2006: 692) about the nature of law than as *organising efforts towards solving specific problems*, whether of legal discourse or in social research on legal phenomena. The tendency to present concepts of law as embodying truth about law may explain the radical inconclusiveness of some debates in legal philosophy. Behind this tendency is an assumption that all scholars are engaged in the same inquiry, about the same legal experience, with the same ends in view. When the participants in debates are theorists whose shared experience is of modern Western state legal systems this assumption may be understandable. But in confronting the challenges posed by the interaction of many kinds of national, transnational, and international regulation, as well as by intimations of legal pluralism in unitary nation-states (e.g. Grillo et al eds 2009) and a new 'jurisprudence of difference' in legal thought,[12] it seems increasingly untenable.

Various concepts of law could be helpful in understanding global legal pluralism depending on the tasks in hand. Perhaps the most urgent task at present is to be able to map legal plurality, to use legal theory to show the interrelating legal structures that exist and to explore the kinds of legal reasoning possible (and hence the possibilities for a transnational rule of law) given this regulatory diversity.

A concept of law serving such purposes would need to be able to represent not only legal thinking familiar to lawyers in modern nation-state legal systems but also relationships between regulatory regimes not identified in terms of nation-state jurisdictions. The experience to be represented in a transnational concept of law will be simultaneously that of 'internal' participation in the use and interpretation of regulation and 'external' observation of how potentially conflicting or competing regulatory structures and practices interact. But legal interpretation – increasingly,

12 On which see Chapter 11.

interpretation *across* as well as within normative regimes – will not be possible except in the context of this observation. And observation of global legal pluralism will require interpretive understanding of its diverse normative practices. Thus, the distinctions between 'internal' and 'external' views of law, so familiar in legal philosophy, will be hard to maintain.

Politics, communities, doctrine, practices

Beyond the need for this kind of responsiveness to a plurality of regimes of legally relevant regulation, two other general suggestions about a transnational concept of law can be made, both of them developing points made earlier about problems of Hart's concept of law.

First, a Hartian concept of law that draws close analogies between legal rules and the rules of games, rather than emphasising radical differences between them, is useful for many purposes, but in the complex, rapidly evolving political and social contexts of global legal pluralism, concepts of law emphasising law's links to *political structures* or its roots in various kinds of *community structures* are especially important.

The political link suggests a need to consider new arguments about structures of national and international sovereignty and, more generally, to examine the extent to which a useful concept of transnational law must incorporate a sharp awareness of the power structures of globalisation and international relations. Correspondingly, linking law with structures of community would address a need to explore the many new and diverse networks of social relations that support various forms of transnational regulation. For example, it might reflect the ways in which transnational business and financial networks, as well as segments of legal and other professions operating transnationally, both shape and give authority to transnational regulation, an authority that might, in some cases, be as significant as the traditional forms of state-based legal authority. More generally, this approach would portray transnational law as representing networks of different types of social relations of community with different (often competing or conflicting) legal implications and problems.[13]

A second suggestion also relates to the emphasis on impersonal rules in Hart's concept of law. If this tends to direct attention away from seeking what is distinctive about law in favour of highlighting what is common to many systems of social rules, a good strategy in developing a transnational concept of law might be to reintroduce the personal element of human action by focusing not only on rules but also on the *institutionalised practices of managing them*. Indeed, the emphasis should be on these practices in relation to legal doctrine in general, including rules, principles,

---

13 The following chapter develops this idea, and it is applied to the specific case of transnational criminal law in Chapter 10. On law as the regulation of communal networks, see generally Cotterrell 2006 and Cotterrell 2008c: ch 2 and Pt 4.

concepts, or values of law. Law thus requires relatively stable, recognised, established agencies existing to create, interpret, or enforce doctrine.

To see law in this way as *institutionalised doctrine*, as proposed in the previous chapter, is to emphasise the specific, identifiable mechanisms by which legal doctrine is socially managed in organised, patterned ways.[14] It is to emphasise that law is never normative ideas alone but always ideas that are the focus of specific practices designed to serve them. Such an emphasis necessarily brings political or communal elements back into a concept of law, the nature of these depending on where the agencies or processes of doctrine-management are seen to be socially located and by whom and in what ways they are controlled. Whatever their other roles and effects, these agencies or processes should be seen as controlling the assertion of authority by law. They are the primary institutional (patterned, established, and recognised) links between law as doctrine and its specific social contexts.[15]

In the context of global legal pluralism, it would be wise not to insist on the presence of *all* of these three kinds of institutionalised practices – for creation, interpretation *and* enforcement of doctrine – as necessary to law. Some degree of formal institutionalisation is required to mark 'the legal'. But the purposes of a concept of law in this context are best served by recognising that, while institutionalising one or more of these functions of creation, interpretation, or enforcement is necessary to law, not all are found in every legal regime or legal type.

For example, much well-developed and effective 'soft law' lacks formal enforcement mechanisms. And standards of various kinds that it might be very important to take into account in interpreting transnational regulation are not necessarily created by anything like orthodox courts or legislatures. Again, transnational doctrine sometimes lacks distinct adjudicatory or interpreting institutions or agencies; and where these exist they sometimes compete or conflict – a matter familiar in international law as well as new transnational regulatory regimes (Higgins 2006; Berman 2007a). The authority of transnational regulation as law might well vary depending on the extent of its institutionalisation.

14 This approach can be compared with that of Abbott et al. 2000 conceptualising 'legalisation'. My concept of doctrine implies the idea of obligation, which they also stress, and similarly embraces diverse normative phenomena (not just rules). But Abbott et al. address this diversity using 'precision' as a variable, while I think types of doctrine are differentiated in other ways. Their idea of 'delegation' refers to aspects of what I call institutionalisation but begs questions about the variety of types of authority underpinning legal processes.

15 To talk of 'agencies', 'processes', 'practices', and 'institutions' is not necessarily to restate a Hartian emphasis on (secondary) rules, since one should not assume or emphasise the rule-governed nature of these phenomena in all cases. Their customary, purposive, charismatic, or prudential basis might not necessarily be best formulated in terms of governing rules (though in relation to many regulatory structures this will surely be possible). As Max Weber (1968: 215–6, 226–54) taught, not all legitimate authority is based on rules. A general concept of law taking account of the great variety of global regulatory structures will thus emphasise institutionalised practices from which rules may (or may not) emerge or around which they may (or may not) cluster.

Concepts of law useful in analysing transnational regulation are likely to be less developed and more exploratory than many earlier characterisations of law in the literature of legal theory. Any such concept will be a work in progress, a provisional frame, a practical tool in organising new fields, an idea tailored to specific contexts and projects. But it would serve new purposes of a reinvigorated general jurisprudence, helping to redirect analytical jurisprudence towards a sustained engagement with the problems of understanding law's changing transnational arenas.

8

THE NATURE OF
TRANSNATIONAL LAW

The scope of transnational regulation

The idea that law has 'spilled out' beyond the borders of the nation-state is commonplace. Merchant communities that operate across national borders make regulation that effectively binds them as law in their dealings with one another. Europeans have long experienced the fact that much of their law comes not from their own nation-state sources but from Europe-wide institutions. International criminal justice increasingly claims to reach out to catch gross violators of human rights irrespective of the state they happen to be in or the place of their alleged crimes. Judges in different nations draw on one another's ideas in what are beginning to appear as transnational judicial communities. Conventions authorised by international law create rights and duties for people in cross-border relationships. Human rights instruments and agencies carry legal ideas around the world, creating new expectations of rights and protections not limited by national borders.

For many scholars, a new term has seemed necessary to indicate legal relations, influences, controls, regimes, doctrines, and systems that are not those of nation-state (municipal) law but, equally, are not fully grasped by extended definitions of the scope of international law. The new term is 'transnational law', widely invoked but rarely defined with precision. In this chapter the problems of analysing transnational law as a general idea are the focus of attention.

Often 'transnational law' is taken to refer to extensions of jurisdiction across nation-state boundaries, so that people, corporations, public or private agencies, and organisations are addressed or directly affected by regulation that originates outside the territorial jurisdiction of the nation-state in which they are situated, or is interpreted or validated by authorities external to that jurisdiction. Sometimes it refers to regulation guaranteed neither by nation-state agencies nor by international legal institutions or instruments such as treaties or conventions. Sometimes it signals a space for regulation not yet (fully) existing but for which a need is felt in cross-border interactions.

The international lawyer Philip Jessup (2006: 45) wrote that transnational law includes 'all law which regulates actions or events that transcend national frontiers'. In his view national and international law would be part of it insofar as they have these effects, and it could address both public (state and governmental) and private (nongovernmental, civil society) actors (Tietje and Nowrot 2006). But other writers treat transnational law as conceptually distinct from national and international law because its primary sources and addressees are neither nation-state agencies nor international institutions founded on treaties or conventions but private (individual, corporate, or collective) actors involved in transnational relations (see Zumbansen 2002; Calliess 2007: 476).

Another controversy is as to whether substance or procedure should be emphasised. Is transnational law primarily made up of rules applying directly across national borders, or is it mainly coordinating regulation harmonising or linking substantive rules that may differ between states? The latter suggests a pluralistic approach (Berman 2007b) recognising and preserving legal difference but smoothing interactions between legal regimes – a kind of transnational conflict of laws system. Its main focus might be procedural. The substantive approach, by contrast, could envisage convergence in regulation, a potentially monistic approach, a 'universalist harmonisation' (ibid: 1164, 1189–91) in which transnational law aims at a gradual spread of legal uniformity across national boundaries and moves towards a 'world law' (cf Berman 1995). Perhaps more realistically, it might emphasise the way regulatory regimes seek uniformity across limited (usually functionally defined) transnational operational spheres.

Thus, basic questions about transnational law remain. First, does this law still rely fundamentally on nation-state law and international law (the latter supported by and recognising the sovereignty of states), or does it entail a new relationship between law and state – in which some sources of law now exist entirely outside the ambit of state authority? Second, if transnational law regulates transnational relations, are these specifically the relations of individuals, corporations, and associations in civil society, or, as Jessup thought, can it also embrace relations involving state and governmental agencies? In other words, is it centrally transnational *private* law, or is that too narrow a conception? Third, is transnational law building a new regime (or regimes) of substantive law existing alongside state law, or is it mainly a procedural, coordinating law, linking state and other legal regimes to serve transnational networks? Does it point towards a gradual transnational unification of regulation, or must it remain a vast array of intersecting, often conflicting regulatory regimes?

These questions defy conclusive answers. But areas of established or embryonic regulation often associated with transnational law can easily be listed. Individually many items on the list might be assigned to traditional legal categories (municipal law, international law, nonlegal regulation), but, taken together, perhaps they imply a change in the legal landscape, if only because of the vast regulatory scope they cover. The list could include international human rights law, international criminal law, international trade law, international financial law, international environmental law, Internet regulation, international commercial arbitration practice and the transnational regulation of merchant communities (*lex mercatoria*), European Union law, the law of the World Trade Organization, private self-regulation in transnational industries, and transnational corporate governance codes or principles.

Equally available for consideration is a mass of regulation (guidelines, standards, norms, principles, and codes, together with procedures for norm creation, adjudication, and enforcement) established by associations, nongovernmental organisations, and administrative agencies, in addition to the 'internal' collective regulation of transnational corporations and corporate groups. Finally, also in the mix of transnational legal phenomena could be the extraterritorial application and effects of national laws, as well as extradition practices by which the practical reach of national jurisdiction is extended into foreign states.

The value of models and maps

The range of all this seems disconcerting. Is transnational law a category at all? And is it all 'law'? Lawyers often quickly make judgments as to what is and is not law in such a motley regulatory mix. They judge on the basis of common understandings: most centrally the idea that all law is, in one way or another, the *law of the nation-state*. If international law is significant as law, a matter that even now is not universally assumed (Goldsmith and Posner 2005; cf Berman 2006), this is often on the basis that it is a projection of the sovereignty of nation-states (which authorise the making of treaties and international conventions and the recognition – explicitly or through their practice – of international customary norms). From this viewpoint, transnational law, when properly called law, is an extension of national sovereign jurisdictions or the creation (through recognised mechanisms of international law) of law by international agencies or through international instruments ultimately validated by the express or tacit authority of sovereign states. Viewed in such a perspective, a category of transnational law apart from municipal or international law might seem redundant.

However, the range and variety of regulation operating beyond nation-state boundaries may now have become so considerable and its impact so substantial that a different view is needed. To invoke an idea of transnational law is to suggest that law has new sources, locations, and bases of authority. Adding 'transnational' to 'law' is like adding a question mark: querying modern Western jurisprudence's state-centred understanding of law. It is also to query whether ideas and methods in international law need revising (e.g. Koh 1996; Berman 2005) to accelerate the ongoing development of this field away from its traditional focus on the relations of states and towards a broad concern with the regulatory problems of international society.

Is it enough to look merely at *specific* fields of regulation – for example international criminal justice or *lex mercatoria* – and ignore any *general* category of transnational law? From a sociological standpoint, a general inquiry about the nature of transnational law might offer a *framework* for comparing empirical sociolegal studies in different cross-border contexts. If a useful *model* of transnational law could be devised – a working notion of what might link social phenomena under this conceptual label – there might be better possibilities for relating studies of transnational legal developments in seemingly disparate areas. Theoretical interpretations of historical sociolegal developments in diverse fields – viewed through a 'transnational' lens – might show commonalities or interesting parallels and divergences otherwise missed. A concept of transnational law could assist in selecting problems for empirical study and formulating hypotheses. It could help in mapping a field of phenomena and organising ideas (to be tested in research) about their nature.

Juristic interests in a concept of transnational law are likely to be different from sociological ones. For the jurist and practical lawyer, crucial issues may be about conflicts of laws and of legal authorities. Is it becoming harder to identify valid law in a transnational context? Juristically, what is to be made of 'soft law'[1] (often linked to legal authorities but ambivalent in its legal significance)? Is it an irrelevance or a confusion in strictly legal terms or something whose half-hearted designation as law (but not as 'hard' or enforceable law) suggests that *some* account must be taken of it, if only as doctrine (e.g. rules, principles, guidelines) that may be *on the way to becoming law* and acquiring some legal authority.

Closely related may be juristic concerns about the 'deformalisation' and 'fragmentation' of established legal regimes (and so of their authority), noted especially by scholars and practitioners of contemporary international law (Michaels 2009: 249; Calliess and Zumbansen 2010: 271; Higgins 2006). But fragmentation seems a growing feature of law in general, so that, as was argued in Chapter 6, some concept of legal pluralism must now be a part of the discourse of well-informed jurists. In a situation in which old ideas of unity and system in law are insecure (Graver 1990), the need to find new ways to interpret and manage legal complexity juristically is easily felt.

Practising lawyers, as a professional group, have an interest in getting a sense of the whole range of law so as to be able to order and develop their activities in this realm of 'the legal'. They need ways to orient themselves to the changing character of legal phenomena. To adopt John Austin's metaphor in defending his idea of a general jurisprudence, they need *a map of law* – a chart to give perspective on its range and structure (Austin 1885b: 1082) and the lines of its past, present, and likely future development. Providing it is a central juristic task.

Private and public in transnational regulation

Gralf-Peter Calliess's and Peer Zumbansen's (2010) important book on the nature of transnational private law can be seen as an effort at provisional and partial mapping of law's contemporary transnational dimensions. I shall focus in detail on their approach here and try to build from it. The starting point is an idea of private law,

---

1 Usefully defined as 'regulatory instruments and mechanisms of governance that, while implicating some kind of normative commitment, do not rely on binding rules or on a regime of formal sanctions' (Di Robilant 2006: 499).

of some kind, which can extend transnationally or have transnational effects. So the question of distinguishing public and private presents itself immediately. One of Calliess's and Zumbansen's main themes is that public and private cannot realistically be separated in their inquiry, yet the designations public and private can still be of use. In their view, anything that can be recognised as law, even if developed essentially by 'private' actors such as traders in transnational commercial networks (as *lex mercatoria*) or corporations and corporate groups (as transnationally operating norms of corporate social responsibility), will have important public aspects.

These public aspects are matters of government or governance that go beyond a mere compromising of private interests in transnationally operating groups or networks. However, the 'private' in transnational law suggests that the dynamo of norm-production, development, interpretation, and enforcement is primarily located in civil society actors rather than public authorities of the state or public international law. And the kinds of matters regulated are those which (if legally relevant at all) would be the concern of municipal private law if they were limited within the jurisdiction of the nation-state.

The examples which Calliess and Zumbansen focus on are the regulation of corporations and their relations with civil society, regulation governing the practice of transnational merchant groups, governance frameworks for e-commerce between business and consumers, and transnational technical standard setting. Often more significant than legislation by state authorities or international agencies is the working out of regulatory practices in social (especially economic) interaction within networks of individuals, corporations, organisations, and associations. Yet, echoing many other writers in this field, Calliess and Zumbansen emphasise that state authority is still important in many contexts.

Corporate governance codes may gain official authorisation and support from state legislation (as in Germany, discussed in some detail in the book), even if these remain voluntary in the sense of lacking official enforcement. Organisations, corporations, or associations set up to manage regimes of transnational private regulation may also be created, recognised, or guaranteed by public authority. Soft-law mechanisms may be attached to hard law or introduced as a prelude to the 'hardening' of guidelines into state or international law. When the focus of attention ceases to be the settled jurisdictional reach of the nation-state, the public-private line becomes blurred.

Common lawyers often tend to confront the undermining of the public-private dichotomy with pragmatic adjustments to their reasoning. But for Continental civil law scholars, used to a firmer conceptual association of law and state, perhaps the issue is more fundamental: 'without the nation-state as an Archimedean point of reference, the public or private status of regulators becomes fundamentally ambiguous' (Calliess and Renner 2009: 265). Then issues of regulatory legitimacy may arise.

Whatever these conceptual problems, a focus on transnational private law (TPL) is a way of making provisional demarcations in an impossibly huge and diverse field of transnational regulation. The concept of TPL, like almost all concepts in this area, is a pragmatic one. The question is merely whether it helps in mapping and modelling, whether it aids analysis in an area which has few reliable signposts and landmarks.

The private emphasis makes it possible to separate off an area of transnational regulation from the familiar public or governmental regulation of municipal and international law. So TPL might be considered (temporarily) as in a different regulatory category from, for example, international economic law created by the separate or collective acts of nation-states via municipal law or public international law. TPL can be seen (again provisionally and pragmatically) as 'bottom-up' law (created in social inter-action), rather than 'top-down' (legislated) law (Calliess and Zumbansen 2010: 125).

As soon as these terms (bottom-up and top-down), suggesting different ways of lawmaking, are introduced, their problems are apparent. All law is *voluntas* (the expression of coercive authority) as well as *ratio* (negotiated, elaborated reason or principle). Most law is imposed by the regulators through force or pressure of some kind, as well as consented to or at least acquiesced in by those it regulates. Calliess and Zumbansen are well aware of all this, but, in focusing on the 'private' even if they do not really believe in it as a category, they are choosing to start analysis *somewhere*, rather than be paralyzed by conceptual indecision. For the moment, many questions about the specific contribution of municipal and international law to transnational regulation are to be left aside. So, in a rich and complex discussion, they illustrate ways in which transnational economic regulation emerges directly from social inter-action (e.g. in merchant practice, corporate contexts, e-commerce), but always in a dialectic of regulatory power located in a variety of sources, official and unofficial.

Different kinds of theoretical resources structure different parts of their account. The idea of a regulatory dialectic in which established regulatory structures frame and encourage relatively spontaneous processes of norm development implies the significance of theories of reflexive law which emphasise, for example, 'how political governance and corporate self-regulation can be mutually reinforcing and optimis-ing' (Calliess and Zumbansen 2010: 224). Economic theories of social norms are also noted for their helpful emphasis on nonstate mechanisms of regulation but are heavily criticised for their general failure to link up with the extensive, long-established, wider sociolegal literature on norms. These theories are attacked also for simplistic, overgeneralised claims about the greater efficiency (according to what criteria?) of informal norms over formally institutionalised law (ibid: 71–2) and about the widespread regulatory 'incompetence' and inadequacy of courts and (in the view of some critics) of contemporary state regulation as a whole (ibid: 253–4). Soft-law theory is seen as broadly allied with the authors' approach but as insuf-ficiently precise and rigorous (ibid: 255–60).

Law in the toolbox of governance mechanisms

More significant here is a detailed discussion of the economist Oliver Williamson's 'economics of governance'. Williamson distinguishes contrasting kinds of 'good order and workable arrangements' to regulate different conditions presented, for example, by 'spot markets' (involving isolated transactions), long-term contracts (hybrids) providing for ongoing interaction, and 'vertical' hierarchies of control and coordination appropriate to firms and their subsidiaries. Important variables are the relative frequency of transactions and the degree of standardisation or specificity of assets involved in them. The risks and costs that vary with types of transactions and interactive relationships indicate the attractiveness and possibilities of different kinds of regulatory methods (Calliess and Zumbansen 2010: 113–18).

Building on Williamson and other scholars, Calliess and Zumbansen identify 12 possible 'generic governance mechanisms', ranging from state law, courts, and legal sanctions through tripartite arbitration and bilateral negotiation to reliance on social, relational (especially contractual), or corporate norms, and hierarchical corporate control (ibid: 118). What will be optimal or possible depends on the nature of transactions and relations between those engaged in them. But 'this map of governance mechanisms is . . . a toolbox from which tailor-made solutions for the governance of cross-border commerce are formed' (ibid: 113).

Much of this will not fall within the scope of law if, as I have proposed in Chapters 6 and 7, law is thought of as institutionalised doctrine. Again, public and private will be mixed in various combinations. Private ordering mechanisms 'take place in the shadow of national law' (Calliess and Zumbansen 2010: 117, 118), but often state law is not what shapes and guarantees these mechanisms in practice; nor does it necessarily produce or even recognise the regulatory forms seen as binding by those subject to them. What appears is a very complex regulatory picture – a kaleidoscope of governance methods in which the nature of 'the legal' remains to be clarified in transnational contexts.

Calliess and Zumbansen waver between treating the demarcation of 'the legal' as a non-issue – 'Whether transnational law . . . should be regarded as "law" in the traditional sense can remain outside the present analysis' (2010: 20) – and recognising its multifaceted importance as a practical matter (see also Michaels 2009: 250). A sociological approach could easily identify a range of phenomena to label as transnational law, but the issue of the *normative significance* of these phenomena has to be addressed. Several questions are interconnected. What, if anything, does law do which can be considered distinctive? Does law have a specific function? Does it have a specific kind of authority (a claim to bind those it addresses) and legitimacy (recognition as an established order or system)?

Calliess and Zumbansen deal only unsystematically, somewhat inconclusively, and at times opaquely with these questions, approaching them from a number of viewpoints. Following Luhmann's systems theory, they see law as reconstructing conflicts, alienating them from the social contexts in which they arise, and redefining them in terms of the binary legal/illegal code (2010: 44–5, 51), a process which in no way depends on state institutions and can be applied 'into the last corners of societal organization' (ibid: 77). But surely this admitted circularity (law is communication about what is legal) in no way solves the problem of what the term 'law' might embrace or exclude,[2] though it indicates a degree of disembedding of

---

2 As emphasised in earlier chapters, this is not a call for a definition of law. What is needed is a means of (i) recognising (for juristic purposes) degrees of normative significance in various kinds of regulation (such as Calliess's and Zumbansen's generic governance mechanisms), and (ii) provisionally marking out (for sociological purposes) a research field of transnational law.

the legal from the social; a process by which law separates from social relations and seeks a special kind of functional legitimacy.

Elsewhere Calliess and Moritz Renner (2009: 267) have been more explicit. In Luhmann's thinking, they note, the sole function of law is 'the stabilization of normative expectations', the selection and upholding of such expectations even in the face of disappointment (i.e. failure to realise the expectations in practice). Transnational governance regimes that take on this function can develop into legal systems. The function involves more than providing useful regulation (which non-legal social norms can do in many contexts) because it relates to 'society as a whole' (ibid: 266). This description might be taken to mean that law has to be significant for (stabilising normative expectations in) social organisation *in general*, not just for regulating specific social tasks or functions.

Whether this systems theory approach is a useful or even coherent way to iden-tify law in transnational regulation is debatable. Elsewhere, Calliess and Zumbansen write in ways that suggest something like the idea of law as institutionalised doc-trine I advocated earlier. A 'private legal system' would be one that could 'bundle private governance mechanisms which fulfil *legislative*, *adjudicative*, and *enforcement* functions into an effective and operational regime' (2010: 120, my emphasis). But in 'the context of the institutional organisation of modern cross-border commerce . . . purely private legal systems in praxis are rare', and state law 'often suppresses any potential competition to its traditional claim to be the supreme ruler of society' (ibid: 120, 121). Thus, effective enforcement would be crucial for an autonomous private legal system, but Calliess and Zumbansen note that such enforcement devices as diminishing deviant members' reputations, threatened exclusion from the regulated community, or direct coercion will often be controlled or even prohibited by state law. So it seems that – as suggested earlier – the institutionalisation of regulation as law will often be a matter of degree. Calliess and Renner (2009: 268–9, 274–5) have suggested that indicators of steps towards this institutionalisation might be the 'verbalisation of conflicts' in adjudicatory hearings of some kind and the 'stabilising of normative expectations' by publicising past regulatory decisions as precedents.

Internet standard-setting: bottom-up regulation

Whatever the complexities, these ideas point to a need to think about law in radically new ways: emphasising the creation of norms and their authority in 'bottom-up' processes of negotiation and consensus formation. At the heart of Cal-liess's and Zumbansen's book is a model that they use to 'bracket off' for (presumably temporary) purposes of analysis almost all concern with 'top-down' law-making or law-validating by state institutions, or with the element of coercive authority (*vol-untas*) in law.

The concept of 'rough consensus and running code' (hereafter RCRC) refers to a process of global technical standard setting and rule making for the Inter-net, embodied in the long-established 'request for comments procedure' in which technical experts, network designers, system operators, researchers, and Internet

enthusiasts with varying degrees of technical experience engage in collective deliberation and experimentation aimed at producing agreed technical standards for the
operation of the Internet.

As Calliess and Zumbansen describe RCRC, its most important characteristic is
its informal and largely anti-hierarchical orientation. Debate is neither restricted nor
ended by the acts of any established authority nor by majority votes. Nor do membership rules decide participation in the working groups that deliberate on standards;
anyone can be involved. Discussion is guided only by occasional provisional decla-
rations by an ad hoc chairperson that a 'rough consensus' has been reached on an
intermediate issue or a final conclusion. A proposed standard may then be published
for further consideration. A recommended draft standard might eventually follow.
In the 'recognition phase' the deliberating community decides whether to adopt
the standard in practice. Finally, if it gains broad acceptance, it may become a 'full
standard' in the 'binding phase', analogous to 'running code' – that is, to 'a program
that functions in practice and is widespread in terms of its installed basis' (2010: 136).

One might wonder whether this has anything to do with transnational law. After
all, RCRC concerns merely *technical* standards. The Internet Engineering Task Force,
which oversees this governance mechanism, writes on its website: 'We try to avoid
policy and business questions as much as possible.'[3] But, as discussions of implicit
politics in accounting practices have shown, technical norms can have a wider resonance (Calliess and Zumbansen 2010: 256–7) and 'potentially significant values and
policy choices can be embedded into the Internet's technical architecture' (Berman
2007b: 1222–3; see also Froomkin 2003: 809–10).

More problematic is the fact that the Internet as a social network is very different
from, for example, transnational economic networks. Its underlying value (the value
animating those actively promoting it for its own sake) might be seen as one of openness, inclusiveness, and comprehensiveness. The wider its reach and the more uniform
its technology, the more successful its operation. But this is not the case necessarily
for other transnational networks. A business network may prioritise cooperation and
consensus among its members, but its orientation will be to its members' profit, and
it has no need to aim at openness and inclusiveness. Indeed, probably the opposite:
it is likely to protect its collective interest against the interests of outsiders. The issue
of power within such a network, and in relation to those outside it, becomes very
important. What may drive the Internet community is the shared ultimate value of
promoting communication (Froomkin 2003: 810–12), but what primarily drives
commercial networks is usually cooperation for individual profit.

This element of power is absent from Calliess's and Zumbansen's discussion of
RCRC.[4] Indeed, this standard-creating process has appeared to some as a close approxi-
mation of Habermas's communicative rationality in operation – oriented to the

---

3 Accessed June 7, 2017.
4 It is intriguing, however, to contrast the remarkable formal detail of published regulations, e.g. as to
  how, and by whom, deliberative processes are to be overseen (Internet Engineering Task Force 2015),
  with the extreme nonlegalistic informality which the regulations are apparently intended to ensure.

production of mutual understanding (Froomkin 2003). Calliess and Zumbansen make much of it as a regulatory model: it is 'a mixed, public-private, dynamic norm-creation process' and 'a particular form of societal self-governance' (2010: 10) that complements municipal and international regulation. It links substance and procedure, regulation and coordination, and shows a way to legitimise regulation through its multistage facilitation of deliberation (ibid: 134, 143–4; Calliess 2007: 479–81). Whether or not it is really an island of pure communicative rationality in a sea of competing interests, it does at least suggest, as an idealised model of 'bottom-up' rule making, something radically different from familiar models of municipal and international law.

Law and transnational networks of community

Where does this leave the mapping of transnational law? The main mapping tools that have been mentioned here have been dichotomies: private and public, bottom-up and top-down, substance and procedure, *ratio* (principle and reason) and *voluntas* (coercive authority),[5] and doctrine and its institutionalisation. All of these dichotomies are problematic if taken too seriously. They are useful for provisionally orienting initial inquiry, allowing a start to be made somewhere in systematic analysis, and temporarily separating out different aspects of law for purposes of study.

The significance of the dichotomies depends on context. As long as the idea of institutionalised doctrine, for example, remains context-free, it offers a conceptualisation of law only at the most basic and abstract level. To progress further, it is necessary to link this skeletal idea of 'the legal' to an adequate concept of 'the social' – the social realm to which law relates. The nature of the social may, for example, determine what kind of agencies for institutionalising doctrine as law can be envisaged. Sociolegal scholars are used to thinking of the social mainly as (national) 'society' – 'law in society'. But if transnational law relates to social relations extending *across* the borders of national societies, it may be better to see the social in a way that avoids these national connotations.

The social can be thought of as made up of networks of interpersonal relations. But, to be subject to any kind of stable regulation, these networks themselves must have some minimum degree of stability. They might therefore be thought of as networks of *community*. Some scholars have linked transnational law and global legal pluralism to an idea of 'multiple normative communities',[6] seeing these as the source and locus of transnational regulation (Djelic and Quack 2010a). David Held (2010) has written of 'overlapping communities of fate' to emphasise a restructuring of politics beyond and in the state. But it is important to be cautious in invoking the typical, warm, fuzzy, somewhat nostalgic idea of community that, for many, is wholly out of touch with a contemporary Western world of individualistic, transient social relations. As Calliess and Zumbansen (2010: 55) put the matter, with

5 See further, on the significance of the *voluntas/ratio* distinction, Cotterrell 1995: 165–6, 317–20.
6 Berman 2007b: 1157 (citing Robert Cover's work); Berman 2009, 2002: 472–90.

the 'ongoing privatisation of public spaces, the oft-praised notion of "communities". . . turns into a farce'.

I think that the concept of community is useful, indeed essential, to make sense of transnational law in sociolegal theory. However, it is very rare for a *rigorous* concept of community to be put forward in this context. 'Community' has to be drained of any residual romanticism and its different types identified insofar as they have a bearing on regulatory issues. Relations of community need to be seen as much more varied, flexible, fluid, and changeable than is envisaged in most appeals to 'community'.

For example, contractual relations (like all stable *instrumental*, especially economic, relations focused on common or convergent projects) can be treated as social relations of community, but so can social relations based on shared *ultimate values or beliefs* (perhaps, but not necessarily, religious beliefs). Community can also refer to social relations based purely on *affect* (emotional attraction or repulsion) or on a shared environment (for example of locality, language, history, custom) – what might be called common *tradition*. The different kinds of social bonds which these types of community suggest imply different regulatory needs and problems, and as social bonds they can be relatively enduring or transient, strong or weak. Most important, communal relations are not mutually exclusive. So any given person can participate simultaneously in a range of them.

It makes sense, therefore, to think of communal networks[7] that combine different types of social relations of community – instrumental, belief-based, affective, or traditional – but may be dominated by one or more of these types. It is easy to think of local, religious, financial, commercial, professional, scientific, kinship, friendship, linguistic, or ethnic networks of community in this way. These ideas about types of community and their regulation have been elaborated fully elsewhere (Cotterrell 2006; 2008c: 17–28, 363–72), but two aspects are especially important here: first, thinking in this way suggests that all relations of community are based on a degree of *mutual interpersonal trust* among their members (which gives them some stability and continuity); second, all have *regulatory needs* (for 'justice' and 'order') (Cotterrell 1995: 154–7, 316–7) that may or may not give rise to law in the form of institutionalised doctrine of some kind.

One might think of transnational networks of community as the ultimate source of their own legal regulation but, equally, as being subject to legal regulation created in other such networks that impinge on them. The socioeconomic networks in which Calliess's and Zumbansen's examples of transnational private law develop (e.g. transnational merchant law, corporate governance regimes, e-commerce arrangements, standard-setting organisations or associations) can easily be thought of in this way. So it is possible to envisage a kind of paradigm shift in legal inquiry provoked in part by the development of transnational law: a shift away from a

---

7 Throughout this book the terms 'communal network' and 'network of community' are used interchangeably.

limited nation-state focus and towards a new emphasis on the law-creating potential of complex, interpenetrating networks of social relationships of community.

Calliess and Zumbansen see the idea of analysing transnational private law in terms of community as 'promising' (2010: 39) but ultimately do not pursue it far. Two aspects, in particular, would certainly need examination. First, relations of community are almost always unequal, structured by power differentials, and the regulation created in them will reflect this. Municipal law reflects the power structures present in the networks of community that make up the national society; international law reflects the power relations of the 'international community'. Similarly, transnational law will reflect the distribution of power in transnational communal networks. Second, as most writers on transnational law regimes emphasise, a major issue for these regimes is their legitimacy (their recognition and acceptance as established) and authority (their capacity to bind those subject to them). So it is important to ask where their authority and legitimacy can come from if they cannot appeal to the democratic foundations on which municipal law is usually assumed to rely. From a law-and-community perspective, the answer would have to be found in the structure of networks of community themselves.

While the nature of relations of community is not Calliess's and Zumbansen's concern, their book contains discussions that indirectly bear on this. For example, they consider the operation of 'trustmark' systems in e-commerce, designed to build the confidence of economic actors, especially consumers, in the reliability of others with whom they plan to trade. In Internet transactions, where the usual resources of municipal law and the possibilities of dealing securely 'in its shadow' may not be available, the need to build confidence in the general reliability of potential trading partners becomes especially important, though clearly it is relevant in any environment where few opportunities exist to assess such matters personally. Trustmarks, like credit rating mechanisms, consumer satisfaction ratings, professional accreditations, and transaction insurance systems, are examples of devices for supporting mutual interpersonal trust in primarily economic networks of community. Thus they help (insofar as they are effective) to stabilise context-specific (Schultz 2011) expectations of justice and order.

In fact, the most interesting aspect of transnational trustmark and related systems, as described by Calliess and Zumbansen, is their *fragility*: the vulnerability of trusting relations, especially where interacting members of networks of community are (as in many Internet dealings) (i) physically remote from and entirely unknown to each other, (ii) single-shot transactors (as individual purchasers or sellers) rather than repeat players, and (iii) unable to judge probity on the basis of any personal, face-to-face interaction. Mutual interpersonal trust is fundamental to all social relations of community. Supporting it in the case of transnational networks is one of the most vital tasks of transnational regulation. Hence the development of 'trustmarks of trustmarks' (secondary trustmarks) and reliance on municipal law or, in the European context, Europe-wide regulation to support mutual interpersonal trust through its enforcement mechanisms wherever this is feasible (Calliess and Zumbansen 2010: 169–78).

Elaborating transnational legal doctrine

Where can transnational law find its legal authority and legitimacy or, more broadly, its practical guarantees of effectiveness? Most writers find these guarantees in an unstable mix of (i) the politically established authority of municipal law and international institutions, (ii) social sanctions having varying degrees of authority rooted in the nature and organisation of the regulated population, and (iii) considerations of mainly economic necessity and self-interest among the regulated. But some further progress might be made in considering how transnational regulation in general is developing and seeking effectiveness by emphasising its locus in networks of social relations of community. Here, analysis of transnational law parallels that of municipal law, because the authority and legitimacy of the latter are usually traced to the assumed structure of the national community, and democratic theories, elite theories, and social contract theories are the main tools employed in explanation.

In the national context the coercive authority (*voluntas*) of law is mainly associated with state power. The reason and principle of law (its *ratio*) is associated mainly with the expert elaboration of doctrine (primarily by judges in the common law world but also through legislative drafting, code-making, jurists' conceptualisations, and lawyers' practical problem-solving creativity). Both *voluntas* and *ratio* as essential elements of law can be seen as components of its overall authority: the former as law's political authority, the latter as what might be called its moral authority – its resonance with shared cultural understandings. As suggested earlier with regard to all such dichotomies, their separation is a matter of analytical convenience, a provisional contrasting of ultimately interdependent aspects of law.

How might the *voluntas* and *ratio* of transnational law be identified? In some respects it is easier to see how the transnational development of regulation creates new forms of *ratio* than how it builds *voluntas*. It may be that the nature of the sources of *ratio* of international law is not radically changed by the increasing application of this law to nonstate actors, even if the range of locations in which the *ratio* of international law is being developed is extending – a matter of the fragmentation of international law noted earlier. Equally, the processes of producing *ratio* in municipal law may not be changing in a fundamental way specifically as a result of transnationalism.

However, in the relatively 'bottom-up' creation of transnational private law, considerable change is surely occurring. Alongside familiar kinds of law-creating or law-interpreting agencies (courts, legislatures, administrative agencies, and international organisations), other agencies increasingly take part in shaping transnational regulatory doctrine. A space has been created, outside the normative reach of municipal authorities and international agencies established by treaties or conventions, for new agencies to elaborate the emerging *ratio* of transnational law.

Examples are commissions of private law experts drafting new 'model laws' available for adoption in national law or European law or through the choice of transacting parties. Notable products of this kind of enterprise are the Principles of International Commercial Contracts created by the International Institute for the

Unification of Private Law (UNIDROIT) and the Principles of European Contract Law drafted by the independent Commission on European Contract Law,[8] organised by the Danish lawyer Ole Lando. Insofar as these are 'private' (nongovernmental) productions of legal doctrine, they are elaborations of *ratio* without *voluntas*. They depend on voluntary adoption by those they are intended to regulate or on 'public' political incorporation into law.

Here, as elsewhere, however, the line between public and private is hard to draw. The Lando principles, for example, have contributed to broader private law unification initiatives pursued 'in the shadow' of the ongoing development of European Union law and political integration. The independently operating UNIDROIT is an intergovernmental organisation supported by 63 states as members. International public organisations or conventions often authorise the production of model law codes. The Convention on Contracts for the International Sale of Goods 1980, prepared by the United Nations Commission on International Trade Law (UNCITRAL), applies in general to contracts between parties based in states that have ratified the convention (currently 85) or where contracting parties have chosen this law to regulate their agreement. The UNCITRAL Model Law on International Commercial Arbitration has been used by many countries as the standard for reform of their national arbitration laws. The International Bar Association and the International Federation of Insolvency Practitioners were actively involved in UNCITRAL's drafting of a model law to regulate major corporate bankruptcies across national borders (Halliday and Carruthers 2007: 1183–4).

In general, jurists, whether independent or serving, directly or indirectly, state or international bodies, have acquired many new opportunities to serve as expert elaborators of *ratio*, as the possibilities for transnational law expand (Quack 2007).

Experts and nonexperts as law creators

It might be appropriate to introduce here yet another pragmatic (and ultimately problematic) dichotomy; one between 'experts' and 'nonexperts' as elaborators of *ratio*. In municipal law, legal doctrine is created mainly by legal experts (judges, legislative drafters, jurists, lawyers) but sometimes by others (nonlawyer legislators, administrative officials). Controversially, the idea has been mooted that 'lay' citizens can be seen as elaborators of legal doctrine when they interpret law in principled opposition to state authorities as a justification for their civil disobedience (Dworkin 1978: 206–22). In a transnational context, however, the scope for both expert and nonexpert elaboration of legal ideas seems greatly expanded. Much transnational regulation and policy formation now develops through the work of innumerable associations, organisations, or corporate bodies engaged in setting and developing standards.

Familiar examples of private transnational standard-setting organisations include the Forest Stewardship Council, 'a non-governmental, non-profit organization that

---

8 Succeeded by the Study Group on a European Civil Code; and see Jansen 2010: 59–76.

promotes the responsible management of the world's forests';[9] the European Advertising Standards Alliance, organised to promote 'responsible advertising by providing detailed guidance on how to go about advertising self-regulation across the Single Market'; and the food standards regulator GlobalG.A.P., which sets 'voluntary standards for the certification of agricultural products around the globe'.[10]

Alongside such bodies, others, established, authorised, or sheltered by municipal or international law, exist to elaborate transnational standards. How far these should be seen as public or private is often unclear (confirming the insecurity of the public-private dichotomy). Also often unclear is what counts as 'expert' in standard setting. Yet the authoritativeness of standard setting or rule declaring by bodies that lack access to some kind of coercive (*voluntas*) authority and rely on voluntary compliance may depend on how far these bodies enjoy respect for their (not necessarily legal) expertise or on the basis that they adequately represent the participants in the networks of community they purport to regulate.

Possibilities of *democratising* (beyond domination by experts) the elaboration of regulatory *ratio* are surely greatly expanded in transnational settings. The power of state legal authorities in national contexts to destroy any competing nonstate sources of law – what Robert Cover (1983: 40, 53) described as their 'jurispathic' role – is typically great. In transnational contexts, however, where the writ of municipal law does not necessarily run, or run smoothly, these jurispathic possibilities are far fewer. Numerous sources from which competing kinds of *ratio* could be created may exist. What could give them authority? What could make their doctrinal *ratio* persuasive? One important factor might be democratic mandate, or the overwhelming authority of mass popular support.

Calliess's and Zumbansen's invocation of Rough Consensus and Running Code as a regulatory model provides food for thought here. Recall, first, that the members of the working groups whose deliberations produce binding Internet standards are not necessarily 'experts', and no one, it seems, inquires into the levels of expertise of those participating. What determines whether the ideas formed in the process of deliberation prevail is simply the evolution of 'rough consensus'. Second, recall that there are no membership rules for working groups – anyone can join. So there are no fixed boundaries of the communal network of these Internet standard makers. Yet, through a process of collective deliberation and consensus formation, they build standards.

Can wider lessons be learned from this? First, the development of transnational law might imply a revision of the whole idea of 'legal' expertise. Regulation intended to be meaningful, authoritative, and capable of attracting support in networks of community could be produced not necessarily by people with juristic expertise but by standard setters knowledgeable in the specific kinds of regulatory problems that exist in those networks, that is, experts in functionally specific areas

9 On the FSC's certification system, see Maguire 2013: 273–92.
10 Quotations in the text are from the websites of the organisations mentioned (accessed June 7th 2017). See further e.g. Scott et al 2011: 6–11.

rather than juristic generalists. Taking the point one step further: is the whole idea that the expert's view should be privileged put in contention? In municipal law contexts, the authority of lawyers, judges, and legislators is supported by their position in the structures of 'official' power in the nation-state. If these power structures no longer operate in the transnational realm or at least are contested and unclear, the authority of expertise may dissolve into the issue of how acceptable is the *ratio* – the reason and principle of regulatory doctrine – which people claiming expertise actually produce.

Second, the RCRC example is a reminder that, in thinking about the production of *ratio*, boundaries around networks of community are not needed. Membership can be open and in constant flux. Ralf Michaels (2009: 253) criticises appeals to 'community' in analysing transnational law partly on the ground that there would be a need for 'some kind of boundaries, a distinction of inside and outside', and it may be hard to identify such boundaries. But this problem does not arise if communities are seen as types of social relations combining and recombining, and not as 'fixed' social objects.

The open communities of RCRC might be seen as not unconnected with the open organisation of mass opinion on a huge scale through the Internet by transnational organisations such as the online activist community Avaaz, which (as of 2017) claimed to have 44 million members worldwide. Internet 'referenda', coordinated by such campaigning bodies, mobilise the sheer power of numbers – mass transnational plebiscitary voting from the computer keyboard or smartphone – to influence legislators and governments by means that entirely bypass any appeal to expertise or any membership rules for participation in opinion formation.

Coercion and effectiveness in transnational law

Where can transnational law find its coercive authority (*voluntas*)? And how far is some kind of *voluntas* necessary to guarantee its effectiveness? As Calliess's and Zumbansen's book makes clear, and as most discussions of transnational law confirm, this law relies in many ways on the established coercive authority of municipal law, and of international law underpinned by the support of nation-states. Thus, contemporary *lex mercatoria*, developed through private arbitration practice and sometimes described as an autonomous nonstate transnational commercial law, in fact involves 'a continuous competition and interplay between state and non-state institutions' (Michaels 2007: 465), and the UN Convention on the Recognition and Enforcement of Foreign Arbitral Awards has been called an 'historic milestone' in linking 'the private law' created by international commercial arbitration to the enforcement guarantees of municipal law (Rödl 2008: 746–7). Prospects for further harnessing the coercive authority of municipal law may also lie in the development of conflict of laws rules to allow a wider recognition in state law of regimes of regulation chosen by transnational transacting parties (e.g. Rödl 2008; Wai 2008: 123–5; and see Muir Watt 2016).

Ultimately, the coercive authority of *municipal* law reflects the power structures of networks of community that make up the nation-state and the mechanisms of consent formation that exist within them – matters that political theorists have usually analysed in terms of democratic theory, elite theory, and social contract theory. Can parallels exist in transnational networks of community? I referred earlier to processes of mass opinion formation through organisations such as Avaaz. Mainly because of the communication possibilities opened up by the Internet, opportunities for democratic will formation can be extended transnationally, theoretically without limit. Transnational referenda and plebiscites, as well as the organisation of lobbying and campaigning unconstrained by national borders, now become entirely feasible as a matter of technical organisation, with issues of representativeness obscured to some extent by the availability of huge numbers of participants. While such devices seem limited as a means of producing any adequately elaborated *ratio* of regulation (often being restricted to yes/no answers to referendum questions), they may indicate ways of giving a kind of democratic foundation for coercive authority (*voluntas*) to be exerted by transnational agencies. The idea of a global public opinion – however crude the means of measuring it may be for the foreseeable future – is not fantasy.

To suggest that possibilities for *voluntas* depend on the structure of transnational networks of community is not inconsistent with the claim made earlier that 'community' should be thought of in terms not of bounded entities but of often flexible and fluid social relations (nevertheless with a degree of stability based on mutual interpersonal trust). It can be assumed that participation in communal relations – even if temporary and limited in scope – is often valuable to members of networks of community. Hence, as legal sociologists have long emphasised, social sanctions of expulsion from or ostracism by those networks can be powerfully coercive – indeed, often far more so than the sanctions of municipal law in practice (e.g. Bernstein 2001: 1737–9). And studies of transnationally organised business networks often identify strong pressures for conformity in them to their dominant norms of self-regulation (Djelic and Quack 2010a: 389–90). Among specific sanctions are reduction in reputation among peers and business partners; loss of opportunities for productive dealing with other members of the communal network; denial of access to knowledge available to other members; blacklisting; less favourable terms and conditions of trade; less availability of cooperation from other members; and, ultimately, exclusion from the communal network.

To understand how these sanctions work it would be necessary not only to differentiate among different types of social relations of community and the different ways they combine in networks but also to examine the structure of power relations in communal networks. So, just as sociolegal research has examined the power structures that surround the operation of municipal law, the sociology of transnational law requires further empirical study of corresponding power structures in transnational networks and their bearing on regulation.

For most networks of community, the coercive authority supporting their regulation will be seen to come partly, as suggested earlier, from the internal structure of the network concerned. Clearly this is an image of *self*-regulation, consistent with the experience of participants in many such networks and also with many current assumptions about the limited utility of 'external' (e.g. state) regulation. A focus on transnational private law tends to direct attention to internally generated regulation in communal networks. But it is vital to note that networks of community do not exist in isolation. Their members are usually members of other networks, and networks of community may exist within (or in the field of influence of) larger or more powerful networks or in complex articulation with other networks. So the regulatory authority that operates will usually be a mix of internally and externally generated regulation.

Again, there is no need to think in terms of rigidly bounded communities confronting each other. The appropriate image is rather of intersecting (but fluid and frequently changing) networks of social relations of community. So sources of coercive authority in any given network may be varied. Transnational networks will often be subject to the regulatory authority of states, international networks of states, and other nonstate networks of community.

Conclusion

In this chapter, the problem of conceptualising transnational law has been addressed in terms of recent sociolegal literature on transnational private law. Only a few themes in a vast subject have been brought to light. Nevertheless, taken together they suggest a necessary displacement in thinking about the nature of law and society.

Jurists, at least, may find it hard to accept a reconceptualisation of the idea of 'law' to make possible an analysis of the whole range of types of doctrine (e.g. guidelines, principles, concepts, codes, norms, standards) that are now being associated with transnational law. There may, similarly, be resistance to a reconceptualisation of the social, to see it no longer as (national) 'society' but instead as networks of community that may be subnational, national, or transnational in extent. Yet, calls to discard a focus on 'society' and to view the social in more flexible terms to take account of the development of transnational social relations are now familiar in sociological literature (e.g. Beck and Sznaider 2006; Urry 2000). As regards transnational regulation itself, lawyers and sociolegal scholars are busy analysing its many aspects and its diverse social contexts.

Indeed, large forces are at work encouraging new thinking about the nature of law and about the nature of the social. I referred earlier to debates about the efficiency or 'competence' of state regulation. The capacity of the state to regulate is often an ideologically charged issue, but, whatever the nature of the debate, it feeds into queries about the general regulatory capacity and limits of state law and so of the significance (or insignificance) of 'law' as it is most commonly understood by governments and lawyers. Interest in soft law, in self-regulation, in informal regulation, 'voluntary' standards, and social norms, is spurred in part by neoliberal political and other campaigning movements interested in reducing as much as possible the use of law in its usual 'hard' sense as municipal law and often also suspicious of international law. At the same time, doubts are often expressed about traditional ideas of state sovereignty that assume nation–states have full control or direct supervision of all socioeconomic regulation inside their territory. In the face of these accumulating doubts, the idea of analysing regulatory needs and problems by reference to a social realm not defined by nation–state boundaries becomes theoretically attractive and increasingly realistic.

Transnational law remains an imprecise notion. The concepts available for its analysis are often no more than fragile dichotomies applicable only provisionally and pragmatically. Nevertheless, the transnational extension and transformation of law is likely to become ever more clearly one of the most urgent foci for the development of practical strategies by jurists. As has been suggested, the most difficult juristic problems of transnational law are (i) to map its scope (and so to rethink the scope of the juristic role transnationally), and (ii) to locate the kinds of authority that can support transnational regulation and find reliable ways to assess these juristically. The first of these problems has been the central focus of this chapter. The second is examined more fully in the next.

9

TRANSNATIONAL LEGAL AUTHORITY

Many attempts by legal scholars are now made to conceptualise the authority that can support transnational regulation. Almost invariably – and perhaps unsurprisingly – these adopt juristic orientations strongly reflecting the experience of Western state law. In this chapter I want to argue, however, that such orientations are inappropriate in considering transnational regulatory developments that are not easily subsumed into state law or into international law treated as a consensual exercise of states' law-making authority. A better starting point, it will be claimed, is to treat authority generally as a *practice* and *experience* to be identified and interpreted sociologically. On the basis of such an approach, possibilities for reshaping juristic outlooks in realistic ways arise.

Drawing on Max Weber's analyses of legitimate domination, the chapter identifies a variety of bases of authority on which transnational regulation may rely; it also considers the cultural sources of legitimacy for this regulation that can arise in what I called, in Chapter 8, communal networks. It concludes that, given the complex conditions of existence of transnational legal authority, this authority will be shifting, variable, and constantly renegotiated. It is hard to capture in illuminating ways by means of projects aimed at presenting authority as a universal phenomenon having the *same essential character* wherever found. Understanding the variety of sources, types, and expressions of authority requires study of the kinds of political structures and communal networks in which transnational regulation arises and in which authority claims are made, recognised, and judged.

Conceptualising authority for *explanatory*, descriptive purposes involves empirical study of practices and experiences associated with such claims. The central question is: which phenomena are to be seen as involving authority? Conceptualising authority *normatively*, to consider how it might be justified, involves asking for whose benefit justifications are needed and by whom these justifications are to be accepted. So, in transnational regulatory contexts, attention to context seems especially needed.

The transnational problem

It seems that the idea of authority creates much uncertainty even before the task of adapting it to an increasingly complex world of transnational regulation is attempted. In the context of municipal state legal systems, lawyers often avoid difficult questions about authority by talking instead of *validity*. They test the validity of rules, procedures, or decisions as 'legal' by tracing their formal derivation from largely settled and accepted sources of legal authority in constitutions, statutes, or judicial precedents. Issues of authority become, in everyday legal practice, mainly technical questions about the proper normative interpretation of actions and situations in relation to these sources. For legal philosophers, deeper questions about the ultimate meaning and justification of authority remain.

As it becomes necessary to consider the nature of legal authority beyond state law – that is, beyond the context of law established and enforced by agencies of a state having a jurisdiction over what John Austin (1885a: 220ff) called an 'independent political society' – familiar juristic assumptions are fundamentally challenged. Juristic thought, reflecting state law experience, tends to presuppose authority as a matter of settled *hierarchy*. This can be theorised as 'chains' or 'levels' of authority such as those in which secondary rules authorise the production and management of primary rules (Hart) or in which more 'concrete' or specific norms are authorised by 'higher' or more fundamental ones (Kelsen). Typically, the state is seen as the ultimate focus of all governmental authority – exercising, in Austin's (1885a: 220) simple image, the sovereign authority of a 'determinate and common superior'. This conception of authority ties law to the political structures of the state; it could be termed a conception of the political authority of law.

Insofar as this outlook prevails, lawyers in modern advanced societies are comfortable with a largely *monistic* view of authority.[1] All legal authority is seen as traceable to a *single* unifying source or at least to a strictly limited number of sources existing in adequately settled relation to one another. Federal structures pose no theoretical problems as long as the allocation of powers which federalism makes possible is defined by an effective state constitution. Disputes over the boundaries of federal powers are then usually seen as practical issues of interpretation rather than issues about the very nature of legal authority. And the authority of international law need not be problematic either. Seen as grounded in the consent of states, it can be subsumed in a monistic approach. A state's legal authority may be exercised across the whole political society (statewide), or localised to regulate only certain parts or aspects of it (intrastate), or applied to legal relations in the international sphere which consenting states together agree to regulate (interstate). Even when 'an international law above the state' is advocated, a jurist such as Kelsen could portray the authority of such a law monistically, extending the model of hierarchical (municipal) legal authority into a single, unifying, hierarchical structure of authority of the entire international order (Bernstorff 2010: 93–100).

---

1 See Chapter 6.

However, the gradual expansion of the range of types of *transnational* regulation recognised, in some degree, by various regulated populations as legally authoritative disrupts traditional juristic approaches to legal authority – challenging both the idea of hierarchy and that of monism. The well-recognised challenge now is of a 'collision' of legal 'discourses' (Teubner 1996; 2004) or an overlapping or confrontation of different regulatory regimes claiming independent jurisdiction over the same legal space (legal pluralism). Any hierarchies existing among these regimes are only partial and incomplete and may be controversial and readily challenged.

We have noted that international law itself is increasingly fragmented into diverse, not necessarily cohesive jurisdictions and regimes of regulation,[2] and relations between these international regimes and municipal state law and EU law are sometimes contested or unpredictable. And, as discussed in the previous chapter, forms of transnational regulation often now called transnational private law are produced 'bottom-up' through, for example, the interactions of lawyers organising cross-border transactions, arbitrators processing transnational commercial disputes, the economic networks of transnationally organised industries, the articulation of international financial systems, and the transnational effects of communications technology.

From a juristic perspective, the need is to establish reliable ways of working in a transnational environment in which previously stable anchors of authority often no longer hold. The central juristic challenge is ceasing to be merely to interpret and apply *established* legal authority; it is increasingly to identify, conceptualise, and evaluate authority as it operates *in an evolving practice*. The prospect of having to recognise legal authority as inherently relative arises. That is to say, lawyers will have the responsibility of assessing the relative weight of the authority claims of different legal orders which conflict or compete with one another or even deny one another's existence as valid, operative law. They will have to judge *to what extent and for what purposes* (rather than whether or not) particular kinds of regulation can be authoritative as valid law.

My claim is that neither traditional, state-oriented, juristic experience (however imaginatively reinterpreted) nor the mainstream of contemporary legal philosophy (which has, until recently, shown little interest in examining the new forms and conditions of regulation) has the resources at present to organise adequately even the main elements of this new transnational world of law. There is a preliminary need for a sociologically focused consideration of the way authority is being understood as a practical matter, though often in contested, contradictory, and inchoate ways, in its various contemporary regulatory contexts.[3] It is necessary to examine authority empirically as a social phenomenon (as the *practice* of claiming it and the *experience* of accepting it) in these changing contexts, recognising that their relations with state law are often unclear, fluid, shifting, or evolving.

Given the rapidly changing landscape of authority as practice and experience and the array of unpredictable regulatory challenges arising in it, this is a more

---

2 See p 106, and e.g. Varella 2013, Broude 2013, and Koskenniemi and Leino 2002.
3 Quack 2016 provides an excellent window on important parts of this terrain.

pressing inquiry than that of asking whether any essential and timelessly 'true' justification for authority can be found. And a sociolegal inquiry might indicate ways of going beyond the important and extensive efforts of forward-looking legal scholars today to explore 'outwards' from established legal experience gained in nation-state contexts. Jurists may need to draw 'inwards' (into their legal worldview), material – for example principles, institutional forms, normative problems, and conceptualisations – from kinds of regulatory experience and practice existing entirely outside the familiar thought-ways of state law.

Some limits of juristic approaches

In general, juristic scholars seek to engage with transnational developments by adapting, extending, or transforming ideas that are important in Western municipal legal systems or applying familiar juristic theories[4] of law that are themselves grounded in the experience of these systems.

Thus, some important approaches to legal transnationalism in the juristic literature have extended ideas of constitutionalism and principles underlying constitutional law in advanced Western polities to the transnational arena (e.g. Walker 2002). Other approaches extend procedural or organisational principles of public law familiar in these polities into a vision of 'global administrative law' (Kingsbury 2009). But constitutional approaches tend to search for some sense of ordered hierarchy in the transnational arena by analogy with the constitutional structures of states. Global administrative law, in Benedict Kingsbury's well-known conception, seeks 'the attributes, constraints, and normative commitments that are immanent in public law' and recognises a need to emphasise and build universally 'the (tempered) requirements of publicness in law' (2009: 30, 55).[5] On such a view, regimes of private ordering are hard to recognise as legally authoritative (ibid: 57). But it has been claimed (and the discussion in the previous chapter may support this claim) that private actors 'are now at the heart of the production of transnational law' (Devaux 2013: 843–4; see also Duval 2013: 824).

As Nico Krisch has emphasised, a focus on constitutionalism is hard to adopt in the transnational arena because, in its dominant modern form (providing the normative foundation for government), constitutional authority has been thought to presuppose some idea of a supporting, legitimising community – 'the people' – which hardly seems to exist on a transnational basis (Krisch 2010: 55–6; cf Walker 2015: 101). In fact, I shall argue, transnational legal authority *does* need to be understood in relation to an idea of 'community', but this idea must be understood

---

4 The literature shows, for example, frequent efforts to apply Hart's concept of law, a theoretical model that ultimately presupposes a hierarchically ordered, bounded body of rules founded on a unifying rule of recognition: see e.g. Daniels 2010, Kingsbury 2009, and Duval 2013.

5 For commentary see Somek 2009, suggesting that the point of the GAL project 'is to emphasize that what used to be the paradigmatic make-up of the modern "regulatory state" is merely a limiting case of how administrative processes have come to be reenacted on a global scale' (p 986).

sociologically and examined empirically. It is not productive to try to build on rhetorical appeals to a global 'international community', understood as a diffuse *demos*, to find democratic legitimacy for transnational constitutionalism. Neil Walker notes that constitutional law, '*the* framing law of the modern age', always presents itself 'as the authoritative voice of the people of a particular place over that same particular place' (2010: 22; italics in original). Perhaps 'place' is not as essential as this suggests, but *some kind* of particularity of a constitutional community is essential, and a sociological perspective is needed to examine empirically what kinds of community exist transnationally to support regulation.

In fact, 'a constitutional, hierarchical order seems contrary to the world we inhabit' (Shaffer 2012: 571). But Krisch notes that many juristic approaches that seek to escape ordered hierarchy and adopt a pluralistic approach (emphasising the diversity of distinct, autonomous legal regimes and forms of legal authority in the transnational world) ultimately overlay this pluralist openness and tolerance with some overarching, organising, *controlling* principles. He sees, for example, Mattias Kumm's 'cosmopolitan constitutionalism' as 'embedded in a thick set of overarching norms, such as subsidiarity, due process, or democracy, that are meant to direct the solution of conflicts'; Mireille Delmas-Marty advocates 'overarching rules, softened by way of margins of appreciation and balancing requirements', and Paul Schiff Berman's ideas for managing conflicts in global legal pluralism recall 'constitutionalist instruments for accommodating diversity' that reflect devolutionist ideas and models of consocation (Krisch 2010: 74–5).

However, Krisch himself is forced to ask which polities 'deserve respect and tolerance' in the global legal pluralism that he terms postnational law. He answers that this will depend on how far these polities are 'based on practices of public autonomy: on social practices that concretize the idea of self-legislation', on the strength of 'participatory practices' supporting them and on how convincingly they try 'to balance inclusiveness and particularity' (ibid: 101). These are terms that seem to carry a freight of implicit Western public law principle.

From a quite different perspective, Hans Lindahl (2010: 54) insists that all legal orders in the postnational world must be understood as unities with distinct jurisdictional boundaries 'because boundaries are the necessary condition of legal order'; the possibility of integrating political plurality 'in a higher order legal unity' thus depends on legal boundaries being 'open to reformulation'. Juristic thought has often sought normative unity in law, and legal theory has found many ways to conceptualise this (Cotterrell 2003: 8–11).

But it may be that transnational regulation does not operate – or does not operate only – in terms of bounded regimes and that the idea of such regimes is a projection of the idea of state territorially focused jurisdiction that may be waning in transnational conditions in favour of more 'porous', graduated, indistinctly delimited spheres of shifting, negotiated authority and jurisdictional reach. For example, the more that law in transnational conditions can be seen as providing guidance (through a variety of normative devices) as well as control (through positive mandatory rules), the more it becomes possible to think of law as contributing to a complex normative web of indefinite and changing shape, rather than as the defining structure of a fixed jurisdictional entity.

In the light of such illustrations of recent juristic work, it appears that legal scholars seeking ways to manage transnational conflicts of authority tend to be drawn back to prescriptions and principles that in some way (perhaps inevitably) reflect the juristic techniques or underlying political principles of the state legal systems most familiar to them. It may be that juristic thought, insofar as it operates independently of sociological and historical inquiry, lacks the resources, at present, to organise normatively (while respecting the diversity of) global legal pluralism – the largely chaotic overlay of (i) municipal (state) jurisdictions including their extraterritorial extensions, (ii) international legal regimes of many kinds, (iii) established transnational systems of (what is usually seen as) 'private' legal ordering, and (iv) forms of regulation emerging to govern communal networks that are transnational in scope or effect.[6]

There is a tendency in conceptualising legal transnationalism not only to interpret empirical reality through the lens of established juristic thought but also sometimes to apply wishful thinking to it, imagining a global normative realm that is hard to relate to sociopolitical reality. Harold Berman, for example, writes of an emerging 'world law' governing 'emerging world society'. To speak of the 'transnational', he suggests, is to refer back to the 'national' and so does not adequately indicate 'the new era that all humanity has entered', one of 'global interdependence' in which 'all inhabitants of Planet Earth share a common destiny' (Berman 1995: 1619, 1621).

Other writers herald a world in which rights might be effectively asserted without reference to state power. Cosmopolitans, writes Jean Cohen, 'construe the expansion and individualization of international criminal law, the proliferation of human rights discourse, and calls for humanitarian and democratic interventions as indicative of an emergent consensus on the basic values of the "international community"'; the task is 'to order and regulate the world community so as to *protect the rights of world citizens*' (Cohen 2006: 485–6; italics in original). But Cohen insists that this cosmopolitan portrayal of law is no more than a cloak for the self-interested interventionist strategies of some states in relation to others.

Idealised global visions of law (to which not only juristic thought is susceptible) are often dreams of new kinds of monistic authority or reference points from which an overarching legal order might be created. Yet such general visions of law's future are hard to support empirically. Similar criticisms can be made of visions of a 'global legal culture' (Menyhart 2003; Friedman 2002) as emergent or desirable. These are close relatives of the premature or overgeneralised 'convergence' claims sometimes propounded by sociologists and political scientists to suggest that polities, societies, or cultures are gradually tending towards a practically comprehensive global uniformity.

---

6 See Chapter 7.

Authority and legitimacy in Weber

It may be best to set aside, temporarily, all juristic presumptions in examining transnational legal authority and to consider how the issues might be approached sociolegally – seeing the practices and experiences of authority as empirical social phenomena and considering how they can be observed and interpreted in the varied contexts of transnational regulation. Max Weber (1968: 953, 954) noted 'the generally observable need of any power . . . to justify itself. . . . [H]e who is more favoured feels the never ceasing need to look upon his position as in some way "legitimate". . . . [T]he continued exercise of every domination . . . always has the strongest need of self-justification through appealing to the principles of its legitimation.' But, in ordinary usage, terms such as power, legitimacy, and authority are often imprecise or confused. And many different conceptions appear in the scholarly literature.

Victor Muñiz-Fraticelli writes that 'only by making a *claim* to legitimacy does the exercise of power become authoritative' (2014: 563). Susan Marks sees legitimation as 'the process by which authority *comes to seem* valid and appropriate' (2000: 19). In other formulations, legitimacy is 'the right to rule and the *recognition by the ruled* of that right' (Jackson et al 2012: 1051). It 'is generally defined as the reasons why citizens accept power' entailing 'a voluntary *subjection to a claim* to authority' (Devaux 2013: 845).[7]

A sociolegal approach needs not conclusive, timeless definitions of authority and legitimacy but only ways of understanding these ideas that can help in provisionally identifying relevant social practices. It might be tempting, then, to think of authority as something primarily *claimed* in support of power by its holders and legitimacy as something primarily *conferred* on power by those subject to it or who observe it; that is, legitimacy indicates an acceptance of the claim of authority as successfully made. Some such rough distinction could be useful in recognising authority and legitimacy as social phenomena despite much variation in usage of these terms.

It has been suggested that legitimacy, seen in such a way, 'must be projected *by* someone' (Thomas 2014: 747–8; italics in original); there 'must be some social group that judges the legitimacy of an actor or action based on the common standards acknowledged by this group' (ibid, quoting K. P. Coleman). 'Legitimacy is generated in a social sense through the creation of communities of practice' (ibid: 745). This suggests the importance of studying social groups and networks that may confer legitimacy on the authorities that purport to address them, that is, the importance of studying the various regulated populations over whom authority is claimed. It has been noted that the same authority claims may be legitimised by different communities[8] applying different standards of recognition (Thomas 2014: 748). At the same time, there may be conflicts between these standards.

---

7 Emphasis added in each of the quotations in this paragraph.
8 I prefer to call them communal networks to avoid the now often unrealistic idea of communities as distinct, bounded, and perhaps somewhat static entities.

Once it is recognised that networks of communal relations on which the legitimacy of regulation may depend can exist *intranationally, nationally*, or *transnationally*, the situation becomes potentially very complex. The authority of transnational regulation might rely on many different social sources of legitimacy. These sources (communal networks) may support the authority of many different kinds of regulation. Equally, the values, interests, allegiances, and established practices of these networks may conflict, so that different networks favour different kinds of authority and reject others.

In stable political societies, conflicts between different social sources of legitimacy for legal authority do not usually seem very significant. Politico-legal structures of state power are typically sufficiently firmly established as authoritative. The situation may, however, be far more complex when the question of legal authority beyond state borders is to be considered. Then it may be necessary to ask what kinds of authority claims can realistically be made and where support for them can be found.

How far can transnational regulatory authority be successfully claimed by extending – or developing analogies with – the established 'official' authority of law embedded in the political structures of the state? Alternatively, how far must it be traced to communal networks that exist transnationally? These networks are likely to foster their own kinds of authority to support the regulation they create for themselves, regulation reflecting their own cultural characteristics (that is, the shared values, beliefs, interests, traditions, history, and allegiances of their members). A sociolegal approach to transnational law must ask how far and in what ways available *political* or 'official' authority for this law (reflecting and extending that of state law) can interact with what can be called the *cultural* authority produced directly in communal networks, that is, authority arising from their own internal needs for regulation.

Weber's celebrated analysis of 'legitimate domination' (Weber 1968: 212–6) offers a useful way to consider claims of authority made for state law (and perhaps the extension of these claims into the transnational arena) in a far broader manner than is often done in juristic writing. Famously, Weber identified three pure types of authority in terms of the fundamentally different kinds of legitimacy that can support them. *Legal-rational authority* relies on an appeal to rational rules that are seen to confer such authority, and Weber notes that today 'the most common form of legitimacy is the belief in legality' (ibid: 37). It is easy to see that much juristic thought assumes this as its model of legitimate authority. The idea of legal-rational authority signals the importance of the clarity, rationality, hierarchical structure, consistent application, and practical effectiveness of rules conferring authority on officials of the state legal system. It suggests the central importance of constitutionalism and the rule of law.

But it is very important (particularly if something beyond established juristic thinking is needed in studying transnational regulation) to remember the two other pure types of authority in Weber's analytical scheme. He sees *traditional authority*, based on reverence for 'that which is customary and has always been so' (ibid: 954), as declining in importance in the modern world. Certainly, it may have limited relevance to the rapidly changing transnational arena. But the third Weberian type, *charismatic authority*, deserves careful consideration (Adair-Toteff 2005). It is authority founded on a belief, held by a leader's followers, in that leader's (real or imagined) exceptional personal qualities, such as invincibility, heroism, capability, foresight, wisdom, infallibility, saintliness, or rhetorical skill.

Charisma can be a property attributed not only to individual leaders but also to regimes, institutions, and offices (Weber 1968: 1139–41; Turner 2003: 9–10) which are thought to deserve special respect and deference because of some extraordinary quality they are seen (rightly or wrongly) to possess. Unlike the legal-rational and traditional types, charismatic authority is inherently unstable since it exists only as long as the followers' faith is sustained. So it tends in modern conditions to be routinized gradually into the more enduring form of legal-rational authority. In the sociological literature the concept of charismatic authority has uncertain status,[9] often being seen as a catch-all category for diverse kinds of authority that are hard to envisage in terms of the other two types (Turner 2003).

This Weberian schema allows a breakout beyond most juristic thinking about authority. First, authority *need not be wholly demarcated by rules*. For example, the charismatic authority of the 'great' common law judge, who develops the law in new ways not imagined by others (and perhaps at first considered bizarre and eccentric) but recognised ex post facto as valuable, is a personal authority grounded in a perceived[10] 'extraordinary' wisdom, foresight, and imagination. In effect, it is an authority superimposed on, or supplementary to, the 'routine' legal-rational authority that defines the judge's office and jurisdiction.[11]

Second, charismatic authority *makes a direct appeal to the regulated population* to acclaim acts done in the population's name or for its benefit. And such acts may include declaring policies or issuing guidance, no less than creating legal rules. For example, a belief in a regime's unfailing ability to provide economic prosperity can support its legitimacy. Charisma, as legitimate authority, can support any kind of governmental act aimed at the welfare of the communal network that sustains it. Hence it is not confined by the orthodox parameters of constitutionalism. To emphasise its significance is to recognise realistically the diverse ways in which regulatory authority is actually used in social life but also to highlight many potentially authoritarian, instrumentally justified forms of rule.

Finally, it seems reasonable to see the *authority of expertise* (Quack 2016) as a kind of charismatic authority. As already noted in Chapter 8, this is important in relation

---

9 See Joosse 2014 on misinterpretations of Weber's concept that have made it hard to use effectively.

10 It is important to see this as rooted in perceptions of those (lawyers) who observe and interpret the judge's acts, rather than in actual special qualities of the judge (though these special qualities may well exist). On charisma as residing solely in the perceptions of followers see Joosse 2014: 276.

11 Hence it can sometimes lift a judge's reputation significantly above that of many others holding formally superior judicial office. A well-known historical example is that of the American judge Learned Hand: see Dilliard 1960: vi, xxvi.

to many forms of transnational organisation where standard-setting bodies exist to regulate communal networks, such as those of transnational industries, cross-border trade and finance, information technologists, sports authorities, and transnational professions. These standard setters sometimes shelter under the authority of state or international law but often rely for their authority on their claim to special expertise in their field and on the support of those they regulate who believe the regulators' work to be useful for the well-being of the communal network. The rulings of such 'expert' bodies are often much more than guidance; they are intended to be followed. In some cases, indeed, the line between guidance and prescription may become blurred when membership in communal networks depends significantly on conformity to the governing norms of the network, but, equally, members' participation in the network may be more productive for them when they treat regulatory standards as best practice and as a valuable guide to achieving success.

For Weber (1968: 266–7), democratic processes involving the popular acclamation of rulers can be a way of legitimating charismatic authority. However, voting in periodic routine elections can probably best be seen as an exercise of legal-rational authority (to select representatives through formal electoral processes) by citizens. Standard-setting agencies are rarely democratically created, but they rely on *recognition* by the regulated, often on the basis of assumed expertise (Devaux 2013).

It can be said that the idea of charismatic authority indicates kinds of supplementary and transformative authority that play a major role (as expert authority) in those emerging structures of transnational regulation that are *entirely independent* of the established political structures of states. It might further be suggested that charismatic authority is the presently essential means by which transnational legal authority is *projected 'outwards'* beyond state legal authority (including its extension through the consent of states as international legal authority). For example, many writers have noted the emergence of transnational communal networks of judges (e.g. Slaughter 2002; 2003; Frishman 2013), as a consequence of which courts sometimes influence one another's practices across national boundaries and recognise the purely persuasive (that is, expert) authority of their fellows beyond their own jurisdictions.[12]

Expert authority as charismatic authority is a vehicle for both (i) sharing a kind of (persuasive) legal authority 'horizontally' between state-centred constitutional structures, and (ii) building new 'vertical' hierarchies of authority (through standard setting) outside these structures in the 'no-man's land'[13] of transnational interactions not effectively governed by states or international jurisdictions.

---

12 Glenn 1987 and Slaughter 2003: 193, 199–201. See also Flanders 2009. For a broader perspective see Glenn 2013: Part IV, especially 207–13, 220–22; and the country surveys in Groppi and Ponthoreau eds 2014. On limitations of such developments and controversies around them, see Lambert 2009 and McCrudden 2000.

13 Because of this location, expert authority has attracted understandable juristic criticism: e.g. Devaux 2013. Yet the operation of such authority is a sociolegal reality to which it will surely be necessary to adapt.

The practical authority of states as lawmakers

Today, political authority (the authority of states and their agencies and the extension of this authority into the transnational realm through international law) is largely Weber's legal-rational authority, supplemented with elements of charismatic and traditional authority. Weber thought that legal-rational authority in modern conditions was largely self-sustaining (legitimacy being produced through legality), but this is doubtful (Cotterrell 1995: 146–59). It relies ultimately on cultural sources of legitimacy (grounded in the interests, beliefs, values, allegiances, and traditions of the regulated population), even if in normal circumstances in stable, independent political societies these can typically be taken for granted.

Treating authority as a social phenomenon, a matter of practice and experience, we can ask how far law's political authority – its political frameworks seen as legitimate – is changing. How great is the capacity of states to supply political authority to support transnational law? If this question can be answered, it may become easier to see how and in what ways legitimacy for this law needs to be found elsewhere, in the cultural conditions of transnational communal networks themselves – that is, inside transnational law's diverse regulated populations.[14]

Clearly it is not possible to generalise far about the practical legal authority of contemporary states because this varies greatly. Legal philosophy might describe state authority normatively in universal theoretical terms (e.g. Raz 2009a: ch 13), but a sociolegal approach has to recognise many factors that affect a state's capacity successfully to claim authority over its citizens and attract legitimacy to the exercise of its governmental power through the use of law.

It is important to recognise that even in many strong, stable representative democracies this political authority is weakened in ways that seem often invisible to juristic thought. For example, *corruption* can break ties of official allegiance, seriously distorting the hierarchical flow of legal-rational authority and undermining the acceptance and exercise of it.[15] External *private forces* (powerful corporate interests, mass media pressure) sometimes affect the practical exercise of authority.[16] Tax evasion and avoidance and misuse of *public finances* can diminish financial resources available to make the exercise of state authority effective.[17] Where ideologies that

---

14 For a discussion of this issue in relation to transnational criminal law see Chapter 10.
15 See e.g. Graycar and Villa 2011 (New York City legislation on health, safety, human services, town planning, and other regulatory behaviour circumvented); Linde and Erlingsson 2013 (negative effect on attitudes to government); Clausen, Kraay, and Nyiri 2011 (negative effect on confidence in public institutions).
16 See e.g. Wilmarth 2013 (financial industry undermining or deterring government regulation).
17 Official UK statistics (HM Revenue and Customs 2016) estimate a 'tax gap' ('the difference between the amount of tax that should, in theory, be collected by [Revenue and Customs], against what is actually collected') in 2014–15 of £36 billion (6.5% of national total tax liabilities). Of this, £5.2 billion is attributed to 'evasion', £2.2 billion to 'avoidance', £3.6 billion to 'non-payment', £6.2 billion to the 'hidden economy', and £4.8 billion to 'criminal attacks'. See also e.g. Kleinbard 2011, 2013 (current practices of and possibilities for large-scale corporate tax avoidance); Avi-Yonah 2000 (consequences of international competition and the use of tax havens); Schaeffer 2002 (causes and effects of misuse of public finances).

consistently favour the 'private' over the 'public' and attach little significance to ideas of 'public interest' and the 'common good' (Tamanaha 2006; Antonio 2013) become dominant, they may eventually *demoralise public officials* and representatives and affect their projects and policies, perhaps leading to a general decline in their quality.[18] And resources of *expertise* available to parts of the 'private sector' are often superior to those on which public regulatory agencies can draw. The costs of regulating or enforcing regulation sometimes seem too great to incur, so that a situation of *impunity* is seen by the regulated to exist.

Practical political authority for law also varies with the *strength of states* relative to one another. Globalisation pressures limit freedom of action for all but the most powerful states, often directly affecting the content of legislation, for example in areas of economic policy. Official or unofficial extraterritorial law enforcement by some states affects the practical legal authority of others over their citizens (e.g. Cross 2015). Extradition provisions can sometimes have similar effects,[19] appearing in effect to hand over the exercise of legal authority in particular cases to another state. Some states are able even to exercise punitive force in others without permission, including the power (e.g. through clandestine raids or use of remote technology) to execute or seize residents of weaker states in the territory of those states.[20] In this way they undermine weaker states' capacity to assert their own authority within their borders. Disparities of power between states are reflected in the shape, use, and effects of international law (Simpson 2004; Krisch 2005), so that its legitimacy as an extension of the political authority of states, founded on their *consent* as an international community, is often doubted. And competition between even powerful states may limit their regulatory capacity (Rixen 2013).

Conditions such as these, where they exist, do not usually directly affect judgments about the validity of legal rules and decisions insofar as this validity can still be traced in juristic analysis to formal sources of legal-rational authority in statutes, precedents, administrative orders, constitutional provisions, treaties, and so on. But they may eventually affect the extent to which authority claims are popularly accepted. Respect for law has been shown in empirical sociolegal research to be affected by perceptions of the fairness, consistency, and reliability of legal procedures (Tyler 2001: 382; Jackson et al 2012: 1052–3). Hence, uncertainties about the nature and effectiveness of political authority and the variables that determine how and when it is legally used can unsettle the legitimacy of law.

All of these matters could be discussed at great length. They are listed here only indicatively and schematically to preface an argument that questions about legal authority should be considered beyond the usual parameters of juristic analysis focused

---

18 For a general discussion of determinants of authority and effectiveness in government see Ringen 2013.

19 See Chapter 10, pp 144–5.

20 See Heyns 2013, stating that the 'use of drones by states to exercise essentially a global policing function to counter potential threats presents a danger to the protection of life, because the tools of domestic policing (such as capture) are not available, and the more permissive targeting framework of the laws of war is often used instead' (para 103).

on the essentially legal-rational structures of authority in political societies governed by state law. Equally, to introduce such matters is a means of suggesting that an inquiry into transnational legal authority cannot limit itself to examining efforts to project into the transnational arena the diverse conditions of legitimacy that surround municipal law. These conditions may be themselves shaped to a significant extent (for example through the globalisation pressures mentioned earlier) by transnational developments. So, transnational legal authority should be considered by focusing directly on the social nature of the transnational world which emerging structures of law seek to address.

Political authority and communal legitimacy

Recent social scientific literature has developed the idea of transnational communities and sought to identify such communities and study their forms of governance (Djelic and Quack eds 2010b). Transnational communities are said to be more than merely instrumental (often contractually structured) networks, markets, or hierarchies; community is said to imply a common culture of some kind and its members' sense of belonging together in it (Djelic and Quack 2010a: 384–6). Thus, transnational communities have regulatory needs and may create regulation for themselves through the interactions of their members. It is very easy to envisage some such communities – for example religious, ethnic, linguistic, regional, scientific, or economic.

However, it is also easy to see the limitations of thinking of communities in this way. The concept suggests bounded entities – organisations or social groups that could be called communities. But it is clear that the transnational arena cannot be wholly or even mainly described in terms of these (Michaels 2009: 252). The idea of communities as distinct, bounded, perhaps somewhat static entities seems to have only limited relevance today. Few exist. Social relations (especially those that concern transnational law) tend to flourish and decay, contract and expand, assume varying forms and transmute in complex, intersecting, overlapping patterns. But one can envisage these relations as having a *communal character* when they have *some* (even if temporary) degree of stability and endurance and when they are built on mutual trust between the participants.

Bonds of community can lie in the common or convergent projects of the participants (as long as these projects last), in their shared beliefs and ultimate values, in emotional bonds of common allegiance, or simply in the fact that the participants must (for the time being) share some common environment and relate to it collectively. People can potentially be linked in relations of community in any or all of these ways, briefly or for some considerable time, so that the patterns of these linkages can be very complex. We can then speak of communal networks, in which probably one or more of these types of bonds dominate but not exclusively. Instead, a web of communal relations exists. So, 'community' is not a thing but a *quality of social relations*.[21]

---

21 For convenience I sometimes use the word community, in line with common usage, to refer to groups or population categories, but always intending this as a reference to communal networks as discussed in this book.

The transnational arena – the world regulated by transnational law – is thus best seen as made up of networks of communal relations continually changing in character and shape. These can consist of individuals, groups, or corporations. Their essential character is that, on the one hand, they are not strictly bounded and their scope may be poorly defined, debatable, and variable, so that they do not necessarily create the basis for sharply delineated jurisdictions of the kind familiar to lawyers. On the other hand, they seek and require collective regulation to express and support the bonds of community that give them some stability. This stability depends on mutual trust between participants insofar as they wish to remain members of the network, on attitudes that support this trust, and, where necessary, on regulation that reinforces and facilitates it. Communal networks are not necessarily democratically structured. Members may rarely participate in them on a footing of equality. In many, perhaps most, such networks, they may have very unequal power.[22]

The notion of communal networks helps in identifying sources of legitimacy for transnational legal authority. Transnational communal networks (for example transnational business and financial networks or networks of religious believers) may produce more or less organised forms of regulation to govern themselves. Within those networks, this regulation may certainly possess authority. It may be possible to observe agencies operating in them creating, interpreting, and applying law-like doctrine. So, to varying extents in communal networks, normative doctrine may be institutionalised with agencies set in place to develop and manage it. As this development occurs, doctrine may seem to take on characteristics of 'law' – at least it may become hard to say why it should not be recognised as law unless one falls back on assumptions, based on state law experience, about the characteristics that all law must have.[23]

A communal network may therefore create its own law, with legitimate authority derived directly from the cultural conditions of the network itself (e.g. the common interests of its members, its unifying beliefs or values, its traditions, or its collective allegiances). Emerging patterns of transnational legal authority can be seen, in part, as relying on this kind of self-generated authority of transnational networks. Much of what is now widely called transnational private law surely relies significantly on such a 'bottom-up' production of legitimate authority. But this is far from being adequate to conceptualise transnational legal authority for several reasons.

First, as noted earlier, much reliance is placed in developing transnational law on the *political authority of states* as creators and guarantors of law. And, insofar as much transnational law is being developed out of international law, it relies also on the traditional sources of legitimate authority for international law. So its claims to legitimate authority are linked to the established ways in which the authority of states is extended into the international arena through the general principle of the

---

22 A circumstance influencing how, and by whom, claims to authority in networks are made.
23 See the discussion of law as institutionalised doctrine in Chapters 6 and 7.

'consent' of states, expressed in treaties and conventions, and especially in the setting up of international agencies on the basis of these 'consensual' instruments.

The fragility of such ideas of consent, as well as the uncertainty or variability of states' political authority when viewed in terms of the empirical conditions surrounding it, was considered earlier. We could visualise the political authority available to transnational law as an extremely thin, fragile arm stretched out from states over a vast transnational realm. This extended, state-derived political authority surely has little connection with the collective life conditions (cultural experience) of most of the communal networks that make up the regulated population of transnational law.

Consider, for example, the international economic law of the World Trade Organisation, which certainly affects the economic and other circumstances of the members of many global communal networks. We could visualise this law as suspended far above them, engulfed in clouds of international diplomacy, its remote political authority hardly visible from below. It surely gains such legitimate authority as it has not from the global populations of economic actors it affects but from the overstretched scaffolding of the notional agreement of states applying their own political authority, an authority itself mainly appealing to some democratic validation by their citizenry.[24]

What guarantees these fragile structures of political authority supporting transnational law is, above all, the influence of particular dominant states or groups of states.[25] Just as configurations of power in international relations affect the practice and experience of authority in international law,[26] so they will for transnational law insofar as international law and international legal agencies contribute to its development. But the use of this 'great power' influence, itself gradually evolving and changing shape (Cai 2013), cannot in itself produce legitimacy for transnational law. It would do so only to the extent that a centralised sovereign power was accepted to direct transnational legal development.

Then transnational law could be unified as a monistic, hierarchical structure, no doubt involving structures of delegation, federalism, complementarity, and subsidiarity infinitely more complex and elaborate than anything yet experienced. In such conditions Austin's theory of law (1885a: lects 5 and 6), centred on a single, common, and determinate law-making sovereign habitually obeyed, on the delegation from it of law-making powers of command, and on the universal association of law with sanctioning processes, might come into its own again. But these conditions are presently inconceivable. No world state is in the process of forming to provide reliable universal political authority for transnational law.

---

24 See Bacchus 2004, defending WTO legitimacy as an extension of the democratic legitimacy of nation-states but recognising the WTO's remoteness from the knowledge and understanding of those it regulates.

25 And, it should be added, the influence of transnational elites (especially economic elites) on these states.

26 Which is not to deny a reciprocal influence of international law on these relations: see e.g. Reus-Smit 2004.

A conception of legitimate authority for transnational law as being produced 'from below' is, however, also inadequate because of the nature of transnational *legal pluralism*. While communal networks might produce regulation for themselves that enjoys legitimate authority, they cannot produce regulation that can adequately govern their relations with other networks by this means. This might seem to throw the inquiry back towards the juristic approaches, mentioned earlier, that invoke 'overarching' principles to coordinate different regimes of transnational regulation. But at this stage in the development of transnational regulation, when its overall shape and scope is still unclear and its development continues rapidly and to some extent unpredictably, it would be a mistake (and perhaps fruitless) to follow such approaches.

They involve trying to apply established juristic ideas to a world that cannot be confined within such ideas, because the forces shaping it are only partly informed by typical Western juristic assumptions and preconceptions as to what makes regulation authoritative and legitimate.

Coping with legal pluralism

The problem comes down to a choice of strategies to address the problems of transnational legal pluralism – to navigate normatively in a realm consisting not only of inconsistent regulatory regimes but also of regimes founded on differing, sometimes incompatible principles of authority and legitimacy. These differences and incompatibilities reflect the different cultures of communal networks and the different kinds of authority (such as those conceptualised by Weber in terms of their bases of legitimacy) that can be claimed and accepted. There are at least four such strategies.

First, a broadly *monistic* approach may not try to organise all transnational law into a single system, which most jurists now see as impossible; it may rather invoke 'overarching' procedures or principles to police the limits of plurality. As suggested earlier, this approach is premature because of the impossibility of justifying any particular 'overarching' devices except by stipulation.

A second approach is *agnostic* about the nature of transnational law and avoids specifying any criterion of legitimate transnational law in general. It merely recognises what counts as authoritative regulation for a particular regime in a particular context. This surely represents much current practice in transnational law. Regulation in particular spheres exists in indeterminate relation with other kinds of regulation; their relative authority is left to be decided pragmatically only when conflicts arise.

A third, *statist* approach judges as 'law' regulatory regimes beyond the reach of the political authority of the state on the basis of criteria modelled on those applied to recognise state law or insofar as these regulatory regimes can be seen as alternatives to or extensions of state law. But this approach is surely unsatisfactory as long as it remains tied to the model of state law and confines the imagination in this way, deterring it from recognising that transnational law (while it contains much state law and state-derived law) also contains entirely new ideas of what might be legally significant.

A final approach would accept a genuine legal pluralism – perhaps, in a sense, a *supra-juristic* legal pluralism. This does not mean that it is a juristically irrelevant approach but suggests merely that it searches for different modes of analysis beyond established Western forms of juristic thought. It focuses most sharply on identifying and studying sociolegally the full extent of regulatory authority as practiced and experienced in the transnational realm.

This fourth approach recognises that the practice and experience of authority can take very different forms in different contexts (in different communal networks and their cultures), that it is useful to think of a continuum or scale of legality (regulation might be more or less legal judged against different criteria adopted in different contexts), and that no uniform principles can decide where legitimate authority lies in many cases of conflict between different transnational regulatory regimes (there cannot be comprehensive general principles of transnational conflicts of laws). Even seemingly established structures of legal authority governing the relations of state law, intrastate law, and international law may seem disturbed when the full range of criteria and conditions of legitimacy is examined in sociolegal perspective.

This may seem to suggest only hopelessly negative conclusions: that the question of transnational legal authority cannot be addressed, that the situation is too chaotic with too many variables in play, and that too much uncertainty exists both about the present and the future. But it should not be concluded that progress is impossible. New methods are necessary, and, for the moment, these should be methods of empirical sociolegal inquiry – but methods that aim at finding ways back towards addressing practical juristic questions.

- First, existing hierarchies of transnational legal authority created by *state and international law* need to be examined in terms of the sociolegal conditions that guarantee or undermine these hierarchies. This is necessary to make a realistic assessment of the shape, quality, and forms of political authority that are available to shape a transnational legal order.
- Second, the conditions in which regulation is developed, enforced, and seen as authoritative in *communal networks* need further study beyond the extensive existing literature on 'living law', social norms, private legal systems, transnational private law, and transnational standard setting. This is necessary to examine potential sources of social legitimacy for the various kinds of transnational regulation taking shape.
- Third, further work can be done on processes of *negotiation and conflict-resolution* between communal networks, and on the conditions for effective communication between legal cultures. This is necessary to explore the possibilities for creating institutional frameworks for managing the coexistence of transnational regulatory regimes.
- Finally, *the idea of law* needs to be shorn of definitional criteria that tie it permanently to state law forms and prevent the possibility of finding phenomena that might usefully be recognised for various purposes as legal regulation exist-

ing entirely outside the scope of municipal or international law. Some minimal model of law as institutionalised doctrine as elaborated in earlier chapters might be a working basis for ongoing negotiations of potential transnational legal authority to take place.

In some respects, progress in establishing transnational legal authority will depend on the slow building of reliable hierarchies of coercive authority (*voluntas*) for transnational law through efforts to strengthen (i) the political authority supporting international law, and (ii) the legitimacy of the independent authority of states. In other respects, it will depend on processes of communication, negotiation, and reasoning across transnational communal networks aimed at developing bodies of legal principle that, if not uniform between these networks, can at least become increasingly intelligible across and between them. By this means something that could be recognised as the *ratio* (reason and principle) of transnational law may also be slowly developed. As in all law, the reliable combination of *voluntas* and *ratio* (Cotterrell 1995: 317–20; Neumann 1986) will be what finally creates convincingly legitimate authority for transnational law.

10

A TRANSNATIONAL CONCEPT OF CRIME

Politics, culture, crime

Crime is one of the most basic juristic categories. But what is the relation of this category to popular ideas about wrongdoing and to changing social and political conditions, especially those linked to the transnational extensions of law? This chapter illustrates how juristic understandings can be challenged, and perhaps destabilised in some respects, by the shifting social foundations of a legal concept. The concept of crime is fundamental to all modern legal systems. Here it is taken as a focus for exploring why juristic understandings need empirically and theoretically informed social insight – that is, a sociological jurisprudence – especially in the face of transnational extensions of law.

It is said that 'there is no "ontological reality" of crime' (Hulsman 1986: 300); the term seems to refer to no irreducible, distinctive social phenomenon existing independently of legal definition. Crime is what the state (or some international agency authorised by states) declares it to be through law. By designating an offence as 'criminal', state law links it to established assumptions about kinds of punishment appropriate for criminal behaviour. And, it seems, *any* conduct might be so designated. Crime is merely what criminal law in a given society at a given time states it to be.

Yet the immense variety of kinds of conduct labelled as criminal sometimes attracts comment and even concern (Stuntz 2001) because 'the sheer number of criminal offences has grown exponentially' (Husak 2004: 768). In this situation, doubts about the coherence of 'crime' as a category have tended to be pushed aside in practice – so William Stuntz (2001: 512) has suggested – by making criminal law 'not one field but two. The first [field] consists of a few core crimes. . . . The second consists of everything else. Criminal law courses, criminal law literature, and popular conversations about crime focus heavily on the first. The second dominates criminal codes.' In other words, crime as a basic social category is assumed to be well understood, but perhaps that understanding depends on generalising from a few seemingly prominent kinds of criminalisation, often leaving aside much else.

Whatever the truth of this as regards juristic and popular perspectives, criminologists have been concerned to conceptualise crime and have divided mainly into two broad camps in doing so. One camp expressly or tacitly adopts a broadly legal demarcation of crime as its practical focus: what the state, through its law, marks out as crime provides criminology with its basic subject-matter and its scholarly field. But, for strong intellectual and moral-political reasons, many other criminologists have rejected the idea that the subject-matter of their field is given to them by legal-political fiat. Fearing to be 'kings without a country' (cf Van Bemmelen 1951), they have wanted to produce their own concept of crime or to discard crime as a concept in favour of a more independent focus for their knowledge-field (Henry and Lanier eds 2001). Alongside this, efforts have been made for moral and political reasons to open up or replace the idea of crime so as to cover types of behaviour typically not criminalised by state law or thought to be treated insufficiently seriously by the state or those in which the state and its agents are themselves implicated (e.g. Rothe and Friedrichs 2006).

Until recently, such efforts to escape the state law focus have surely had limited effect. If the state is not to hold a monopoly in declaring what is to count as crime, where else can the authority to define crime be found? If critical criminologists, setting out to challenge state law definitions of crime, have sometimes found a hearing, it is because they have appealed to widespread concerns about serious wrongdoing. They have aimed to link established popular notions about the seriousness of 'crime' to other widely felt social concerns. Beyond popular assumptions that crime is what criminal law says it is, other popular ideas exist as to what are serious social wrongs,[1] about what *should* be treated as criminal, or about what is 'really' criminal even if law does not declare it to be so. But what authoritative conceptualisations of crime could come from such diffuse popular understandings?

Is it possible to speak of a *cultural* authority underpinning ideas of crime, as contrasted with the *political* authority of the state and its juristic servants – 'cultural' referring here broadly to bonds of shared tradition, interests, beliefs, values, or emotional allegiance that may hold people together in conditions of relatively stable social coexistence? In some circumstances, can this cultural authority be important? Studying its character would be an essentially sociological enterprise.

Where the state extends criminalisation beyond certain limits cultural attitudes might not support this; popular ideas of crimes as 'mala in se' (wrong by nature) might be significantly out of alignment with the scope and character of some state 'mala prohibita' (that is, acts that are wrongs merely because prohibited). The same position might arise where the state is seen to 'undercriminalise', to condone impunity or provide inadequate punishments. More generally, it might arise where the

---

1 General issues about the relationship between governmental and popular views of social wrongs are further considered in Chapter 14.

state, in punishing or not punishing, is seen to serve special interests rather than a broad public interest – or where the very idea of public interest becomes confused. Cultural definitions of crime might matter when the state's general practice in criminalising begins to be questioned.

Thus, when cultural authority *does* largely support the state's political authority in treating crime, this may depend on the state being seen as a secure, reliable regulator – as holding what Max Weber (Gerth and Mills eds 1948: 78) called a monopoly of legitimate violence in its territory – together with a popular sense that the state and its law represent a relatively stable sociopolitical and economic order against which crime is easily seen as a serious threat which the state identifies and addresses.

In this chapter I shall argue that the state monopoly on defining crime is being weakened, especially by the transnational spread of criminal jurisdiction – that is, by the increasingly felt need to apply ideas of crime coherently across and irrespective of national boundaries. If this is so, the question of how and by whom the meaning of 'crime' is to be settled assumes renewed importance. Cultural authority (the authority of popular ideas arising in everyday social life) to shape the concept of crime may have new significance as the political authority to shape it becomes less clear. So, in what follows, suggestions are made of ways in which the state's independent power to determine what is criminal is becoming destabilised or restricted. The question then arises: where can the idea of crime in transnational context find a supporting input of cultural authority? The answer suggested is in emerging transnational networks of community – networks that now extend beyond the various social networks from which national popular ideas about crime have arisen.

State and crime: perspectives from social theory

If the state's sole authority to criminalise has usually been popularly accepted, this is surely partly because no other authority has seemed sufficiently focused to compete with it. But it may also be because popular assumptions about what the state criminalises have tended to conform to popular views about what crime is. In this respect Stuntz's idea of 'two fields' of criminal law, one known, the other unknown, seems important. What has been popularly seen as the state's management of the idea of crime – and accepted as legitimate as such – has actually been *only a part of its extensive practice of criminalisation.*

Some warrant for this view might be found in Weberian and Durkheimian sociolegal theories.[2] Weber has little to say directly about crime, presumably because in his perspective the state's power to criminalise is just one of many regulatory techniques it possesses and can deploy pragmatically. Central to these techniques is the relatively formal character of modern law, which sustains the idea of both its autonomy as a rational system and its usefulness as an all-purpose regulatory device,

2 For a somewhat parallel comparison see Terpstra 2011.

available equally for private purposes and to enable the state to fulfil its administrative functions. If the modern state typically successfully claims a monopoly of legitimate violence,[3] much of its power, in Weber's view, is exercised through enunciated rules, and administration (rather than politics) typifies the everyday life of state and society.[4] His emphasis on rational administration easily morphs into more abstract contemporary social theories that envisage systems and networks as somehow taking on lives of their own, perhaps even ultimately unbounded by the jurisdictional reach of nation-states.

One might imagine that as the administrative structures and tasks of the state extend and its law proliferates to frame these, the possibilities of criminalisation also expand – but into esoteric areas of regulation that reflect the sheer complexity of modern social and economic organisation – what can be called forms of 'administrative' criminalisation. 'Crime' does not appear at all in the index of the English edition of Weber's magnum opus, *Economy and Society* (1968), but we might imagine that, in his typical modern state, categories of mala prohibita proliferate. So if criminal law is, indeed, actually two fields – one highly visible in popular consciousness, the other largely unseen – perhaps the growth of the unseen part really typifies the progress of modernity and the flourishing of the state.

Can we then speculate that, as the state grows more ambitious (Weber's theory suggests no strong reasons why it should not), the contours of crime as a category change – that the process of politico-legal criminalisation potentially embraces more and more wrongs that are distant from everyday popular conceptions of crime? And can it also be assumed that no particular problems arise from this divorce from popular conceptions?

Émile Durkheim (1984) provides a striking contrast to such an outlook. He too sees the modern state's regulatory capacities and ambitions as vastly expanding; there is surely more and more law. But, unlike Weber, he pays careful attention to assessing how much of it is properly to be seen as penal. Whereas Weber's modern state seems to need no specific cultural authorisation for its criminalisation practices, Durkheim's does. Punishing crime has to be seen as a *special* focus of law, to be distinguished clearly from all the many other regulatory objectives which law and state must address.

As modern regulation expands, most of this expansion is aimed not at defining and punishing crime but at peacefully and nonviolently coordinating and repairing social relations: for example by guaranteeing compensation, rectifying arrangements turned sour, providing useful administrative structures, and facilitating cooperation and interdependence. Despite all the many new regulatory demands on the state in modern conditions, the idea of crime remains something that 'society', not the state,

---

3 Gerth and Mills eds 1948: 78. See also Weber 1968: 314: 'Today legal coercion by violence is the monopoly of the state.'

4 A striking illustration of this point is that a stable state may be able to continue administrative functions effectively even when political processes fail to produce a government: see e.g. Bouckaert and Brans 2012, and Devos and Sinardet 2012.

determines. So the state operates through what I earlier called cultural authority in criminalising and punishing.

There is something both powerful and unreal in this Durkheimian picture – a paradox which has long produced deeply polarised views in the criminological literature. Crucially, as regards Stuntz's postulated 'two fields' of criminal law, how does Durkheim analyse the 'unseen' field – the areas of mala prohibita largely unknown to most people; the realm of regulatory, technical, managerial, administrative, public health, and other offences not necessarily seen as 'wrong in themselves'? Occasionally Durkheim refers to examples of such offences, but they are clearly not his concern, and he mainly ignores them. When he writes of crime he means something popularly condemned generally in society – affronting the shared moral outlooks of average people. So he sees only part of what criminal law addresses.

On the other hand, a strength of Durkheim's view is that the idea of crime in it is something powerful, enduring (despite all regulatory changes), and stable. The political authority of the state (acting on behalf of society) in punishing crime meshes with the cultural authority that makes crime a readily intelligible concept. Crime is a distinct moral phenomenon (however varied the forms it takes). It consists of wrongdoing regarded generally by citizens as constituting such a serious threat to the moral security of society (not just particular interests of individuals) that it is to be repressed by collective action through the agency of the state. Crime, as Durkheim puts it, offends the collective consciousness (or conscience) of society.

From a Weberian perspective, the main problem of transnational criminalisation must be to ensure adequate political authority to support appropriate regulation. The key question will be: what happens to the state's monopoly of legitimate violence? Can it be extended transnationally, shared with other states, or somehow conferred on transnational political authorities? In a Durkheimian perspective, however, as ideas of crime become transnational, cultural authority must be found for them if they are to be coherent and meaningful (Nimaga 2010).

The implications of this can, however, be pushed well beyond anything in Durkheim's writings. If the idea of crime were somehow to be loosened from the state's modern monopoly of criminalisation, could it become a focus for potentially unlimited *struggle and dispute*? Does the power to fix the meaning of crime potentially become a political prize to be fought over? If the idea of crime has been used to identify threats to a social order and to justify the use of penal violence to repress these threats, what if *competing* claims are made to harness the idea of crime for such purposes? What if the nature of the threats and their sources are viewed in competing ways? Finally, what if those who could once be securely labelled by the state as criminals now invoke the idea of crime to *condemn the state* and its agents as criminal? The ultimate scenario is that the idea of crime might become uncontrollably contested and unstable. So the issue of cultural authority returns to haunt insecure political authority in conceptualising crime and legitimising criminal punishment.

In the transnational development of criminal justice, debates around the meaning of crime assume increasing importance. For example, both extradition and extraterritorial law enforcement sometimes attract popular controversy as to whether 'crime' is being given the same meaning in all states involved or whether one state is seeking to impose its own understanding of crime (and the way it should be dealt with) on another. As transnationalism advances, nationalistic views of crime find new prominence. 'Loose interpretation' of strict dual criminality requirements[5] for transnational criminal justice cooperation or reliance on 'analogies' between offences in different jurisdictions can be causes for concern (Lardo 2006: 889–92, 898–902). Popular, nationalistic 'extradition fury'[6] fanned by media reports suggests that the idea of crime is not something to be entrusted entirely to the state to negotiate with other states; cultural resonances are important. This may be specially so where extradition offences are outside Stuntz's field of popularly 'known' crimes and so their wrongfulness may depend on technical definition.[7]

Aspects of cybercrime provide other illustrations. Hacking and cyberattacks are perpetrated not only by individuals or organised crime groups targeting state or other public facilities or private businesses, bank accounts, and databases. They may also be acts of state agencies trying to crush opposition or attack other states (e.g. Billo and Chang 2004). So, transnational crime can destabilise distinctions between the state and the criminal and between cybercrime, cyberterrorism, and cyberwarfare (e.g. Lin 2016). The idea of the *criminal state* (or its agents) arises as an aspect of the broader relocation of the state from a position of overall supervisor and controller of criminal justice processes to that of a participant or subject in these processes – sometimes as victim, agent, offender, or promoter or obstructer of criminal justice.

The state is said to be 'losing control over the monopoly of coercion hitherto under its aegis' (Mittelman and Johnston 1999: 123), but it is unwise to generalise so broadly. Certainly, in some cases the state is subject to attacks (from terrorism, corruption, and organised crime) which it struggles to criminalise in the face of weakening resources and authority (e.g. Garland 1996). Instead of being above the criminal fray, some states find themselves in the midst of it, battling to enforce their view of criminality in the face of disinterest or controversy – so that the crime label may seem to cease to matter (only the balance of coercive forces counts) or is harnessed to the interests of those who wish to use it to condemn opposing interests. Otherwise criminalisation in practice is partially taken from the control of the state through privatisation initiatives or by being entrusted to the care of transnational criminal justice agencies (such as international tribunals) or merely to stronger states with greater power to impose it.

---

5 Requirements that the act for which extradition is sought must amount to an offence in both the requested and the requesting state. Cf Kester 1988: 1461 (claiming that in US practice 'the double criminality requirement often does not mean much'); Lardo 2006: 890 (noting the 'liberal interpretation of dual criminality espoused by US prosecutors'). Under the European Arrest Warrant procedure the requirement has been either weakened or removed.

6 Outcry against the handing over of fellow-citizens to another state for trial and potential punishment.

7 Kester 1988: 1492 (stressing that 'social norms and business ethics and duties vary considerably, and not improperly, even among the Western democracies'); and see Lardo 2006: 898–9 on UK-US controversies.

The concept of crime and international criminal law

The emergence of international criminal law (ICL), especially in the past half century, represents perhaps the most visible emergence of a transnational arena of criminalisation in which some states (at least, their agents) have become potentially subjects (rather than controllers) of criminal justice. It is necessary to say 'some' states because others surely dominate in practice in this transnational arena, lending their continuing monopolies of legitimate force within their territory to guarantee ICL in operation. Because this guarantee is limited, selective, and uneven, so that it is presently hard to imagine some state authorities being subject to it, ICL is seen as both embryonic and insecure in its legitimacy.[8] And although it is called *international* law, it might be best described as transnational (Leonard 2005: 6) because it is individuals rather than states that are addressed by it, in some cases irrespective of nationality or citizenship (Werle and Jeßberger 2014: paras 119, 123, 270–1).

Like criminal law in national contexts, ICL can be rationalised juristically into a system of thought (e.g. Ambos 2007: 2667–71), but it displays no general idea of crime as a social phenomenon. Crime is primarily what the statute of the International Criminal Court and the court's interpretations declare as offences. The statute lists specific crimes organised under headings of genocide, crimes against humanity, and war crimes, the headings not themselves being defined apart from the specific offences they encompass.[9] The assumption seems to be that – in the light of ICL's history – these offences need only be stated in order to be accepted as instances of crime: a reasonable assumption insofar as they include such matters as 'murder', 'extermination', 'enslavement', 'torture', 'rape', 'causing serious bodily or mental harm', 'enforced sterilization', wanton 'destruction and appropriation of property', and 'pillaging'. Central ideas of crime in ICL are clearly built out of categories of crime accepted in both juristic and popular understandings in all modern Western societies – that is, as transnational extensions of ideas of crime in the first of Stuntz's two fields of criminal law, the 'known' field that most obviously defines crime in popular understandings. Beyond these ideas of crime in ICL is, however, much else which invokes, for example, established categories of illegality enshrined in the 1949 Geneva Conventions or in other principles of international law and includes acts aimed at destroying specific victim groups, wanton destruction of natural environments or cultural heritage, and a range of outlawed weapons and tactics for waging war.

Looked at in terms of possibilities for cultural legitimation, the category of crime in ICL seems a strange compendium – a packaging of disparate elements. They include:

---

8 The issues have long featured in public debate: e.g. Copnall 2010 (focus of ICL only on African cases); and Milne 2012 (effective impunity of NATO leaders in ICL). See generally Köchler 2017 and Henham 2007.

9 ICC Statute Arts 5–8. The statute does add requirements of context; for example that crimes against humanity occur as part of a widespread or systematic attack on a civilian population. And a 2010 amendment to the statute now defines the crime of aggression, previously merely signalled in the text.

- efforts to 'humanise' modern warfare (for example, outlawing the use of certain kinds of weapons or tactics) – that is, rules about the way to conduct violence that surely find little or no presence in domestic (national) cultural understandings of crime;
- concerns to protect natural and cultural environments, which are present in many Western legal systems but often as civil rather than criminal matters; and, when criminal, perhaps popularly seen as mala prohibita as much as, if not more than, mala in se; and
- much that in popular perceptions is usually very obviously crime (e.g. deliberately inflicting serious harm to the person or to property without lawful excuse).

If some kind of popular legitimation is available for ICL, it might be hard to spell it out in general terms. But could it be that this is not needed, that adequate politico-legal authority, relying on the combined monopolies of violence possessed by the treaty-supporting states, sustains the somewhat incoherent transnational concept of crime?

Politico-legal authority alone seems, however, an unstable basis for extending transnationally the concept of crime. The spectre of victors' justice that has hung over ICL since the Nuremburg trials is now transformed into suspicion that ICL is a means by which some states try to impose a global criminal justice system on other (usually weaker) ones. So, the concept of crime appears as a mechanism of military-police control extended beyond the national arena to control foreign populations, perhaps by analogy with the 'dangerous classes' or 'underclasses' addressed by state criminal justice. It may be that the only way to avoid ICL being seen in this way is clearly to identify forms of cultural legitimation on which it can draw but also to recognise that in present conditions there is no single global culture that can legitimise fully a transnational concept of crime. Instead, what may exist are important networks of community existing not only within nations but also transnationally that can support the extension of ideas of crime across national boundaries.

The serious violent acts that constitute crimes against humanity according to the legal definitions may seem to epitomise 'crime' so obviously that universal cultural authority for their recognition is undeniable – the cultural appeal is to a global idea of 'humanity'. But what one population sees as atrocities are sometimes dismissed as justified retaliation by another; wanton destruction can appear as collateral damage, targeted killings as suppressing terrorism, and terrorist violence as action against injustice and in the service of achieving freedom. Where acts such as killing, rape, enslavement, or appropriation of property are directed against people seen as enemies or as utterly alien, their criminal character is sometimes totally denied.

A popular understanding of crime presupposes a degree of *solidarity in a network of community*, whether that network is national or transnational. It is doubtful that 'humanity' designates such a communal network of solidarity today, except as an aspiration for the future (cf Gould 2007). But something less may exist – an evolving transnational arena in which some ideas of human rights and human dignity are acquiring relatively stable meanings and can thus inform criminalisation.

Without stable cultural understandings of crime, its politico-legal designation risks ongoing challenge, especially because, being ultimately guaranteed by the authority of states, it cannot escape controversy about the extent of this state authority. Attitudes to war as an instrument of the state reveal this starkly. During the twentieth century, the idea became established that criminal liability could arise from the mere pursuit of war by states (as distinct from anything occurring in the course of that pursuit) (Werle and Jeßberger 2014: Pt 6). So, to that extent, rights of nation-states in international law were scaled down. The military historian Martin van Crefeld writes: 'Once the legal monopoly of armed force, long claimed by the state, is wrested out of its hands, existing distinctions between war and crime will break down' (quoted in Cohen 1996: 16).

One consequence could be that war (involving invasion, military intervention, imposed regime change), although distinguished legally in modern times from the idea of punishment, might come to be treated as a sanction against criminal activity by states. One writer has suggested that the idea of war as punishment 'remains alive and well in the moral imaginations of modern societies, even if diplomats and lawyers carefully scrub it from official justifications for armed conflict' (Luban 2011: 300–1). While he rejects this view of war, he sees no reason why states, like corporations, should not be capable of assuming criminal responsibility.

The idea of criminal acts by states has been debated juristically, but it has been suggested that such acts should not be called crimes 'as they do not provoke punishment in a way analogous to that of domestic law' (Nimaga 2010: 62). Punishability is surely a key issue. But various sanctions against states are possible, including economic sanctions (which might be analogised to fines in domestic law); or isolation, boycott, or exclusion as a 'pariah' from the international intercourse of states (which might be analogised to exclusion from 'the social' produced by imprisonment of an offender); or military action to effect regime change (which might even be imagined as 'capital punishment' of a state).

These speculations remain unreal if acts against an 'offender' state are seen only as serving the special interests of another state (or a limited coalition of states). Such acts could be legitimised as punishment only if they were aimed at addressing not the 'private' interests of particular aggrieved states[10] but serious threats to the 'international community' of states as a whole, that is, action to protect the existence of a common transnational sociopolitical order which international criminal justice is seen to serve.

Generalising to current forms of transnational criminalisation, two basic requirements for a transnational concept of crime are highlighted by this discussion: first, the existence of *mechanisms to punish offenders*, and, second, *transnational communal*

---

10 That war is usually a matter of such 'private' interstate conflicts is a key reason why Luban (2011) denies that it can be accepted as a form of punishment.

networks on behalf of which criminalisation and punishment are undertaken. Efforts to address the first of these requirements are being made through transnational cooperation between states. The streamlining of extradition and European Arrest Warrant procedures, on the one hand, and the willingness of coalitions of states to engage in humanitarian intervention, on the other, represent strongly contrasting examples (whatever controversies may surround them). But the nature of transnational social networks supporting criminalisation needs much more analysis. References to an 'international community' or 'community of humanity'[11] served by ICL remain for the most part purely rhetorical because ungrounded in any sociological inquiry about what 'community' might mean and what kind of existence it might have.

Locating ideas of crime in communal networks

This chapter has referred to cultural (as contrasted with politico-legal) authority to conceptualise crime. That cultural authority can best be seen as arising in many different communal networks. As discussed in earlier chapters, bonds of community of varying degrees of stability, fluidity, transience, or permanence can arise from (i) common or convergent interests, (ii) shared beliefs or ultimate values, (iii) coexistence in particular cultural or physical environments, or (iv) emotional allegiances. In social life, these different types of bonds are combined (often with some types dominating) in social networks of varying size, complexity, and stability: examples include trading or financial networks, networks of religious believers, social or ideological movements, ethnic or kinship groups, and local or linguistic populations linked primarily by coexistence in the same territory or by common history or traditions. Membership in such networks overlaps; people move in and out of and are usually involved simultaneously in many of them. Crucially today, as we have noted, such communal networks can be not merely national in extent but also intranational or transnational and thus not limited in their extent by the boundaries of nation-states. Just as emerging forms of transnational law find (or need) cultural bases of authority in such transnational networks, so do transnational ideas of crime.

Can anything be said in general terms about ideas of crime that emerge from such communal sources? It was noted earlier that, when scholars' efforts to replace politico-legal definitions of crime have gained a sympathetic hearing, this has happened because, in various ways, they have reflected widespread popular ideas about crime. Three such broad approaches in criminological and penological literature are most prominent.

First is a *social harm conception* of crime. On this view, the essence of crime (or perhaps the fundamental problem that legal ideas of crime only partly address) is serious social harm or injury (e.g. Lasslett 2010), or the creation of danger,

---

11 See e.g. Renzo (2012: 454) claiming that accountability for crimes against humanity is 'to the members of the international community (rather than just to their fellow citizens)'.

significant risk, or insecurity to individuals or society. A second approach views *crime as upsetting a 'moral balance'* in society, so that justice requires punishment of the offender to reestablish this balance – to proclaim society's condemnation, its recognition and its judgment of the gravity of the wrong done; in this perspective, law in practice might not always provide what criminal justice is thought to require.[12] A third approach is grounded in a *need to protect human rights and dignity* so that what the idea of crime recognises (or should recognise) are serious denials of or attacks on basic conditions of life that humans are entitled to enjoy.[13]

In the context of the discussion here, these approaches suggest possible broadenings of or amendments to politico-legal ideas of crime – ones that might reflect sentiments, interests, values, or traditions not always seen as fully reflected in criminal law. Because these approaches tend to focus on what crime does, more than on the nature of the criminal, some criminologists extend them to embrace not only acts of individual offenders but also those of corporations, groups, states, state agents, or international organisations (Friedrichs and Friedrichs 2002) and even – at the extreme – to include wrongs (such as poverty, racism, sexism, imperialism, colonialism, and exploitation) that are not necessarily seen as always having specific, identifiable agents.

However, doubts among critical criminologists themselves who view such ideas as 'too woolly and polemical' (Cohen 1996: 6) may suggest that they go beyond what most popular ideas of crime will encompass. Jeffrey Reiman (2006: 363), criticising such expansive concepts of crime, claims: 'Individuals think about their actions, they respond to arguments and moral considerations, and their actions are subject to their choices. None of this applies easily to groups or structures.' Thus, he argues, the idea of individual responsibility is basic to most contemporary ideas of crime. Extensions outside it need special justification.

To go beyond these limited suggestions about conceptualising crime it is necessary to return to the notion of networks of community. No meaningful concept of crime could encompass *all* kinds of popularly recognised harms, injustices, or infringements of rights. What could distinguish those that are covered? Crime surely involves some harm, injustice, or dehumanising right-infringement produced by the acts of others in *a common social environment* (embracing both victim and offender) that presupposes basic conditions for coexistence in it. Absence of such a common environment can, as noted earlier, make ideas of crime so controversial as to be practically unworkable.

So, popular ideas of crime in fact presuppose the context of some network of community. Even if it is individuals who are victims of crime, the seriousness of the crime has to be judged ultimately by its consequences for that network *as a whole*. If criminal punishment rather than individual redress is required, it is because the wrong is viewed as sufficiently serious to threaten the order or security of the

---

12 Cf West 2005 on the 'criminal' judge.
13 For discussion of these various orientations see e.g. Henry and Lanier eds 2001.

entire communal network, the general ideas of justice widely presumed within it, or the basic conditions of trust and interdependence (solidarity) that underpin it. People can be passionate about crime because they treat it as *a threat to the way that social life — that is, the communal networks in which they see themselves as involved — must be organised.*

This is a view of crime clearly much closer to Durkheimian than Weberian perspectives. Weber's image of powerful modern states extending their regulatory capacities suggests a growing scope of what I earlier called administrative criminalisation (focused on managing socioeconomic complexity), and it allows us easily to imagine its expansion transnationally through the cooperation of states. But it does not address issues of cultural authorisation of ideas of crime. So it is necessary to see, through some examples, how ideas of crime might be shaped and stabilised by transnational networks of community and what the limits of any transnational cultural legitimation of ideas of crime may be.

The international crime of piracy provides an interesting illustration since it seems, both historically and today, the perfect example of a globally recognised crime, long established in international custom and supported by universal jurisdiction. The nationality or state allegiance of both offenders and victims is largely irrelevant, and the authorities of any state have authority in international law to prosecute piracy. The pirate is said to be the 'enemy of all humanity' (*hostis humani generis*) and criminally punishable on this basis (e.g. Randall 1988: 792–5).

Is this then a rare example of criminalisation supported by a genuinely universal (global) network of community — a true community of humanity? Perhaps unfortunately, the answer has to be negative. What supports this idea of crime is not a global community of belief or ultimate values (perhaps focused on universal human rights and dignity) but rather the existence of common or convergent interests in transnational trade. The relevant transnational communal network is primarily economic in nature. States now address piracy to protect their nationals from physical harm, but more fundamental (certainly in establishing customary piracy jurisdiction) is the need to protect property and *economic interaction* via the high seas or air routes.[14] In this respect, states act on behalf of transnational trading networks from whose welfare and success they benefit.

Much other transnational criminalisation is similarly grounded in the interests of transnational economic networks. Hence its cultural legitimacy comes from those networks — not from any wider constituency of global authorisation. Much administrative criminalisation[15] is concerned to facilitate effective instrumental relations on which the increasingly complex structures of productive economic interaction across national boundaries depend. Crimes of money laundering, fraud,

---

14 Piracy is defined as a crime committed for 'private' (i.e. typically economic, not political) purposes; and under old customary international law it covered robbery but not murder: see e.g. Kontorovich 2010: 252–3.

15 The phrase, though not Weber's, surely reflects the outlook of his sociolegal theory.

counterfeiting, insider trading, corruption, price fixing, racketeering, environmental pollution, and similar infractions proliferate in this context.

But many of these crimes are poorly understood by most people; the exact nature of the criminality involved – the practical meaning of these crimes – is given mainly by understandings internal to the primarily economic networks of community (e.g. business and financial networks, and networks of state and international enforcers policing them) that are involved. Hence what might be readily understood *inside* these networks as crime – as mala in se – might well be seen outside them as criminality only in some vague sense: as offences because designated as such – mala prohibita.[16]

In this light, Durkheimian approaches to understanding crime in transnational contexts surely need substantial modification to be convincing. Transnational crime in general cannot be seen as an affront to some all-embracing transnational collective consciousness (Henham 2007: 84–5). The idea of such a global consciousness as a basis of universal cultural authority for criminalisation is a myth, just as the idea of a global 'international community' is a mythical foundation of a universal politico-legal authority.

More plausible is the idea of limited transnational networks relying on different kinds of dominant relations of community. Many are networks of primarily instrumental (economic) community. Others are territorially based – regional networks dominated by traditional (e.g. historically evolved) relations of community based on coexistence in a single environment. Often there is overlap, so that the European Union's transnational criminal law can be seen as supported by the EU's nature both as a region of geographically and historically determined coexistence (a matter of common fate and common tradition) and as a relatively integrated economic network (a matter of increasing instrumental interaction in industry, commerce, and finance). But it might also be seen as based in a Europe-wide community of belief – in 'European values' – lending it cultural authority, or even in an emotional allegiance to a presumed distinct European identity requiring protection.

Despite its difficulties, the Durkheimian understanding of crime as related to a collective consciousness – a set of beliefs and ultimate values held in common by people and uniting them in social relations of community – should not be discarded. Durkheim saw this collective consciousness as a reality in modern political societies, however limited the scope of universally shared beliefs and values might have become in complex, diverse modern life. He saw 'moral individualism' – the value system that defends the autonomy and dignity of every human being as of equal value – as not only possible but necessary as the overarching moral bond of complex modern societies. Only by treating every other person as of equal human worth with oneself would it be possible to relate constructively to people in conditions where their experiences, lifestyles, aspirations, and understandings might differ radically from one's own. Durkheim thus saw moral individualism – which can be

---

16 By contrast, attacks on the person and property (e.g. homicide, theft) that threaten local environments of coexistence are easily and widely 'visible' as crime insofar as these environments are essential to life.

seen as the prototype of universal human rights discourse – as actually essential for basic solidarity in diverse, complex, and fragmented modern societies.[17]

If the value system of moral individualism is very limited in scope (it leaves much to be filled in as to what dignity and autonomy entail), it is nevertheless powerful in its demands. As regards criminal law, it mandates condemnation of fundamental human rights violations but also humane treatment of offenders and prisoners. It outlaws all cruel and unusual punishments, including capital punishment, and it marks out all serious physical and psychological harms deliberately inflicted on individuals (whether free citizens or prisoners in custody) as the most important crimes. Hence, one might think, this value system offers powerful moral authority to support international criminal law in many of its most central designations of offences.

Up to a point, this is so. ICL can be seen as gaining cultural authority from a transnational network of community held together primarily by a common commitment to beliefs and ultimate values centred on human rights. Its authority derives politically not only from the acceptance by states of the Rome Statute and the jurisdiction of the International Criminal Court. It comes also from the fact that this law and its court reflect a widely held popular aspiration to the realisation of humanitarian values. However, it seems important to accept that this network of community is not worldwide. It coexists with other networks that may espouse different beliefs or values or not be characterised by any public agreement on ultimate values or beliefs. It is sometimes said, indeed, that the human rights constituency reflects a specifically European experience, with which non-European states and populations may or may not find reasons to link themselves. The idea of networks of community emphasises always the *relativity* of cultural authority: the diversity and contingency of its locations.

Though human rights embodying the values of an international community are often said to underpin ICL, it is important to note that Durkheim's value system of moral individualism is justified not juristically or philosophically but *sociologically as appropriate to complex, secular, highly diverse modern societies.* This value system is necessary (even if often violated in practice) to unite and underpin networks of interdependence in such societies. One could speculate that, insofar as more and more of the world takes on the characteristics of these societies, moral individualism will spread, extending a transnational network of community emphasising human rights understood in a Western European sense. But, in a sociological view, this extension might not be inevitable. Ideas of human rights remain the property of *certain* networks of community, not of a 'community of humanity'.

The relativity of the concept of crime

As argued earlier, crime, treated as a cultural rather than a purely politico-legal idea, is best seen as action threatening the very existence of a communal network of community – its basic conditions of order, underlying ideas of justice, or fundamental supports of solidarity. Because there are innumerable networks of community

17 For full discussion see Chapters 12 and 13.

reflecting different combinations of communal bonds – common interests, shared beliefs or ultimate values, emotional allegiances and rejections, or the mere fact of coexistence in a common environment – it follows that ideas about crime will vary. Crime is a relative idea, rooted in specific social settings. The idea of criminal responsibility presupposes not some irreducible characteristics of human beings but a *social environment* that gives meaning to the concept of crime. Insofar as states retain the monopoly of legal violence in their territory, any cultural legitimacy comes from the national political society as a communal network. But, as criminalisation increasingly crosses state boundaries or even ignores them, this social environment, to give cultural legitimacy, must itself become transnational.

So, criminalisation has to reflect transnational ideas of order, justice, and solidarity. If it does not do so, the popular support it obtains for law enforcement may be inadequate. Like all transnational law, transnational criminal law has to find secure grounding in populations that can culturally 'own' this law. To ignore that requirement is to risk stretching the politico-legal authority of regulation beyond the point where its success can be assumed. The message is hardly new. It is one that Eugen Ehrlich (1936) taught a century ago: official state-created and state-supervised law, if it is to be strong, has to take account of the 'living law' of popular experience: in this chapter's terms, politico-legal authority has to be grounded in cultural authority.

The relativity of the concept of crime as understood in networks of community is certainly troubling in important respects. Relations of community judged valuable by the members of such a network may sometimes be condemned as pathological and evil when viewed from outside that network. And what is seen as criminal in one such network may be the opposite in another. Within Nazi networks of community shaped by a common purpose of organising genocide, any form of brutality could be justified for the larger shared aims. And such networks were also based, for some members at least, on bonds of shared belief. Individuals challenging such aims and beliefs in any way could be and often were judged as heinous criminals (Koch 1989).

Today, from the standpoint of some transnational communal networks of community united especially by shared beliefs, Western secular states can be condemned as criminal. At the same time, acts condemned in many networks of community as terrorist crimes can be hailed in others as heroic deeds. Again, economic networks of community (e.g. some business communities) may have different 'internal' conceptions of acceptable or expected behaviour, so that what might be seen in one communal context as corrupt or otherwise criminal could be seen in another as normal and necessary practice. And transnational networks of community may exist specifically to pursue enterprises that are seen as obviously and seriously wrongful (transnational organised crime) beyond them.

As transnational processes of criminalisation accelerate, the problem of different understandings of the nature of crime may be addressed partly by forceful repression of some understandings by others – as in the destruction of the Nazi regime in war and the criminalisation of its leaders. In such circumstances, the old Weberian claimed monopoly on legal violence by the nation-state is transformed into organised repression by coalitions of international states or by international agencies supported by adequate military power supplied by states. In other cases, forms of coercion, influence, or persuasion not involving the use of military force may be available.

Broadly speaking, it is necessary to envisage the process of transnationalisation of the idea of crime on two planes. The first is that of the *political* relations between states and the dynamics of international organisations supported by the politico-legal authority of states. The other is that of *intercultural* dialogue, involving the interaction, interpenetration, and eventual coordination of networks of community. Both of these planes are ones on which juristic ideas have to be formed.

Durkheimian theory gives some grounds for predicting the ongoing spread of ideas of human rights, though not necessarily their global universalisation or the removal of major differences of interpretation of their meaning. On both the politico-legal and the cultural planes, however, it seems clear that the ongoing trans-nationalisation of the idea of crime will be pursued most effectively and enduringly through negotiation and compromise. This, in turn, will depend on an ongoing effort to translate, transnationally, innumerable communal understandings of what can be assumed as universal aspirations for order and justice within a framework of solidarity. The possibilities and limits of that process indicate the extent to which the concept of crime can acquire stable transnational content.

PART III

Legal values in sociological perspective

11

CULTURE AS A JURISTIC ISSUE

A multicultural context

Previous chapters have discussed conditions under which what I have been calling cultural authority seems, at least sometimes, to be needed to underpin legal ideas and legal regulation. These discussions at least suggest that 'culture' matters for law, that it designates phenomena that lawyers have to understand. However difficult it may be to define the idea of culture in a way that is juristically useful, it must somehow be taken into account systematically in juristic theory. Most of the final part of this book focuses specifically on societal or group values as an element of culture. But in this chapter the juristic significance of culture is considered more generally. And it might be thought that there is much urgency about the task of exploring this significance. Cultural diversity and pluralism – and legal responses to multiculturalism – are now constant topics for debate in contemporary Western societies.

This chapter's central concern is with the challenges and possibilities for juristic thought that are presented by *multiculturalism* – that is, by the situation in which self-defined cultural groups make widespread and (at least to some extent) successful efforts to assert and preserve what they see as their cultural distinctiveness in a political society and to achieve public recognition and validation of this distinctiveness. What general issues are posed for juristic theory – jurisprudence – by multiculturalism in complex Western societies today? How might jurists approach these theoretical issues?

I shall argue that it is helpful in this context to link ideas of 'community' and 'communication' in legal theory. The concept of 'community' is often adopted to refer to culturally defined groups, but I shall use it differently, following this book's approach, to indicate relatively stable types of social relations that law has to regulate. As will appear, the related idea of 'communication' highlights aspects of law that may be particularly significant in relation to multiculturalism.

Juristic images of society

For sociologists and anthropologists of law it seems obvious that culture is an important idea in considering generally the nature and functions of law. But juristic scholarship has been more wary of the idea. Nevertheless, in many ways, this scholarship explicitly addresses culture today. If it rarely defines 'culture', it usually takes it to include such matters as shared beliefs or values, customs, traditions or inheritances, and allegiances, attachments, and outlooks.

Examples of these references to culture include discussions of the idea of legal culture in comparative law; legal definitions of cultural statuses such as tribal identity[1] or membership of ethnic or religious groups; the invocation of cultural defences or excuses in criminal law and other legal fields; the work of critical race scholars interpreting law through the experience of cultural minorities; and the use of law to protect cultural heritage in various forms (Cotterrell 2006: 97–102). Cultural rights now feature in international and human rights law. Courts in Britain often have to judge the significance of marriages and divorces conducted according to the particular religious practices of minority groups and have sometimes tried to give official effect to legally unofficial arrangements through 'presumptions of marriage' (Shah 2007). In other cases it has been necessary to confront the issue of providing redress for otherwise legally unprotected wives and children of polygamous marriages (e.g. Shah 2005: ch 5). In many European countries, controversies over Muslim female dress have produced legal questions spawning a huge literature. In Britain, legal issues have arisen prominently about the wearing of religious dress in schools and workplaces (e.g. McCrea 2014; Sandberg 2009). Examples could be multiplied easily. If culture was once largely invisible to law in so far as law assumed a monocultural jurisdiction, it is now becoming, ever more, an issue influencing regulatory choices in many legal fields.

Juristic legal theory has not caught up with this state of affairs. The issue here is how this theory has viewed *the social* – the realm of social life or society that law regulates. Modern legal theories have usually conceptualised law's regulated population as an undifferentiated social field made up of citizens or subjects assumed to be treated equally by law. In this social totality, according to the modern tenets of liberalism, the legal situation of individuals should, as far as possible, vary only in consequence of their own voluntary acts (e.g. duties acquired through their contracts, torts or crimes) or the right-conferring acts of others (e.g. under wills or contracts or as a result of wrongdoing against them). As Will Kymlicka (1995: 26) notes, 'In all liberal democracies, one of the major mechanisms for accommodating cultural difference is the protection of the civil and political rights of individuals.' By focusing on these rights, which usually make no reference to culture, law has enabled population groups to organise themselves in culturally distinctive ways, but without explicit legal recognition of this situation.

---

1 See *Mashpee Tribe* v *Town of Mashpee* 447 F Supp. 940 (D Mass 1978), affd, 592 F 2d 575 (1st Cir), cert denied, 444 US 866 (1979).

Anglo-American juristic legal theory presents two contrasting images of the social (Cotterrell 1995: ch 11). One is an image of *imperium*. This portrays society as a collectivity of individual subjects or citizens united only by their common subjection to a superior power. For Jeremy Bentham and John Austin, an independent political society is characterised by the habit of obedience of the bulk of the population (an undifferentiated mass for this purpose) to a single sovereign. For H. L. A. Hart (1994), by contrast, a society regulated by law is made up of citizens and officials whose relationships are fixed by the operation of social rules, of which the most important are legal. Citizens must at least obey primary rules of law, and officials must accept from an internal point of view the rules that make possible the operation of the legal system. So, social life is subject to the rule of law. But in both the theory of sovereignty and Hart's 'model of rules' the image of society is that of legally undifferentiated individuals united by being subject to a hierarchical order – the authority either of a sovereign person or body, or of the rule structures of the legal order.

Superior, 'vertically structured' authority provides the unity of the social as viewed through the prism of this kind of legal theory. The image is of individuals subject to official power which controls them, but – in a responsive, well-organised legal system – this power also lends support to their individual purposes and protects their valued conditions of life.

The converse image is that of *communitas*.[2] It underlies much of classical common law thought (e.g. Postema 1986: 19, 23, 66–76) and is present in nonpositivist theories of law such as those of Roscoe Pound and Lon Fuller. But this image appears most clearly in Ronald Dworkin's (1986) explicit theory of a political community as the author of its law.

In Dworkin's view, this community consists of interacting, legally empowered, rights-possessing individuals. Law derives from an active community that, in some sense, owns and creates it and in any case provides law's ultimate meaning and moral authority. Law's roots are in a social group conceived as a unified entity whose values, beliefs, common interests, allegiances, or traditions (we might say its culture) provide its foundation. The community source of law is seen theoretically as a single unified entity. Each nation-state legal system has one political community that it belongs to; indeed, Dworkin (1989: 496) equates the political community with the nation or the state. He does not assume that such a community is morally homogeneous but does see it as supporting a common culture and language (ibid: 488–9). No resources are offered for considering possible cultural variation – the matter is not seen as theoretically significant. The political community that makes and owns law is seen for the purposes of Dworkinian theory as a cultural unity (see also Kymlicka 1995: 77), a single, united source of law.

---

2 Communitas as an *image of society* should not be confused with the empirical concept of communal networks used throughout this book, which refers to sociologically identifiable forms of communal organisation.

In contrast to the image of imperium, that of communitas suggests a 'horizontal' rather than a 'vertical' structure of law's authority – an authority conferred through the interaction of individuals in community, rather than through the imposition of power. In the imperium image, law and the state power that supports it unify the social; in the communitas image the social is already unified through interaction and consensus, and that unity is expressed through law.

All of the most influential modern legal theories tend towards one or other of these two opposing images of society. They portray the social as *unified*, insofar as this issue is relevant in conceptualising the nature of law. And they portray the social as composed, for the most part, of *individuals* – legally identical citizens or subjects (corporations being, for many purposes, assimilated to the position of individuals as regards legal capacities). In the imperium conception, the social consists not of communities but of citizens or subjects. Even where the idea of community is made central, as in the communitas conception, the community is typically seen, under the influence of liberalism, as made up of individuals, rather than groups. By this means it remains possible to conceptualise the social as a single political community, rather than one fractured into different groups. This community (or its lawyer representatives) is assumed to establish law in a process of collective interpretation. In Dworkin's legal philosophy, the question of whether debate to find a 'best' meaning of law is possible between different cultural groups is not a theoretical issue. A common language and culture are assumed.

Legal theory and the differentiation of the social

Surely this theoretical state of affairs is highly unstable. In fact, the idea of the unity of the social has been challenged within juristic legal theory in three main ways.

The jurisprudence of difference

The first of these has been the emergence of approaches that base themselves explicitly on an idea of the *patterned differentiation of the social*. Marxist legal theory pioneered this orientation with its emphasis on the fundamental division of the social by class. If it had little real impact on mainstream juristic thought, more inroads were made by feminist legal theory, emphasising the significance of gender divisions and insisting that the very meaning of legal ideas becomes contested and destabilised in the face of feminist reinterpretations. More recently, critical race theory and other minority jurisprudences have invaded legal thought. The result has been the establishment of a 'jurisprudence of difference' which builds its insights directly from claims about the differentiation of the social (Cotterrell 2003: ch 8).

Ultimately, these critical approaches to juristic theory point to the idea that law can no longer be analysed as an object. It must be understood as a form of experience. When jurists were recruited from a single stratum of the social, their subjective views of the meaning and character of law could appear objective. Now, the jurisprudence of difference shows that what law is 'in reality' depends on the standpoint from which it is seen and the way it is experienced. The sense of social differentiation has invaded juristic thought – carried into it through the work of feminist lawyers, critical legal scholars, and lawyers linked to minorities of many kinds. They experience law in different ways, so its meaning differs for them.

How much impact has all this had on juristic thought? It is still, for the moment, possible to marginalise the jurisprudence of difference, to quarantine it in distinct chapters in jurisprudence textbooks or to see it as addressing special constituencies. The edifice of mainstream legal thought survives, but cracks are beginning to show. Legal philosophy that ignores these developments seems out of touch with sociolegal reality.

If the jurisprudence of difference were to succeed in reshaping juristic thought where would that lead? A recognition of the patterned differentiation of the social must demand attention to the categories used to conceptualise that differentiation – categories of gender, ethnicity, race, and so on. How meaningful or restrictive are these categories for the purposes of legal analysis? How far do they really capture the identity of individuals? Essentialism – the false assumption that essential characteristics of individuals or their experience can be deduced merely from their categorisation by characteristics such as gender, class, race, or ethnic group – is a problem for the jurisprudence of difference, one that is well recognised in, for example, feminist literature.[3] It suggests that ultimately the categories (e.g. race and ethnicity) of this new jurisprudence are not adequate. Insofar as the recognition of cultural differentiation is part of what is at stake here, new ways of understanding the complexity of culture are needed.

Culture inside law

A second challenge to juristic assumptions about the unity of the social arises from the fact that, as noted earlier, legal scholarship already addresses many issues of cultural diversity, and yet the scope of the concept of culture is unclear. For juristic purposes, culture needs to be broken down into component elements and in practice often is. In one aspect it relates to shared beliefs or ultimate values, in another to matters of tradition, including common language, environment, or historical experience. In a third sense it refers to shared affective allegiances and emotions. In a fourth, it reflects levels of technological and productive development (material culture) and instrumental (especially economic) social relationships.

Law may not relate to these contrasting elements in similar ways. The legal issues they raise – how law should express and protect social relations of community based on beliefs or values, on tradition, on affective or emotional bonds, or on common instrumental (primarily economic) projects – may be radically distinct. Society is made up of fluctuating, continually reshaped networks of community, which combine aspects of all of these different components of culture. As Samuel

---

3 One consequence is the advocacy of 'intersectional' approaches recognising the overlapping and interaction of race, gender, and other categories. But the problem of categorisation itself remains.

Scheffler (2007: 119) notes, 'cultures are not . . . sources of normative authority, for they are not explicitly justificatory structures at all.' Culture is not a definable unity that can in itself justify legal decisions and strategies. People relate to its different components rather than to an amorphous cultural aggregate. Scheffler (ibid: 124) advocates 'the elimination of the language of culture' from arguments about political and legal claims.

But in multicultural societies, different elements of culture readily become *superimposed* on one another. The development of multiculturalism can threaten to turn the normal plurality of modern societies – the different interests, value commitments, traditions, and allegiances that are combined in communal networks – into rigid, unbridgeable social divisions. This occurs when particular social groups appear to be separated from other groups along *all or most* of the four distinct cultural dimensions of (economic) interests, traditions, beliefs/values, and allegiances.

It is easy to see how this can occur. Instrumental (economic) relations of trade and employment can become relatively self-sufficient and closed. For example, employment practices may tend to exclude members of other racial or religious groups or those having different languages or customs. Trade and commerce networks may become discriminatory, exclusive, and self-enclosed. Thus, the boundaries of networks of community that exist primarily for instrumental (especially economic) purposes may come to mirror those of networks defined primarily by religious or other beliefs, or those shaped mainly by affective allegiances based on racial or other preferences and attachments, or those defined by shared customary practices, languages, or environments of coexistence.

All of these boundaries may merge into one. Social divisions based on divergent beliefs/ultimate values, affective allegiances/rejections, conflicting group interests, and contrasting traditions may reinforce one another, so that they create rigid, almost total separations between networks of community, which can then easily be seen as impenetrable, monolithic cultures or subcultures confronting each other.

Confronted by these problems, juristic theory's task is surely not to develop a legal concept of culture but to explore how far the regulation of social relations of community based on shared beliefs and values, on aspects of tradition and common experience or environment, on affective or emotional relationships, and on instrumental (primarily economic) relationships pose fundamentally *different technical problems* for law,[4] problems which sometimes converge dramatically and urgently in the particular conditions of multiculturalism.

What does unify the social?

A third challenge for juristic legal theory follows from what has just been said. If culture is a problematic idea when invoked to explain differences between social groups and their legal demands and aspirations, it must be no less problematic when

---

4 See Cotterrell 2006: 121–6, 153–8; 2008c: 23–5, 26–7.

invoked to presuppose the unity of the social. The question is not whether culture unifies the social but how far any of its component parts – the separable elements of culture – can contribute to this. And do these elements of culture contribute to a social unity in support of law?

Without overarching societal beliefs or values, common projects or convergent interests, elements of tradition, or emotional allegiances that sufficiently underpin law, its mobilisation may become an unlimited free-for-all (cf Tamanaha 2006). In multicultural societies, tradition may divide as much as unify populations that consist of diverse immigrant groups who carry their own traditions in such forms as common language, historical experience, and collective memory. Emotional ties (including the unifying feelings of patriotism) can be strong but volatile; it can be difficult to approach them rationally or to predict their effects. Purely instrumental ties of common interest focused on mutually beneficial projects can be transient, ephemeral, and changeable – providing social bonds only as long as advantage continues to be gained from them.

Something more fundamental, however, may come from the individualistic value systems that both American and European scholars have seen as underpinning, in different ways, law and the social in their societies. Utilitarian and expressive forms of individualism (supplemented with republican and other ideas), proclaimed as unifying 'habits of the heart' in the American context (Bellah et al 1996), run parallel with a European moral individualism, expressed, for example, in Durkheim's sociology.[5] In both contexts, an ideology that demands universal respect for the human dignity and autonomy of others as individuals, whatever their gender, race, ethnicity, or sexual orientation, might seem to offer the only *universal* value system that can help to unite contemporary Western multicultural societies, in which beliefs and values are otherwise very diverse. It is broadly consistent, in many respects, with the liberal individualism that informs much contemporary juristic legal theory. But it needs to be not merely assumed, as in this theory, but argued for theoretically as a necessary underpinning of cultural pluralism.

It might be suggested that it is enough to continue to appeal to liberalism to unify the social in conditions of multiculturalism. Will Kymlicka claims that liberalism can, indeed, address multiculturalism's challenges. In Western societies, he argues, there is a normal process of integration into the larger social unity for ethnic groups that have arisen from immigration but not for national groups such as those whose homelands were originally incorporated by conquest. Kymlicka (1995: 76) sees the difference in terms of how far minority populations possess what he calls societal (self-sufficient, all-embracing) cultures providing 'meaningful ways of life across the full range of human activities, including social, educational, religious, recreational, and economic life'. In his view national groups can have such a culture, but immigrant groups tend not to. They link in many ways into the larger society, and some of their elements of cultural differentiation soften in a few generations.

5 See Chapters 12 and 13.

Thus, for Kymlicka, different kinds of rights are appropriate to meet the aspirations of these diverse groups. Self-government rights might be necessary to allow national groups to affirm their own societal culture, while 'polyethnic rights' of immigrant groups, which support their cultures and may exempt them from some laws of the wider society that are fundamentally inconsistent with their particular cultural practices, might be warranted as a way of easing their integration into this wider society (ibid: 27–31). Kymlicka suggests not that cultural differentiation will, or should, disappear but merely that it might be appropriate to relate it legally to different kinds of social unity. He sees these kinds of legal strategies as compatible with liberal individualism, as long as individuals retain essential liberal freedoms in their cultural group, including the freedom to leave it.

There are problems with this approach, however, if an overall value system is needed to allow diversity in a structure of social unity. First, it is clear that many claims of cultural difference challenge liberal principles. They often demand ways of understanding individual dignity and autonomy that differ from liberalism's understandings but nonetheless place great emphasis on these values and may see liberalism as, to some extent, inconsistent with them. Consequently what may be sought in practice is X's recognition of the dignity and autonomy of Y, which, however, involves also recognising that the way Y may wish to express that dignity and autonomy may be different from and even inconsistent with the way X would do so.

A value system focused on individualism might therefore need to recognise that the meaning of the value system itself will be developed in a process of communication between cultural groups – a continuous effort of these groups to learn from each other. So it is necessary to hold firmly to values that can unify across cultural divides, yet be prepared to reflect on and revise one's interpretations of those values in the process of seeking to understand the other.[6]

Second, Kymlicka's characterisation of ethnic groups originating with immigration may not be convincing. The implication is that in these groups cultural difference is unstable, and law's task is to integrate them into the larger society. But, in Europe at least, including the UK, demands on law from these groups are not merely for special support or for concessions – 'opt-outs' from general rules. Often, the demand is that law should represent cultural diversity generally as one of its major purposes. It should not treat cultural differences as exceptions to the norm but should evolve towards becoming a law appropriate for a society of permanent cultural diversity.

This is a considerable challenge. It may involve more than legal exceptions (for example, exceptions for elements of religious dress as modifications to uniforms in the school or workplace). A process of *collective reinterpretation of legal concepts* might be entailed – involving new understandings of familiar common law ideas, such as 'reasonableness'. The unity of the social, in these circumstances, is not, then,

---

6 Cf Raz 1998: 204–5, emphasising that multiculturalism involves the recognition that 'universal values' can be realised in different ways in different cultural contexts and that, in the effort to understand such values, these different ways are worthy of respect, not merely toleration.

something to be presupposed or to be engineered through specific exceptional legal changes. It seems best to see it as an aspiration – a special purpose set for law in the context of multiculturalism – to facilitate and guide a permanent cross-cultural conversation by which mutual learning between groups takes place.

How can legal theory embrace this conversation, given its established outlooks? An imperium outlook would imply the promotion of unity between citizens through law's coercive authority (*voluntas*). Any cross-cultural conversation will appear, in this image, as strongly shaped and directed by hierarchies of legal official-dom. Legal authority being seen as a 'vertical' structuring of the social, the tendency may be to emphasise 'deep conflicts between the state-centred assumptions of offi-cial law . . . and the postulates governing ethnic minority communities with their own kinship networks and religious spheres' (Shah 2005: 10). Communication across cultural divides may be subject to official or state legal control.

A communitas orientation, by contrast, would more easily see law reflecting or expressing cultural conditions but would need to be adjusted to recognise explicitly the diversity of legal interpretive communities. The Dworkinian search for the 'best' meaning of law to be derived through interpretation would now appear as a search for the best mutual understandings as to how society should be governed that can be derived from cross-cultural conversation.

Law as communication

Focusing on these challenges to legal theory, it seems natural to use words such as 'conversation' and 'communication'. Legal ideas are changing in the face of the challenges of multiculturalism, but my emphasis has been on processes of commu-nication by which these changes are brought about, not on the changes themselves. Indeed, it is hard to generalise about these because legal changes, in the main, relate not to unified ideas of culture or cultural pluralism but to social relations reflecting diverse aspects of culture in complex ways. If law's most distinctive tasks in relating to multiculturalism are tasks of *communication* and of *facilitating communication*, it fol-lows that the main reorientation of legal theory required by multiculturalism is a new emphasis on these communicative purposes of law.

It has long been argued that the concept of purpose cannot define the nature of law because it represents nothing objective (Berolzheimer 1912: 350). It is necessary to know *whose* purposes are being considered; otherwise the attribution of purpose to law is arbitrary. Criticisms of this kind have often been made of Lon Fuller's purposive theory of law, which identifies communication as law's key purpose (Fuller 1969: 186).

Yet the idea of law as communication and as a facilitator of communication has a special significance for multiculturalism. Cultural groups must communicate with one another to obtain the benefits of coexistence. And the jurisprudence of difference can be understood, in part, as an effort to communicate minority experiences and interpretations of law in the forums of juristic debate. If, in legal theory's communitas conception, communication among law's interpreters creates law's meaning, then in multicultural societies this involves communication across cultural difference. In an imperium conception, failure of communication by courts and legislatures is a hurdle that law must overcome to carry its authority and commands to groups that appear deaf or resistant to it. Communication cannot be the basis of a comprehensive theory of law, but it is an aspect of law that is central to its engagement with cultural pluralism.

Legal communications, Koen Raes writes, '*make possible* a dialogue between different views of life' (Raes 1996: 38; italics in original). For Mark van Hoecke (2002: 7, 8), reflecting ideas of Habermas and others, law gives 'a framework for human communication . . . the taking into account of differing points of view and . . . some dialectical exchange of viewpoints'. James Boyd White (1990: 261) sees law as mediating among virtually all discourses but creating a new one in the process; it is a means of translation. Raes (1996: 38–9) emphasises the 'emptiness' of legal subjectivity (its abstractness), which facilitates legal communication by simplifying the contexts law must communicate between and about. Postmodernist writers see law as a form of knowledge without foundations, which might fit it for the task of mediating between different cultural understandings. For White (1990: 267), law 'partakes of the radical uncertainty of the rest of life, the want of firm external standards'.

But law is not an empty vessel. It carries cultural presuppositions. It does not regulate communication channels neutrally but directs them in accordance with dominant cultural understandings. Law is a prism through which particular cultural claims are refracted in predictable ways. But this does not make law incapable of being a facilitator of communication. Because culture is not a single thing but only an aggregate of different types of social relations of community, each component of the aggregate is a site of communication, a point at which the negotiation of new understandings can be attempted when these social relations are addressed by law. Invocation of law can thus enable many kinds of cultural dialogue to occur.

Once that dialogue has occurred in some area, it may be possible for law to provide a relatively peaceful and passion-free ordering of affairs. That will depend on how far law has addressed in a plausible way the diverse aspects of cultural relations – instrumental, belief/values-based, affective, and traditional – that bear on it. Much will depend on the sensitivity with which courts or legislatures communicate their understanding of the issues involved and on the way information about the law is conveyed (for example by reporting in mass media) to those it purports to regulate. But where this dialogue has not occurred or is not completed satisfactorily, legal processes may remain a site of furious, often passionate, conflicting communications, efforts to influence, persuade, demand, or threaten – not just battles of rights but battles of interests, ideas, allegiances, or traditions.

One much discussed case before the House of Lords (then the UK's highest court) may illustrate the potential complexity of law's role as a medium and site of communication in relation to multiculturalism. In *Begum*,[7] the respondent, age 17, argued that, contrary to Article 9 of the European Convention on Human

7 R (on the application of Begum, by her litigation friend, Rahman) v Headteacher and Governors of Denbigh High School [2006] UKHL 15.

Rights, which guaranteed her right to manifest her religion or beliefs, she had been excluded from her school because she had insisted on wearing a *jilbāb*, 'a long coat-like garment' (case report, para 10) covering her head but not her face – a form of Islamic dress which she considered that her faith required her to wear. The court noted that the issue was not the rights and wrongs of schoolchildren wearing Islamic female dress – permitted in very many UK schools – but the school's right to maintain its school uniform policy. After much consultation with parents and with Muslim advisers, a variable uniform (including optional Islamic headscarves) had been devised, intended to satisfy the religious requirements and traditions of all sections of the school's multicultural student population, and parents.

The court dismissed the respondent's claim that her Article 9 rights had been infringed. When, after wearing the school uniform for two years, she had decided to wear the *jilbāb*, she could, in the court's view, have moved without 'any real difficulty' (para 25) to another school that allowed this attire. The court found the school uniform policy justified and proportionate given the school's perceived needs. The school saw a uniform as important to promote 'a positive sense of communal identity', to avoid 'manifest disparities of wealth and style' in students' dress that could be divisive (para 6), and 'to promote inclusion and social cohesion' (para 18). 'It had taken immense pains to devise a uniform policy which respected Muslim beliefs but did so in an inclusive, unthreatening, and uncompetitive way' (para 34). The court noted evidence that Muslim girls at the school feared pressure to wear the *jilbāb* if some were allowed to do so. One judge, Lord Hoffman, noted that compromise solutions had been rejected by the respondent and by her elder brother, who often spoke for her; he thought that they had 'sought a confrontation' (para 50).

My concern is with the social messages communicated by and through this case.[8] It communicated (as it was clearly intended to) the strength of the conviction of the respondent and her supporters about the importance of a particular kind of Islamic dress for the faith it represented. Also communicated were messages about the needs of social cohesion, symbolised in the school's view of its uniform policy. One judgment (by Baroness Hale) quotes extensively from academic literature on the significance of the Islamic headscarf and other forms of female Islamic dress and on the religious, family, political, and other reasons why they are worn. These ideas are thus written into the judicial record, potentially communicating them to those who read the judgments or other reports of the case. Communication here is certainly not just about what is or is not lawful under UK law. It is also about the way problems such as those in the case should, in the court's view, be reasoned out. The school's approach to addressing multiculturalism is explained and approved and

---

8 David Nelken (2014) criticised an earlier version of the arguments in the following paragraphs for ambiguity, asking how far they were intended as (i) a *juristic* evaluation of the *Begum* decision or (ii) a *sociological* inquiry into the court's rhetoric. In fact, only the latter was (and is) intended, but, I suggest, such an inquiry might still aid juristic awareness by observing and identifying certain judicial styles and their communicative strategies.

implicitly contrasted with threatening and intransigent behaviour directed against the school authorities.

How does the court manage communication in this case? It does not pit the school as an *institution* (and, still less, the local authority, or the state as an entity) against the *individual* respondent. Communication depends on maintaining a focus on respect for the autonomy and dignity – here, the personal claims (including claims of belief and ultimate values, tradition, interest, and emotional attachments) – of individuals, whether these are before the court or are evoked by the court as actually or potentially concerned with the issues raised by the case. So, the school's uniform policy is portrayed by the court not in an abstract, bureaucratic manner but as a symbol of the balancing of *social relations of community* among individuals in a multicultural environment – hence the emphasis on consultation with parents and with representative religious authorities and on the views of other girls at the school; hence also a stress on social cohesion as a main concern of the school's uniform policy.

It is equally significant that this individualising strategy is sometimes put into reverse, so to speak. The court, in effect, dilutes Shabina Begum's individual claim by implicitly portraying it as something else: perhaps a politically motivated group claim, for which she may serve merely as representative – even perhaps (but barely a hint here) an insincere claim abstracted from her personal circumstances (she had apparently accepted the uniform policy for two years and, on deciding it was unacceptable, could, in the court's view, have moved schools without much difficulty). In general, these matters are touched on only through the reporting of facts in the opinions, with little, if any, comment. The court leaves it to readers of the law report to draw conclusions out of the package of considerations it has carefully assembled.

Of course, messages communicated by the case were not well received in all quarters. But the judicial opinions are clearly designed to communicate directly to the various cultural constituencies concerned with these issues. The methods of the judges are elaborate explanation and description, balancing of evidence, examination of motivations, attention to other case-law (of UK courts and of the European Court of Human Rights), and use of academic legal and other literature. The judges seek to make their communications as authoritative as possible, but they rely not just on legal argument but on appeals to a transcultural reasonableness and the persuasive power of an accumulation of factual detail.

In general this case had some effect in defusing controversy around its particular issues. Whatever the rights and wrongs of the decision (e.g. Sandberg 2014: 258–9), it illustrates especially clearly – precisely because of its context of passionate controversy – a court attempting strategically to communicate across cultural divides while defending its own authority above those divides.

Conclusion

Law's essential purpose in addressing the conditions of multiculturalism is to facilitate communication. What law itself must communicate in a modern society of great diversity is a need for adequate and equal respect for the autonomy and dignity of all individuals. In appropriate circumstances, it must firmly enforce this respect.

Without such a value system of individualism, stable transcultural communication is impossible. And this is no less true once it is recognised that certain aspects of this value system may be themselves matters of ongoing negotiation within the fora of law. Where legal communications around culture take the form of passionate battles of rights, it is important that the eventual outcome of these battles – and the aim in processing them legally – be to produce peaceful, commonsense mutual understandings, routine regulation explicitly recognising cultural differences while facilitating everyday social interaction that makes possible communication across them.

12

CAN SOCIOLOGY CLARIFY LEGAL VALUES?

A template

Can sociology tell us what is right or wrong? For most social scientists (and surely most citizens), the answer is clearly no. Sociology claims to be science, not moral philosophy. Sociology of law, for example, aims to explain the social character of law but not whether any particular law or legal regime is just or morally sound. A few leading modern legal sociologists have disagreed. As we noted in Chapter 5, Philip Selznick claimed that sociology, studying legality as an ideal pursued in practice, could help to clarify and realise that ideal (Selznick 1969; 1992: ch 1). But this has been an unusual minority position.

Nevertheless, classic sociological theory provides some still-useful resources for reconsidering orthodox views about sociology's capacities for informing moral and legal evaluation. Most importantly, these resources are found in Émile Durkheim's elaborately developed sociology of morality. Yet this central aspect of his work has remained largely unexploited and is often ignored as regards its potential relevance for contemporary legal studies, despite all the attention that has been devoted to relating other parts of Durkheim's sociological thought to the study of law (e.g. Lukes and Scull eds 2013; Cotterrell 1999).

Durkheim offers a powerful and distinctive sociological template for examining legal values, aiming to show how they gain such resonance as they have by being congruent with conditions needed to ensure cohesion and integration of the society in which they exist. This chapter explains his main ideas on what he sees as a sociologically necessary framework of values for modern law. It then tries to show the kind of illumination that these ideas may provide by considering, in Durkheimian perspective, two recently prominent legal-moral issues: the acceptability of torture in defence of national security, and restrictions on the wearing of the Islamic headscarf.

These issues may seem wholly distinct and unrelated, but, in the context of this chapter, they provide convenient vehicles for exploring aspects of moral individualism – the value system that, *for sociological reasons*, Durkheim argues must be a foundation of all law in modern complex Western societies. The central element of Durkheimian moral individualism is universal respect for the equal human dignity and autonomy of every member of society, whatever differences there may be in the outlook, position, life conditions, or roles of society's members. I suggest that Durkheim offers, through his analyses of moral individualism, a thought-provoking, critical sociological alternative to familiar juristic debates on human dignity.

I argue that this alternative provides important insights relevant to contemporary issues. It can be used, for example, not only to show unambiguously why the use of torture is morally indefensible for contemporary complex societies but also to clarify the context (in terms of various conceptions of national security) in which efforts have been made to *defend* torture. In relation to Islamic dress, an application of Durkheim's ideas on solidarity and the body suggests that prohibiting *certain* forms of dress but not others contravenes values of human dignity. Beyond this, I argue that Durkheim reveals the complexity of human dignity and autonomy as legal values and raises important issues about their scope of application. This is to claim not that these values *must* be seen in Durkheimian terms but merely that doing so casts a new, revealing light on their scope and significance.

Durkheim consistently advocated a 'value-free' sociology of morals – purporting to study moral values objectively as these are expressed in the practices, proclamations, and assumptions characteristic of particular societies or social groups. But Gabriel Abend (2008) has argued that Durkheim's actual sociological practice was very different, since he was committed – as he made clear – to the idea that 'science can help in finding the direction in which our conduct ought to go, assisting us to determine the ideal that gropingly we seek', and that, having observed reality, 'we shall distil the ideal from it' (Durkheim 1984: xxvi).

Abend calls Durkheim a 'normative relativist' who believes that what is moral is, basically, what people in a certain time and place think is moral. So, sociologists can record a society's morality as what its members assume it to be. On this basis, one can decide (sociologically) whether or not conduct is 'moral' with regard to a particular society or type of society (Abend 2008: 92, 102). Yet, for Durkheim, matters are more complex than this. Durkheimian morality is *not* just what people think in a given time and place. Sociologists can also point out what is morally (and legally) appropriate for societies *of a certain type*, and this depends on a sociological understanding of what is needed to ensure their integration or cohesiveness.

Following this Durkheimian approach, sociology cannot reveal *universal moral truths* (at least, it would need adequate empirical evidence to suggest that any particular moral principles are appropriate to all societies). Social science is not engaged in the pursuit of timeless moral understandings (as moral philosophy might be). Any criteria governing what is morally appropriate will relate to the sociological character of the particular type of society concerned. Durkheim claims that sociology can study social life objectively as a matter of 'social fact'. In doing so, it can identify moral principles and practices compatible with (or even necessary to) stable social relations in particular kinds of societies. To this extent, sociology can provide guidance on moral issues. It is not limited to describing what people think in moral terms and what moral choices they actually make. To some extent, it can also provide criteria to evaluate and criticise those choices. Thus, sociology can sometimes advise on what law should prescribe or permit. When sociology reveals the fundamental importance of certain moral principles in particular social conditions, the question of whether these should be expressed and defended through law needs to be faced (Cotterrell 1999: ch 13).

Clearly, a sociolegal approach such as that sketched here is wholly alien to most established research orientations in sociology of law. Law has been seen less as an expression of morality (as Durkheim sees it) than as an expression of power. In Western societies it has increasingly been understood in purely instrumental terms (Tamanaha 2006), perhaps especially by legal sociologists (Cotterrell 2009). Yet it may be that more is now being asked of law by citizens[1] and that its morally expressive potential needs more exploration (e.g. Zeegers et al eds 2005; Van Der Burg and Taekema eds 2004). In such a context, the idea that sociology might help to clarify certain legal values is at least worth considering (e.g. Thacher 2006), especially in times when uncertainty exists about their substance and grounding and the appropriate direction of their development. The issue is: in what sense, if any, can law be more than merely an instrument to achieve any chosen governmental or private end?

A sociology of legal values would thus be an enterprise of seeking law's moral meaning, not philosophically but in terms of the empirically identifiable conditions of coexistence of individuals and groups in a certain time and place, that is, in the circumstances of a particular kind of society at a particular point in its historical development.

Durkheim on justice and moral individualism

It is necessary initially to outline Durkheim's general treatment of morals. Sociology, for him, cannot explain *why* particular moral beliefs exist in any given society. Sociology does not claim that moral ideas arise through social necessity. 'However strong a need may be, it cannot create *ex nihilo* the means for its own satisfaction,' he writes (1992: 35); 'just because [a particular institution] . . . was desirable it does not follow that it was possible.' Morality is 'an infinity of special rules' (Durkheim 1961: 25) related to particular social circumstances and historical conditions. Choices and practices acquire their moral meaning in specific contexts. Generalisation of principles comes later, if at all, and gives only 'a schematic expression' (Durkheim 1975: 268). To understand morality, it is necessary to study social life *empirically*, as it exists in specific times and places.

---

1 See further, Chapter 14, discussing tensions between popular and governmental expectations of law.

Progress will not be made by talking abstractly about 'human nature' or 'humanity' as if these had a timeless, context-free character as a source of moral and legal ideas. As Norberto Bobbio remarks, 'many rights have been derived from the generous and obliging nature of man' (1996: 4), but scholars disagree on what this nature is, so human rights clash, are open to varying interpretations, change over time, vary in range of application, and lack absolute foundations and uncontroversial definitions of their contents (ibid: ch 1; Laughland 2002).

In a well-integrated society, the most important moral precepts – those on which fundamental social relations depend – are expressed in law. But the state and its law cannot take sides in many moral disputes. Social groups of all kinds and sizes need to sort out moral structures for themselves and provide self-regulation. Durkheim emphasises the vast moral pluralism of complex modern societies but does not go far in analysing it, except to emphasise the variety of occupational groups and their need for self-regulation (e.g. Hearn 1985). A strong emphasis in his work, after the publication of his first book *The Division of Labour in Society* (1984), is on the need for a framework of ultimate values to underpin unifying, society-wide regulation in which moral pluralism can flourish without leading to a fragmentation of society.

This framework of values is *moral individualism* or what Durkheim (1957: 54, 69–70, 172) often calls 'the cult of the individual' or 'cult of the human person'. It demands unconditional respect for the dignity and autonomy of all individuals by virtue of their common humanity (Durkheim 1969). In Durkheim's view, this is the only moral basis on which interaction between people can occur spontaneously and with calculability, security, stability, and mutual confidence in complex modern societies. These societies are characterised by ever-increasing specialisation of social roles and economic functions, so there are proliferating differences in citizen's lifestyles, moral outlooks, and social understandings. Moral individualism affirms what unites people – their basic, irreducible human worth – despite their being divided from one another in innumerable other ways. It provides an essential basis for interpersonal and intergroup communication, especially about rights and responsibilities, one that can link human beings in bonds of mutual respect and human empathy, despite all social differences in conditions of great social complexity.

Crucially, moral individualism is not liberalism (cf Cladis 1992), although, like liberalism, it puts the individual at the centre of its moral universe. It does not give the individual a kind of primacy over society, as liberal thought typically does. It is *society* (its need for solidarity in circumstances of modern complexity and diversity) that invests each individual with absolute moral value (irrespective of personal conditions or character). Society does not exist only to fulfil the needs of the individual; rather, individualism is valuable because it corresponds with (a particular kind of) society's requirements for solidarity and unity. The autonomy and dignity of the individual are what society decrees (and needs) them to be. Autonomy as a value requires that the individual be able to interact freely and spontaneously with others, but this is not an idea of freedom *from* society. And the state, law, and regulation are indispensable to make possible the autonomy and dignity of the individual. Certainly, the state can be a threat to this autonomy and dignity, but potentially so can almost any action by other people, whether politically organised or not. So, what is important is to create participatory structures to ensure that regulation, whatever its source, reflects and promotes moral individualism.

How does moral individualism relate to the value usually most directly linked to law, that of *justice*? In *The Division of Labour*, Durkheim portrays justice as what is required to ensure the normal functioning of the division of labour (the differentiation and reintegration of specialist tasks and social functions) in a complex modern society; justice might be thought of as the oil to lubricate the mechanisms of interdependence in such a society – to ensure the smooth, complex interplay of social and economic roles and functions. So, justice should be embedded in everyday social relations and transactions, a matter of *practice* rather than moral theory. Anne Rawls (2003), for example, sees Durkheimian justice as having nothing to do with shared beliefs or abstract value systems. On one interpretation, this justice does not seek significantly to disturb the existing 'natural' character of society at all but merely stabilises and regularises expectations attaching to transactions within it (Sirianni 1984); on another, justice may pull towards larger ideals of equality but still remains largely constrained by the practicalities of existing social organisation (Green 1989).

Durkheimian justice is not an integrated value system in itself but a set of basic practical conditions to be satisfied if social interactions, in complex societies, are to be founded on reliable expectations and stable mutual understandings. It is the minimum of regulation needed for that purpose. So, the need for justice seems to grow directly out of economic transactions and social relationships themselves, so as to fulfil them and allow them to flourish. It is 'a functional necessity, not an ideal' (Rawls 2003: 299).

Justice must, at least, as Durkheim explains, (i) outlaw arbitrary discriminations and official disabilities that prevent people dealing freely with one another and participating in social and economic relations (what he calls the 'forced division of labour'), (ii) guarantee proper reciprocity in dealings (an idea of 'just contracts'), (iii) remove arbitrary economic advantages in the form of inherited wealth, and, in general, (iv) provide clear, consistent regulatory understandings to govern social interaction (preventing anomie) (Durkheim 1984: bk 3 chs 1 and 2; 1957: ch 18). The last of these aspects of justice entails the whole apparatus of the rule of law, including due process and legal equality (Rawls 2003). And law attracts respect by 'clearly expressing the natural interrelation of things' and being 'appropriate to the nature of the facts' (Durkheim 1957: 107) – in other words, by expressing the particularistic moral demands of justice, rooted in specific kinds of social relations and transactions.

It may be that when Durkheim wrote *The Division of Labour*, he thought that justice, in this sense, expressed through law, was enough to underpin regulation to promote solidarity in modern societies. In his later writings, however, he saw a need for something more: a broad system of shared beliefs or ultimate values – moral individualism. Why, then, is this value system needed to supplement a justice rooted in particular kinds of transactions and social relations? Durkheim never makes the connection between justice and moral individualism clear, but his ideas can be developed to suggest why the latter must supplement the former. Justice encourages trust between people as they transact, cooperate, plan common projects, try to avoid friction, compromise interests, and recognise their interdependence. But it does not create the sense, for them, of being *part of a larger whole*, a cohesive, unified, integrated society. Such a society needs a value system that affirms the full membership status of each of its members, and without this it 'cannot hold together' (Durkheim 1969: 66).[2]

Given the moral diversity of modern societies, this overarching value system will be strictly limited in scope. It will not only recognise difference but support and celebrate it; it will not impose moral uniformity. But it will uncompromisingly condemn acts and policies that *exclude* individuals or groups from society because they are seen as different or that *prevent* or discourage them from interacting freely with others on a society-wide basis – that is, playing their part as effectively as possible in the networks of interdependence on which modern social solidarity depends. It will be a value system that not only removes barriers to interaction but also *actively motivates* all individuals to play their part in society, giving them the confidence and status to do so by strongly affirming their human worth. It will foster *communication* across all social divides. It will be *inclusive*, opposing all forms of social marginalisation.

So, moral individualism is justified not philosophically, by deduction from abstract ideas of 'humanity' (cf Mautner 2008), but *sociologically*, as needed to facilitate society-wide economic and social integration and to affirm the moral unity of a diverse society. It is, in Durkheim's view, 'the only system of beliefs' that can fulfil this need (1969: 66). Whether or how far moral individualism is actually respected in practice, supported in popular opinion, or affirmed in government policy is not the issue; it is uniquely appropriate to modern complex societies, *whether recognised or not*. But Durkheim sees it as a yardstick against which, increasingly, Western laws and legal systems are widely judged in practice.

A sociology of human dignity

Two other matters need to be considered before applying Durkheim's arguments to specific problems. First, why, in his analysis, has moral individualism become more prominent and explicit in Western societies – for example, in legal ideas of human dignity? Second, can sociology clarify what human dignity and autonomy mean as legally relevant values? These questions can be addressed together.

Human dignity has been condemned as 'a useless concept' and 'hopelessly vague', at least in some legal contexts (Macklin 2003: 1420). Yet it is very widely invoked

---

2 Compare Radbruch's recognition of 'justice' and 'fitness for purpose' (i.e. the cultural purpose set for law by the environment in which it exists) as distinct values inherent in the idea of law: see Chapter 3. In a Durkheimian perspective, promoting moral individualism might well be seen as an overriding cultural purpose that is set for law by 'modern' (complex, highly differentiated) societies.

in contemporary law. Some writers see it as at the core of human rights (Mautner 2008). For Oscar Schachter (1983: 851), human dignity 'includes recognition of a distinct personal identity, reflecting individual autonomy and responsibility', but 'the individual self is a part of larger collectivities', and dignity presupposes a level of material well-being because it cannot be sustained by someone lacking the basic means of economic subsistence.

Some writers distinguish a subjective sense of dignity from 'real dignity' objectively measured (Lee and George 2008: 174). Thus, objectively, one can be judged as having sacrificed one's dignity even though subjectively one may not feel or care about this – and vice versa. So, society can decide whether individuals' dignity is infringed irrespective of what they themselves think (Dworkin 1993: 167–8), and one can lose human dignity through one's own voluntary acts (e.g. Wheatley 2001: 322–3). Thus, human dignity as a legal value does not mean liberty free of all constraints. It refers (as expressed, for example, by German courts) to the 'individual's right to personality' and 'the flourishing not the deterioration of the personality' (Fletcher 1984: 179). Unfettered liberty to degrade oneself as a human being is not an expression of dignity or autonomy.

Such ideas are consistent with Durkheim's understanding of dignity and autonomy as defined by society, not rooted in some pre-social notion of individual freedom. Yet, if the dignity and autonomy of the individual are necessary to *society* to secure its integration, cohesion, and moral unity, they can be meaningful only insofar as they are experienced by the *individual*. What then, sociologically speaking, does society need the individual to experience? To participate fully in society, one must feel in control of one's life conditions, which means free from the tyranny of instincts that dominate one's choices, from external controls and arbitrary prohibitions, and from exploitations that undermine one's sense of identity.

For example, the publication, without permission, of intimate photos might well be experienced as an invasion of privacy and a loss of human dignity. But there might be no such negative experience if the photos were published with the permission of those photographed who welcomed the resulting publicity and the opportunities it brought. Subjectively, loss of human dignity and autonomy is loss of personal control over one's conditions of existence.

This is still highly complex, however, because what counts as 'control' is a relative matter depending, in part, on the kind and amount of control seen as possible (by the individual concerned and by society at large). Someone terminally ill may have little control over the timing and circumstances of his or her death, but it may be possible to speak of dying 'with dignity' in such conditions, which means being able to exercise such personal control as the circumstances allow and continuing to promote 'the flourishing not the deterioration of the personality' as far as possible up to the end of life. It means retaining a consciousness of personal identity and integrity and continuing to assert these, despite all obstacles to doing so. Punishments condemned as 'cruel and unusual' are often seen as ones that remove all possibility of retaining dignity in this sense.

Means of control of conditions of dignity may differ also according to the status accorded to individuals by society. For example, indebtedness in a 'respectable' working-class household might amount to a personal indignity of a kind unknown to an aristocrat for whom living on credit is not at all a badge of shame. People having limited possibilities, for example because of poverty, to assert their 'right to personality' effectively may value badges of dignity that appear relatively unimportant to other individuals who, because of their material wealth, have many ways to assert such a right. Durkheim has been criticised for paying insufficient attention to status in analysing the conditions of social solidarity (Adair 2008). But it is clear that, from his sociological perspective, the dignity and autonomy demanded by moral individualism are very much concerned with individuals' ability to control the conditions of their existence in relation to other people and to maintain a status that makes it possible for them to play a role appropriate to their talents and abilities in the economic division of labour of modern complex society.

However, if that were all, social and economic interactions could remain limited, restricted within particular social or economic groups or by locality or shared traditions. Control of one's personal conditions of existence (the aspect of human dignity and autonomy that is subjectively experienced) has to be linked also to the more objective aspect of dignity and autonomy which society defines – especially through law. This is the aspect that defines human worth as irreducible and dignity as non-alienable by the individual.

Why, sociologically speaking, is this aspect necessary? The answer is suggested by the 'dying with dignity' example mentioned earlier. The subjective sense of dignity, taken alone, cannot indicate whether, say, the execution of a human being is, in itself, an affront to human dignity – or, indeed, whether any constraints on individual freedom are attacks on dignity. Because everyone lives subject to constraints, moral individualism has to define what human personality is and what constitutes an unjustified constraint on its expression. It has to do this in terms of not what the individual thinks and feels but what society needs human personality to be so as to fit the conditions of social interaction in a diverse, well-integrated society.

Seen in this light, it seems that *moral individualism becomes more important the more complex and differentiated societies become.* Ideas of common humanity, in the form of human rights and human dignity, are sociologically necessary to modern, but not necessarily to premodern, societies. Conceptions of justice arising out of the particularities of social relations need generalising in these modern societies. They also need supplementing with an overarching individualistic value system as social interactions become less localised, more varied, and wider-reaching in their effects, as they become elements in ever more extensive networks of economic and social interdependence.

As these networks become more complex, transactions within them become more anonymous; people rely on confidence in impersonal systems as much as on interpersonal trust (Luhmann 1979). More must be assumed, because it cannot be known, about the innumerable 'faceless' people an individual must deal with in these systems, and such assumptions need moral-legal guarantees. Developed ideas of human dignity and autonomy become more and more the basis of these assumptions and guarantees. Hence, *universal ideas of human dignity are a function of social and economic complexity*.

These values are needed to promote *society-wide* interpersonal communication, spontaneous social interactions, economic confidence and coordination, social inclusion and collective commitment, and mutual appreciation of diversity. Their appropriate content is determined by these objects which they serve. And since, in Durkheim's view, the modern state has the responsibility to promote these objects, values of human dignity and human rights are not inevitably set up in opposition to the state as weapons for the individual to wield against it in the form of legal claims. They are values that sociology advises the state to champion and are in no way opposed to necessarily extensive state regulation of ever more complex social and economic life.

Punishment and torture

Durkheim assumes that central to human dignity and autonomy is the integrity of the human body and mind. Thus, one of the most important things moral individualism does, in his analysis, is to constrain the ferocity of *punishments*: 'there is a real and irremediable contradiction in avenging the offended human dignity of the victim [of crime] by violating that of the criminal. The only way, not of eliminating the difficulty (for strictly speaking it is insoluble), but of alleviating it, is to lessen the punishment as much as possible' (Durkheim 1992: 42). Moral individualism requires that punishment no longer act on the body (Durkheim 1961: 182–3). Even in serious cases, it should act only on the offender's liberty (imprisonment). All physically cruel forms of punishment are unacceptable because they directly affront human dignity. The same applies to any physical maltreatment of the individual inflicted by agencies of the state. On this basis, Steven Lukes has argued that Durkheimian sociology condemns *torture* absolutely, as wholly inconsistent with the moral foundations of modern societies (Lukes 2006; see also Levey 2007).

The matter is not as straightforward as Lukes suggests, though I think his conclusion is correct. Note Durkheim's caveat, quoted earlier: the difficulty of the morality of punishment (or we might say, more broadly, the morality of society deliberately inflicting harm on those who themselves threaten harm to society) is, he says, 'strictly speaking . . . insoluble'. The value system of moral individualism is justified sociologically because it promotes the inclusion and participation of all in society and society's cohesion and integration. But that aim is undermined not just by violence against the body but also by imprisonment, which excludes the offender from the networks of social solidarity. In fact, any punishment may loosen the offender's ties to society insofar as it obstructs the individual's participation in society. Durkheim saw the punishment of individuals who transgress society's values as necessary to defend those values for the law-abiding, but once we see the values themselves being compromised in the process of punishment, the morality of what is being done becomes ambiguous.

The logic of Durkheim's position (which he does not develop, no doubt because he wants to defend the necessity of punishment) seems to be that *all punishment, of whatever kind, is an attack on human dignity and autonomy* and in conflict with moral individualism (see also Joas 2008: 171).

Is the moral contradiction presented by punishment (defending society's values by transgressing them) removed only by thinking of the offender as being *outside* society anyway – not part of the networks of solidarity, an enemy of society who can properly be sacrificed for the good of society? Such an unattractive conclusion would fly in the face of Durkheim's humanitarian outlook, which rejects any idea that the individual, even if a criminal, can be used as a means to an end. It is also a conclusion that might justify torture if the torture victim, like the offender, is seen as 'outside' society and can be sacrificed as a means to an end: the defence of society against its enemies.

Clearly, however, Durkheim does not see offenders as outside society, because he insists that society's value system of moral individualism applies to them too. This is why 'cruel and unusual' punishment of body or mind is not morally permissible. In his writings, the idea of the offender being punished for the benefit of society is gradually supplemented with that of punishment as a communication process between society and the offender – it is important that the offender be shown society's values and their meaning (Cotterrell 1999: 77). Whether punishment is useful in doing this is another matter, but this is now seen as part of its justification. The offender, it seems, is to be drawn back into society's networks of interaction and interdependence if possible.

So, I think, the best way to see Durkheimian punishment is as an uneasy *compromise*, a process in which the dignity and autonomy of the offender are indeed sacrificed, but in a strictly limited, measured way and always with the idea that the damage to these values is, as far as possible, to be repaired.

Seen in this way, it is not self-evident that attacks on the body are always the most serious penal transgressions of moral individualism. A long period of imprisonment does not obviously infringe the 'individual's right to personality' less than might corporal punishment in schools, which Durkheim (1961: 182) explicitly condemns as incompatible with the values of moral individualism. But where the object is to *destroy completely* the individual (as in capital punishment) or the individual's personality, this is clearly the most flagrant affront to these values, as Durkheim understands them. Since the object of *torture* is to destroy every vestige of the victim's personal control over his or her conditions of existence so as remove any autonomy or subjective experience of dignity that would allow resistance to the interrogator's demands, it is absolutely incompatible with moral individualism and not a matter of value compromises like those that surround punishment.

We noted that, for Durkheim, the normal offender is not outside society. Punishment is a process *within* society. But must the value system of moral individualism be extended to protect nonmembers of society? Rare recent attempts to justify torture practices have presented these as regrettably necessary to protect a national society against *external* threats to its very existence (former US Vice President Cheney, as quoted in Danner 2009). As one official put it: 'you had a whole bunch of people all of whom agreed on basic admirable humane principles. . . . They were all grappling with this extremely difficult problem of how do you defend the system against enemies of this kind' (former US Under Secretary of Defense for Policy Doug Feith, quoted in Sands 2008: 231).

Durkheim's words (1969: 70) give an answer: 'what a deplorable calculation to make – to renounce, in order to live, all that constitutes the worth and dignity of living.' He was writing in the context of the Dreyfus Affair, a late nineteenth-century panic about enemies *within* French society, and he rejects any internal bifurcated friend/enemy view of society: the idea of solidarity (cohesion, integration, inclusion), which moral individualism serves, is wholly incompatible with such a divisive view. But what of enemies from outside society – people for whom there is no warrant to seek their integration within it, to make them part of its networks of solidarity?

Philosophical ideas of human rights and dignity can simply declare the universality of these values beyond any political borders, however contested may be the idea of humanity on which they base that universality. But a sociological justification of such universality seems on weaker ground. The value system of moral individualism serves the needs of a certain kind of society, not of abstract humanity. It supports social solidarity in complex modern societies. Is there any reason to invoke or apply it beyond them, to people who are not members of these societies?

A Durkheimian answer will not be a simple declaration in favour of universal humanity. It will be based on a weighing of conditions for and threats to social solidarity. Society, acting through its agent, the state, must deal with 'external' threats to its solidarity in the same way that it deals with the 'internal' threats posed by crime: through calculated compromise. But it will not 'renounce, in order to live, all that constitutes the worth and dignity of living'.

Clearly, as Durkheim recognised, the identification and targeting of outsiders of society (scapegoats) is often a way of defending assumed unifying values in crisis conditions (Goldberg 2008; Gane 1992: 109). Hence, it is convenient if lawbreakers, terrorists, foreigners, or the culturally different can be seen as 'beyond the pale' so that repressive acts against them do not appear as acts against society's members. In such conditions, acts expressing the greatest contempt for the dignity and autonomy of the 'outsider' (e.g. 'alien', 'suspected terrorist') victim can sometimes be portrayed as emergency defences of society's values; violence against such victims may, in some conditions, be unlimited (cf Durkheim 1961: 192–3). But this strategy is ultimately self-defeating for several reasons.

First, in an increasingly interconnected world, the borders of societies are porous, and it is not easy to restrict the values of moral individualism to citizens of a particular society or even a particular type of society. People in complex contemporary societies are increasingly linked through social interaction and mutual awareness with others beyond the borders of those societies. In a globalising world, the moral borders of societies are becoming blurred. The line between insiders and outsiders is less easy to draw, or is drawn in different ways by different people, or is simply rejected by many who may perhaps be unsure about their own insider/outsider status.

Second, even if moral individualism is ultimately given coherence by sociological relativism (an analysis of the distinct characteristics of particular types of society) rather than by philosophical universalism (speculations on human nature), it acquires strength the more it can be generalised in popular consciousness into a simple idea of respect for common humanity. The effectiveness of moral individualism, in Durkheim's view, depends on it being an ideal that can be believed in, and, since the ideal focuses on human individualism as an abstraction, it is hard to confine that abstraction, *as popularly understood*, within particular, empirically specified social milieux.

Third, moral individualism, even if shaped by the experience of complex modern societies, has now become, to some extent, and especially for political reasons, a total value system seen as fitted for export to all societies. While such a view may be sociologically very problematic, the fact that it exists poses obstacles for attempts to treat some people as 'less human' than others, whoever and wherever they may be (cf Gould 2007). Such attempts would create the danger of making the value system appear hypocritical.

Sexuality and headscarves

The significance of Durkheim's sociology of morals in addressing legal issues can be further illustrated by reference to a very different area of his sociological thought (though one that raises some issues parallel to those considered earlier): his discussion of sexuality. An interesting aspect of this, as will appear, is that, indirectly, Durkheim's writings in this area can be made to offer new insight into one of the most fiercely contested of recent legal issues in Europe – that of the regulation of female Islamic dress. But a Durkheimian position on this matter has to be constructed out of his general ideas on what he sees as the problematic character of sexuality viewed in the light of the sociological necessity of moral individualism.

The body is at the heart of Durkheim's ideas of human dignity: 'we keep our distance from our fellows and they keep their distance from us . . . we conceal our body as well as our inner life from prying eyes; we hide and isolate ourselves from others, and this isolation is at once the token and the consequence of the sacred character which has been invested in us' as human beings by moral individualism (Durkheim 1979: 146). The context of this statement by Durkheim is a discussion of sex education. If punishment presents one set of circumstances that pose contradictions for moral individualism, then sexual relations present another, at least as discussed in his writings.

From one point of view, sexual freedom is part of the modern autonomy of the individual. But, seen from Durkheim's standpoint, it is highly problematic. In his discussions, a late nineteenth-century prudishness and the tendency to formality and severity that seem to have been part of his character (Greenberg 1976) combine with hardheaded, sometimes startling insights on the complexities of reconciling sexual intimacy with dignity and autonomy.

For Durkheim, sexual relations 'by their very nature . . . violate the boundaries of the individual so carefully erected by society' (Gane 1992: 120); 'the sexual act is the immodest act par excellence' (Durkheim 1979: 142) in which the normal defences of individual autonomy and dignity are disarmed to produce 'a communion of the most intimate kind possible between two conscious beings' (1979: 147). This 'curiously complex act' contains, through its deliberate invasion of another's most intimate being, 'the seed of basic immorality' which is, however, not only redeemed but turned into something 'profoundly moral' when it produces or affirms the unique bonding of two people as one (1979: 145, 146–7).

My concern here is not with Durkheim's much debated writings on the relations between the sexes but only with his comments relating sexuality to human dignity and autonomy. We find in them a *moral ambivalence* which strikingly parallels the ambivalence underlying his analysis of punishment: both sexual relations and punishment involve a calculated sacrifice of dignity and autonomy, as Durkheim sees it: a sacrifice that amounts to a vaguely defined but essential exception in societies where the values of dignity and autonomy are fundamental.

Suppose we accept this image of islands of exception in the midst of the value system of moral individualism and accept also Durkheim's view that modern law's tasks are focused mainly on defending and expressing this value system. On those premises, it might be reasonable to conclude that these areas of exception will pose particular problems for law. Indeed, profound ambivalence does often surround the practical enforcement of prisoners' rights: the effort to protect dignity and autonomy in circumstances where important aspects of these have already been forfeited through imprisonment. Correspondingly, where sexual intimacy invades individual autonomy (as Durkheim sees it), rights protecting dignity and autonomy, if clear in theory, often become ambiguous in practice.

Consider, for example, the never-ending dilemma of achieving successful prosecution and punishment of rape. In Britain, until 1991, law did not recognise rape within marriage.[3] Thus, before the removal of this anachronism, an island of exception existed in which important claims of dignity and autonomy simply could not be legally asserted. Legal clarity had been bought at the price of ignoring these claims. Today, as the assertion of sexuality becomes more casual and often freely commercialised and as social relations in general become more sexualised (e.g. Orbach 2009) in contemporary Western societies, it sometimes becomes harder to judge definitively the moral-legal meaning of sexual acts.

Durkheim sees sexual intimacy as a momentous breach in the edifice of moral individualism, which could be interpreted in one of two ways: it could be either a glorious, if strictly limited, consensual discarding of some of the protections of

---

3   The law was changed by *R* v *R* [1992] 1 AC 599 and the Criminal Justice and Public Order Act 1994. For the old law see e.g. *R* v *Clarence* (1888) 22 QBD 23.

these values so as to achieve something greater, or it could be an obvious, flagrant transgression of them that therefore deserves punishment. Either way, the meaning must be clear for law to be able to define the situation. But, to the extent that sexual activity becomes a relatively casual aspect of social relations, its moral ambiguity is displayed. The issue of consent becomes crucial, but in many cases it also becomes elusive because of the ambiguity of social circumstances.

At the same time, as gender relations become more equal (itself a necessary expression of moral individualism), the victimisation of women is more clearly seen as a special focus for legal redress. Legal protection is a more urgent priority at the same time that legal concepts become harder to apply in practice (e.g. Temkin and Krahe 2008; Larcombe et al 2016). Thus, some of the problems surrounding practical protection of women's rights (e.g. in domestic violence and rape) directly parallel those of prisoners' rights, or rights in almost any circumstances in which the individuals concerned are somehow isolated from the ordinary networks of social solidarity that provide the foundation of moral individualism and so of the law shaped by this value system.

Clearly, from a Durkheimian viewpoint, sexuality is a disruptive force, acting on the normal conditions that govern the application of moral individualism. To protect those conditions, 'we conceal our body as well as our inner life from prying eyes', partly to make it easier to relate interpersonally on the basis of the neutral individuality that moral individualism celebrates. It is easy to understand in these terms many professed justifications given by women for wearing the Islamic head-scarf (*hijāb*) or body-covering gown (*jilbāb*). Although these justifications are very varied, the most relevant here are expressed in such statements as these: 'The Muslim woman wears *al-khimar* [head covering] in order to desexualise public social space when she is part of it'; 'she does not want her sexuality to enter into interactions with men' and 'is concealing her sexuality but allowing her femininity to be brought out' (quoted in Shadid and Van Koningsveld 2005: 37, 38).

Whether or not the wearing of Islamic dress achieves this effect, these justifications for it are clearly consistent with Durkheimian moral individualism. They relate to values of individual dignity and autonomy, as distinct from liberal ideas of freedom, because they *bypass* all questions about individual choice and liberty, peer or family pressure, religious fundamentalism and *laïcité*, which have been the focus of much discussion in Europe in this connection (e.g. Shadid and Van Koningsveld 2005: 43–8; Coene and Longman 2008; De Galembert 2009). Moral individualism, as noted earlier, does not demand uniformity in attitudes, beliefs, or lifestyles; instead, properly understood, it celebrates diversity. It prescribes minimum basic values within which this diversity can flourish: that is, those needed to facilitate society-wide participation, communication, cooperation, and interdependence in social interaction so as to secure the cohesion, integration, and moral identity of society. So, in Durkheimian terms, through the wearing of the headscarf, sexuality's ambivalent messages about dignity and autonomy might, as far as possible, be legitimately excluded from the normal interpersonal everyday interactions that social solidarity requires.

It follows that moral individualism will condemn deliberately erected barriers to communication between individuals and groups. No doubt the conditions of communication, like other aspects of this value system, will involve compromises in practice. No one is to be forced to communicate with each and every individual or with all social and economic groups. Perhaps realistically this is not possible anyway. But conditions of free communication and interaction across society are very important when society is diverse because of the specialisation of roles and functions within it and, we might add (though Durkheim pays little attention to this), because of cultural differences. So, the sociological logic of moral individualism will require it to condemn the creation of serious barriers to society-wide communication and interaction.

In contemporary multicultural societies these are sometimes cultural barriers – for example, certain religious or customary dietary rules or other restrictive rules – that make it virtually impossible for people of different ethnic or religious groups to mix socially. As regards Islamic dress, the adoption of the full veil – that is, a complete or almost complete face covering (*niqāb*, *burqa*, *chadrî*) – might be such a barrier to communication.[4] It seems to me that the sociological logic of moral individualism may well declare this form of dress contrary to the values of individual dignity and autonomy, to the extent that it actively impedes the social purposes which moral individualism serves. While moral individualism, properly understood as a defence of diversity, celebrates multiculturalism, it also demands society-wide social and economic integration. Yet how far any particular practice in fact supports or opposes this value system is an empirical question. In considering it, it will be necessary to take account of both the subjective and objective aspects of dignity and autonomy discussed earlier in this chapter and of the varied conditions of social interaction in complex contemporary societies.

A Durkheimian view thus bypasses much preexisting debate on the 'headscarf issue'. On the one hand, it would surely treat the wearing of female Islamic dress as justifiable insofar as it expresses an intention to take part in social interactions normal in an integrated and cohesive society but to do so while deliberately controlling the impact of sexuality as a factor in those interactions. On the other hand, such an approach presumes that individual choices in dress in a modern complex society should ultimately be governed morally by the value system of moral individualism, which, in turn, reflects the needs of social solidarity in such a society.

One of those needs is not to prevent the interpersonal communication that can facilitate routine social interaction and encourage social interdependence. Insofar as forms of dress seem seriously to impede (perhaps, indeed, seem intended to impede) this communication, Durkheimian moral individualism will surely condemn them. Whether such a sociological assertion of relevant legal values should lead to their direct support through law, and, if so, how, are presumably matters to be clarified further empirically – by examining the conditions and possibilities of social interaction in a particular time and place.

---

4 The issue of the wearing of the full veil as a barrier to communication has been addressed in cases in various jurisdictions: see e.g. Bakht 2009 and Szustek 2009.

Conclusion

Durkheim's sociological analysis of contemporary values presents one perspective in which to view these. It would be possible to take issue with his understanding of the prerequisites of social solidarity, of the particular significance which he attaches to moral individualism in relation to this, or indeed with the idea that complex contemporary societies need social solidarity in anything like the terms he describes. It would be appropriate, certainly, to criticise his conception of social solidarity as focused mainly on functional (especially economic) coordination and interdependence and its lack of attention to bases of solidarity that lie in emotional allegiances and commitments, or in customary practices.

It would, in any case, be important to consider more fully how diversity of beliefs and values (as well as an overarching ultimate value system) may contribute to solidarity. Admittedly, Durkheim (1957) does discuss this matter in his lectures on professional ethics and civic morals, but his emphasis is on diversity among occupational groups, not on the many other forms of differentiation to be found in complex contemporary societies. Nevertheless his arguments about a sociological foundation of legal values deserve serious consideration because of their sophistication, broad scope, and striking contemporary relevance.

Durkheim's sociology of law has been criticised for its focus on law's links to morality, rather than to power (for discussion see Cotterrell 1999: 204–7). Indeed, the very idea of a sociology of morality is still controversial, though perhaps becoming less so (Thacher 2006; Abend 2008). It raises, however, many important issues that often bypass the agendas of moral or legal philosophy. For example, it directs attention, as this chapter has indicated, to the *social boundaries* of legal and moral values – their jurisdictional reach and applicability beyond the membership limits of particular societies or types of society. It detaches morality from seemingly timeless philosophical debates and grounds analyses of it in *empirical study* of specific types of social relations and social organisation (Thacher 2006). Durkheim's sociology of morals raises the issue of the *justification* of legal values. It addresses the particular character of *justice* as an expression of requirements for stable social interactions and for predictable expectations in social relations. It emphasises that legal and moral values usually associated (in legal and moral philosophy) with the rights and responsibilities of *individuals* should be thought of primarily as prerequisites for *society's solidarity and unity*.

Taking all of these matters into account, it may be that sociology of law's traditional avoidance of the possibilities of a general sociology of legal values has resulted in some missed opportunities. In contemporary conditions when law and its practice are often condemned for an instrumental orientation that pays little attention to the moral needs and bases of regulation or to the necessary moral frameworks of legal relationships (e.g. Tamanaha 2006; Kronman 1993; Trotter 1997), the time may be ripe for a new focus, for which Durkheim's pioneer work still provides insights that can be related directly to important juristic issues of today.

13

HUMAN RIGHTS AND DIGNITY

A Durkheimian perspective

Egoism and individualism

From the time he wrote his first book, *The Division of Labour in Society*, until the end of his career, Émile Durkheim was convinced that only a single, particular value system could be universally shared by people living in complex, intricately structured modern Western societies. He sometimes called it simply 'individualism', or otherwise the cult of the individual, the cult of humanity or of the person, or the religion of humanity.

In these societies with a very extensive specialisation of social roles and economic functions (a highly developed division of labour), the lifestyles, beliefs, attitudes, and experiences of citizens and of different social groups would inevitably become increasingly diverse. A belief in common humanity – in the supreme moral importance of the individual as a human being, the sacredness of the person – would be the only ultimate belief that *all* could subscribe to; as Durkheim put it, 'the individual becomes the object of a sort of religion', 'the unique rallying-point for so many minds' (1984: 122, 333). Without this, people might be thoroughly *alien* to one another: their life positions too varied to unite them; their allegiances, beliefs, and convictions too diverse to bridge; their personal experience too limited to allow empathy beyond their own occupational, family, or local environment.

Durkheim initially, in *The Division of Labour* (1984), saw citizens in these societies as sharing a consciousness that amounted to turning in on themselves: glorifying their personal individuality in a world of differentiation, uniformly asserting their total autonomy from others. Such a turning inwards to value a privatised individuality[1] could hardly create a social bond (ibid: 122). Instead, it pushed towards

---

1 Often mocked by the dehumanising conditions of much work: its frequent 'dull, mediocre, spirit-crushing uniformity': see Watts Miller 1988: 648.

an atomisation of society. Durkheim initially thought that what would check this atomisation would be not shared values of any kind but a *functional interdependence* produced by the division of labour itself.

People are linked, on this view, by the specialised roles and functions they sustain for the benefit of others (and hence for themselves) in the groups and networks to which they belong. Social integration arises directly primarily from economic interdependence. But shared values that glorify individual autonomy do not, as such, contribute anything to social solidarity. Indeed, they may just excuse antisocial egoism, reinforcing individuals' moral isolation.

However, Durkheim's view of individualism soon changed dramatically. The first developed expression of his new view is in *Suicide*, published in 1897 (Durkheim 1952), four years after *The Division of Labour*, but it is most often associated with his essay 'Individualism and the Intellectuals' (Durkheim 1969), which appeared the following year and was his primary response to the political and social crisis of the Dreyfus Affair. Now, individualism, while retaining the same substance as before – a quasi-religious sanctification of the human person – was to be understood no longer as directed inwards to the self but as a *turning outwards*, potentially towards humanity at large.

The value system of individualism, in this new view, glorifies not any particular individual but the abstract human person; hence, it demands recognition of the equal humanity of others *beyond oneself* – in principle, the humanity of *all* others, since all are humans possessing human worth and as such are entitled to equal dignity, autonomy, and respect. The 'individualism' that merely justifies me in asserting *my* rights and defending *my* interests against others is no longer to be characterised properly as individualism but instead is to be seen merely as *morally empty egoism*. The true value system of individualism points not towards selfish, absolute assertion of one's rights but to recognition of human rights – the rights of each and all by virtue of being human, irrespective of all differences of personal situation, interests, allegiances, convictions, and beliefs. In that way it supports a social bond of shared humanity.

This chapter asks how far Durkheim's revised understanding of individualism – which in the previous chapter I introduced as *moral* individualism[2] – provides a convincing sociological basis for understanding the idea of human rights, treating this idea as itself a social phenomenon with a history and a cause. Durkheim's sociology aims to explain moral individualism as such a phenomenon. His concern is not philosophical but sociological. He tries not to find ultimate philosophical justifications of the value system which he sees as fundamental to complex modern societies but rather to show how this system has emerged in history and why, viewed

---

2 I adopt this term from the usage of Mark Cladis, who notes (1992: 29) that Durkheim himself rarely used it. Strictly, the adjective 'moral' is redundant since, for Durkheim, individualism is *always* a moral phenomenon (Cotterrell 1999: 113n). But, after his change of view, the individualism recognised in *The Division of Labour* appears as just a rational universalisation of egoism, a self-interested outlook which for Durkheim is not moral at all. To avoid confusion with this, it is useful to identify the value system expounded in his later writings as *moral* individualism.

in sociological perspective, it must be recognised as necessary to such societies, so that they deny or discard it at their peril.

I shall argue that he offers two different types of analysis of the nature and significance of moral individualism – a *functional* analysis and a *historical* analysis. It will be suggested that, while these are interrelated, they provide different and to some extent incompatible characterisations of moral individualism both as the underlying value system on which modern law depends and as the basis for the idea of human rights which occupies an increasingly important position in this law. And the tension that emerges between these characterisations is highly instructive. It points to ambivalence and uncertainty in the very idea of human rights.

Durkheim enthusiastically supported and promoted movements for human rights in his day, and he surely saw these as expressing the value system of moral individualism in important respects. But his analyses present an interestingly ambiguous account of moral individualism. His functional analysis raises doubts about the viability of rooting claims to rights and dignity in an idea of common humanity unconfined to particular societies, while his historical analysis indicates a trajectory of cultural development that suggests why it is hard to limit the scope of human rights. It will be suggested here that, to 'rein in' human rights within an intellectually and morally manageable compass, it is necessary to question sociologically what the adjective 'human' as a concept in regulation can properly be taken to embrace. And Durkheim helps in doing this.

The social function of moral individualism

Why was it necessary for Durkheim to present the concept of moral individualism as the guarantee of social solidarity when originally this had played no part in his thinking? His first book assumed that the division of labour itself would structurally produce the conditions for social solidarity and emphasised that the necessary moral principles to govern most of the law in complex modern societies would arise directly from the conditions of socioeconomic interaction and interdependence. As seen in the previous chapter, the focus would be on justice and equity as essential moral principles. These would be entailed by the requirements of orderly social interaction and functional interdependence (Rawls 2003; Adair 2008). In Book 3 of *The Division of Labour*, however, Durkheim noted 'pathological' circumstances in modern society that, in practice, often defeat such a mundane, everyday emergence and maintenance of justice in social relations. They include practices of discrimination, exclusion, or limitation of some groups or individuals from full participation in economic life; unequal bargaining power and unfair contracts; industrial and commercial exploitation; uneven distribution of work; and inadequate or insensitive regulation.

As critics have noted, however, these 'pathological' forms of the division of labour seem often normal in modern societies (Pope and Johnson 1983). Durkheim may have silently set aside his early distinguishing of organic solidarity (based on spontaneous functional interdependence) from mechanical solidarity (based on shared values and beliefs) once he fully appreciated that working principles of justice for organic solidarity would not reliably arise directly out of the modern division of labour. His new focus, from around 1897, was on the necessity and availability of shared beliefs in moral individualism as the value system needed to ensure solidarity in modern societies (Hawkins 1979). This may well have arisen from Durkheim's clearer focus on, first, the chronic structural problems of modern societies and, second, the effects of acute moral crises such as the Dreyfus Affair or sudden economic changes (cf Goldberg 2008: 302). Certainly, he now saw moral individualism as filling a void in moral life and countering social malaise: promoting 'sympathy for all that is human, a wider pity for all sufferings, for all human miseries, a more ardent desire to combat and alleviate them, a greater thirst for justice' (Durkheim 1969: 64).

As noted in Chapter 12, Durkheim's stress on moral individualism is not a defence of liberalism because the individual, for him, has no foundational, ontological priority over social forces and imperatives. As a moral being, the individual is *created by* society. It is society's need for solidarity that puts the human person at the heart of its unifying moral system, and society decides (with sociology to guide it) the appropriate scope of individual rights and duties. Moral individualism is functionally necessary for modern complex societies.

Durkheim sometimes seemed to suggest that this value system is inevitable for modern societies, its emergence dictated as 'a law of history', and that modern societies 'no longer have the right to ignore it' or 'to dispose of this ideal freely' (1952: 336, 337). But elsewhere he stressed an urgent need to foster it and the existence of threats to it that 'cannot rest unpunished without putting national existence in jeopardy' (1969: 69). Perhaps, then, it is not moral individualism but only the pursuit of egoism that is an inevitable aspect of social life and that promotes a growing insistence on individual *rights*. By contrast, the moral imperative to embed the *duty* of all to respect the dignity and autonomy of others as 'sacred' in their common humanity is something to be worked for constantly and vigilantly protected, and the state has a major responsibility in doing this (Durkheim 1957: 70; Cotterrell 1999: 117).

It is not clear that Durkheim has adequate answers to give when it is *the state itself* that undermines moral individualism, denying or ignoring the human rights and dignity of its citizens. He presupposes a rationally organised state, directed to organising efficient functional interdependence to cope with the complexity of modern society. Such a state is therefore necessarily concerned to foster social solidarity based on this interdependence and to promote moral individualism as the only moral system that can serve it (Pickering 1993: 56–7). Presumably, however, a state that consistently fails to pursue such policies must, in the long run, be following self-defeating policies, ones that will ultimately produce social friction, conflict, and disorder, as well as economic inefficiency and political instability; even perhaps 'putting national existence in jeopardy'.

Much remains unclear. How precisely must moral individualism be translated into social regulation? What exactly are the rights that this value system will support? It would be unwise to assume that they include all those covered by current legal conceptions of human rights, because it is by no means obvious that functional integration in contemporary, complex societies requires all these rights. Nor does it necessarily require that these rights be universal. How far should their reach extend? One way of interpreting moral individualism is to see it as a value system to inform the meaning of justice in social relations – to remedy the inadequacies of assuming that justice can spontaneously arise out of conditions of functional interdependence in a modern complex society.[3] Some overarching value system is needed to enable concepts of justice and equity to be applied reliably and consistently *on a society-wide basis*, rather than ad hoc on the basis of what is practically efficient or broadly acceptable to participants in the 'local' circumstances of their particular transactions or interactions.

To do justice coherently and predictably throughout society, a sense of the overall purpose of regulation in that society is needed, informing an understanding of the general moral position of participants in transactions and interactions. This requires an understanding of the conditions for solidarity in that society. But it does not necessarily require an elaborate idea of abstract humanity or of the universal 'sanctity' of the abstract human person. A functional analysis of the needs of integration and interdependence in contemporary societies will carry the analysis as far as establishing a need to recognise many general individual rights and duties but not perhaps as far as universal human rights, 'by definition, equal and inalienable' (Donnelly 2007: 283), or the quasi-religious aura that Durkheim saw as attaching to belief in the sanctity of the person. There may not be any need for what he sometimes (e.g. 1969: 63) calls a 'religion' of humanity.[4]

A functional explanation of moral individualism focuses on the way it integrates the society in which this value system exists. It indicates a set of individual rights and duties essentially tied to membership and participation in such a society, but this is different from *human* rights. Human rights could be considered membership rights in a society only if humanity itself could be thought of as constituting such a society – a vast communal network. The dream of human brotherhood 'cannot be satisfied unless all men form part of one and the same society, subject to the same laws' (Durkheim 1984: 336), 'a solidly organised collectivity' (1970: 297). No communal network of individuals embracing the entirety of the human race exists, except as an aspiration. Actual societies are made up of particular humans, excluding others. Therefore, *universal* human rights seeking sociological grounding in such a functional analysis could themselves be no more than aspirational.

This is clearly Durkheim's view. If we try to extend his perspective today, only perhaps in one aspect is the idea of worldwide functional interdependence currently realistic – that of interdependence in sustaining coexistence in a common environment, interdependence in collectively pursuing ecological survival. International human rights to environmental protection and to worldwide security for coexistence could thus be partly explained and justified in Durkheimian functional terms. But, seen in this way, these are rights given not by the sanctity of the human person as such but by the need for existence in a common environment. What these rights

---

3 See Chapter 12, pp 176–7.
4 See Pickering 1993, also noting (p 73) that very few of Durkheim's close collaborators seemed to subscribe to the idea of the 'sacred' individual.

seek to project on to a global scale are the concerns for coexistence of people living in any shared locality, however large or small.

Universalising moral individualism

In the previous chapter, it was suggested that moral individualism is, in practice, likely to be carried as a value system beyond the boundaries of the societies for which, on Durkheim's analysis, it is needed to promote functional integration. At least three reasons were suggested: first, the effect of greater transnational social interaction in an increasingly interconnected world; second, the tendency in popular consciousness to generalise and simplify moral individualism into an ideal of universal respect for common humanity; and, third, the tendency, especially for political reasons, for this value system to be actively promoted as fit for export to all societies. But these are contingent reasons not related directly to Durkheim's logic of functional interdependence.

Even within the particular kinds of societies in which Durkheim saw moral individualism as functionally necessary, its scope of application can be queried. If it is needed to ensure integration of roles and functions in these societies, who is to be included in the social networks of interaction and interdependence? Is this value system truly universal in reach even within the societies to which it is to apply?

Durkheim clearly thought that moral individualism's embrace would extend to require inclusion of all human individuals in a society, as members in that society's network of interaction. Barriers based on differences of religion, race, or ethnicity would weaken as the recognition of common humanity reinforced social solidarity. But it is not clear how far he saw gender relations as affected by this recognition, and his writings tend to assume the obvious application of moral individualism to both men and women and, at the same time, a broadly settled division of labour and social position between them. More generally, it can be asked what kind of equality of treatment, uniform markers of dignity, and scope of autonomy the sanctity of the human person actually requires.

He recognised in *The Division of Labour* the urgent need to counter forced exclusions, such as deliberate discrimination against individuals or groups. But surely not everyone can be in a position to play a part in the networks of interdependence arising from the division of labour. Some who suffer from various kinds of disability or disadvantage may be unable to play fully such a role. Presumably moral individualism demands their inclusion to the greatest extent possible. Children, too, as dependents, are assumed to be outside these networks of interdependence and so, if the functional analysis is followed, must be seen in terms of their *potential* future membership in them. More generally, it would seem that the inclusion of every individual in the embrace of social solidarity – seeing them all as members of a society integrated and structured in terms of the interdependence of functions within it – is a policy choice or a moral decision but not an inevitable result of the complexity of modern societies, even though that complexity might suggest strong reasons why the ideal of full inclusion should be followed.

Looking from a different standpoint at inclusion, it is not clear what the position of modern business corporations is in terms of the functional analysis of moral individualism. While they are not human beings, they have sometimes been recognised as entitled to benefit from human rights regimes where human rights documents have included references to the rights of 'persons', and this has been accepted as including 'legal' as well as 'natural' persons, so that corporations can claim in this way notionally 'human' rights (Scolnicov 2013; Emberland 2006).[5] Such an approach might be intelligible in a functional analysis that requires recognition of the equal entitlement, in principle, of all persons to interact in the networks of functional interdependence. On such a basis there is not necessarily any convincing reason why the 'sacredness' of the person should not embrace the equal 'sacredness' of the corporate person as a participant in legal interactions.

But this takes us very far from Durkheim's own vision of human individuals integrated into a society of solidarity in which their personal dignity and autonomy are respected and enhanced. The vision of social relations facilitated by an emphasis on what unites and equalises actors as human beings, despite all differences among them, can hardly apply to relations between business corporations and their individual consumers or employees or between different corporate actors or different groups.[6] All this suggests a need for much caution in talking about the sacralisation of the *person* rather than that of the individual, although this has sometimes been advocated (Joas 2013: 51) so as to avoid any mistaken associations of the latter with egoism.

It seems that a functional view of moral individualism cannot convincingly suggest a basis for the *universal* reach of human rights and human dignity claims today. At least this analysis must be supplemented by other sociological arguments, as noted earlier, identifying factors that may encourage an extended invocation of the value system of moral individualism beyond the boundaries of the societies whose solidarity it exists to serve. Durkheim's writings do not, however, explore any lack of fit between the apparent functionally limited scope of moral individualism, on the one hand, and the aspirations to universality of human rights, on the other. The idea of moral individualism described most notably in the 'Individualism and the Intellectuals' essay clearly points towards such broad humanistic orientations, although he was certainly cautious about the possibility of a truly universal human rights regime when the institutions to support it were not in place (Cotterrell 1999: 117, 195).

---

5 See also *Burwell* v *Hobby Lobby Stores Inc.* 573 US (2014), in which the US Supreme Court decided that a closely held for-profit corporation could assert its right to 'exercise of religion' as a person under the Religious Freedom Restoration Act 1993 to claim exemption from general law on religious grounds.

6 Scolnicov 2013: 16, rejecting the idea that corporations can have human rights, asserts that such rights are 'based on the inherent worth of individuals, whether concerning the right to express themselves or protecting their physical and moral integrity, or other aspects of their innate personality'. Emberland (2006: 39) notes in relation to the European Convention on Human Rights that, given 'the impersonal character of the company, the inclusion of corporate entities in the Convention system will enjoy little direct support on the basis of the value of human dignity'; the status of 'corporate human rights in Strasbourg practice must primarily be explained on the basis of other Convention values'. See also Paul 2011. On recent invocation of human rights by foreign investment entities see e.g. Alvarez (2017).

I think it can be suggested both that Durkheim wanted such a regime to become a reality at some future time and that he saw no reason in principle why this could not happen; why appropriate institutions could not arise eventually to promote human rights and dignity on a global scale. For the moment, he notes (1970: 294), our allegiances are to nation-states, but 'there is another [country] in the process of formation, enveloping our national country; that of Europe or humanity [*la patrie européenne, ou la patrie humaine*]'.

It is interesting that Europe and humanity are juxtaposed in this claim, suggesting that it is in the culture and future of Europe that the transnational extension of rights and allegiances is to be envisaged, that the ideals of humanity and human rights are rooted in a specifically European experience, and that the hopes for carrying them forward lie with Europe, which he equated with 'the civilised world' (1970: 295). So, in Durkheim's work, alongside the functional perspective which originates with *The Division of Labour* and evolves to recognise moral individualism as a value system conceptualising membership and participation rights in complex modern societies, there exists a historical perspective, focused specifically on an interpretation of Europe's past and a vision of its future.

To supplement the limitations of Durkheim's functional perspective, it is necessary to elaborate this historical one, which points much more clearly towards a universalisation beyond national borders of the individual's moral obligation to others as fellow human beings and hence towards the possibilities of universal human rights and a distinctive view of their nature.

The sacred individual in history

Today, numerous accounts of the history of ideas of human rights and human dignity exist, and much controversy remains about this history – and indeed as to what it is a history about. Different histories portray the progress of what they identify as human rights in different cultures and in relation to different intellectual and moral traditions. Some treat human rights as a distinctively European innovation eventually transplanted to other cultures. Others find indigenous human rights traditions in many of the world's cultures and in the precepts of many of the world's religions (cf Donnelly 2007: 284ff). Some accounts portray human rights as prominently carried through religious traditions and eventually secularised, while others view them as emerging in clear reaction against the repressions of religion or in the face of religious opposition. Durkheim's Europe-focused account stands at a relatively early stage in the writing of these various histories. It is merely a sketch presented in brief passages in some of his writings, but its importance in his thinking is not to be underestimated.

Durkheim's historical view centres not on principles of morality developed in philosophical systems[7] but on the emergence and diffusion of certain popular

---

7 Despite, for example, Kant's strong influence on him, he rejects attempts to ground morality in philosophical absolutes and insists on the need for sociological explanations of it as a phenomenon rooted in the historically varying conditions of social life. See Cotterrell 1999: 56–7 and Stedman Jones 2001: 65ff.

currents of thought. Most notable in it is the focus on the significance of religious – and very specifically European Christian – traditions: thus, 'the originality of Christianity has consisted precisely in a remarkable development of the individualist spirit' (1969: 68). As Hans Joas notes, Durkheim 'presents his call for human rights as a continuation of the Christian tradition', although this 'is not a matter of embedding the belief in human rights in Christianity; instead; this belief is to replace Christianity', which has paved the way for it (Joas 2013: 54).

Christianity, Durkheim (1969: 68) writes, 'was the first to teach that the moral value of actions must be measured in accordance with intention, which is essentially private. . . . [T]he individual was set up as the sovereign judge of his own conduct', accounting only 'to himself and his God'. It is 'a singular error to present individualist morality as antagonistic to Christian morality; quite the contrary, it is derived from it'; with moral individualism 'we do not disown our past' but build on it (ibid). But Christianity's demand for concern for the other must, in Durkheim's view, be extended far beyond that expressed in its historical practice; we are, for example, 'no longer electrified by those principles in whose name Christianity exhorted the masters to treat their slaves humanely', and 'Christianity's idea of human equality and fraternity seems to us today to leave too much room for unjust inequalities. Its pity for the downcast seems to us too Platonic. We would like one that is more vigorous' (Durkheim 1995: 429).

Durkheim's picture of Christian history and its significance for human rights is clearly controversial. Jack Donnelly remarks that 'No widely endorsed reading of Christian scriptures supported the idea of a broad set of equal and inalienable individual rights held by all Christians, let alone all human beings' and adds that 'virtually all Western religious and philosophical doctrines through most of their history have either rejected or ignored human rights', although today 'the moral equality of all human beings is strongly endorsed by most leading comprehensive doctrines of all regions of the world' (Donnelly 2007: 287, 290, 291).[8]

On the other hand, elements of Christian teaching (the ideas of the soul as the core of the human person and of human life as a gift incurring obligations) are 'often claimed to have paved the way for human rights and to be essential to sustaining them' (Joas 2013: 7). On Hans Joas's view, human rights 'draw on cultural traditions such as Christianity' alongside others but demand that these traditions 'be articulated in novel ways' (ibid); he sees the history of human rights as, indeed, one of sacralisation of the person, drawing on and transforming elements of these traditions extending back to the American and French revolutions and combining secular and religious influences. Certainly, surrounding secular rights with a religious aura was unremarkable. In Durkheim's time, the idea of a 'religion of humanity' was current, well rooted in a long history of French thought (Pickering 1993: 62–6).

---

8 Recently, the importance of Christianity in the development of modern human rights thinking immediately after the Second World War has been argued in Moyn 2015.

It is not necessary here to assess the validity of diverse historical accounts of the sources of human rights. The issues are: how does Durkheim's particular historical perspective colour his view of 'the belief in human rights and human dignity as an expression of the sacralization of the person' (Joas 2013: 51), and what implications follow from this for following this view? At the time when he expressed it most clearly in *Suicide* and then in 'Individualism and the Intellectuals', he was still in the process of integrating in his thought broad anthropological perspectives on the sacred (Maryanski 2014) and had not yet produced his final great study of religion (Durkheim 1995) based on these perspectives. It seems reasonable to suppose that, at this time, Western religious traditions – and especially, given its prominence in his writings, Christianity – remained very strong influences in shaping his sense of the individual as sacred.

Hence the aspiration towards human rights and dignity as universal ideals can be presented by him as the extension of a historical trajectory which starts mainly from what he calls 'Christian morality' and proceeds through a gradual, still to be completed transformation of this into a universal 'individualist morality' (Durkheim 1969: 68). This transformation can surely be understood only as a radical generalisation and eventual universalisation of the Christian 'neighbour principle',[9] also firmly rooted in Jewish tradition.[10] The ancient command to 'love your neighbour as yourself' is extended in Christian teaching into an injunction to 'do good to' not only those who are members of the group with which one identifies but also and perhaps especially those outside it, even one's enemies and 'those who hate you' and 'persecute you';[11] we might say today, to aliens and refugees and also to terrorists and combatants in war.

It is easy to see in this particular tradition a moral insistence on complete universalisation of respect for the sanctity of the individual, an injunction to reach out in some way to others, as human individuals, beyond any boundaries of nationality, ethnicity, locality, tribal loyalty, religious belief, friendship, reciprocity, or natural affection. Christianity historically has rarely been able to inspire such a totally universal commitment to others; its followers usually have at best conformed to another commandment to 'love one another' (that is, fellow believers),[12] even then sometimes failing to do so and provoking schisms and often viciously pursued claims of heresy. But this human failure, mirrored by similar common frailties in the practice of other religions (Joas 2013: 9–10), does not entirely cancel the significance of the universalising message of the Christian New Testament as an ideal, though it might reveal the ideal of consistent universalisation as extremely remote from practice.

Durkheim does not carry his invocation of Christian tradition into these problematic regions. His focus, restricted for this purpose to Europe, surely enabled him to imagine that a religiously inspired sacralisation of the individual ought eventually

---

9 Mark's Gospel, ch12, v31.
10 Leviticus, ch19, v18.
11 Luke's Gospel, ch6, vv27–35; Matthew's Gospel, ch5, v44.
12 John's Gospel, ch13, v34.

to sweep aside all divides between insiders and outsiders of any of the old religious creeds that modern (European) society still harboured. One's 'neighbour' would be anyone whom one might encounter as a fellow inhabitant in society. But this sacralisation is seemingly not, in Durkheim's thought, what an invocation of religious tradition suggests it might be. It is not 'love of neighbour' alongside and inseparable from 'love of God' – God as a force external to humanity.[13] For Durkheim, the belief in God that is central to the old religions of Europe no longer has any chance to retain its hold over individuals generally in modern conditions.

We could say that 'love of neighbour' is all that can remain as an article of faith; a generalised love of one's neighbour, extended to all members of society, is simply a love of society itself. Joas (2013: 52) suggests that Durkheim 'has by no means shown that the human being is also the source of his own holiness'. But Durkheim's answer to this is surely that *society* is the source of it. Thus, when he later developed an elaborate defence of religion as, in some sense, 'indispensable' to and 'eternal' in social life (1969: 66; 1995: 429, 432), he presented it as focused on society itself, seeing religion as a means of representing and recreating the identity of society in the consciousness of its members. So, however universal the idea of the sacred person could be, Durkheim's (1995) last major work in sociology ultimately reasserts the foundational idea that society (and not the individual) is the central focus for analysis. At the end of his career he presents society – a condition of living together that can give meaning to individual lives – as the sole object of any viable future unifying religious faith.

This is a process of argument that seems to move attention to some extent away from the sacralisation of the individual. Perhaps a love of (a religious attachment to) *society* could be limitless. As such; in Durkheimian perspective, it might necessarily be beneficial in its lack of limits if it (i) promoted solidarity and communally oriented actions expressing the interdependence of society's members, and (ii) embodied, in the conditions of complex modern societies, moral perceptions enabling individuals to be recognised as having the autonomy and dignity that allow them to be active members. This would be a reversion to the mainly functional understanding of moral individualism discussed earlier.

But a different direction would be followed if the sacredness of the *individual* is kept in the centre of attention, rather than the religious representation of society. Then questions arise: Can love of the sacred individual actually be limitless, would such a lack of limits be a good thing anyway, and what in practice could it mean? Perhaps it is the need to answer these questions in terms of an extension of what he calls 'Christian morality' that Durkheim avoids by putting society firmly back in the centre of religious veneration in his final book (1995).

Christian morality requires *unlimited* love for the other (however far its human adherents have distorted this or been unable to come to terms with it). And this is

---

13 But such an 'externality' is qualified in Christianity e.g. by the doctrine of the Trinity, affirming that God, taking human form as Jesus and active in the world as the Holy Spirit, is ever-present as well as transcendent.

surely entirely impossible to operationalise in legal regulation such as human rights law, just as it may be impossible for most people to operationalise in actual religious practice. When, in English law, the Christian 'neighbour principle' was explicitly invoked to provide shape and inspiration for a legal concept of negligence, it was turned into an injunction to take reasonable care not to do reasonably foreseeable harm to one's neighbour, and 'neighbours' were defined as those 'so closely and directly affected by my act' that I ought reasonably to consider the effects on them of the act (or omission) when I contemplate it.[14] Ideals of human rights and dignity clearly extend far beyond the scope of such a formula. They require not just avoidance of careless injury but a recognition of the humanity of others by affirming (and legally expressing) their integrity and autonomy as persons and their basic entitlement to satisfy human needs.[15]

The translation of an ideal of universal love for the other into rules that embody an affirmation of humanity certainly goes beyond what a functional justification of moral individualism implies. It can suggest a need to recognise not just civil and political rights of individuals but also social, economic, and cultural rights insofar as these are part of the guarantee of personal human flourishing that a meaningful reaching out to others entails. But all such rights must be directly in the service of universalising the autonomy and dignity of individual human beings. And, if this universalisation to cover all humanity seems problematic in a *functional* view of moral individualism, it appears, by contrast, mandated by the *historical* trajectory which Durkheim suggests towards a sacralisation of the individual beyond what the old religious practices of Europe could achieve. The question this leaves, however, is: what limits are there to the scope of legal protections mandated by humanity itself?

Durkheim's historical perspective gives no answer to this: a religious command to boundless, universal love translated into legal terms suggests that human rights could cover anything that contributes to human flourishing. While the Durkheimian functional justification for legal rights of the individual may circumscribe these too much to be able to fit with contemporary human rights thinking, the historical perspective gives no obvious basis for putting practical limits on what these rights should embrace. Is the only clear limit that love of fellow creatures cannot possibly translate legally into any human rights for *corporations*? The ambivalence on this matter that the functional view of moral individualism suggests is surely entirely dispelled in a Durkheimian historical trajectory which builds human rights out of religious traditions that root personality in such ideas as the possession of a human soul and the sacred gift of human life (Joas 2013: 143ff).

14 *Donoghue* v *Stevenson* (1932) AC 562, 580.
15 The unifying aim of human rights has been said to be to secure a 'self-determinate, meaningful, and responsible way of leading one's life' for every human being: Brugger 1996: 601.

Durkheim's legacy and its limits

How can these Durkheimian ideas aid a juristic understanding of contemporary ideas and practices of human rights and dignity? It should first be stressed that while this chapter has separated the functional and historical perspectives on moral individualism that Durkheim's writings indicate, he does not himself distinguish them in this way. So, these perspectives might be seen as reinforcing and, at the same time, perhaps correcting or supplementing each other. Nevertheless, I think that their analytical separation aids a clear assessment of the legacy they offer for contemporary thought and also shows the highly instructive divergence, even potential incompatibility, in the conclusions to which they point.

The key claim to be drawn from the functional perspective is that individual rights and duties are meaningful and have the possibility of being effective (practically recognised, popularly understood, and juristically well defined) *if they are rooted in the socioeconomic conditions of particular societies* or types of societies. Seeing them in that way makes it possible to explain in sociological terms what rights and duties are for, as long as a certain analysis of the conditions of these societies is accepted and the need to foster social solidarity in such conditions is accepted.

Human rights, like other rights, are, on this view, essentially *membership and participation rights in a society or in some other communal network*. It is necessary to include the idea of communal networks here to indicate the possibility that a network of functional interdependence could extend beyond the boundaries of a politically organised society such as a nation-state or, indeed, that it could be less extensive than such a society. From this Durkheimian functional perspective, viable rights are rights within societies or communal networks. But they cannot properly be characterised as 'human' rights until *humanity itself* forms a recognisable communal network in which interdependence is a reality and solidarity can be seen as important and achievable.

Perhaps only as ecological threats to worldwide coexistence become universally apparent can humanity be viewed as beginning to accept some such communal network of interdependence as existing. What international lawyers call the 'international community' is usually quite different from any such conception and presumes a consortium of states rather than a potentially solidary integration of the world's population. Certainly, as seen in earlier chapters, the extension of regimes of rights and duties of individuals beyond the boundaries of politically organised societies is happening widely today in various fields of international and transnational law, but from a sociological perspective the question always remains: what are the societies or communal networks to which these rights and duties relate, where they have a sociologically intelligible function and a culturally given legitimacy?

In analysing how far human rights can realistically be considered universal, Jack Donnelly identifies three forms of partial, contingent, or what he calls 'relative' universality, while rejecting the plausibility of universality in any other senses. Relative universality can take 'functional', 'international legal', and 'overlapping consensus' forms.

As regards the first, Donnelly (2007: 288) claims that human rights emerged as a response to social hardships brought about by the 'modernisation' of Western states and are now 'the only proven effective means to ensure human dignity in societies dominated by markets and states'; thus they have 'functional' universality wherever this domination exists. But it might be asked whether the hardships arising in such societies are worse than those of other societies without extensive market systems or strong states. Durkheim's functional arguments, which similarly emphasise the consequences of modernity but see moral individualism as consistent with these rather than as compensating for them, seem more plausible once it is accepted that modern societies can bring a wide variety of consequences for their members.

Donnelly's idea of human rights underpinned by an 'overlapping consensus' between different moral systems in the world suggests the possibility of partial agreement between them on some human rights principles despite disagreement on other matters. This is surely plausible but leaves the scope of human rights dependent on the contingencies of such a consensus, which may shift over time and appears to have no necessary basis in any unifying justificatory principle.

'International legal' universality, by contrast, simply reflects the current topography of international human rights law. It properly recognises that international human rights have indeed taken legal form, with a flourishing body of legal doctrine and many established agencies, such as national and international courts, to secure their institutionalisation. From a sociological perspective, however, there remain important issues as to how to strengthen the social underpinnings of these legal rights, even when they may be well supported politically. In particular, where do social and cultural foundations lie for human rights law and its institutions? To what communal networks do they relate from which they might derive cultural legitimacy, and how do human rights serve the needs for integration of these networks? In other words, what constituencies exist to support an ongoing universalisation of human rights?

Restated in these terms, Durkheim's insistence that it is *society*'s needs that define the practical scope and function of rights surely retains relevance. Today, as has been seen, it is the needs of particular communal networks that are providing legitimacy for the transnational development of law[16] and may do so also for the extension of human rights law. And – leaving aside transnational dimensions – when states trample on moral individualism and human rights in their own political society, it will be only in the various communal networks of this society that a determination to maintain or repair solidarity may be able to provide moral resources to defend these rights against the state.

What should be made of Durkheim's historical perspective? It seems to be the main basis for his strong emphasis on a link between human rights and religious traditions informing his idea of 'sacred' humanity. In his last book, he famously wrote that 'the former gods are growing old or dying, and others have not been

16 See Chapters 8, 9, and 10.

born' (1995: 429). He meant that the beliefs of the old European religions were in decline. Today, however, we should hesitate over claims about the displacement of religion. As Joas (2013: 52) says, Durkheim's 'dogmatic' atheism 'closes his mind to the idea that religion may continue to be a source of support for human rights into the future'. Among the indigenous populations of Europe, religion may well be in decline, though this is notoriously hard to measure. However, a 2010 demographic study of more than 230 countries and territories estimated that there were 5.8 billion religiously affiliated adults and children around the globe, representing 84 percent of the world's population at that time (Hackett, Grim et al 2012).

Whatever the exact meaning of such statistics, they strongly suggest at least that religion intrudes in the lives of very large numbers of people, helping in some way to shape their attitudes and values. A sociological view of the future of human rights surely must take careful account of this, not merely as regards the significance of a human right to practice one's own religion but also by considering the solidarity which shared religious beliefs and practices promote among adherents and the positive contribution that morally oriented religious practices may make to solidary relations with people beyond the ranks of religious adherents.

On the negative side, a sociological view surely also has to recognise the very serious adverse impact (e.g. Nehushtan 2015) which religion can have on human rights by, for example, aggressive proselytising; forced conversions; apostasy rules denying the freedom to change one's religious adherence; attribution of fixed, divinely sanctioned social statuses that challenge the precept of equality of individuals in terms of their common humanity; and adherents' disrespect, victimisation, and even dehumanisation of those not sharing the same faith.

These suggestions of 'problems' that religion can cause for human rights presuppose an essentially Durkheimian conception of these rights, which can certainly be challenged. But the Durkheimian approach – combining functional and historical perspectives on the nature of human rights – does at least offer an elaborate template for conceptualising them, not philosophically, as derived from timeless, rational moral systems or absolute principles but sociologically and in terms of a perspective on history that can be assessed against evidence and challenged by rival interpretations. And such an approach can guide juristic thought: suggesting how analyses of the scope and limits of human rights can be practical and realistic because rooted in systematic social inquiry.

It can be said, on the basis of this Durkheimian template, that human rights, rooted in an interpretation of European history but projected beyond this,

- are always rights of human individuals, not of groups or corporate entities;
- focus always on the need to guarantee the dignity and autonomy of the individual;
- have as their function the promotion of social solidarity, so that they are essentially social in orientation, despite their individual focus;
- hold to a vision of universalisation and harmonisation of entitlements, an outreach that transcends the sectarian claims of particular groups or any selfish unlimited pursuit of private interests;

- being tied to the recognition and facilitation of interdependence, are necessarily coloured by the need to foster communication between individuals in society or in other communal networks; and finally
- should, by insisting on recognising equal human worth, promote respect for the diversity of lifestyles, beliefs, customs, and experiences within a morally unified social milieu.

This is no small agenda. Human rights and dignity as ideals are probably fated to be denied, corrupted, and abused in practice in all present and future societies, at least to some degree. But a Durkheimian template offers a conceptualisation of the ideals themselves and a means of interpreting them in a distinctive, historically informed sociological (and ultimately juristic) analysis. Such an interpretation may suggest that consistently recognised *universal* human rights, disconnected from any specific, identifiable communal networks of solidarity, are no more than a dream, a religiously inspired dream in some important respects, if Durkheim's historical interpretation is given credence. Beyond such a dream, human rights are realistically the full membership and participation rights of everyone in a certain society or communal network, rights that go beyond the needs of functional interdependence to recognise a full moral interdependence. Differently put, the *legal* meaning of universal love can be realised, if at all, only in the solidary relations of particular communal networks.

14

LEGAL INSTRUMENTALISM AND POPULAR VALUES

There ought to be a law!

In Britain and no doubt elsewhere, popular expectations as to what law should be doing are often seriously at odds with what it actually does. 'There ought to be a law about that! Why isn't there?' 'Why isn't he prosecuted?' 'Why is that sentence so light? It's a scandal that they aren't properly punished.' 'Why isn't the law enforced?' 'Why can't those poor folks get justice? – Everyone knows they deserve it.' Or, conversely, 'Why are they being prosecuted? They aren't to blame. Why are they being victimised? It's a witch hunt.' This chapter considers what may explain some such polarities of popular and official views of law, which touch on basic juristic concerns about the authority, interpretation, meaningfulness, and legitimacy of law. It suggests that they may reflect more than mere misunderstandings, special pleading, or popular ignorance of legal processes and that the root issues can be brought to light by analysing a fundamental dichotomy in understandings of modern law.

Western legal theory has often been structured around opposing visions of law's nature. The most familiar opposition has been between natural law and legal positivism, but most scholars viewing law from a sociolegal perspective have avoided that particular debate. In practice, for the purposes of their empirical or policy-related research, they usually treat as law what is accepted as such by lawyers and officials, or they adopt some provisional working idea of the scope of the 'legal' for the purposes of their particular projects. Neither the problem of conceptualising 'law' nor the theoretical relationship between law and fundamental social values has normally been a major concern.

However, two sharply conflicting visions of law have been present in sociology of law from its pioneer days, although the general significance of this conflict has been little discussed. These two views are traceable back directly to the writings of Durkheim and Weber at the beginning of the twentieth century, and the conflict between them remains significant a century later. I shall suggest that it underlies pervasive dilemmas surrounding the use of law as a regulatory tool by government today. Equally, it explains much about general popular dissatisfactions with law as a means of satisfying individuals' legitimate expectations and aspirations. And it sets in a new context juristic debates about the significance of moral principles and ultimate values as a basis of legal regulation.

Two social visions of law

Durkheim wrote that 'moral ideas are the soul of law [*l'âme du droit*]. What gives authority to a code [of laws] is the moral ideal that it embodies and which it turns into precise prescriptions' (1970: 150), thus making these moral resources 'an effective discipline of wills' (1975: 277). Durkheim's entire sociological analysis of law is oriented towards showing an intimate connection between law and ultimate values – that is, abstract values accepted by people living in a certain cultural environment, values justified 'as such' and not for any utilitarian purposes they might serve for the individuals who accept them. These values are not a universally valid natural law, though those subscribing to them might think of them that way. They are merely the most fundamental, generally shared values of the particular society which the law serves. Hence, sociology can observe these values in existence – proclaimed and acknowledged as self-evidently sound by people in a particular society at a particular time.

As has been seen, Durkheim argued that all modern, advanced Western societies would tend to subscribe, at least officially, to certain values.[1] It is not clear why he used the word 'soul' to refer to law's dependence on ultimate values, but in his writings the concept of soul expresses an idea of continuity in group life, something rooted in and yet transcending individual lives (Durkheim 1995: 265–7; Fields 1996). One might think that what is being signalled is law's rootedness in society as a whole, in its past, present, and future, an idea that law reflects a common good resonating with the experiences of citizens in general, but more fundamental than the sum of their individual interests.

At almost exactly the same time as Durkheim wrote, Weber, in Germany, proposed an entirely different view of law. He distinguished between an idea of action oriented to ultimate values (*wertrational*) and an idea of action that is instrumental – a means to some delimited end, to achieve some project (*zweckrational*) (1968: 24–5). He writes that the discrediting of natural law thought has made it impossible to give modern law 'a metaphysical dignity'; most of its main provisions are no more than 'the product or the technical means of a compromise between conflicting interests' (ibid: 874–5). So, Weber sees law, for the most part, not as an expression of ultimate values but as a technical instrument for balancing or choosing among incompatible interests.

1 See Chapters 12 and 13.

Brian Tamanaha (2006) has argued in a United States context that the idea of law as an instrument (*legal instrumentalism*), which was once linked firmly to a sense of law promoting the common good, has over the past century lost that association; it has become detached from any sense of common good or an ultimate value (or set of values) served by law. Long before Tamanaha, however, Weber signalled the ultimate triumph of legal instrumentalism. In Durkheim's way of thinking, this would be the triumph of law without a soul, yet Weber saw such law as potentially supremely useful, calculable, and efficient in ordering the complexities of modern life. Indeed, perhaps law lost its 'metaphysical dignity' because it no longer needed it. In a secular modern world shaped by science and technology, law itself might best be seen as a technology without any stable moral commitments, an infinitely adaptable, fluid law, responding to rapid socioeconomic development and helping to facilitate this. By contrast, Durkheim's vision might suggest a law weighed down with heavy value commitments embedded in culture, a censorious, preaching, hortatory kind of law measuring all change against deep-rooted, relatively enduring cultural understandings, expectations, and ideals.

Instrumentalism and expressivism

This Durkheimian outlook, linking law to abstract, deep-rooted values independent of private or particular group interests, can be called *legal expressivism* (law seen as expressing such values) in contrast to Weberian legal instrumentalism. I shall argue that there are indeed strong reasons for assuming the general dominance of legal instrumentalism in the practice of modern legal systems. Treated as a pure type, instrumentalism links law directly to private or sectional interests (including the interests of government as a body of official decision-makers and policy-setters whose personal and organisational agendas may or may not coincide with any general 'public interest'). Instrumentalism focuses on making decisions and policies specific and concrete; it treats law as a technology, a technical means to any chosen ends (of governments, individuals, groups, or corporate entities).[2] By contrast, expressivism's focus tends towards abstraction and an aspirational view; it treats law as the partial embodiment of ideals.

This dichotomy might no longer be significant if Tamanaha's thesis about an almost total triumph of legal instrumentalism is indeed correct and can be generalised beyond its US context. He sees 'rampant instrumental manipulation of the law' (2006: 250), unconstrained by any strong sense of a common good and reflected in the following conditions: lawyers have little concern except to further their clients' interests (and so their own) by any means short of illegality; the selection of judges (by political appointment or election in the US) depends on whether they are thought likely to protect the interests of those who decide their appointment;

---

2 For a different conception of legal instrumentalism which ties it essentially to governmental interests in steering society *rather than* the private interests of individual actors, see Morawski 1997.

legislators tailor their votes on legislation to the demands of those who can influence their re-election; law students are taught that skill in arguing legally on either side of a case is more important than working out how the case should be resolved; further, the legal system is characterised by lawyers' 'brutish' means of maximising profit, out-of-control legislative lobbying, and the encouragement of unmeritorious litigation practices. Tamanaha suggests that when law loses its integrity, built on inherent values, the rule of law itself is threatened or at least (given the difficulty of specifying exactly what the rule of law demands in practice) *belief* in the rule of law is undermined – perhaps a *faith*[3] in law as embodying values to which lawyers can subscribe.

Tamanaha's specific claims about the pernicious effects of instrumentalism are hard to evaluate. Much depends on an assumption – difficult to test empirically – that the sense of the common good has declined and on uncertainties as to how far such a sense ever actually shaped the operation of law or was truly more important in practice a century ago than it is now. The different circumstances of different countries and legal systems can be debated, and Tamanaha's thesis depends on generalising across vast amounts of disparate data. It may be that instrumentalism and expressivism have long been vying for influence on the workings of law (Van Der Burg 2001). If so, this influence will be hard to assess in any general way. However, I shall argue that certain factors typically promote one or the other of these two approaches to law in particular conditions and that these factors can be identified through sociolegal inquiry. Further, it will be suggested that what is important here is not to assess Tamanaha's claim that one of them has triumphed – which ultimately he himself is not entirely sure about (2006: 236, 240–1, 248–9) – but to identify consequences of their coexistence in legal practice and policy. This is the focus of this chapter.

Can a dichotomy between interests and values be operationalised?[4] One can speak of the *value* of something to someone as representing a material or other *interest* of that person. If values focus on the common good in a culture, they can be seen as representing the interests of an indefinite number of people in that culture. But *ultimate* values tend towards the general, the impersonal, and the universal and are understood as such. Interests tend towards relative specificity – the identifiable, definable advantage of individuals or particular groups. Values in the sense intended here might be seen as universalised, abstracted, depersonalised interests, 'non-instrumental ends', 'intrinsically valuable' and 'free-standing', 'absolutely or inexplicably valuable', and 'ends in themselves'.[5]

---

3 See Smith 1999 (a thoughtful paper that sets out, on a more theoretically developed basis, arguments later developed in Tamanaha's book) and DeGirolami 2008.

4 On interests and values see e.g. Swanton 1980 (descriptive and normative uses of the concept of interest) and Skeggs 2014 (ultimate values remain socially significant in capitalism). On sociological approaches to the study of values see Spates 1983 and Wuthnow 2008.

5 The quoted phrases are from Green 2010: 175–6.

It is possible to distinguish (i) ultimate values that are seen as abstracted (common or public) interests of an indefinite range of people at large (perhaps of a certain civilisation or of humanity in general) from (ii) those that derive from 'pure belief' such as the teachings of a religion accepted on a basis of faith. That distinction is unimportant here. What is important is to recognise the tension between legal instrumentalism focused on supporting private, corporate, or governmental interests and legal expressivism focused on supporting ultimate values. And I shall suggest why instrumentalism – with its cost-benefit analyses of legal intervention – is likely to be the approach to law increasingly favoured by *those officially concerned with law* especially as lawmakers and law enforcers.

How instrumentalism triumphs in the use of law

A key factor as regards governmental attitudes to the use of law must be the sheer complexity and scale of governmental tasks and responsibilities in complex, advanced Western societies. Weber portrayed modern politicians as having to face the 'ethical irrationality of the world' (Gerth and Mills eds 1948: 122) – the fact that no single scheme of value can govern all practical political choices. Political pursuit of ultimate values (what Weber calls the ethic of conviction or ultimate ends) is impossible, he claims, without compromising these or adopting an absolutist view that good ends justify any necessary means; the politician should follow an ethic of responsibility and weigh practical consequences, not blindly ignore them in following a vision. Even where policies are inspired by ultimate values they typically involve compromising interests. Weber does not argue that the ethic of responsibility always trumps the ethic of conviction: politicians who seek to serve ultimate values to which they are committed usually will and should compromise these 'responsibly', but perhaps only up to a point if they are to retain their self-respect (ibid: 127).

Ultimate values can be too rigid or vague to determine most government action; often it is hard to see how to translate them into precise regulatory form, and laws may be ambiguous in their value reference. The practical complexities of regulation encourage piecemeal rationality (the formulation of limited regulatory aims in isolation from other related regulatory concerns) rather than expansive, overarching principle. Those who formulate government regulatory policies often rely on large amounts of gathered data. At least, the modern expectation is that they should be well informed about the conditions to be regulated and the legal techniques available.

So, insofar as law is seen in government as a means of addressing socioeconomic complexities, it needs to be justified on the basis of detailed knowledge of the interests and conditions to be addressed. And as law addresses more and more areas of life and the specialist knowledge required to enable it to do so proliferates, governmental thinking is likely to drift further from overarching principles and towards pragmatic calculations of the costs and benefits of managing the numerous interests and conditions involved.

This is not, however, the only way to consider how law's regulatory capacities should be mobilised.[6] For example, they may look very different when viewed by a mass public relatively ignorant of and unconcerned with the technical capacities and conditions of legal regulation and governmental policymaking. It is hard to know how far generalised (neoliberal and/or realist) ways of thinking that favour instrumentalist, cost-benefit, and interests-focused approaches to law have penetrated popular consciousness. Tamanaha's concern was only with the way that they had penetrated the minds and motivations of professionals involved in the maintenance of the legal system. It can certainly be assumed that popular instrumental views will be widespread (individuals will want law to protect their private interests), but they may not always dominate. A purely expressive view of law may be much more viable in *popular consciousness* than in the consciousness of officials of the legal system.

For example, even citizens with little knowledge of law, its contexts, or the philosophical ideas that surround it can hold strong views about law's links to ultimate values. To some extent values such as 'liberty', 'equality', 'justice', 'security', 'dignity', and the 'rule of law' are almost intuitively understood in popular consciousness. They are not difficult to grasp in essence, and no specialist knowledge about lawmaking and law enforcement is a prerequisite for having firm opinions as to how far such values should be promoted. Actually operationalising them through law is another matter and leads to problems of interpretation (and often to instrumental, cost-benefit analyses to determine how, if at all, to implement them). But where these problems are unknown to citizens they will not complicate popular affirmation of values and demands to protect them through law. Some values are seen as mandated unambiguously by adherence to a particular religion or form part of a political ideology unquestioned by its adherents whatever the consequences of pursuing it. Thus, a large space exists for popular demands for purely value-driven uses of law, whereas in most ordinary conditions of professional involvement with law the Weberian ethic of responsibility is expected to operate as an ultimate guide and limitation.

The mass media reflect almost daily instances of populist legal expressivism which can create demands for legal intervention to which policymakers or law enforcers seem reluctant to accede. Thus, strong popular calls for action in the UK against female genital mutilation (FGM) have led to government responses mainly focused on promoting educational initiatives to persuade recalcitrant minorities of the wrong involved in this practice. But calls for effective legal action have fallen for

---

6 Black (1973: 126) refers to mobilisation as 'the process by which a legal system acquires its cases' and 'the link between the law and the people served or controlled by the law'. For him the concept focuses on invocation of law by citizens and on law enforcement decisions by state agencies. I use it here to refer to both of these but also to governmental *policy decisions* to use law (and as to how to use law) to address some issue; law is not mobilised when a decision is made to use means other than law or not to address the issue officially at all.

a long time on deaf official ears, and for nearly 30 years no prosecutions took place despite the existence of laws against FGM since 1985.[7]

Demands for legal and other measures here appeal generally to ultimate values while being supported by empathy with victims. In terms of a Weberian ethic of responsibility, however, it is easy to see many instrumental, cost-benefit, interest-focused reasons for legal caution. These might include the considerable difficulties and costs of law enforcement, a wish not to inflame tensions between cultural groups, and perhaps a hope that cultural changes will remove the problem. Undoubtedly, conflicting beliefs or values in society have a part in this. Instrumental reasoning, however, seems to produce a paralysis of efforts to operationalise law against a problem widely seen throughout society as a fundamental matter of values. Many people might wish for a law genuinely expressive of these values, but instrumental considerations have surely tended to encourage legal inaction.[8]

One can similarly analyse many recent legal responses to the popular furore over corporate financial fraud and aspects of the dominant culture and practices of investment banking. It has been argued (Rakoff 2014: 4) that a lack of prosecutions in the United States arising out of the 2008 financial collapse was due to (i) the understaffing, overburdening, and inadequate expertise of prosecutors, (ii) the government's own involvement in creating conditions that could lead to fraud (and its consequent reluctance to encourage public scrutiny), and (iii) a policy shift away from devoting large resources (of time, money, and expertise) to building cases against individual executives and towards routinely proceeding against corporations themselves (very often settling cases after corporate assurances of better self-regulation).

There is no need here to assess these reasons; what is important is that all of them concern the management of resources or the protection of interests. Such instrumental thinking may refer to the entire national economy, the welfare of which has sometimes been said (for example, until recently by the US Department of Justice) to be potentially threatened by aggressive prosecution of corporations – the 'too big to jail' argument (Rakoff 2014: 8). So a reason to bypass pressure to act in defence of *values* (e.g. business probity) might be that each citizen's material *interests* will suffer.

How the expressive use of law nonetheless survives

Among many ordinary citizens these stances seem at odds with popular aspirations for justice, understood as an ultimate value. Parts of the mass media express a sense of despair: 'The state is simply outgunned by private sector powerhouses' (Birrell 2013); 'politics feels entirely opportunistic', and 'a pervasive air of resignation has taken over' (Orr 2013). Yet it would be wrong to see Western legal thinking in

---

7 Prohibition of Female Circumcision Act 1985; replaced by Female Genital Mutilation Act 2003, amended by Serious Crime Act 2015 sections 70-5. The first prosecutions under the legislation, announced in 2014, resulted in acquittals a year later.

8 See Bindel 2014, explaining inaction in terms of difficulties in identifying the crime, gathering evidence, and securing testimony; inadequate knowledge and training in the relevant institutions; and failure to identify and record victims and potential victims. Bindel notes that FGM 'has been presented as a cultural issue' (p 40).

general as overtaken by instrumentalism. The expansion of human rights discourse provides new scope for idealism in law, since human rights law is at its core an effort to translate ultimate values of human dignity and autonomy into legal form. As discussed in the previous chapter, this law can be seen as an attempted expression of the value system of moral individualism which Durkheim thought necessary in complex modern societies. To this extent, human rights might well be seen as the 'soul' of contemporary Western law.

But two general problems exist with this project of translating values into law. First, the clarity of a basic, widely recognised value is inevitably weakened as it is turned into specific legal provisions and efforts are made to enforce these. The obviousness and seeming simplicity of the popularly understood value gives way to texts requiring elaborate technical interpretation. The popular idea is handed over to professional legal interpretive techniques or to a pragmatic balancing against particular local political or cultural realities. Second, it may be hard to avoid the transmutation of ultimate values expressed in law into instruments to serve merely private interests. This can work to undermine the sense that popularly understood values justify the law. Individual human rights claims are sometimes seen as unmeritorious because they appear in public opinion not as vindicating values (of dignity and autonomy) but as a means to secure controversial personal, sectional, or corporate interests.[9]

All of this might provoke disbelief at the idea that law in practice can be expressive in any significant sense. But such a conclusion seems premature. Human rights have often been seen as a new religion for a world without religion. And, since the ultimate validity of religions is not destroyed by cost–benefit considerations or the play of private interests, it is reasonable to suppose that the 'religion' of human rights cannot be so destroyed either and will continue powerfully to haunt law. More generally, established religions are seen by many as resurgent in the world, and, with population movements, clashes between religious and secular ultimate values or between the belief-commitments of adherents of different religions are notoriously more frequent. A growing visibility of religion as a factor in public life and the need to mediate between opposing beliefs and values create demands for law to take careful account of ultimate values and beliefs.[10] And the fact that religiously stated legal claims may be linked with individual or group interests does not diminish this.

In fact, the presence of ultimate values as a foundation of law is more pervasive and timeless than debates around religious resurgence might suggest. For example, as Durkheim emphasised, criminal punishment performs expressive functions in condemning offenders as transgressors of society's ultimate values and symbolically expressing popular beliefs and convictions about moral behaviour (Cotterrell

9 A UK Equality and Human Rights Commission study (Donald et al 2009) reported widespread popular perceptions that the Human Rights Act 1998 was being improperly used to pursue such interests but also that human rights were seen as valuable: 'surveys of general public opinion . . . reveal . . . hostility to the way in which the HRA is perceived to operate as a charter for people . . . to cheat the system' (p 162).

10 See Chapter 11.

1999: ch 5). It would be wrong to understand punishment entirely in these terms, as Durkheim seemed to do, because instrumental and expressive elements surely intermingle in it. Furthermore, the dangers of expressivism as a basis for punishment are obvious: how is it possible to decide how far and in what ways law should express, through violent action against an offender, the values seen as having been transgressed? Durkheim's answer takes us back to human rights. As explained in Chapter 12, moral individualism demands respect for the human dignity and autonomy of every individual, *not excluding the prisoner*: the legal assertion of values requires compromise between protecting those values for the law-abiding *and* protecting them for the prisoner. But in both popular consciousness and legal policy a basis of criminal punishment in ultimate values remains important.

Such values may be significant for law even if not directly expressed in its substance or procedures. They may be part of law's 'self-understood' (Daube 1973) – that is, understandings and values that are so widely assumed by legal officials and citizens alike that they need no legal expression.[11] Yet they may give essential keys to understanding law; they are presupposed yet not expressed directly in it. And legal doctrine may provide 'triggers' to invoke the self-understood.

An important example of such a trigger is the concept of 'reasonableness' in many legal systems and many areas of law. This impels a legal judgment of appropriateness based substantially on 'commonsense' understandings. In English law the 'reasonable person' (Moran 2003) – one whose actions or responses are judged reasonable and therefore legally acceptable or excusable – is not necessarily a rational calculator. As discussed earlier, he or she is best seen as having an outlook circumscribed by *generally accepted parameters* of rationality and moral judgment. And these parameters themselves are rarely explored in general terms in legal analysis; they are settled in relation to actual circumstances in which specific legal issues arise.[12] But the use of the 'reasonableness' concept opens law to infiltration by and dependence on shared values and understandings that are legally fundamental while remaining in important respects legally opaque.

Mutual dependence of instrumentalism and expressivism

Tamanaha's analysis of the progress of legal instrumentalism in the United States leads him to dramatic conclusions. His last two chapters are titled 'Collapse of higher law, deterioration of common good' and 'The threat to legality', and he supplies much factual evidence to support his claims about the parlous state of legal practices and key legal institutions seemingly governed by rampant self-interest rather than public spirit.

The blame for the situation is put at the door of legal instrumentalism, yet, as Tamanaha recognises, an instrumental approach to law has long existed and has not

---

11 See also Eng 1997 and Carmichael 1997: 6 ('By and large, lawgivers addressing societal problems are not motivated to set down in writing what no one questions').
12 See Chapter 5.

produced until relatively recently the dangerous consequences he observes. Hence the pernicious effects of instrumentalism are tied in his analysis directly to what he sees as a general decline in belief in the common good among those who professionally serve the legal system. But this decline is shown neither through empirical evidence (it is hard to know what evidence could be conclusive) nor by theoretical argument. Equally, he is not able to show that such a belief has actually controlled or directed the mobilisation of law at any time. So, its decline and the possible significance of any such decline remain matters of speculation.

Rather than trying to identify a general belief in the common good at any given historical time and in a particular society, it is productive to identify general sociolegal conditions that encourage instrumentalist rather than expressive approaches among those who make and apply law. At the same time, it is important to recognise that expressing ultimate values is probably an inevitable part of legal experience: legal expressivism is seen in value orientations informing legal doctrine (Witteveen 1999); it is also seen in popular aspirations for justice that demand expression through law.

The conscientious lawmaker, judge, jurist, or law enforcer has to work in an environment in which (i) instrumental considerations are likely to dominate but (ii) law still needs to have moral meaning for those it regulates. It has this moral meaning when its criteria of justice and the values that it seems to represent harmonise at least to some extent with popular opinion and convictions. To this extent, as Durkheim said, moral ideas are indeed the soul of law.

A legal system needs to rely on innumerable cognitive and normative assumptions existing in the consciousness of those it regulates, and understood as such by the official creators, interpreters, and enforcers of law. However, partly because these assumptions will typically vary within the regulated population, the mobilisation of law by officials often requires a choice of which assumptions to respect and which to reject. When the ultimate value-convictions of citizens conflict, law may have to *compromise them* as if they were private interests; in other words, the recognition of ultimate values in law may be dealt with more or less instrumentally, on a cost-benefit calculation, and values are treated as interests to be weighed and balanced. Since ultimate values are by their nature abstract and typically absolute in their own terms, their 'scaling down', so that they are transmuted in legal interpretation and legal policy into the interest-claims of those individuals or groups that hold them, may be the only way that law can practically deal with conflicts between them. In such a situation, law compromises values in much the same way as it compromises interests.

Nevertheless there are good reasons for suggesting that this compromising cannot go too far without instability entering into the idea of law – a sense that the operation of the legal system lacks direction or coherence. If law is no more than a means of compromise, what *justifies* it in effecting such compromises; why is law *rather than anything else* the means to be chosen; and when and why is *compromise* needed anyway (rather than a preference for one side over the other)?

Such questions go beyond the scope of this chapter,[13] but their salience indicates that law is not automatically justified by its capacity to effect compromise. At a minimum, one can associate the idea of law with ultimate values such as justice and security which are needed to guide its pragmatic interventions and are popularly demanded from it (Cotterrell 1995: 154–7). To suggest that the juristic idea of law has at its heart such values is in no way inconsistent with affirming that the meaning of and relationship between these values may vary in popular and official contexts. Nor is it inconsistent with acknowledging that the promotion of specific interests and not the desire to affirm abstract values dominates the mobilisation of law.

So, the relationship between legal instrumentalism and ultimate values is complex. Fundamentally, it is one of symbiosis. It is not necessary to postulate wide agreement either among legal officials or citizens on ultimate values in order to see that the general acceptance of certain ideas of justice and order (or security) as basic to law is fundamental to its juristic integrity and its popular legitimacy. One can go further and suggest that the prominence of the idea of human rights is symptomatic of the significance of the Durkheimian value system of moral individualism as an inspiration for contemporary Western legal thought. Instrumental approaches to law ultimately rest on and presuppose value foundations. Nevertheless, as has been argued earlier, these instrumental approaches dominate the ways in which law-makers and law enforcement operate.

Varieties of pathology: legal populism and legal inertia

Populism: the case of penal policy and practice

The modern symbiosis of instrumentalism and expressivism is certainly not free of problems, and on the basis of the previous discussion suggestions can be made as to where difficulties may arise. Some of them may reflect the potentially unbounded scope of aspirations to mobilise law *expressively*. Where these aspirations dominate a particular area of legal policy, they may direct law's mobilisation in ways that seem irrational to many observers when judged in instrumental terms.

Instrumentalism's hold over official law-making and law enforcement is usually so strong that this difficulty is unlikely to be widespread in normal circumstances. Nevertheless, criminal justice sometimes shows the effects of a dominant expressivism in a sector of the legal system (Feinberg 1965). In some legal systems, such as those of the UK and the United States, penal policy has been seen as gripped by a 'punitive obsession' (Playfair 1971). The claim is made that sentences are unjustifiably harsh for many offences that could be dealt with more effectively by other means and that, in general, punishment is ratcheted up to levels of severity not justifiable on any utilitarian basis. In a cost-benefit balance any gain is said to be

---

13 They are issues that may be considered by reference to the juristic idea of law elaborated in Chapter 3 and the responsibilities involved in safeguarding it.

far outweighed by the destructive consequences of these punishment regimes on offenders themselves and their families, the high costs of maintaining the regimes, and the absence of significant reformative effects or material benefits to society (Allen et al 2014).

The 'penal obsession' is often traced to *penal populism* (e.g. Pratt 2007; Roberts et al 2003) and it seems justifiable to see this as a prominent – yet, within the scope of law as a whole, rare – instance of popular ultimate values being directly expressed (or manipulated) in legal policy. It seems that this can be accompanied by the marginalising of many obvious instrumental considerations that operate routinely in the rest of the legal system, such as cost-effective deployment of the resources available for implementing law, and identification of conflicting interests at stake and their pragmatic ordering. The problem is not that mobilising law in this field is informed by popularly understood ultimate values (e.g. just deserts, general security) but that the interpretation of these values in practice remains permanently controversial, as does the setting of appropriate limits to their legal expression.

A Durkheimian perspective has no difficulty in accounting for this prominent legal expressivism. For Durkheim it is in penal law above all that ultimate values (the normative heart of society's collective consciousness) find expression; and they can animate penal law with immense force, giving powerful direction to it. Yet the Durkheimian position seems overstated. In many modern legal systems the punitive obsession is curbed or seemingly absent (e.g. Nelken 2006); penal law is firmly tamed by cost-benefit, instrumental thinking. Penal populism is hardly universal. Government interests in some countries may, however, be served by riding and, indeed, encouraging punitive public opinion.[14] None of this, however, reduces the significance of the fact of official recognition that certain ultimate values are to be affirmed by the criminal justice system and that legal policies must express them.

Inertia: the case of whistleblower protection

A different kind of problem can arise where expressivism is *too weak to guide instrumental use of law*. Sociolegal issues around whistleblowing in business contexts may illustrate this. UK law provides protection under certain conditions for people who 'blow the whistle' on some types of wrongdoing at their place of work in an effort to have it sanctioned or rectified.[15] The law makes crucial a motivation to promote 'the public interest' (not personal interest), and it gives redress against retaliation by the employer or fellow employees against the whistleblower. The public interest is not legally defined, however, so it seems that it is treated here as part of the

---

14 See Roberts et al 2003: 63–4, noting that, in both the United States and the UK, a 'complex interactive process developed, in which politicians simultaneously shaped and responded to [public] opinion'; equally, news media and special interest groups 'help frame and construct . . . the direction of public opinion'.

15 Public Interest Disclosure Act 1998, amended by Enterprise and Regulatory Reform Act 2013.

law's self-understood and presumably reflects popularly championed ultimate values applicable to business conduct.

In this area of regulation many interests are at stake. For example, businesses do not usually want wrongdoing in their operations to be publicised; fellow workers may not want the company to suffer as a result; whistleblowers have an interest in being protected from retaliation and in good work conditions; government has an interest in not antagonising the business sector unnecessarily and in using valuable law enforcement resources in what it sees as the most efficient ways. Good businesses have an interest in seeing bad practices rooted out of their sector; bad businesses may wish to protect dubious practices that underpin their profitability; citizens in general have an interest in how the economy is working, and so on.

Whistleblowing remains controversial and its protection inadequate surely because of this array of conflicting interests and the lack of precise definition in law or official practice of the values served by the protecting law. One might speculate that law is here trapped in a web of competing interests, many of which push against devoting substantial resources to mobilising it to protect whistleblowers.[16] Yet, where governmental security interests are seen as threatened by whistleblower action, law may be powerfully mobilised *against* whistleblowers even in the face of contrary public opinion asserting ultimate values, such as those of freedom of information. Apart from such cases, whistleblower support is sometimes organised independently of any legal protections by agencies offering a safe conduit for anonymous complaints (and either providing stories for the mass media in the process or serving corporate needs for 'social responsibility').[17]

One way to interpret the business whistleblower situation sociolegally is to say that, here, ultimate values are legally marginalised, especially by being left unexpressed or undefined (except as 'the public interest'). In such circumstances the allocation of legal resources and the criteria to determine the scale and nature of legal mobilisation are likely to be determined mainly by the interplay of interests at stake. But the complexity of this interplay, the array of interests, and the sheer difficulty of compromising them can produce significant *legal inertia*. Thus, instrumentalism may sometimes seem to stand alone, unmediated by the effective influence of ultimate values. When that occurs, its weakness is that it may be *overwhelmed* by the task of compromising interests, and it may *retreat from the task* or use law merely *symbolically*[18] – asserting a position that in practice is not effectively pursued. This is not to claim that whistleblower law can be seen only in this way but to suggest that the deterrents to mobilising this law in this particular area indicate more general weaknesses of legal instrumentalism that could even sometimes amount to a paralysis of effective legal action.

16 Vandekerckhove et al 2013 found that common action against whistleblowers, despite the legislation, included closer monitoring, ostracism, verbal harassment, blocking of resources, relocation, demotion, job reassignment, suspension, disciplining, and dismissal.

17 UK examples are the Whistle Blowers Press Agency www.whistleblowers.uk.com/ and the Whistle B Whistleblowing Centre https://whistleb.com/.

18 See Rixen 2013, on 'ineffective and symbolic' reforms in the face of conflicting interests.

Unstable instrumentalism

Paralysis of legal action might arise in various circumstances: for example, (i) when there seems, from a governmental perspective, to be nothing to choose between conflicting interests, so they are left to 'fight it out' among themselves in free-market competition because no overriding concerns dictate that law should intervene; or (ii) the interests to be challenged or controlled are strongly opposed to legal intervention and the risks of intervening are judged too high;[19] or (iii) the costs of legal intervention are seen as greater than any benefit that intervention might offer to the interests asserted; or (iv) the interests at stake are too hard to identify and so cannot be made distinct objects of legal protection or control; or (v) there are no discernible interests at stake to which law can be addressed. Where, however, there are popular aspirations for law to operate in the public interest (for example to punish serious wrongs committed in financial systems) but cost-benefit calculations lead to regulatory inaction, the public perception may be that impunity exists for certain wrongdoers – a situation which can induce popular cynicism about law.

In situations where expressivism does not adequately temper and give direction to legal instrumentalism, another possibility, apart from regulatory inertia or paralysis, is its opposite: over-regulation or juridification – a situation of *too much law* (at least in popular perceptions). This can occur because law tries to reflect every interest at stake and every claim or demand in some way, yet cannot find any conclusive means to balance them or assess their ultimate normative justification. In such situations law works incessantly in unstable conditions and with *unlimited attention to regulatory detail*. Again the fundamental issue is that legal instrumentalism taken alone (not stabilised by values that are part of popular common sense) cannot provide its own secure self-justification or set its own limits. As is well known, widespread perceptions of over-regulation encouraged the reaction of deregulation. The progression of debates around over-regulation and deregulation might be considered a political projection of the career of legal instrumentalism in one of its relatively recent phases.

$$***$$

We may conclude that, despite the many difficulties in rigorously conceptualising the two poles of the instrumentalism-expressivism symbiosis in contemporary law, it provides a useful vehicle for exploring many familiar modern phenomena of Western legal regulation. It offers a means of judging the health or sickness of law's 'soul' as well as law's general practical utility as a technical means to chosen ends. For juristic inquiry it suggests some very important dynamics of official action and popular reaction: a dialectic in which the authority and legitimacy of law are shaped in practical regulatory experience.

---

19 These may include electoral risks: see Holland 2015 on non-enforcement of law, or forbearance, as an electoral strategy.

15

CONCLUSION

Horizons of sociological jurisprudence

In the thick of events

The previous chapters are not intended to survey comprehensively how jurisprudence should incorporate sociological insight about law. One way to read them is as separate but interconnected studies of different aspects of what I see as the juristic role and its dependence on systematic social inquiry. But they are intended to develop a single theme about the purposes and methods of jurisprudence as well as a consistent critique of some contemporary understandings of its nature.

Under the influence of dominant strands of recent Anglophone legal philosophy, jurisprudence may have too often been seen as an enterprise entirely dominated by a search for analytical rigour in expounding concepts of law, concepts that are assumed to have a validity and significance not directly related to empirical study of any specific social and historical contexts of their application. Relatively rarely has the question been asked: what are general concepts of law for? The same is true with concepts of authority, legal system, rules, and so on. What work are these concepts supposed to do if they are devised as timeless and beyond context? How are they to be put to practical use in interpreting or explaining the experience and practice of law when they are confronted with specific sociohistorical contexts? Is such application necessary, or do they exist solely in an intellectual world of their own, requiring no justification beyond a pleasing rational consistency, the satisfactions of philosophical rigour?

This book has tried to show that jurisprudence is important, and certainly has much work to do. It is crucially necessary to the juristic role – as that role has been sketched in Part I. This is a role *actively engaged with legal life* – that is, with the practice and experience of law in its time and place. The jurist seen in this way is 'in the thick of events', as I characterised Radbruch's juristic practice in Chapter 3. It is true that legal theory can, almost inevitably, seem removed from practicality. The theorist stands back to survey legal experience from some distance, trying to see the whole wood, not the mass of individual trees. But the distancing is solely to gain perspective, and the point of gaining perspective should be to benefit from it to inform and interpret immediate experience.

That experience should also set priorities for theory. I have tried to show, especially in the chapters in Part III, that values matter in legal experience – but that the way they matter is often very complex. Conflicts or tensions between values arise in the practice of law. So do tensions between impulses towards instrumental aims for law (immediate usefulness, 'getting the job done', keeping the legal 'show on the road') and towards representing wide social values (ensuring that law has a moral 'soul'). At the beginning of the book, in Chapter 2, I attempted to show this tension in examining the ambiguities of lawyers' claims of expertise. And, near the end, in Chapter 14, I addressed it in a very different way by exploring the confrontations of instrumentalism and expressivism in popular and governmental perceptions of the tasks and capacities of law.

A concern to safeguard and promote certain values has to be central to juristic work and therefore has to have a central place in jurisprudence. But it is obvious that the age is long past when philosophers, theologians, or other sages could lay out any universal, timeless precepts of moral philosophy to which the Western jurist is obliged (like all morally upright citizens) to subscribe. As Weber (1968: 874) wrote a century ago, 'the axioms of natural law have lost all capacity to provide the fundamental basis of a legal system.' Jurists are not given, as part of their professional formation, ready-made theoretical answers to moral conundrums that law must address. A key part of the art and craft of juristic work is to confront those conundrums and find answers that will work in the practice of the time and place.

The reason why Radbruch's effort to clarify an idea of law with which modern jurists can work seems so instructive and powerful is that it does not appear to legislate solutions to the problem of infusing law with appropriate values, but neither does it discard the problem itself or shift it away from jurisprudence. On the contrary, it makes it central. Through what I interpreted in Chapter 3 as Radbruch's subtle 'variable geometry' of legal values, a template within which the jurist can work can be provided. Certain values – of justice, security, and fitness for cultural purpose (*Zweckmassigkeit*) – are identified as juristically fundamental, but their interpretation and concrete application are left for jurists to work out as a central part of their job ('in the thick of events', not speculating on legal eternity). In terms of my expansion of Radbruch's approach, this involves trying to understand the diversity of popular aspirations for justice and security (a matter of sensitive social observation of law's regulated populations and their actual experience of law) and also recognising what, as an objective matter, is required of law for the social integration of the society whose law the jurist serves.

It should not be hard to recognise that these juristic responsibilities demand a well-developed sociological sensibility. The jurist must be concerned – as Pound (to give him proper credit) clearly understood in his pioneer sociological jurisprudence – to understand the claims and aspirations that people project on to the legal system.

But, beyond this, jurists must find, in social theory and elsewhere, insights about the conditions under which the cohesion of social life under law becomes possible and sustainable *in a given social environment.* Just as jurists typically work to promote the sense of coherence in law, so they must as an overriding concern (which also informs the pursuit of values of justice and security) promote the cohesion of the social environment of which law is a part.

Solidarity as juristic focus

In modern Western societies the key insight about the basis of social cohesion is, I think, the one to which Durkheim's sociology so clearly points. That is the insight that if social solidarity is to be achieved, this will be in two inseparably interconnected ways: (i) by actively ensuring (by law and other means) the ever more complex *interdependence* of all members of society (involving the removal of all barriers to free interaction and communication among individuals and groups to promote the sense of that interdependence), and (ii) by an uncompromising legal insistence on the promotion of *moral individualism* as the only possible (and entirely indispensable) unifying value system in modern society.

This view might seem too idealistic. Isn't any search for solidarity made pointless by the vast disparities in power that exist in politically organised societies? Power differentials are a feature of almost all communal networks. Hasn't power been forgotten in this Durkheimian imagery of law in society? Isn't the typical situation one of dependence and domination, not *inter*dependence? Certainly it is! When Durkheim wrote in *The Division of Labour in Society* about 'forced' and 'abnormal' forms of this division (1984: bk 3), he explicitly recognised these barriers to solidarity. The most important failing of his sociology was his assumption that such forms were exceptional, rather than normal. But to recognise the existence of vast, uncontrolled disparities of wealth and opportunity, the exclusion of many from the actually existing relations of interdependence and reciprocity on which social organisation depends, and the frequent lack of concern of governments and lawmakers with the needs of social solidarity does not make the values that are necessary to social cohesion unimportant.

First, it is important to emphasise that the jurist is not merely an observer of society. Jurists, as has been stressed earlier, are not social scientists explaining and recording the character of social life. They have the responsibility to promote the well-being of the idea of law as an affair of particular, crucial values. Where law acts against solidarity, and against popular aspirations for justice and security, jurists have the responsibility to promote the translation of the idea of law into better practical forms and processes. They should act to help to make the substance, procedures, and practices of law conform better to value structures on which social cohesion ultimately depends. They have, if necessary, to be fierce, uncompromising critics of law – in the service of the idea of law.

Second, and following from this, jurists (alongside sociologists) can properly point to eventual consequences of ignoring the regulatory requirements of social solidarity in complex contemporary societies. Informed with social insight, and perhaps with many lessons from history, they can sound warnings about the economic disorganisation, political incoherence, and social disorder that are likely to arise when the requirements of social cohesion are blatantly ignored in legal policy for a significant period of time. Law as more than just a technical instrument of government is also a repository of popular aspirations. The literature of sociology of law explores empirically many of these aspirations, as well as ways in which they are often defeated in the experience of people who call on law for aid or have learned that its promises of justice and security are, for them, *simply empty*. Much of this literature can be read as precise warnings to lawmakers, law enforcers, and administrators, lawyers and jurists. So too can some critiques of law that come from a wide range of popular opinion formers.

Solidarity is an *ideal* of optimally (not perfectly) harmonious social cohesion and inclusion – an ideal that one might choose or not choose to pursue. But it can also be understood as something that may or may not exist as a matter of fact, in the form of a commonly held recognition that people are indeed interdependent, that they actually depend on each other, and so this must be reflected in their behaviour in relation to each other. In this latter sense it is a matter of social psychology, of the way people understand and evaluate their existence together in social relations. Solidarity, finally, can also be understood in a way closer to that in which Durkheim understood it: as a form in which social life can be *organised*. In this last sense, solidarity is expressed in the organisation and operation of institutions, in the structures of law, in the aims and practices of education, in the forms and manner of social communication, in economic life, and in the avenues and processes of political participation.

Crucially, solidarity is not, as Durkheim seemed to think, a natural or normal state of affairs in politically organised societies. If it is considered important, it has to be worked for, and the wise crafting of law is a very important means of doing so, although not the only or perhaps the most fundamental one. Also, there is a limit to the amount of progress in practical regulation that can be achieved by elaborating a concept of solidarity as a value in general terms. There are many different kinds of solidarity that are possible and valued in different communal networks and social relations of community. The kind of solidarity possible will depend on the type of social relations involved, the reasons for their existence, and the basis on which mutual interpersonal trust can be built in them. There is no single form of community or of solidarity. Relations of community serve different needs and reflect the different reasons and conditions that bring people together. The different forms of community have to be analysed in their regulatory dimensions (Cotterrell 2006: ch 4; 2008c: ch 2).

Finally, it is important to note that solidarity can be promoted by appreciating (not merely tolerating) important *differences* in the conditions and needs of different groups, networks, and relationships, as well as by seeking means of communicating among these: that is, by looking for ultimate points of similarity or consensus to circumvent difference without denying its significance. In Durkheimian terms, a key contribution to the vocabulary of this communication has to be a sense of common humanity – translated into a language of outreach across different material conditions, belief systems, affective allegiances, traditions, and local environments. Jurists have a vital task to perform in developing this language of communication, law being one of its vehicles. It would be dangerous – to the well-being of law as an idea, as well as to the society to which this idea relates – to neglect this task. So, the juristic role has a clear critical focus whenever law seems to stand against the conditions of unfettered social interaction, transcultural communication, and economic interdependence that promote possibilities for solidarity.

Concepts as frames and models

Earlier chapters devoted much attention to distinguishing jurisprudence from legal philosophy – at least as legal philosophy is widely understood today in the Anglophone world. The main reason for doing this is to free jurisprudence from seemingly strong tendencies in some legal philosophy to treat conceptual analysis as an end in itself, as noted earlier. In such an approach, conceptual inquiries in no way depend on empirical inquiries about law's specific contexts – inquiries that might reveal the variety and contingency of these contexts. In fact, if contextual variability had to be taken into account, this would pose insuperable obstacles to any assumption that a well-formulated concept can usefully clarify the 'essential' nature of any social phenomenon (such as law) abstracted from time and place,[1] that it can crystallise an understanding of this nature as, in some way universal or timeless.

The threat which sociological inquiry could pose to this conceptual 'essentialism' would be (i) in raising doubts about the utility of any abstractions that do not indicate explicitly the limits of their contextual application, and (ii) in insisting that the range of application of any given concept, understood as a means of clarifying social experience, be made explicit so that the concept's usefulness can be tested systematically. Insofar as sociological jurisprudence is committed to bringing methods and ideas of social science inside jurisprudence – which is necessarily concerned with conceptual analysis in and about law – these challenges to conceptual essentialism cannot be avoided.

The effect of them is that conceptual inquiry in sociological jurisprudence rejects essentialism. All jurisprudential thinking has to be related to time and place – to the practice and experience of specific historically existing legal systems and regimes. In

---

1 Often such an assumption is merely implicit, arising from statements being made about the nature of some phenomenon without recognising any need to specify the range of contexts to which the statement is to apply. On problems of essentialism in conceptual inquiries about law see e.g. Tamanaha 2017 (doubting claims by analytical jurisprudents that they are identifying necessary, universal truths about the nature of law); Tamanaha 2011 (philosophical concepts of law tend to be highly parochial, despite universalistic pretensions, and have potentially harmful real world consequences); Schauer 2010 (an insistence that inquiring about the nature of law must mean searching for law's essential features distracts attention from important, commonly found nonessential features); Giudice 2011 (concept of law must recognise contingent aspects of law).

sociological jurisprudence no concepts can be presented as designating universally necessary or essential characteristics of law. Concepts can be so presented only if their applicability or significance can be demonstrated in empirical and theoretical study of all possible contexts – past, present, and future – which is impossible.

Nevertheless, jurisprudence is rightly concerned with conceptual clarification. Concepts and categories are central to the lawyer's stock in trade. They are means of classifying and distinguishing situations and issues for the purposes of legal analysis. They are crucial to the organisation and systematisation of legal doctrine. And they are crucial also to social inquiry – fundamental in the construction of social theories and in the rational structuring and interpretation of empirical social research. We cannot speak or write without concepts; they are tools for the organisation of thought. So, their clarification is an obviously important aspect of juristic as of social scientific work.

In this book a few theoretical value concepts have been treated as juristically fundamental. The most prominent are justice, security (or order), and solidarity. And an ideal typical role of the jurist has been suggested as organised around an 'idea of law' (another fundamental concept) developed from Radbruch's work. Are these concepts then, despite what I have written earlier, timeless, meaningful beyond any specific references to context, valid in and of themselves? The answer to this question requires the asking of others. What are the concepts for? What work should they be required to do? In what ways and in what circumstances are they to be used?

A juristic 'idea of law', as sketched in Chapter 3, is a way of thinking about and linking, for the purposes of juristic practice, certain values that are very familiar in *modern Western* juristic experience. It is a framework for organising practical tasks of regulation in a coherent way congruent with juristic and popular experience. It does not purport to convey universal truth or a self-sufficient characterisation of the essence of law. It is a template on which to arrange a set of practical problems for jurists in thinking about values of justice, security, and 'fitness for cultural purpose' as these values can be understood in the time and place where the jurist works. The idea of law is nothing but a formulation of the tension between these values in regulatory practice and of the juristic responsibility to balance them. The tension *might* be inevitable (although we cannot know that) wherever and whenever jurists work. But in any case it is present in the juristic experience of modern legal systems.

The jurist's obligation to take values of justice and security seriously is an invitation not to adopt a timeless, universal concept (still less, theory) of justice or of security but to identify empirically (i) the meanings attached to these ideas among the regulated population, (ii) the diversity of demands for justice and security that are popularly made and the conflicts between these demands, (iii) the priority which people give to one or the other of these two fundamental values as they understand them in particular circumstances, and (iv) the complexities and dilemmas that arise in professional practice and popular experience in trying to reconcile these values. And values of justice and security are given meaning in juristic experience and modern legal practice – most basically in the ideas of equal treatment of similar cases and of predictability and certainty in legal procedures and in the interpretation of legal doctrine. So, the words 'justice' and 'security' are receptacles for aspirations, expectations, and experiences – those of the jurist along with everyone else.

Clearly, then, these are far from meaningless ideas: everyone knows that justice and security are important. They understand that even when they cannot define or generalise these ideas – except as related to their own particular circumstances or to concrete instances of which they are aware. And *juristic* conceptualisations of justice and security are far from unimportant – they are among the intellectual resources available for guiding legal development and the classifications of legal doctrine. But neither jurists nor philosophers exclusively *own* these concepts, and a sociological jurisprudence requires that their social meaning be found in the lived experience of citizens beyond the legal scholar's study.

A juristic sense of the social

The idea of law cannot be simply handed over to popular experience.[2] Jurists surely have to try to lead legal development – the development of legal thinking. It is not enough for them merely to reflect popular experience and try to organise it so that people can feel that, as far as possible, justice has been done and order guaranteed. Juristic practice has to cut clear, viable paths for legal regulation through the tangle of conflicting popular views about and demands for justice and security. And it should also exert influence on the way the concepts of justice and security themselves are perceived.

This requires a standing back, a distancing from the tangle of popular views. It involves the third value in the 'triangle' of Radbruch's juristic values – the value of making law fit for cultural purpose, guiding it towards the pursuit of purposes that are fundamentally important for the integrity and identity of the particular cultural environment in which law exists. Again, there is nothing timeless or universal here. The purposes to which law should be directed according to juristic understandings are given not by human nature (as in some classic forms of natural law theory) or by some inherent essence of law but by specific cultural conditions: we might say, by the sociologically identifiable regulatory needs and possibilities of law's environment, in a particular time and place.

Juristic work, I suggest, ultimately aims at promoting the overall unity of this social environment, just as it has promoted the idea of the *unity of law*.[3] Jurispru-

---

2 An interesting case of a jurist seemingly claiming this in effect is that of the French theorist Emmanuel Lévy, who understood law as a structure of ideas dependent for its sustainability on popular convictions and beliefs. On Lévy see Cotterrell 2008c: ch 6.

3 'When somebody takes his starting point somewhere other than in the unity of the legal system . . . he is not a legal scientist in the classic sense. The societal role of the latter is . . . to interpret the legal roles so that they comprise a single legal system': Aleksander Peczenik, quoted in Petrusson and Glavå (2008: 100). But the relevance of an overriding juristic emphasis on law as 'system' today is debatable: see Chapter 6, especially p 86. The role of the jurist has to be 'outward facing' towards the social, where boundaries of law can be best seen in important contexts as a matter for practical judgment or negotiation, rather than comprehensive systemic elaboration.

dence has usually, at least in the modern Anglophone world, sought to portray law as an integrated body of doctrine. The idea of the rule of law depends on the assumption that the legal order forms a reasonably coherent whole, not an array of contradictions in which it might often be impossible to know which of the contradictory precepts would or should apply and not a situation of parallel, unrelated jurisdictions where it might be hard to know when cases will fall under one jurisdiction or another. In general, jurisprudence presupposes that ideas of unity, consistency and coherence in legal thought matter (Cotterrell 2003: 8–11).

A juristic sense of the unity of the social is probably merely a further extension of this presupposition of the overall unity of law. This is not to say that well-integrated legal systems correlate with highly cohesive societies; this is often clearly not the case. Jurists in reality frequently serve unequal, divided societies, where law is used as a weapon to ensure privilege for some groups and to repress others. Juristically, the presupposed unity of the social is, most fundamentally, the idea that law structures the patterns of social life in a comprehensive, all-embracing way, at least as regards the most important institutions of society and the most important determinants of social organisation. Law takes ultimate, society-wide responsibility for social order and social justice, as these values are understood by the regulators; it translates lawmakers' perceptions of justice and order into regulatory form, and it imposes these values of justice and order on society as a whole. So, legal thought envisages the unity of the social as a constructed, *official*, normative unity, a unity of common citizenship in civil society, not necessarily as a general condition of social cohesiveness consciously experienced by citizens.

Nevertheless, this normative unity entails a juristic sense of how the population regulated by law is actually structured. I have argued elsewhere that jurisprudential theories have tended to visualise 'society' – the social entity that law purports to govern – broadly in two fundamental ways: as a mass of autonomous individuals linked only by their common recognition of a unifying legal authority (imperium) and as an integrated community (communitas) that collectively authorises its own law.[4] So, juristic thought implies certain general images of the social world in and for which law exists. When Radbruch wrote of fitness for purpose (*Zweckmassigkeit*) as one of the three fundamental values of the idea of law, he surely meant its fitness for embodying and promoting the essential cultural expectations, understandings, and assumptions of this social world.

Juristic images of it can (and should) be sharpened, corrected, and enriched by empirically oriented social theory. This book has devoted most attention to one type of such theory, that of Durkheimian sociology. This, as has been seen, emphasises the ever-increasing complexity of contemporary social life – its diversity, division, and fragmentation. At the same time, it indicates how law's normative construction of the unity of the social might be translated into a genuine social unity (through

---

4 See Chapter 11, and more generally Cotterrell 1995: ch 11.

law's promotion of moral individualism).[5] Solidarity is the value concept that represents the fundamental problem of securing social *unity in diversity*, a problem increasingly familiar and central in juristic experience. So, the concepts of justice, security, and solidarity should be understood as rough frameworks of thought, value orientations that are to be given detailed, precise juristic meaning in their time and place. In other words, they are devices to help make law fit for purpose.

The Durkheimian focus on moral individualism as a unifying value system might be challenged. Could not other values – for example, the more elaborate and less minimal precepts of some religion – provide a unifying structure of values for a society? Certainly they could. But no unifying value system can be appropriate for complex modern societies, I suggest, unless it entails the *appreciation (not merely tolerance) of difference* (for example, in beliefs and customs) at the same time that it insists on the *similarity* of all individuals (in entitlement to human dignity and respect).

One could seek elsewhere for social stability: for example in a free interplay of individual interests without appeal to any overarching values except those of unfettered individual choice. Solidarity might then be admittedly a frail thing, dependent on the vagaries of contractual ties, pragmatic cooperation in transient projects, and the fluctuating judgments of where one's self-interest lies in dealings with others. Solidarity might also be based on bonds of affection and emotional ties, but emotions can be volatile and so the solidarity based on it can be volatile, too. Finally, it might be based merely on coexistence in a shared environment – a physical locality where people live in proximity, a shared history and collective memory, or common traditions or a common language – but this is a form of solidarity often resistant to or suspicious of inevitable social change. All of these, however, are possible bases of a unity of the social which can explored via social theory.

Jurisprudence in movement

Sociological jurisprudence is distinguished from sociology of law, according to the approach of this book, because of jurisprudence's explicit commitment to the pursuit of values through law, indeed its recognition of values as at the heart of legal practice and experience. With this emphasis, values seem more fundamental to the idea of law than are specific legal forms (for example, the idea that law must be made up of positive rules and well-defined procedures) and institutions (such as courts, legislatures, and enforcement agencies). In established municipal legal systems, the forms of law are in the centre of juristic attention and a crucial locus of juristic work. But in considering transnational law earlier in this book, it was suggested that jurists might be wise not to be too rigidly prescriptive as to what they may recognise as legal form and legal institutions in transnational contexts. Perhaps relatively simple, serviceable models of what could be treated for practical purposes as legal phenomena – and thus as potentially juristically relevant – might be adopted as a

---

5 See Chapters 12 and 13.

starting point in juristically exploring and ordering the shifting, evolving, inchoate transnational regulatory arena.

The model advocated earlier in this book of law as institutionalised doctrine offers a minimal working idea of law's regulatory mechanisms.[6] In practice, of course, jurists must understand law in any particular jurisdiction in far more sophisticated terms. But the combination of a minimal model of law as institutionalised doctrine and a tenacious commitment to the pursuit of basic legal values may be a realistic starting point to allow jurists to address theoretically many new, unfamiliar regulatory phenomena in transnational and perhaps intranational contexts and in contexts in which municipal state law must interact productively with transnational nonstate regulation. Forms and institutions of law should be shaped to embody the idea of law in the contexts where that idea is to be nurtured.

Some scholars might reject such an open approach as giving up too much of their established learning about the juristic nature of law. It would be possible to say that the kinds of nonstate regulatory phenomena that this flexible approach is designed to bring into the juristic orbit should in fact be put firmly outside it; they are simply not to be included in what jurists can, or should, treat as law. But the consequence of such a view would probably have to be a recognition that the relative significance of law is *shrinking* in the whole transnational regulatory landscape. Law would then appear as surrounded by numerous kinds of burgeoning regulation that jurists would treat as outside their fields of expertise and responsibility; perhaps it could be left to other nonlawyer professionals to address, organise, and manage this regulation. Jurists could generally feel no need to extend beyond the experience of their own legal systems or of other such systems familiar to them. All that would be someone else's job.

This would, however, certainly be to diminish the juristic role, to make it less able to serve the value of making law fit for the purpose of ordering the cultural environment in which it exists. The jurist could act as a critical servant of the positive law of the state but without the possibility of understanding juristically the evolving regulatory prospects and limits of this law – in other words, without being able to work actively to safeguard values of justice, security, and solidarity in an environment shaped by many regulatory forms apart from state law.

Changing times can dislodge theoretical certainties. Recently, nationalist and populist currents have strongly resurfaced in Western politics. They have aimed, among other things, to halt or slow the previously seemingly unstoppable forward march of transnational regulation. Protectionism; regulatory isolationism; the desire to reassert national control over the making, interpretation, and enforcement of law; a strengthening and firmer policing of jurisdictional borders; and a suspicion of transnational regulatory structures of all kinds: these have seemed to be characteristic of a new politics – or, more accurately, the rediscovery of an old one. These developments have often been greeted with shocked surprise in the countries where

---

6 See Chapters 6 and 7.

they occurred. Yet various themes of sociological jurisprudence developed in earlier chapters of this book offer a range of conceptual resources for interpreting their meaning and for understanding some of their likely causes.

Insofar as many kinds of international and transnational regulation have been objects of attack, the urgent question of regulatory legitimacy, considered especially in Chapter 9, is directly relevant, indeed central, in understanding some bases of this attack. Transnational authority claims have often seemed overextended, and the legitimacy for them that comes from democratic processes in politically organised societies tends to seem thin and insecure. In Chapter 9, I visualised the political authority available to transnational law as 'an extremely thin, fragile arm stretched out from states over a vast transnational realm'. This book has frequently emphasised the great but often insufficiently juristically recognised importance of cultural bases of legitimacy, rooted in the experienced social relations of communal networks.

International law is often characterised as rooted in an 'international community', a fragile communal network of states based on their self-interest and the coalitions that form and reform as the interests of states are collectively pursued. However, when international law is seen as affecting the life conditions of the individuals who inhabit the political societies of these states, a need for cultural legitimacy becomes increasingly apparent: law needs to reflect and express the communal bonds that are experienced by individuals. International law needs to descend from the clouds of diplomacy to address the life conditions of the actual human beings affected by it (and not just the perceived interests of states). Insofar as transnational law directly impacts on these life conditions, it too has to find its legitimacy in the communal networks to which it relates. This issue was discussed earlier most fully in connection with the development of transnational criminal law.[7]

Behind everything is the general regulatory problem which can be regarded as the foundational theme of sociology of law – a theme central to the work of Eugen Ehrlich, the foremost pioneer of this research field – the problem of *moral distance*, a multifacetted and disabling remoteness of regulators from the regulated.[8] It is a problem affecting the municipal law of modern Western democratic states as well as the regulatory structures of international and transnational law. It is certainly not solved merely by the existence of formal structures of representative democracy in modern polities. It is properly seen as a juristic problem of infusing into legal operations adequate sensitivity, information, and insight into the relations between those who make laws and those who live under them.

Jurists drawing on sociological perspectives should treat the need to address the problem of moral distance as central to their work, as well as emphasising related issues surrounding the legitimacy of regulatory authority. Doing so requires attention to perspectives on the unity of the social discussed earlier in this chapter. I noted that there might theoretically be several very different underpinnings of this

---

7 See Chapter 10.
8 See Chapter 1, pp 10-11.

unity – or at least different perceptions of the essential bases of social unity. Amongst them is the idea of convergent or common economic interests or projects as providing this basis (the existence of a primarily instrumental communal network) or the idea that familiar, established, common conditions of coexistence in a certain environment (traditional relations of community centred on common language, ethnicity, history, geographical locality, and so on) might provide that basis of unity.

Law focused on transnational economic interests and projects – for example, international economic law and much transnational private law – needs cultural bases of legitimacy in the communal networks of economic actors who benefit from this law. But populist counter-movements challenging these kinds of law might be seen as especially rooted in communal networks centred on bonds of *tradition*, as described earlier. These networks seek regulation that relates to traditional conditions of 'local' coexistence; they do not want those conditions disrupted or undermined by transnationalism.

Undoubtedly much more than this is at stake, but the reassertion of bonds of traditional community in the face of their perceived marginalisation by transnational structures of instrumental (economic) community is surely part of the picture. For jurists these developments should suggest the central legal importance of different types of community relations as components of culture. The unifying conditions of the diverse social environments in which law exists have to be taken into account if jurisprudence is to rise to the challenge of understanding and reshaping itself in the face of change.

Alongside this, new or newly powerful forms of regulation have to be assigned their place in juristic understanding. The plurality of regimes of regulation has to be juristically analysed. And jurists need to explore afresh the bases of regulatory authority and legitimacy in contemporary circumstances where the role of the state as monopolist of law has now become controversial.

Sociological jurisprudence should examine the legal present and try as best it can to envisage the regulatory future. Perhaps this will be a future of halting steps towards more transnationalism and an increasingly integrated world legal order or at least towards the eventual greater legal integration of large transnational blocs. Perhaps the future will see the forceful reassertion of the state's claim to monopolise the making and application of law and a greater fragmentation of the international legal community of states, with all its attendant risks for stable international relations. Perhaps another, different scenario will take shape, one that cannot yet be envisaged even in outline.

One thing is certain: jurisprudence can play its part in the mapping and guiding of law's development in uncertain times only if a sociological sensibility becomes integral to the jurist's craft and wisdom.

REFERENCES

Aarnio, A., Alexy, R. and Bergholtz, G. eds (1997), *Justice, Morality and Society: A Tribute to Aleksander Peczenik*. Lund: Juristförlaget i Lund.

Abbott, K. W., Keohane, R. O., Moravcsik, A., Slaughter, A.-M. and Snidal, D. (2000), 'The Concept of Legalization', 54 *International Organization* 401–19.

Abend, G. (2008), 'Two Main Problems in the Sociology of Morality', 37 *Theory & Society* 87–125.

Adair, S. (2008), 'Status and Solidarity: A Reformulation of Early Durkheimian Theory', 78 *Sociological Inquiry* 97–120.

Adair-Toteff, C. (2005), 'Max Weber's Charisma', 5 *Journal of Classical Sociology* 189–204.

Alexander, L. (1998), 'The Banality of Legal Reasoning', 73 *Notre Dame Law Review* 517–33.

———and Sherwin, E. (2008), *Demystifying Legal Reasoning*. Cambridge: Cambridge University Press.

Alldridge, P. (2015), 'The Spirit and the Corruption of Cricket', in A. Diduck, N. Peleg and H. Reece eds, *Law in Society: Reflections on Children, Family, Culture and Philosophy: Essays in Honour of Michael Freeman*, pp. 331–46. Leiden: Brill.

Allen, R., Ashworth, A., Cotterrell, R., Coyle, A., Duff, A., Lacey, N., Liebling, A. and Morgan, R. (2014), *A Presumption Against Imprisonment: Social Order and Social Values*. London: British Academy.

Alvarez, J. E. (2017), 'The Use (and Misuse) of European Human Rights Law in Investor-State Dispute Settlement', in F. Ferrari ed, *The Impact of EU Law on International Commercial Arbitration*. Huntington, NY: Juris.

Ambos, K. (2007), 'Toward a Universal System of Crime: Comments on George Fletcher's *Grammar of Criminal Law*', 28 *Cardozo Law Review* 2647–73.

Anderson, J. (2006), 'An Accident of History: Why the Decisions of Sports Governing Bodies Are Not Amenable to Judicial Review', 35 *Common Law World Review* 173–96.

Antonio, R. J. (2013), 'Plundering the Commons: The Growth Imperative in Neoliberal Times', 61 *Sociological Review*, Suppl S2, 18–42.

Arnold, T. W. (1935), *The Symbols of Government*. New York: Harcourt, Brace & World reprint, 1962.

Aroney, N. (2008), 'Julius Stone and the End of Sociological Jurisprudence: Articulating the Reasons for Decision in Political Communication Cases', 31 *University of New South Wales Law Journal* 107–35.

Astorino, S. J. (1996), 'The Impact of Sociological Jurisprudence on International Law in the Inter-War Period: The American Experience', 34 *Duquesne Law Review* 277–98.

Austin, J. (1885a), *Lectures on Jurisprudence or the Philosophy of Positive Law*, 5th edn. London: John Murray.

———(1885b), 'On the Uses of the Study of Jurisprudence', in Austin ed (1885a), pp. 1071–91.

Avi-Yonah, R. S. (2000), 'Globalization, Tax Competition and the Fiscal Crisis of the Welfare State', 113 *Harvard Law Review* 1573–676.

Bacchus, J. (2004), 'A Few Thoughts on Legitimacy, Democracy, and the WTO', 7 *Journal of International Economic Law* 667–73.

Bakht, N. (2009), 'Objection, Your Honour! Accommodating *Niqab*-Wearing Women in Courtrooms', in Grillo et al eds (2009), pp. 115–33.

Balkin, J. M. (1996), 'Interdisciplinarity as Colonization', 53 *Washington and Lee Law Review* 949–70.

———(2011), *Constitutional Redemption: Political Faith in an Unjust World*. Cambridge, MA: Harvard University Press.

Banakar, R. (2016), 'Law, Policy and Social Control Amidst Flux', in K. Dahlstrand ed, *Festskrift till Karsten Åström*, pp. 47–74. Lund: Juristförlaget i Lund.

Barzilai, G. (2008), 'Beyond Relativism: Where Is Political Power in Legal Pluralism?', 9 *Theoretical Inquiries in Law* 395–416.

Beck, U. and Sznaider, N. (2006), 'Unpacking Cosmopolitanism for the Social Sciences: A Research Agenda', 57 *British Journal of Sociology* 1–22.

Bell, J. (1986), 'The Acceptability of Legal Arguments', in N. MacCormick and P. Birks eds, *The Legal Mind: Essays for Tony Honoré*, pp. 67–82. Oxford: Oxford University Press.

Bellah, R. N., Madsen, R., Sullivan, W. M., Swidler, A. and Tipton, S. M. (1996), *Habits of the Heart: Individualism and Commitment in American Life*, updated edn. Berkeley: University of California Press.

Berman, H. J. (1995), 'World Law', 18 *Fordham International Law Journal* 1617–22.

Berman, P. S. (2002), 'The Globalization of Jurisdiction', 151 *University of Pennsylvania Law Review* 311–546.

———(2005), 'From International Law to Law and Globalization', 43 *Columbia Journal of Transnational Law* 485–556.

———(2006), 'Seeing Beyond the Limits of International Law', 84 *Texas Law Review* 1265–306.

———(2007a), 'A Pluralist Approach to International Law', 32 *Yale Law Journal* 301–29.

———(2007b), 'Global Legal Pluralism', 80 *Southern California Law Review* 1155–237.

———(2009), 'The New Legal Pluralism', 5 *Annual Review of Law and Social Science* 225–42.

———(2012), *Global Legal Pluralism: A Jurisprudence of Law Beyond Borders*. New York: Cambridge University Press.

Bernstein, L. (2001), 'Private Commercial Law in the Cotton Industry: Creating Cooperation Through Rules, Norms, and Institutions', 99 *Michigan Law Review* 1724–90.

Bernstorff, J. von (2010), *The Public International Law Theory of Hans Kelsen: Believing in Universal Law*, transl. T. Dunlap. Cambridge: Cambridge University Press.

Berolzheimer, F. (1912), *The World's Legal Philosophies*, transl. R. S. Jastrow. Boston: Boston Book Co.

Billo, C. and Chang, W. (2004), *Cyber Warfare: An Analysis of the Means and Motivations of Selected Nation States*. Hanover, NH: Institute for Security Technology Studies, Dartmouth College.

Bindel, J. (2014), *An Unpunished Crime: The Lack of Prosecutions for Female Genital Mutilation in the UK*. London: New Culture Forum.

Birrell, I. (2013), 'Which Politician Will Dare Dismantle Crony Capitalism?', *Evening Standard* (London), November 25th. www.standard.co.uk/comment/ian-birrell-which-politician-will-dare-dismantle-crony-capitalism-8961935.html (accessed June 7th 2017).

Black, D. J. (1973), 'The Mobilization of Law', 2 *Journal of Legal Studies* 125–49.

————(1976), *The Behavior of Law*. New York: Academic Press.

————(1989), *Sociological Justice*. New York: Oxford University Press.

————(1998), *The Social Structure of Right and Wrong*, revised edn. New York: Academic Press.

Blythe, R. (1983), *The Age of Illusion: Glimpses of Britain Between the Wars 1919–40*. Oxford: Oxford University Press.

Bobbio, N. (1996), *The Age of Rights*, transl. A. Cameron. Cambridge: Polity.

Bouckaert, G. and Brans, M. (2012), 'Governing Without Government: Lessons From Belgium's Caretaker Government', 25 *Governance* 173–6.

Brewer, S. (1996), 'Exemplary Reasoning: Semantics, Pragmatics, and the Rational Force of Legal Argument by Analogy', 109 *Harvard Law Review* 925–1028.

Brock, B. J. (2011), 'Modern American Supreme Court Judicial Methodology and Its Origins: A Critical Analysis of the Legal Thought of Roscoe Pound', 35 *Journal of the Legal Profession* 187–207.

Broude, T. (2013), 'Keep Calm and Carry On: Martti Koskenniemi and the Fragmentation of International Law', 27 *Temple International and Comparative Law Journal* 279–92.

Brubaker, R. (1984), *The Limits of Rationality: An Essay on the Social and Moral Thought of Max Weber*. London: Allen & Unwin.

Brugger, W. (1996), 'The Image of the Person in the Human Rights Concept', 18 *Human Rights Quarterly* 594–611.

Cai, C. (2013), 'New Great Powers and International Law in the 21st Century', 24 *European Journal of International Law* 755–95.

Calliess, G.-P. (2007), 'The Making of Transnational Contract Law', 14 *Indiana Journal of Global Legal Studies* 469–84.

————and Renner, M. (2009), 'Between Law and Social Norms: The Evolution of Global Governance', 22 *Ratio Juris* 260–80.

————and Zumbansen, P. (2010), *Rough Consensus and Running Code: A Theory of Transnational Private Law*. Oxford: Hart.

Carmichael, C. M. (1997), *Law, Legend, and Incest in the Bible: Leviticus 18–20*. Ithaca: Cornell University Press.

Carson, N. P. (2011), 'Thick Ethical Concepts *Still* Cannot Be Disentangled: A Critical Response to Payne, Blomberg, and Blackburn'. Paper presented at the Central Division Meeting of the American Philosophical Association, March 2011. http://blogs.baylor.edu/nathan_carson/files/2011/11/Thick-Ethical-Concepts1.pdf (accessed June 7th 2017).

Cassese, A. (2012), 'For an Enhanced Role of *Jus Cogens*', in A. Cassese ed, *Realizing Utopia: The Future of International Law*, pp. 158–71. Oxford: Oxford University Press.

Chesler, M. A., Sanders, J. and Kalmuss, D. S. (1988), *Social Science in Court: Mobilizing Experts in the School Desegregation Cases*. Madison: University of Wisconsin Press.

Chroust, A.-H. (1944), 'The Philosophy of Law of Gustav Radbruch', 53 *Philosophical Review* 23–45.

Cladis, M. (1992), *A Communitarian Defense of Liberalism: Émile Durkheim and Contemporary Social Theory*. Stanford: Stanford University Press.

Clausen, B., Kraay, A. and Nyiri, Z. (2011), 'Corruption and Confidence in Public Institutions: Evidence From a Global Survey', 25 *World Bank Economic Review* 212–49.

Clifton, J. (2014), 'Beyond Hollowing Out: Straitjacketing the State', 85 *Political Quarterly* 437–44.

Coene, G. and Longman, C. (2008), 'Gendering the Diversification of Diversity: The Belgian Hijab (in) Question', 8 *Ethnicities* 302–21.

Cohen, J. L. (2006), 'Sovereign Equality vs. Imperial Right: The Battle Over the "New World Order"', 13 *Constellations* 485–505.

Cohen, S. (1996), 'Crime and Politics: Spot the Difference', 47 *British Journal of Sociology* 1–21.

Cole, W. M. (2012), 'A Civil Religion for World Society: The Direct and Diffuse Effects of Human Rights Treaties, 1981–2007', 27 *Sociological Forum* 937–60.

Coleman, J. ed (2001), *Hart's Postscript: Essays on the Postscript to The Concept of Law*. Oxford: Oxford University Press.

———and Shapiro, S. eds (2002), *Oxford Handbook of Jurisprudence & Philosophy of Law*. Oxford: Oxford University Press.

Collini, S. (2006), 'Book Review', 69 *Modern Law Review* 108–14.

Collins, H. (1986), 'Democracy and Adjudication', in D. N. MacCormick and P. Birks eds, *The Legal Mind: Essays for Tony Honoré*, pp. 67–82. Oxford: Oxford University Press.

Colvin, E. (1978), 'The Sociology of Secondary Rules', 28 *University of Toronto Law Journal* 195–214.

Copnall, J. (2010), 'Bashir Warrant: Chad Accuses ICC of Anti-African Bias', *BBC News Africa*, July 22nd. www.bbc.co.uk/news/world-africa-10723869 (accessed June 7th 2017).

Cotterrell, R. (1992), 'Some Sociological Aspects of the Controversy Around the Legal Validity of Private Purpose Trusts', reprinted in Cotterrell (2008c), pp. 201–33.

———(1995), *Law's Community: Legal Theory in Sociological Perspective*. Oxford: Oxford University Press.

———(1999), *Emile Durkheim: Law in a Moral Domain*. Stanford: Stanford University Press.

———(2000), 'Pandora's Box: Jurisprudence in Legal Education', 7 *International Journal of the Legal Profession* 179–87.

———(2003), *The Politics of Jurisprudence: A Critical Introduction to Legal Philosophy*, 2nd edn. Oxford: Oxford University Press.

———(2006), *Law, Culture and Society: Legal Ideas in the Mirror of Social Theory*. Abingdon: Routledge.

———(2008a), 'Sociological Jurisprudence', in P. Cane and J. Conaghan eds, *The New Oxford Companion to Law*, pp. 1099–101. Oxford: Oxford University Press.

———(2008b), 'Transnational Communities and the Concept of Law', 21 *Ratio Juris* 1–18.

———(2008c), *Living Law: Studies in Legal and Social Theory*. Abingdon: Routledge.

———(2009), 'Spectres of Transnationalism: Changing Terrains of Sociology of Law', 36 *Journal of Law and Society* 481–500.

———(2016), 'Reading Juristic Theories in and Beyond Historical Context: The Case of Lundstedt's Swedish Legal Realism', in M. Del Mar and M. Lobban eds, *Law in Theory and History: New Essays on a Neglected Dialogue*, pp. 149–66. Oxford: Hart.

Cotterrell, R. and Del Mar, M. (2016a), 'Concluding Reflections: Transnational Futures of Authority', in Cotterrell and Del Mar eds (2016b), pp. 387–403.

———eds (2016b), *Authority in Transnational Legal Theory: Theorising Across Disciplines*. Cheltenham: Edward Elgar.

Cotterrell, R. and Selznick, P. (2004), 'Selznick Interviewed: Philip Selznick in Conversation With Roger Cotterrell', 31 *Journal of Law and Society* 291–317.

Cover, R. M. (1983), 'The Supreme Court 1982 Term – Foreword: Nomos and Narrative', 97 *Harvard Law Review* 4–68.

Cownie, F. (2004), *Legal Academics: Culture and Identities*. Oxford: Hart.

Coyle, S. (2013), 'Legality and the Liberal Order', 76 *Modern Law Review* 401–18.

Cross, K. H. (2015), 'The Extraterritorial Reach of Sovereign Debt Enforcement', 12 *Berkeley Business Law Journal* 111–43.

Culver, K. C. and Giudice, M. (2010), *Legality's Borders: An Essay in General Jurisprudence*. New York: Oxford University Press.

Dalberg-Larsen, J. (2000), *The Unity of Law: An Illusion? On Legal Pluralism in Theory and Practice*. Glienicke/Berlin: Galda+Wilch Verlag.

Daniels, D. von (2010), *The Concept of Law From a Transnational Perspective*. Abingdon: Routledge.

Danner, M. (2009), 'The Red Cross Torture Report: What It Means', *New York Review of Books*, April 30th, pp. 48–56.

Daube, D. (1973), 'The Self-Understood in Legal History', 85 *Juridical Review* 126–34.

Davies, M. (2005), 'The Ethos of Pluralism', 27 *Sydney Law Review* 87–112.

De Galembert, C. (2009), '*L'affaire du foulard* in the Shadow of the Strasbourg Court: Article 9 and the Public Career of the Veil in France', in Grillo et al eds (2009), pp. 237–65.

DeGirolami, M. O. (2008), 'Faith in the Rule of Law', 82 *St John's Law Review* 573–607.

Delgado, R. and Stefancic, J. (1994), *Failed Revolutions: Social Reform and the Limits of Legal Imagination*. Boulder: Westview Press.

Devaux, C. (2013), 'The Role of Experts in the Elaboration of the Cape Town Convention: Between Authority and Legitimacy', 19 *European Law Journal* 843–63.

Devos, C. and Sinardet, D. (2012), 'Governing Without a Government: The Belgian Experiment', 25 *Governance* 167–71.

Dickson, J. (2001), *Evaluation and Legal Theory*. Oxford: Hart.

Dilliard, I. (1960), 'Introduction', in L. Hand, *The Spirit of Liberty: Papers and Addresses*, 3rd edn, pp. v–xxvii. Chicago: University of Chicago Press.

Di Robilant, A. (2006), 'Genealogies of Soft Law', 54 *American Journal of Comparative Law* 499–554.

Djelic, M.-L. and Quack, S. (2010a), 'Transnational Communities and their Impact on the Governance of Business and Economic Activity', in Djelic and Quack eds (2010b), pp. 377–413.

———eds (2010b), *Transnational Communities: Shaping Global Economic Governance*. Cambridge: Cambridge University Press.

Donald, A., Watson, J., McClean, N., Leach, P. and Eschment, J. (2009), *Human Rights in Britain Since the Human Rights Act 1998: A Critical Review*. London: Equality and Human Rights Commission.

Donlan, S. P. and Urscheler, L. H. eds (2014), *Concepts of Law: Comparative, Jurisprudential, and Social Science Perspectives*. Abingdon: Routledge.

Donnelly, J. (2007), 'The Relative Universality of Human Rights', 29 *Human Rights Quarterly* 281–306.

Duguit, L. (1921), *Law in the Modern State*, transl. F. Laski and H. J. Laski. London: Allen & Unwin.

Dumas, M. (2018), 'Taking the Law to Court: Citizen Suits and the Legislative Process', 62 *American Journal of Political Science* (forthcoming).

Durkheim, É. (1952), *Suicide: A Study in Sociology*, transl. J. A. Spaulding and G. Simpson. London: Routledge & Kegan Paul.

———(1957), *Professional Ethics and Civic Morals*, transl. C. Brookfield. London: Routledge & Kegan Paul.

———(1961), *Moral Education: A Study in the Theory and Application of the Sociology of Education*, transl. E. K. Wilson and H. Schnurer. New York: Free Press.

———(1969), 'Individualism and the Intellectuals', transl. S. Lukes and J. Lukes, reprinted in W. S. F. Pickering ed, *Durkheim on Religion: A Selection of Readings With Bibliographies and Introductory Remarks*, pp. 59–73. London: Routledge & Kegan Paul, 1975.

———(1970), *La science sociale et l'action*. Paris: Presses Universitaires de France.

———(1975), *Textes vol. 2: religion, morale, anomie*. Paris: Les Éditions de Minuit.

———(1979), 'A Discussion on Sex Education', transl. H. L. Sutcliffe, in W. S. F. Pickering ed, *Durkheim: Essays on Morals and Education*, pp. 140–8. London: Routledge & Kegan Paul.

———(1984), *The Division of Labour in Society*, transl. W. D. Halls. London: Macmillan.

———(1992), 'Two Laws of Penal Evolution', transl. T. A. Jones and A. T. Scull, in M. Gane ed, *The Radical Sociology of Durkheim and Mauss*, pp. 21–49. London: Routledge.

———(1995), *The Elementary Forms of Religious Life*, transl. K. E. Fields. New York: Free Press.

Duval, A. (2013), '*Lex Sportiva*: A Playground for Transnational Law', 19 *European Law Journal* 822–42.

Duxbury, N. (1997), 'The Narrowing of English Jurisprudence', 95 *Michigan Law Review* 1990–2004.

———(2001), *Jurists and Judges: An Essay on Influence*. Oxford: Hart.

Dworkin, R. (1978), *Taking Rights Seriously*, revised edn. London: Duckworth.

———(1986), *Law's Empire*. Oxford: Hart reprint, 1998.

———(1989), 'Liberal Community', 77 *California Law Review* 479–504.

———(1993), *Life's Dominion: An Argument About Abortion and Euthanasia*. London: HarperCollins.

———(2006a), *Is Democracy Possible Here? Principles for a New Political Debate*. Princeton: Princeton University Press.

———(2006b), *Justice in Robes*. Cambridge, MA: Harvard University Press.

———(2006c), 'Hart and the Concepts of Law', 119 *Harvard Law Review Forum* 95–104.

———(2008), *The Supreme Court Phalanx: The Court's New Right-Wing Bloc*. New York: New York Review Books.

———(2011a), 'The Court's Embarrassingly Bad Decisions', *New York Review of Books*, May 26th, pp. 40–41.

———(2011b), *Justice for Hedgehogs*. Cambridge, MA: Harvard University Press.

Dyzenhaus, D. (2000), 'Positivism's Stagnant Research Programme', 20 *Oxford Journal of Legal Studies* 703–22.

———(2006), 'The Demise of Legal Positivism?', 119 *Harvard Law Review Forum* 112–21.

Edwards, H. (1992), 'The Growing Disjunction Between Legal Education and the Legal Profession', 91 *Michigan Law Review* 34–78.

Ehrlich, E. (1917), 'Judicial Freedom of Decision: Its Principles and Objects', in Wigmore et al eds (1917), pp. 47–84.

———(1936), *Fundamental Principles of the Sociology of Law*, transl. W. L. Moll. New Brunswick, NJ: Transaction reprint, 2002.

Elliott, A. and Turner, B. S. eds (2001), *Profiles in Contemporary Social Theory*. London: Sage.

Emberland, M. (2006), *The Human Rights of Companies: Exploring the Structure of ECHR Protection*. Oxford: Oxford University Press.

Encinas de Muñagorri, R., Hennette-Vauchez, S., Herrera, C. M. and Leclerc, O. (2016), *L'analyse juridique de (x): Le droits parmi les sciences sociales*. Paris: Editions Kimé.

Endicott, T. A. O. (2001), 'How to Speak the Truth', 46 *American Journal of Jurisprudence* 229–48.

Eng, S. (1997), 'Hidden Value-Choices in Legal Practice', in Aarnio et al eds (1997), pp. 123–45.

Evan, W. M. (1990), *Social Structure and Law: Theoretical and Empirical Perspectives*. Newbury Park, CA: Sage.

Fauconnet, P. (1928), *La responsabilité. Étude de sociologie*, 2nd edn. Paris: Corpus des oeuvres de Philosophie en langue française reprint, 2010.

Feinberg, J. (1965), 'The Expressive Function of Punishment', 49 *Monist* 397–423.

Féron, H. (2014), 'Human Rights and Faith: A "World-Wide Secular Religion"?', 7 *Ethics & Global Politics* 181–200.

Fields, K. E. (1996), 'Durkheim and the Idea of Soul', 25 *Theory and Society* 193–203.

Finnis, J. (2009), 'H. L. A. Hart: A Twentieth-Century Oxford Political Philosopher: Reflections by a Former Student and Colleague', 54 *American Journal of Jurisprudence* 161–85.

———(2011), *Natural Law and Natural Rights*, 2nd edn with new postscript. Oxford: Oxford University Press.

Fischman, J. B. (2013), 'Reuniting "Is" and "Ought" in Empirical Legal Scholarship', 162 *University of Pennsylvania Law Review* 117–68.

Flanders, C. (2009), 'Toward a Theory of Persuasive Authority', 62 *Oklahoma Law Review* 55–88.

Fletcher, G. P. (1984), 'Human Dignity as a Constitutional Value', 22 *University of Western Ontario Law Review* 171–82.

Flood, J. A. (1991), 'Doing Business: The Management of Uncertainty in Lawyers' Work', 25 *Law & Society Review* 41–71.

Fontaine, L. (2012), *Qu'est-ce qu'un 'grand' juriste? Essai sur les juristes et la pensée juridique contemporaine*. Paris: Lextenso éditions.

Fraser, D. (2005), *Cricket and the Law: The Man in White Is Always Right*. Abingdon: Routledge.

Freeman, M. D. A. (2014), *Lloyd's Introduction to Jurisprudence*, 9th edn. London: Sweet & Maxwell.

Fried, C. (1981), 'The Artificial Reason of the Law or What Lawyers Know', 60 *Texas Law Review* 35–58.

Friedman, L. M. (2002), 'One World: Notes on the Emerging Legal Order', in M. Likosky ed, *Transnational Legal Processes: Globalization and Power Disparities*, pp. 23–40. London: Butterworths.

Friedmann, W. (1960), 'Gustav Radbruch', 14 *Vanderbilt Law Review* 191–209.

———(1967), *Legal Theory*, 5th edn. New York: Columbia University Press.

Friedrichs, D. O. and Friedrichs, J. (2002), 'The World Bank and Crimes of Globalization: A Case Study', 29 *Social Justice* 13–36.

Frishman, O. (2013), 'Transnational Judicial Dialogue as an Organisational Field', 19 *European Law Journal* 739–58.

Froomkin, A. M. (2003), 'Habermas@Discourse.Net: Toward a Critical Theory of Cyberspace', 116 *Harvard Law Review* 749–873.

Fuller, L. L. (1969), *The Morality of Law*, revised edn. New Haven: Yale University Press.

Gabel, P. (1980), 'Reification in Legal Reasoning', 3 *Research in Law and Sociology* 25–51.

Galanter, M. (1983), 'The Radiating Effects of Courts', in K. O. Boyum and L. Mather eds, *Empirical Theories About Courts*, pp. 117–42. New York: Longman.

———(1998), 'The Faces of Mistrust: The Image of Lawyers in Public Opinion, Jokes, and Political Discourse', 66 *University of Cincinnati Law Review* 805–45.

———(2005), *Lowering the Bar: Lawyer Jokes and Legal Culture*. Madison: University of Wisconsin Press.

Gane, M. (1992), 'Durkheim: Woman as Outsider', in M. Gane ed, *The Radical Sociology of Durkheim and Mauss*, pp. 85–132. London: Routledge.

Gardner, J. (2001), 'Legal Positivism: 5½ Myths', 46 *American Journal of Jurisprudence* 199–227.

———(2007), 'Nearly Natural Law', 52 *American Journal of Jurisprudence* 1–23.

Garland, D. (1996), 'The Limits of the Sovereign State: Strategies of Crime Control in Contemporary Society', 36 *British Journal of Criminology* 445–71.

Gerth, H. H. and Mills, C. W. eds (1948), *From Max Weber: Essays in Sociology*, transl. H. H. Gerth and C. W. Mills. London: Routledge & Kegan Paul.

Gierke, O. von (1950), *Natural Law and the Theory of Society 1500 to 1800*, transl. E. Barker. Cambridge: Cambridge University Press.

Giudice, M. (2011), 'Analytical Jurisprudence and Contingency', in M. Del Mar ed, *New Waves in Philosophy of Law*, pp. 58–76. Basingstoke: Palgrave Macmillan.

————(2014), 'Global Legal Pluralism: What's Law Got to Do With It?', 34 *Oxford Journal of Legal Studies* 589–608.

Glenn, H. P. (1987), 'Persuasive Authority', 32 *McGill Law Journal* 261–98.

————(2013), *The Cosmopolitan State*. Oxford: Oxford University Press.

Goldberg, C. A. (2008), 'Introduction to Émile Durkheim's "Anti-Semitism and Social Crisis"', 26 *Sociological Theory* 299–321.

Goldsmith, J. L. and Posner, E. A. (2005), *The Limits of International Law*. Oxford: Oxford University Press.

Gould, C. C. (2007), 'Transnational Solidarities', 38 *Journal of Social Philosophy* 148–64.

Graver, H. P. (1990), 'Administrative Decision-Making and the Concept of Law', in A. Görlitz and R. Voight eds, *Postinterventionistisches Recht*, pp. 177–94. Pfaffenweiler: Centaurus-Verlagsgesellschaft.

Graycar, A. and Villa, D. (2011), 'The Loss of Governance Capacity Through Corruption', 24 *Governance* 419–38.

Green, L. (2010), 'Law as a Means', in P. Cane ed, *The Hart-Fuller Debate in the Twenty-first Century*, pp. 169–88. Oxford: Hart.

Green, S. J. D. (1989), 'Émile Durkheim on Human Talents and Two Traditions of Social Justice', 40 *British Journal of Sociology* 97–117.

Greenberg, L. M. (1976), 'Bergson and Durkheim as Sons and Assimilators: The Early Years', 9 *French Historical Studies* 619–34.

Grillo, R., Ballard, R., Ferrari, A., Hoekema, A., Maussen, M. and Shah, P. eds (2009), *Legal Practice and Cultural Diversity*. Abingdon: Routledge.

Groppi, T. and Ponthoreau, M.-C. eds (2014), *The Use of Foreign Precedents by Constitutional Judges*. Oxford: Hart.

Gurvitch, G. (1932), *L'Idée du Droit Social – Notion et système du droit social: Histoire doctrinale depuis le 17e siècle jusqu'à la fin du 19e siècle*. Paris: Librairie du Recueil Sirey.

Hackett, C., Grim, B. J. et al (2012), *The Global Religious Landscape: A Report on the Size and Distribution of the World's Major Religious Groups as of 2010*. Washington, DC: Pew Research Center Forum on Religion and Public Life.

Halliday, T. C. and Carruthers, B. G. (2007), 'The Recursivity of Law: Global Norm-Making and National Law-making in the Globalization of Corporate Insolvency Regimes', 112 *American Journal of Sociology* 1135–1202.

Halpin, A. (2011), 'Austin's Methodology? His Bequest to Jurisprudence', 70 *Cambridge Law Journal* 175–202.

————(2014), 'The Creation and Use of Concepts of Law When Confronting Legal and Normative Plurality', in Donlan and Urscheler eds (2014), pp. 169–92.

Hart, H. L. A. (1983), *Essays in Jurisprudence and Philosophy*. Oxford: Oxford University Press.

————(1994), *The Concept of Law*, 2nd edn with new appendix. Oxford: Oxford University Press reprint as 3rd edn, 2012.

Hawkins, M. J. (1979), 'Continuity and Change in Durkheim's Theory of Social Solidarity', 20 *Sociological Quarterly* 155–64.

Hearn, F. (1985), 'Durkheim's Political Sociology: Corporatism, State Autonomy, and Democracy', 52 *Social Research* 151–77.

Held, D. (2010), *Cosmopolitanism: Ideals and Realities*. Cambridge: Polity.

Henham, R. (2007), 'Some Reflections on the Legitimacy of International Trial Justice', 35 *International Journal of the Sociology of Law* 75–95.

Henry, S. and Lanier, M. M. eds (2001), *What Is Crime? Controversies Over the Nature of Crime and What to Do About It*. Boulder: Rowman & Littlefield.

Herrera, C. M. (2003), *Droit et gauche: Pour une identification*. Saint-Nicolas, Québec: Les Presses de l'Université Laval.

Heydebrand, W. (2001), 'From Globalisation of Law to Law Under Globalisation', in D. Nelken and J. Feest eds, *Adapting Legal Cultures*, pp. 117–37. Oxford: Hart.

Heyns, C. (2013), *Report of the Special Rapporteur on Extrajudicial, Summary or Arbitrary Executions*. UN General Assembly, 68th Session, A/68/382. New York: United Nations.

Higgins, R. (2006), 'A Babel of Judicial Voices? Ruminations From the Bench', 55 *International and Comparative Law Quarterly* 791–804.

HM Revenue and Customs (2016), *Measuring Tax Gaps 2016 Edition: Tax Gap Estimates for 2014–15*. London: HMSO.

Holland, A. C. (2015), 'The Distributive Politics of Enforcement', 59 *American Journal of Political Science* 357–71.

Howarth, D. (2000), 'On the Question, "What Is Law?"', 6 *Res Publica* 259–83.

Hughes, J. and MacDonnell, V. (2013), 'Social Science Evidence in Constitutional Rights Cases in Germany and Canada: Some Comparative Observations', 32 *National Journal of Constitutional Law* 23–60.

Hull, N. E. H. (1997), *Roscoe Pound and Karl Llewellyn: Searching for an American Jurisprudence*. Chicago: University of Chicago Press.

Hulsman, L. H. C. (1986), 'Critical Criminology and the Concept of Crime' (extract), reprinted in J. Muncie, E. McLaughlin and M. Langan eds, *Criminological Perspectives: A Reader*, pp. 299–303. London: Sage, 1996.

Hunt, A. (1978), *The Sociological Movement in Law*. London: Macmillan.

Husak, D. (2004), 'Crimes Outside the Core', 39 *Tulsa Law Review* 755–79.

Internet Engineering Task Force (2015), *IAB, IESG, and IAOC Selection, Confirmation, and Recall Process: Operation of the Nominating and Recall Committees* (Request for comments 7437). https://tools.ietf.org/html/rfc7437 (accessed June 7th 2017).

Jackson, J., Bradford, B., Hough, M., Myhill, A., Quinton, P. and Tyler, T. R. (2012), 'Why Do People Comply With the Law? Legitimacy and the Influence of Legal Institutions', 52 *British Journal of Criminology* 1051–71.

Jamin, C. (2002), 'Saleilles' and Lambert's Old Dream Revisited', 50 *American Journal of Comparative Law* 701–18.

Jansen, N. (2010), *The Making of Legal Authority: Non-legislative Codifications in Historical and Comparative Perspective*. Oxford: Oxford University Press.

————(2016), 'Informal Authorities in European Law', in Cotterrell and Del Mar eds (2016b), pp. 191–219.

Jessup, P. C. (2006), 'Transnational Law' (extracts), in Tietje et al eds (2006), pp. 45–55.

Jhering, R. von (1913), *Law as a Means to an End*, transl. I. Husik. New York: Macmillan.

Joas, H. (2008), 'Punishment and Respect: The Sacralization of the Person and Its Endangerment', 8 *Journal of Classical Sociology* 159–77.

————(2013), *The Sacredness of the Person: A New Genealogy of Human Rights*, transl. A. Skinner. Washington, DC: Georgetown University Press.

Joerges, C. (2011), 'A New Type of Conflicts Law as the Legal Paradigm of the Postnational Constellation', in C. Joerges and J. Falke eds, *Karl Polanyi, Globalisation and the Potential of Law in Transnational Markets*, pp. 465–501. Oxford: Hart.

Joosse, P. (2014), 'Becoming a God: Max Weber and the Social Construction of Charisma', 14 *Journal of Classical Sociology* 266–83.

Karpik, L. and Halliday, T. C. (2011), 'The Legal Complex', 7 *Annual Review of Law & Social Science* 217–36.

Kaufmann, A. (1988), 'National Socialism and German Jurisprudence From 1933–1945', 9 *Cardozo Law Review* 1629–50.

Kelsen, H. (1967), *Pure Theory of Law*, transl. M. Knight. Gloucester, MA: Peter Smith reprint, 1989.

Kester, J. G. (1988), 'Some Myths of United States Extradition Law', 76 *Georgetown Law Journal* 1441–93.

Kingsbury, B. (2009), 'The Concept of "Law" in Global Administrative Law', 20 *European Journal of International Law* 23–57.

Kleinbard, E. D. (2011), 'Stateless Income', 11 *Florida Tax Review* 699–773.

———(2013), 'Through a Latte, Darkly: Starbucks' Stateless Income Planning', *Tax Notes*, June 24th, pp. 1515–35.

Knepper, P. (2016), 'The Investigation into the Traffic in Women by the League of Nations: Sociological Jurisprudence as an International Social Project', 34 *Law and History Review* 45–73.

Koch, H. W. (1989), *In the Name of the Volk: Political Justice in Hitler's Germany*. London: I. B. Tauris.

Köchler, H. (2017), 'Justice and Realpolitik: The Predicament of the International Criminal Court', 16 *Chinese Journal of International Law* 1–9.

Koh, H. H. (1996), 'Transnational Legal Process', 75 *Nebraska Law Review* 181–208.

Kontorovich, E. (2010), '"A Guantanamo on the Sea": The Difficulty of Prosecuting Pirates and Terrorists', 98 *California Law Review* 243–75.

Koskenniemi, M. and Leino, P. (2002), 'Fragmentation of International Law: Postmodern Anxieties?', 15 *Leiden Journal of International Law* 553–79.

Kramer, M. H. (2011), 'For the Record: A Final Reply to N. E. Simmonds', 56 *American Journal of Jurisprudence* 115–33.

Krisch, N. (2005), 'International Law in Times of Hegemony: Unequal Power and the Shaping of the International Legal Order', 16 *European Journal of International Law* 369–408.

———(2010), *Beyond Constitutionalism: The Pluralist Structure of Postnational Law*. Oxford: Oxford University Press.

Kronman, A. T. (1993), *The Lost Lawyer: Failing Ideals of the Legal Profession*. Cambridge, MA: Harvard University Press.

Kymlicka, W. (1995), *Multicultural Citizenship: A Liberal Theory of Minority Rights*. Oxford: Oxford University Press.

Lacey, N. (2010), 'Out of the Witches' Cauldron: Reinterpreting the Context and Reassessing the Significance of the Hart-Fuller Debate', in P. Cane ed, *The Hart-Fuller Debate in the Twenty-First Century*, pp. 1–42. Oxford: Oxford University Press.

Lambert, H. (2009), 'Transnational Judicial Dialogue, Harmonization and the Common European Asylum System', 58 *International and Comparative Law Quarterly* 519–44.

Lamond, G. (2010), 'Persuasive Authority in the Law', 17 *Harvard Review of Philosophy* 16–35.

Larcombe, W., Fileborn, B., Powell, A., Hanley, N. and Henry, N. (2016), '"I Think It's Rape and I Think He Would Be Found Not Guilty": Focus Group Perceptions of (un)Reasonable Belief in Consent in Rape Law', 25 *Social & Legal Studies* 611–29.

Lardo, A. E. (2006), 'The 2003 Extradition Treaty Between the United States and United Kingdom: Towards a Solution to Transnational White Collar Crime Prosecution?', 20 *Emory International Law Review* 867–903.

Lasslett, K. (2010), 'Crime or Social Harm? A Dialectical Perspective', 54 *Crime, Law and Social Change* 1–19.

Laughland, J. (2002), 'Human Rights and the Rule of Law: Achieving Universal Justice?', in D. Chandler ed, *Rethinking Human Rights: Critical Approaches to International Politics*, pp. 38–56. Basingstoke: Palgrave Macmillan.

Lee, P. and George, R. P. (2008), 'The Nature and Basis of Human Dignity', 21 *Ratio Juris* 173–93.

Leiter, B. (2004), 'The End of Empire: Dworkin and Jurisprudence in the 21st Century', 36 *Rutgers Law Journal* 165–81.

———(2007), *Naturalizing Jurisprudence: Essays on American Legal Realism and Naturalism in Legal Philosophy*. Oxford: Oxford University Press.

Leith, P. and Morison, J. (2005), 'Can Jurisprudence Without Empiricism Ever Be a Science?', in S. Coyle and G. Pavlakos eds, *Jurisprudence or Legal Science? A Debate About the Nature of Legal Theory*, pp. 147–67. Oxford: Hart.

Lempert, R. (1988), 'Between Cup and Lip: Social Sciences Influences on Law and Policy', 10 *Law & Policy* 167–200.

Leonard, E. K. (2005), *The Onset of Global Governance: International Relations Theory and the International Criminal Court*. Abingdon: Routledge.

Levey, G. B. (2007), 'Beyond Durkheim: A Comment on Steven Lukes's "Liberal Democratic Torture"', 37 *British Journal of Political Science* 567–70.

Lin, T. C. W. (2016), 'Financial Weapons of War', 100 *Minnesota Law Review* 1377–440.

Lindahl, H. (2010), 'A-Legality: Postnationalism and the Question of Legal Boundaries', 73 *Modern Law Review* 30–56.

Linde, J. and Erlingsson, G. Ó. (2013), 'The Eroding Effect of Corruption on System Support in Sweden', 26 *Governance* 585–603.

Llewellyn, K. N. (1962), *Jurisprudence: Realism in Theory and Practice*. New Brunswick, NJ: Transaction reprint, 2008.

———and Hoebel, E. A. (1941), *The Cheyenne Way: Conflict and Case Law in Primitive Jurisprudence*. Norman: University of Oklahoma Press.

Lloyd, D. (1965), *Introduction to Jurisprudence With Selected Texts*, 2nd edn. London: Stevens.

Luban, D. (2011), 'War as Punishment', 39 *Philosophy & Public Affairs* 299–330.

Luhmann, N. (1979), 'Trust: A Mechanism for the Reduction of Social Complexity', in T. Burns and G. Poggi eds, *Trust and Power: Two Works by Niklas Luhmann*, transl. H. Davis, J. Raffan and K. Rooney, pp. 2–103. Chichester: John Wiley.

———(1988), 'The Unity of the Legal System', in G. Teubner ed, *Autopoietic Law: A New Approach to Law and Society*, pp. 12–35. Berlin: De Gruyter.

———(2004), *Law as a Social System*, transl. K. A. Ziegert. Oxford: Oxford University Press.

Lukes, S. (2006), 'Liberal Democratic Torture', 36 *British Journal of Political Science* 1–16.

———and Scull, A. eds (2013), *Durkheim and the Law*, 2nd edn. Basingstoke: Palgrave Macmillan.

MacCormick, N. (1993), 'Beyond the Sovereign State', 56 *Modern Law Review* 1–18.

———(1999), *Questioning Sovereignty: Law, State and Nation in the European Commonwealth*. Oxford: Oxford University Press.

Macklin, R. (2003), 'Dignity Is a Useless Concept', 327 *British Medical Journal* 1419–20.

Maguire, R. (2013), *Global Forest Governance: Legal Concepts and Policy Trends*. Cheltenham: Edward Elgar.

Marks, S. (2000), *The Riddle of All Constitutions: International Law, Democracy, and the Critique of Ideology*. Oxford: Oxford University Press.

Marmor, A. (2001), 'Legal Conventionalism', in Coleman ed (2001), pp. 193–217.

———(2006), 'Legal Positivism: Still Descriptive and Morally Neutral', 26 *Oxford Journal of Legal Studies* 683–704.

Maryanski, A. (2014), 'The Birth of the Gods: Robertson Smith and Durkheim's Turn to Religion as the Basis of Social Integration', 32 *Sociological Theory* 352–76.

Mauss, M. (1972), *A General Theory of Magic*, transl. R. Brain. Abingdon: Routledge reprint, 2001.

Mautner, M. (2008), 'From "Honor" to "Dignity": How Should a Liberal State Treat Non-Liberal Cultural Groups?', 9 *Theoretical Inquiries in Law* 609–42.

McCrea, R. (2014), 'Religion in the Workplace: *Eweida and Others v United Kingdom*', 77 *Modern Law Review* 277–91.

McCrudden, C. (2000), 'A Common Law of Human Rights?: Transnational Judicial Conversations on Constitutional Rights', 20 *Oxford Journal of Legal Studies* 499–532.

Melissaris, E. (2009), *Ubiquitous Law: Legal Theory and the Space for Legal Pluralism*. Abingdon: Routledge.

———(2014), 'A Sense of Law: On Shared Normative Experiences', in Donlan and Urscheler eds (2014), pp. 109–21.

Menski, W. (2014), 'Remembering and Applying Legal Pluralism: Law as Kite Flying', in Donlan and Urscheler eds (2014), pp. 91–108.

Menyhart, R. (2003), 'Changing Identities and Changing Law: Possibilities for a Global Legal Culture', 10 *Indiana Journal of Global Legal Studies* 157–99.

Michaels, R. (2005), 'The Re-Statement of Non-State Law: The State, Choice of Law, and the Challenge From Global Legal Pluralism', 51 *Wayne Law Review* 1209–60.

———(2007), 'The True Lex Mercatoria: Law Beyond the State', 14 *Indiana Journal of Global Legal Studies* 447–68.

———(2009), 'Global Legal Pluralism', 5 *Annual Review of Law and Social Science* 243–62.

Milne, S. (2012), 'If There Were Global Justice, NATO Would Be in the Dock Over Libya', *Guardian*, May 16th. www.guardian.co.uk/commentisfree/2012/may/15/global-justice-nato-libya#start-of-comments (accessed June 7th 2017).

Mirchandani, R. (2008), 'Beyond Therapy: Problem-Solving Courts and the Deliberative Democratic State', 33 *Law & Social Inquiry* 853–93.

Mittelman, J. H. and Johnston, R. (1999), 'The Globalization of Organized Crime, the Courtesan State and the Corruption of Civil Society', 5 *Global Governance* 103–26.

Moran, M. (2003), *Rethinking the Reasonable Person: An Egalitarian Reconstruction of the Objective Standard*. Oxford: Oxford University Press.

Morawski, L. (1997), 'Legal Instrumentalism', in Aarnio et al eds (1997), pp. 289–301.

Moyn, S. (2015), *Christian Human Rights*. Philadelphia: University of Pennsylvania Press.

Muir Watt, H. (2016), 'Theorising Transnational Authority: A Private International Law Perspective', in Cotterrell and Del Mar eds (2016b), pp. 325–60.

Muñiz-Fraticelli, V. M. (2014), 'The Problem of Pluralist Authority', 62 *Political Studies* 556–72.

Murphy, L. (2001), 'The Political Question of the Concept of Law', in Coleman ed (2001), pp. 371–409.

Naveen, T. K. (2006), 'Use of "Social Science Evidence" in Constitutional Courts: Concerns for Judicial Process in India', 48 *Journal of the Indian Law Institute* 78–93.

Nehushtan, Y. (2015), *Intolerant Religion in a Tolerant-Liberal Democracy*. Oxford: Hart.

Nelken, D. (2006), 'Patterns of Punitiveness', 69 *Modern Law Review* 262–77.

———(2007), 'Defining and Using the Concept of Legal Culture', in E. Örücü and D. Nelken eds, *Comparative Law: A Handbook*, pp. 109–32. Oxford: Hart.

———(2014), 'Why Must Legal Ideas Be Interpreted Sociologically? Roger Cotterrell and the Vocation of Sociology of Law', in R. Nobles and D. Schiff eds, *Law, Society and Community: Socio-Legal Essays for Roger Cotterrell*, pp. 23–38. Abingdon: Routledge.

Neumann, F. L. (1986), *The Rule of Law: Political Theory and the Legal System in Modern Society*. Leamington Spa: Berg.

Nimaga, S. (2010), *Émile Durkheim and International Criminal Law: A Sociological Exploration*. Saarbrücken: VDM Verlag Dr. Müller.

Northrop, F. S. C. (1959), *The Complexity of Legal and Ethical Experience*. Boston: Little, Brown.

Orbach, S. (2009), *Bodies*. London: Profile.

Orr, D. (2013), 'What Does Idealism Get You Today? Abuse, Derision, or Sometimes Prison', *Guardian* (London), August 3rd. www.theguardian.com/commentisfree/2013/aug/03/what-does-idealism-get-you (accessed June 7th 2017).

Overton, T. W. (1995), 'Lawyers, Light Bulbs, and Dead Snakes: The Lawyer Joke as Societal Text', 42 *University of California at Los Angeles Law Review* 1069–114.

Parker, C. (2008), 'The Pluralization of Regulation', 9 *Theoretical Inquiries in Law* 349–69.

Pashukanis, E. B. (1978), *Law and Marxism: A General Theory*, transl. B. Einhorn. London: Ink Links.

Patterson, D. (2012), 'Alexy on Necessity in Law and Morals', 25 *Ratio Juris* 47–58.

Paul, H. (2011), *Corporations Are Not Human, So Why Should They Have Human Rights?* Oxford: Econexus. www.econexus.info/publication/corporations-are-not-human-so-why-should-they-have-human-rights (accessed June 7th 2017).

Paulson, S. L. (1994), 'Lon L. Fuller, Gustav Radbruch, and the 'Positivist' Thesis', 13 *Law and Philosophy* 313–59.

———(1995), 'Radbruch on Unjust Laws: Competing Earlier and Later Views?', 15 *Oxford Journal of Legal Studies* 489–500.

———(2006), 'On the Background and Significance of Gustav Radbruch's Post-War Papers', 26 *Oxford Journal of Legal Studies* 17–40.

Penner, J., Schiff, D. and Nobles, R. eds (2002), *Jurisprudence and Legal Theory: Commentary and Materials*. Oxford: Oxford University Press.

Perez, O. (2003), 'Normative Creativity and Global Legal Pluralism: Reflections on the Democratic Critique of Transnational Law', 10(2) *Indiana Journal of Global Legal Studies* 25–64.

Petrazycki, L. (1955), *Law and Morality*, transl. H. W. Babb. Cambridge, MA: Harvard University Press.

Petrusson, U. and Glavå, M. (2008), 'Law in a Global Knowledge Economy: Following the Path of Scandinavian Sociolegal Theory', 53 *Scandinavian Studies in Law* 93–133.

Pickering, W. S. F. (1993), 'Human Rights and the Individual: An Unholy Alliance Created by Durkheim?', in W. S. F. Pickering and W. Watts Miller eds, *Individualism and Human Rights in the Durkheimian Tradition*, pp. 51–76. Oxford: British Centre for Durkheimian Studies.

Playfair, G. (1971), *The Punitive Obsession: An Unvarnished History of the English Prison System*. London: Gollancz.

Pope, W. and Johnson, B. D. (1983), 'Inside Organic Solidarity', 48 *American Sociological Review* 681–92.

Post, R. (1987), 'On the Popular Image of the Lawyer: Reflections in a Dark Glass', 75 *California Law Review* 379–89.

Postema, G. J. (1986), *Bentham and the Common Law Tradition*. Oxford: Oxford University Press.

Pound, R. (1907), 'The Need of a Sociological Jurisprudence', 19 *Green Bag* 607–15.

———(1908), 'Mechanical Jurisprudence', 8 *Columbia Law Review* 605–23.

———(1923), *Interpretations of Legal History*. Cambridge: Cambridge University Press.

———(1931), 'The Call for a Realist Jurisprudence', 44 *Harvard Law Review* 697–711.

———(1942), *Social Control Through Law*. New Haven: Yale University Press.

———(1958), *The Ideal Element in Law*. Indianapolis: Liberty Fund reprint, 2002.

Pratt, J. (2007), *Penal Populism*. Abingdon: Routledge.

Priel, D. (2015), 'Toward Classical Legal Positivism', 101 *Virginia Law Review* 987–1022.

Quack, S. (2007), 'Legal Professionals and Transnational Law-Making: A Case of Distributed Agency', 14 *Organization* 643–66.

———(2016), 'Authority and Expertise in Transnational Governance', in Cotterrell and Del Mar eds (2016b), pp. 361–86.

Radbruch, G. (1950), 'Legal Philosophy', in J. Hall et al eds, *The Legal Philosophies of Lask, Radbruch and Dabin*, transl. K. Wilk, pp. 43–224. Cambridge, MA: Harvard University Press.

———(2006), 'Statutory Lawlessness and Supra-Statutory Law', transl. B. L. Paulson and S. L. Paulson, 26 *Oxford Journal of Legal Studies* 1–11.

Raes, K. (1996), 'Communicating Legal Identity: A Note on the Inevitable Counterfactuality of Legal Communication', in D. Nelken ed, *Law as Communication*, pp. 25–44. Aldershot: Dartmouth.

Rakoff, J. S. (2014), 'The Financial Crisis: Why Have No High-Level Executives Been Prosecuted?', *New York Review of Books*, January 9th, pp. 4–8.

Randall, K. C. (1988), 'Universal Jurisdiction Under International Law', 66 *Texas Law Review* 785–841.

Rathus, Z. (2012), 'A Call for Clarity in the Use of Social Science Research in Family Law Decision-Making', 26 *Australian Journal of Family Law* 81–115.

Rawls, A. (2003), 'Conflict as a Foundation for Consensus: Contradictions of Industrial Capitalism in Book III of Durkheim's *Division of Labor*', 29 *Critical Sociology* 295–335.

Raz, J. (1975), *Practical Reason and Norms*. London: Hutchinson.

———(1994), *Ethics in the Public Domain: Essays in the Morality of Law and Politics*. Oxford: Oxford University Press.

———(1998), 'Multiculturalism', 11 *Ratio Juris* 193–205.

———(2001), 'Two Views of the Nature of the Theory of Law: A Partial Comparison', in Coleman ed (2001), pp. 1–37.

———(2009a), *Between Authority and Interpretation: On the Theory of Law and Practical Reason*. Oxford: Oxford University Press.

———(2009b), *The Authority of Law: Essays on Law and Morality*, 2nd edn. Oxford: Oxford University Press.

Redlich, N. (1988), 'Judges as Instruments of Democracy', in S. Shetreet ed, *The Role of Courts in Society*, pp. 149–57. Dordrecht: Martinus Nijhoff.

Reiman, J. (2006), 'Book Review', 46 *British Journal of Criminology* 362–4.

Renzo, M. (2012), 'Crimes Against Humanity and the Limits of International Criminal Law', 31 *Law and Philosophy* 443–76.

Reus-Smit, C. (2004), 'The Politics of International Law', in C. Reus-Smit ed, *The Politics of International Law*, pp. 14–44. Cambridge: Cambridge University Press.

Ringen, S. (2013), *Nation of Devils: Democratic Leadership and the Problem of Obedience*. New Haven: Yale University Press.

Rixen, T. (2013), 'Why Reregulation After the Crisis Is Feeble: Shadow Banking, Offshore Financial Centers, and Jurisdictional Competition', 7 *Regulation and Governance* 435–59.

Roberts, J. V., Stalans, L. J., Indermaur, D. and Hough, M. (2003), *Penal Populism and Public Opinion: Lessons From Five Countries*. Oxford: Oxford University Press.

Rödl, F. (2008), 'Private Law Beyond the Democratic Order? On the Legitimatory Problem of Private Law "Beyond the State"', 56 *American Journal of Comparative Law* 743–67.

Ross, D. (1991), *The Origins of American Social Science*. Cambridge: Cambridge University Press.

Ross, E. A. (1901), *Social Control: A Survey of the Foundations of Order*. New York: Macmillan.

Rothe, D. L. and Friedrichs, D. O. (2006), 'The State of the Criminology of Crimes of the State', 33 *Social Justice* 147–61.

Rottleuthner, H. (1989), 'The Limits of Law: The Myth of a Regulatory Crisis', 17 *International Journal of the Sociology of Law* 273–85.

Roughan, N. (2013), *Authorities: Conflicts, Cooperation and Transnational Legal Theory*. Oxford: Oxford University Press.

———(2016), 'From Authority to Authorities: Bridging the Social/Normative Divide', in Cotterrell and Del Mar eds (2016b), pp. 280–99.

Saltman, M. (1991), *The Demise of the Reasonable Man: A Cross-Cultural Study of a Legal Concept*. New Brunswick, NJ: Transaction.

Samek, R. A. (1974), *The Legal Point of View*. New York: Philosophical Library.

Samuel, G. (2003), *Epistemology and Method in Law*. Abingdon: Routledge reprint, 2016.

————(2009a), 'Can Legal Reasoning Be Demystified?', 29 *Legal Studies* 181–210.

————(2009b), 'Interdisciplinarity and the Authority Paradigm: Should Law Be Taken Seriously by Scientists and Social Scientists?', 36 *Journal of Law and Society* 431–59.

Sandberg, R. (2009), 'The Changing Position of Religious Minorities in English Law: The Legacy of *Begum*', in Grillo et al eds (2009), pp. 267–82.

————(2014), *Religion, Law and Society*. Cambridge: Cambridge University Press.

Sands, P. (2008), *Torture Team: Deception, Cruelty and the Compromise of Law*. London: Allen Lane.

Schachter, O. (1983), 'Human Dignity as a Normative Concept', 77 *American Journal of International Law* 848–54.

Schaeffer, M. (2002), *Corruption and Public Finance*. Washington: Management Systems International.

Schäfer, A. (2006), 'Resolving Deadlock: Why International Organisations Introduce Soft Law', 12 *European Law Journal* 194–208.

Schauer, F. (2006), '(Re)taking Hart', 119 *Harvard Law Review* 852–83.

————(2010), 'The Best Laid Plans', 120 *Yale Law Journal* 586–621.

————(2011), 'Positivism Before Hart', 24 *Canadian Journal of Law and Jurisprudence* 455–71.

Scheffler, S. (2007), 'Immigration and the Significance of Culture', 35 *Philosophy & Public Affairs* 93–125.

Scheuerman, W. E. (1999), 'Globalization and the Fate of Law', in D. Dyzenhaus ed, *Recrafting the Rule of Law: The Limits of Legal Order*, pp. 243–66. Oxford: Hart.

Schultz, T. (2011), 'Internet Disputes, Fairness in Arbitration and Transnationalism: A Reply to Julia Hörnle', 19 *International Journal of Law and Information Technology* 153–63.

Scolnicov, A. (2013), *Lifelike and Lifeless in Law: Do Corporations Have Human Rights?* University of Cambridge Faculty of Law Research Paper 13/2013.

Scott, C., Cafaggi, F. and Senden, L. (2011), 'The Conceptual and Constitutional Challenge of Transnational Private Regulation', 38 *Journal of Law and Society* 1–19.

Selznick, P. (1961), 'Sociology and Natural Law', reprinted in D. J. Black and M. Mileski eds, *The Social Organization of Law*, 1st edn, pp. 16–40. New York: Seminar Press, 1973.

————(1969), *Law, Society and Industrial Justice*, with the collaboration of P. Nonet and H. M. Vollmer. New York: Russell Sage.

————(1980), 'Jurisprudence and Social Policy: Aspirations and Perspectives', 68 *California Law Review* 206–20.

————(1992), *The Moral Commonwealth: Social Theory and the Promise of Community*. Berkeley: University of California Press.

————(1999), 'Legal Cultures and the Rule of Law', in M. Krygier and A. Czarnota eds, *The Rule of Law After Communism: Problems and Prospects in East-Central Europe*, pp. 21–38. Abingdon: Routledge.

Senden, L. (2005), 'Soft Law, Self-Regulation and Co-Regulation in European Law: Where Do They Meet?', 9(1) *Electronic Journal of Comparative Law*. www.ejcl.org/

Shadid, W. and Van Koningsveld, P. S. (2005), 'Muslim Dress in Europe: Debates on the Headscarf', 16 *Journal of Islamic Studies* 35–61.

Shaffer, G. (2012), 'A Transnational Take on Krisch's Pluralist Structure of Postnational Law', 23 *European Journal of International Law* 565–82.

Shah, P. (2005), *Legal Pluralism in Conflict: Coping With Cultural Diversity in Law*. London: Glass House.

————(2007), 'Rituals of Recognition: Ethnic Minority Marriages in British Legal Systems', in P. Shah ed, *Law and Ethnic Plurality: Socio-Legal Perspectives*, pp. 177–202. Leiden: Martinus Nijhoff.

Shils, E. (1985), 'On the Eve: A Prospect in Retrospect', in M. Bulmer ed, *Essays on the History of British Sociological Research*, pp. 165–78. Cambridge: Cambridge University Press.

Simmonds, N. E. (2007), *Law as a Moral Idea*. Oxford: Oxford University Press.

————(2011), 'Kramer's High Noon', 56 *American Journal of Jurisprudence* 135–50.

Simon, J. (2008), '*Katz* at Forty: A Sociological Jurisprudence Whose Time Has Come', 41 *University of California at Davis Law Review* 935–76.

Simpson, G. (2004), *Great Powers and Outlaw States: Unequal Sovereigns in the International Legal Order*. Cambridge: Cambridge University Press.

Sirianni, C. J. (1984), 'Justice and the Division of Labour: A Reconsideration of Durkheim's *Division of Labour in Society*', 32 *Sociological Review* 449–70.

Skeggs, B. (2014), 'Values Beyond Value? Is Anything Beyond the Logic of Capital?', 65 *British Journal of Sociology* 1–20.

Slaughter, A.-M. (2002), 'Judicial Globalization', 40 *Virginia Journal of International Law* 1103–24.

————(2003), 'A Global Community of Courts', 44 *Harvard International Law Journal* 191–220.

Smith, S. D. (1999), 'Believing Like a Lawyer', 40 *Boston College Law Review* 1041–137.

Snyder, F. G. (1999), 'Governing Economic Globalisation: Global Legal Pluralism and European Law', 5 *European Law Journal* 334–74.

————(2004), 'Economic Globalisation and the Law in the Twenty-first Century', in A. Sarat ed, *Blackwell Companion to Law and Society*, pp. 624–40. Malden, MA: Blackwell.

Somek, A. (2009), 'The Concept of "Law" in Global Administrative Law: A Reply to Benedict Kingsbury', 20 *European Journal of International Law* 985–95.

Soosay, S. (2011), 'Rediscovering Fuller and Llewellyn: Law as Custom and Process', in M. Del Mar ed, *New Waves in Philosophy of Law*, pp. 31–57. Basingstoke: Palgrave Macmillan.

Spaak, T. (2009), 'Meta-Ethics and Legal Theory: The Case of Gustav Radbruch', 28 *Law and Philosophy* 261–90.

Spates, J. L. (1983), 'The Sociology of Values', 9 *Annual Review of Sociology* 27–49.

Stedman Jones, S. (2001), *Durkheim Reconsidered*. Cambridge: Polity.

Stein, J. A. (2006), 'Have You Heard the New Lawyer Joke About . . .' 9 *Green Bag 2d* 397–9.

Stone, J. (1968), *Legal System and Lawyers' Reasonings*. Sydney: Maitland.

Strickland, R. (1986), 'The Lawyer as Modern Medicine Man', 11 *Southern Illinois University Law Journal* 203–15.

Stuntz, W. J. (2001), 'The Pathological Politics of Criminal Law', 100 *Michigan Law Review* 505–600.

Swanton, C. (1980), 'The Concept of Interests', 8 *Political Theory* 83–101.

Szustek, A. (2009), *Michigan Judges Can Ask Muslim Women to Remove Veils in Court*. www.findingdulcinea.com/news/Americas/2009/June/Michigan-Judges-Can-Ask-Muslim-Women-to-Remove-Veils-in-Court.html (accessed June 7th 2017).

Taekema, S. (2003), *The Concept of Ideals in Legal Theory*. The Hague: Kluwer.

Tamanaha, B. Z. (2001), *A General Jurisprudence of Law and Society*. Oxford: Oxford University Press.

————(2006), *Law as a Means to an End: Threat to the Rule of Law*. New York: Cambridge University Press.

————(2011), 'What Is "General" Jurisprudence? A Critique of Universalistic Claims by Philosophical Concepts of Law', 2 *Transnational Legal Theory* 287–308.

————(2015), 'The Third Pillar of Jurisprudence: Social Legal Theory', 56 *William and Mary Law Review* 2235–77.

————(2017), 'Necessary and Universal Truths About Law?', 30 *Ratio Juris* 3–24.

Tas, L. (2014), *Legal Pluralism in Action: Dispute Resolution and the Kurdish Peace Committee*. Abingdon: Routledge.

Temkin, J. and Krahe, B. (2008), *Sexual Assault and the Justice Gap: A Question of Attitude.* Oxford: Hart.

Terpan, F. (2015), 'Soft Law in the European Union: The Changing Nature of EU Law', 21 *European Law Journal* 68–96.

Terpstra, J. (2011), 'Two Theories on the Police: The Relevance of Max Weber and Emile Durkheim to the Study of the Police', 39 *International Journal of Law, Crime and Justice* 1–11.

Teubner, G. (1992), 'Regulatory Law: Chronicle of a Death Foretold', 1 *Social & Legal Studies* 451–75.

———(1996), '*De Collisione Discursuum*: Communicative Rationalities in Law, Morality and Politics', 17 *Cardozo Law Review* 901–18.

———(2004), 'Regime Collisions: The Vain Search for Legal Unity in the Fragmentation of Global Law', 25 *Michigan Journal of International Law* 999–1046.

Thacher, D. (2006), 'The Normative Case Study', 111 *American Journal of Sociology* 1631–76.

Thomas, C. A. (2014), 'The Uses and Abuses of Legitimacy in International Law', 34 *Oxford Journal of Legal Studies* 729–58.

Tidmarsh, J. (2006), 'Pound's Century, and Ours', 81 *Notre Dame Law Review* 513–90.

Tietje, C., Brouder, A. and Nowrot, K. eds (2006), *Philip C. Jessup's Transnational Law Revisited – On the Occasion of the 50th Anniversary of Its Publication.* Halle-Wittenberg: Martin-Luther-Universität.

Tietje, C. and Nowrot, K. (2006), 'Laying Conceptual Ghosts to Rest: The Rise of Philip C. Jessup's "Transnational Law" in the Regulatory Governance of the International Economic System', in Tietje et al eds (2006), pp. 17–43.

Titolo, M. (2012), 'Privatization and the Market Frame', 60 *Buffalo Law Review* 493–558.

Toobin., J. (2007), *The Nine: Inside the Secret World of the Supreme Court.* New York: Doubleday.

Trotter, M. H. (1997), *Profit and the Practice of Law: What's Happened to the Legal Profession?* Athens: University of Georgia Press.

Trubek, D. M. and Trubek, L. G. (2005), 'Hard and Soft Law in the Construction of Social Europe: The Role of the Open Method of Coordination', 11 *European Law Journal* 343–64.

Tur, R. H. S. (1978), 'What Is Jurisprudence?', 28 *Philosophical Quarterly* 149–61.

Turner, S. (2003), 'Charisma Reconsidered', 3 *Journal of Classical Sociology* 5–26.

Twining, W. (1974), 'Law and Social Science: The Method of Detail', *New Society*, June 27th, pp. 758–61.

———(1979), 'Academic Law and Legal Philosophy: The Significance of Herbert Hart', 95 *Law Quarterly Review* 557–80.

———(2002), *The Great Juristic Bazaar: Jurists' Texts and Lawyers' Stories.* Abingdon: Routledge.

———(2003), 'A Post-Westphalian Conception of Law', 37 *Law & Society Review* 199–258.

———(2009), *General Jurisprudence: Understanding Law From a Global Perspective.* Cambridge: Cambridge University Press.

———(2012), *Karl Llewellyn and the Realist Movement*, 2nd edn. Cambridge: Cambridge University Press.

Tyler, T. R. (2001), 'Trust and Law Abidingness: A Proactive Model of Social Regulation', 81 *Boston University Law Review* 361–406.

Urry, J. (2000), 'Mobile Sociology', 51 *British Journal of Sociology* 185–203.

Van Bemmelen, J. M. (1951), 'The "Criminologist": A King Without a Country?', 63 *Juridical Review* 24–38.

Vandekerckhove, W., James, C. and West, F. (2013), *Whistleblowing: The Inside Story – A Study of the Experiences of 1,000 Whistleblowers.* London: Public Concern at Work/University of Greenwich.

Van Der Burg, W. (2001), 'The Expressive and Communicative Functions of Law, Especially With Regard to Moral Issues', 20 *Law and Philosophy* 31–59.

———and Taekema, S. eds (2004), *The Importance of Ideals: Debating Their Relevance in Law, Morality, and Politics*. Brussels: Presses Interuniversitaires Européennes/Peter Lang.

Van Hoecke, M. (2002), *Law as Communication*. Oxford: Hart.

———(2014), 'Do "Legal Systems" Exist? The Concept of Law and Comparative Law', in Donlan and Urscheler eds (2014), pp. 43–57.

Van Niekerk, B. (1973), 'The Warning Voice From Heidelberg: The Life and Thought of Gustav Radbruch', 90 *South African Law Journal* 234–61.

Varella, M. D. (2013), 'Central Aspects of the Debate on Complexity and Fragmentation of International Law', 27 *Emory International Law Review* 1–22.

Wai, R. (2008), 'The Interlegality of Transnational Private Law', 71 *Law and Contemporary Problems* 107–27.

Walker, N. (2002), 'The Idea of Constitutional Pluralism', 65 *Modern Law Review* 317–59.

———(2010), 'Out of Place and Out of Time: Law's Fading Co-ordinates', 14 *Edinburgh Law Review* 13–46.

———(2015), *Intimations of Global Law*. Cambridge: Cambridge University Press.

Watts Miller, W. (1988), 'Durkheim and Individualism', 36 *Sociological Review* 647–73.

Weber, M. (1968), *Economy and Society: An Outline of Interpretive Sociology*, transl. E. Fischoff et al. Berkeley: University of California Press reprint, 1978.

———(1977), *Critique of Stammler*, transl. G. Oakes. New York: Free Press.

Weinreb, L. L. (2005), *Legal Reason: The Use of Analogy in Legal Argument*. Cambridge: Cambridge University Press.

Werle, G. and Jeßberger, F. (2014), *Principles of International Criminal Law*, 3rd edn. Oxford: Oxford University Press.

West, R. L. (2005), 'The Lawless Adjudicator', 26 *Cardozo Law Review* 2253–61.

Weyland, I. (2002), 'The Application of Kelsen's Theory of the Legal System to European Community Law: The Supremacy Puzzle Resolved', 21 *Law and Philosophy* 1–37.

Wheatley, S. (2001), 'Human Rights and Human Dignity in the Resolution of Certain Ethical Questions in Biomedicine', 3 *European Human Rights Law Review* 312–25.

White, J. B. (1990), *Justice as Translation: An Essay in Cultural and Legal Criticism*. Chicago: University of Chicago Press.

Wigdor, D. (1974), *Roscoe Pound: Philosopher of Law*. Westport, CT: Greenwood Press.

Wigmore, J. H. et al eds (1917), *Science of Legal Method: Select Essays by Various Authors*, transl. E. Bruncken and L. B. Register. Boston: Boston Book Co.

Williams, B. (1985), *Ethics and the Limits of Philosophy*. London: Collins Fontana.

Wilmarth, Jr., A. E. (2013), 'Turning a Blind Eye: Why Washington Keeps Giving in to Wall Street', 81 *University of Cincinnati Law Review* 1283–446.

Winston, K. I. ed (2001), *The Principles of Social Order: Selected Essays of Lon L. Fuller*, revised edn. Oxford: Hart.

Witteveen, W. (1999), 'Significant, Symbolic and Symphonic Laws: Communication Through Legislation', in H. van Schooten ed, *Semiotics and Legislation: Jurisprudential, Institutional and Sociological Perspectives*, pp. 27–70. Liverpool: Deborah Charles Publications.

Wolf, E. (1958), 'Revolution or Evolution in Gustav Radbruch's Legal Philosophy', 3 *Natural Law Forum* 1–23.

Wuthnow, R. (2008), 'The Sociological Study of Values', 23 *Sociological Forum* 333–43.

Yeager, P. C. (1993), *The Limits of Law: The Public Regulation of Private Pollution*. Cambridge: Cambridge University Press.

Yovel, J. and Mertz, E. (2004), 'The Role of Social Science in Legal Decisions', in A. Sarat ed, *Blackwell Companion to Law and Society*, pp. 410–31. Malden, MA: Blackwell.

Zeegers, N., Witteveen, W. and Van Klink, B. eds (2005), *Social and Symbolic Effects of Legislation Under the Rule of Law*. Lewiston: Edwin Mellen.

Zorzetto, S. (2015), 'Reasonableness', 1 *Italian Law Journal* 107–39.

Zumbansen, P. (2002), 'Piercing the Legal Veil: Commercial Arbitration and Transnational Law', 8 *European Law Journal* 400–32.

———(2013), 'Transnational Private Regulatory Governance: Ambiguities of Public Authority and Private Power', 76 *Law and Contemporary Problems* 117–38.

INDEX

punishment: cruel and unusual 178;
Durkheim on (*see* Durkheim); penal
populism 215; punitive obsession
214–15; values, expression of 211–12,
215; war as 148

Radbruch, Gustav: career 37; continuity
of thought 39; criticisms of 37, 39, 41;
Durkheim and 177; Dworkin and 35–6;
Hart's view of 37; idea of law 35, 38–41,
84, 219, 223, 224; juristic role, and 34–5,
40, 218; justice, on 38, 39, 40, 219; law's
fitness for cultural purpose 38, 40, 219,
224, 225; legal values, on 36; personal
qualities 37; philosophical systems,
rejecting 35; 'recanting' prewar views
37, 38–9; security, on 38–9, 40, 219;
self-questioning outlook 36–7; variable
geometry of law 38–9, 219
Raes, Koen: legal communications, on 168
ratio: reason and principle, as 108, 115;
transnational law, in 112, 115–16, 117, 139
Raz, Joseph: concept of law 90, 97; legal
philosophy and legal sociology, on 52;
multiculturalism, on 166
reasonableness *see* Legal reasoning
Rehnquist, William 18, 42
Reiman, Jeffrey: criminal responsibility, on
150
religion: Christianity 196–9; contemporary
significance of 201–2, 211; humanity,
of 188, 192, 196; human rights and
(*see* Human rights); magic and 19;
minority practices of 160; Muslim female
dress 160, 169, 172, 173, 183, 185–6;
neighbour principle 197–8, 199; schools,
in 160, 169–70; *see also* Begum case
Renner, Moritz 110
rights: egoism and 191; functional analysis
of 192–3; human (*see* Human rights);
membership and participation 192, 195,
200, 203; moral individualism and 190–1;
prisoners' 185; society's needs, defined by
201; solidarity and 187; state, against 201;
women's 185
Rodell, Fred: lawyers, on 19
Ross, Edward: social control, on 2
Roughan, Nicole: relative authority, on 82–3

Saleilles, Raymond 90
Samuel, Geoffrey: French legal science, on 24
Schachter, Oscar: human dignity, on 178
Scheffler, Samuel: culture, on 163–4
Selznick, Philip: legality, on 62–4, 172;
sociology and jurisprudence 65, 69

Shils, Edward: 'sharpshooter' arguments,
on 51
Simmonds, Nigel 41
Snyder, Francis: global legal pluralism, on
93–4
social scientific evidence 59–62, 69–70
society: communitas image of (*see* Communitas); diversity in 226; imperium
image of (*see* Imperium); juristic images
of 160–2, 162–3; religious representation
of 198; unity of the social 164–5, 225,
226, 228–9
sociological jurisprudence: conceptual
inquiry in 222–3; jurisprudence in
general, as 12–13; juristic responsibilities
and 11; juristic use of social science 1–4,
12, 59–62, 69–72, 88, 219–20; nature
of 4, 12–13, 65, 67; new forms of 13;
Northrop's (*see* Northrop); Pound's
(*see* Pound); renewed aspirations of 11;
sociology of law and (*see* Sociology of law)
sociology: enlightenment, as 2, 61–2, 69,
71; fact/value distinction (*see* Values);
jurisprudence and (*see* Sociological
jurisprudence); morality, of (*see* Durkheim); nature of 1–4; philosophy and
64; sociologists and jurists 58–9, 63,
65, 67–9, 82; status of 67; values and
(*see* Values)
sociology of law: aim of 172; critique,
as 221; development of 3–4, 67;
instrumental view of law 174;
jurisprudence and 9, 11, 46, 63, 67, 68,
226; positivist 68; private legal systems in
96, 110; scope of 3–4; sociology of the
case 67–8; values and 12, 187; visions of
law, contrasting 204–6
solidarity: communication and 221–2;
diversity and 187, 221, 226; Durkheim on
(*see* Durkheim); jurists' responsibility for
220; law's contribution to 221; meanings
of 221, 226; power and 220; value, as
30–1, 70, 226; varieties of 221, 226
state: corruption 132; crime and
(*see* Crime); dependent on law 26;
extraterritorial actions by 133; finances
132–3; globalisation affecting 133;
government, without 143; humanitarian
intervention by 149; legal complex 24–5;
modern 80; monopoly of legitimate
violence 142–3, 144, 145, 148, 154–5;
moral individualism and 191; officials,
demoralised 133; practical authority of
80, 132–4; public interest and 141–2;
punishment inflicted on 148; relative

Made in the USA
Las Vegas, NV
10 May 2022

48694635R00149